# MONUMENTS TO THE LOST CAUSE

# MONUMENTS TO THE LOST CAUSE

## WOMEN, ART, AND THE LANDSCAPES OF SOUTHERN MEMORY

EDITED BY

Cynthia Mills and Pamela H. Simpson

FOREWORD BY

Karen L. Cox

THE UNIVERSITY OF TENNESSEE PRESS

KNOXVILLE

Library of Congress Cataloging-in-Publication Data

Monuments to the lost cause : women, art, and the landscapes of southern
memory / edited by Cynthia Mills and Pamela H. Simpson.— 1st ed.
p. cm.

Includes bibliographical references and index.
ISBN 978-1-62190-444-1

1. United States—History—Civil War, 1861–1865—Influence.
2. United States—History—Civil War, 1861–1865—Monuments.
3. War memorials—Southern States—History.
4. Monuments—Southern States—History.
5. Women—Southern States—Political activity—History.
6. Southern States—Politics and government—1865-1950.
7. Southern States—Social conditions—1865-1945.
8. Southern States—Race relations.
9. Political culture—Southern States—History.
10. Memory—Social aspects—Southern States—History.
 I. Mills, Cynthia, 1947–   II. Simpson, Pamela H. (Pamela Hemenway), 1946–
   E468.9 .M77 2003
   973.7'6—dc21

                                                              2002155367

To Sean and Henry

and

The new generation of scholars who have
inspired us to reconsider the nature of
the Lost Cause and its aftermath

# Contents

# Foreword 2019

THE REISSUE OF THIS EXCELLENT BOOK, co-edited by Cynthia Mills and Pamela H. Simpson, coincides with the increased public and academic interest in how the white South sought to remember and restore respect for the defeated Confederacy after the Civil War. This renewed attention has led to more in-depth examinations of what the symbols of this reverence for the Confederacy, especially monuments, have meant to generations of African Americans as well as white southerners. Those who wonder how many of these monuments came to be part of the southern landscape would do well to rediscover this excellent volume of essays and place it on their reading list.

Unfortunately, neither of the editors is still with us to witness this development. Both women died far too soon—Pamela H. Simpson in 2011 and Cynthia Mills in 2014. Their departure is our loss as a scholarly community, and it is the only reason I am writing the new foreword for this reissue. Yet I am pleased to do so in their memory, because I believe in the value of this volume and their vision for it.

* * *

In 2003, when this book was first published, historians had long been in a phase of writing about history and memory. Then and for years to come, one couldn't open the program of the annual meeting of the Southern Historical Association without seeing a paper being presented on southern history and memory, especially the Lost Cause. It was a cottage industry. Yet few had taken up the specific topic of Confederate monuments. Years earlier, in 1987, Gaines Foster explored monuments in his classic text *Ghosts of the Confederacy: Defeat, the Lost Cause, and the Emergence of the New South, 1865–1913* as one of the many ways that southerners came to terms with defeat on the battlefield. Kirk Savage's *Standing Soldiers, Kneeling Slaves: Race, War, and Monuments in Nineteenth-Century America* examined how monumental art extended the debate over Civil War memory and often perpetuated an ahistorical image of slavery. My own book, *Dixie's Daughters: The United Daughters of the Confederacy and the Preservation of Confederate Culture*, also published in 2003, offered a new interpretation of the Lost Cause, featuring women at the center of events, and documented the dominant role they played in the movement to erect Confederate monuments. And yet, Cynthia Mills and Pamela Simpson, the editors of *Monuments to the Lost Cause: Women, Art, and the Landscape of Memory,* presented us with an entirely different book on the Lost Cause that presented new ways of "seeing" monuments. In fact, both women deserve far more credit than they ever received for their innovative approach to the study of these controversial objects.

What made this book different was the interdisciplinary approach of the editors. Cynthia Mills was an art historian and former executive editor of *American Art*, the scholarly journal of the Smithsonian American Art Museum; she was also a scholar of funerary sculpture. Pamela H. Simpson was the Ernest Williams II Professor of Art History at Washington and Lee University, where her scholarly focus centered on vernacular architecture. Together, Mills and Simpson organized this volume of essays that considered Confederate monuments not only as historical objects, but also as art. They recognized, too, that these monuments were the means by which white southerners reinterpreted the region's landscape after the Civil War. Moreover, as editors, they understood the importance of women to the process of memorialization.

Cynthia Mills's introduction demonstrated a keen understanding of the history and the issues at stake in southern white women's memorialization efforts, particularly the United Daughters of the Confederacy (UDC). The Lost Cause, the South's narrative myth about Confederate defeat, served as the driving force behind women's efforts to restore pride to the white South. Mills appropriately referred to this narrative as a "sanitized gospel," which indeed it was. Confederate veterans were lauded as heroes. Defeat was cast as the result of inadequate resources. Slavery was rejected as the cause of war. These beliefs made their way into the very monuments that the UDC placed on the southern landscape from Arlington National Cemetery to Franklin, Tennessee. Mills and Simpson understood this, but they also asked us to "shift [our] focus to the realm of the visual, including sculpture, architecture, and human performance on the landscape."

Even though hundreds of monuments were basic in design and ordered from catalogs, which Mills acknowledged, this volume is concerned with those Confederate monuments intended to make a far more grand statement on the region's urban landscapes. The essays in *Monuments to the Lost Cause*, therefore, treat the reader to the massive undertaking involved in monument building, especially fundraising, but also introduce us to the sculptors who were hired to design them, several of whom were respected internationally for their work. These essays examine Confederate memorials as varied as Stone Mountain in Georgia to the proposed National Mammy Monument intended for the Washington Mall. Richmond, Virginia, is the subject of a few essays in this volume and for good reason. As the former Capitol of the Confederacy, the city is awash in memorials, from those in Hollywood Cemetery to the grand sculptures along Monument Avenue.

Cynthia Mills and Pamela H. Simpson dedicated their book, in part, to "The new generation of scholars who have inspired us to reconsider the nature of the Lost Cause and its aftermath." Still, they left the question about African American reactions to Confederate monuments unanswered. "What did they think of [monuments] built by whites?" Mills asked, only to answer, "That is another area of research that remains for the next generation of scholars." I have no doubt had there been scholarship on the issue of African American responses to southern memorials available they would have sought it for inclusion in this book. As of this writing in 2018, we are still waiting for such scholarship, but it appears to be on the horizon as the issue of Confederate monuments across the South challenges historians to consider the role monuments have played, and continue to play, in southern race relations and politics. As W. E. B. DuBois wrote in 1931 after a visit to the South, "The most terrible thing about War, I am convinced, is its monuments." Generations later, there are many contemporary southerners, black and white, who agree.

The Charlottesville uprising in August 2017 resurrected the debate over Confederate monuments. White supremacists came to the Virginia city, they claimed, to defend the Robert E. Lee statue from removal. In truth, many of the young white men who participated in the uprising were neither from the South nor had Confederate ancestors. Nonetheless, the Lee monument served as a flashpoint for what they saw as the erasure of white history. Since then, the issue of what to do with Confederate monuments and other memorials has been the subject of intense public debates. Should they remain? Should they be removed? Or will adding historical context be enough?

*Monuments to the Lost Cause* is a useful addition to these discussions. Then, as now, the essays in this volume remind us of history's contemporary relevance.

Karen L. Cox
Charlotte, North Carolina

# Introduction

*Cynthia Mills*

The past as we know it is partly a product of the present; we continually reshape
memory, rewrite history, refashion relics.

*David Lowenthal, 1985*

ACROSS THE SOUTH, hundreds of outdoor sculptures and architectural memorials still stand in our midst, telling of the valor and virtue of the Civil War generation. The monuments of bronze and stone are messengers from the past, relaying to us the nostalgic perspectives of the white women, Confederate veterans, and descendants who commissioned them. These loyal southerners tried to come to terms with the region's humiliating defeat and the Reconstruction era that followed by creating a romanticized narrative of the war, known as the Lost Cause, to give meaning to their families' sacrifices.

Built first in grief and later in celebration during a great wave of commemorative efforts that peaked in the early 1900s, public monuments became a central means of rewriting history from the Confederate perspective—"righting history," their patrons said. Unveiled with elaborate ritual and rhetoric, they bear inscriptions speaking of honor, courage, duty, states' rights, and northern aggression.

The memorials usually gloss over uncomfortable aspects of the schism between the states, for example the moral and physical violence of slavery. Some African Americans thus have cited the continuing presence of such monuments as offensive to their own histories. At times, the sculptures also have become rallying points for white supremacists, opponents of governmental intrusion, and advocates of other extreme causes far removed from the patrons' original intentions. In a new millennium, the southern Civil War monuments are playing a central role in a public discourse about how we should remember the period, its people, and the Confederate tradition. What are we, living in an era of greater diversity, to make of these tangible markers of memory? How do they function today?

The meaning of public sculpture is not fixed but changes as audiences' experiences and beliefs grow increasingly distant from original understandings. In this anthology, authors from a wide range of scholarly disciplines reconsider these memorials, their white patrons, and their makers. They ask readers to step outside a binary world of right and wrong to consider the creativity, complexity, and contexts of these commemorative efforts. This volume's exploration of a variety of individual stories results in a fuller picture in which not only patterns emerge but also nuances, and a new richness is added to our understanding of human needs, frailties, and achievements.

One of the most important themes that does emerge is the special role played by white women's organizations, who stepped forward to become a significant force in the postwar monument campaigns. Women often took the lead in commissioning Confederate sculptures, decorating buildings, and funding institutions in the hope of preserving a positive vision of antebellum life. People outside white southern culture—African Americans, for example, or Union supporters —also wrote their histories on the southern landscape, and the alternative ways in which they did so represent another theme explored in this anthology. The essays demonstrate how the relationships and tensions between these various interest groups shifted over time.

Historian James McPherson has called the Civil War "the central event in the American historical consciousness." The conflict divided the nation to such an extent that brother at times faced brother across battle lines, and it cost the lives of more than 600,000 Americans—2 percent of the population. Most of the war was fought on southern soil, and the defeated Confederate troops went home in 1865 to destroyed houses and fields, a collapsed social and economic order, and a ruined land whose slaves had been freed. Southerners viewed the Reconstruction era that followed the war as a punishing decade.[1]

In the years immediately after the war, southern commemorative efforts centered on respectful burial of the dead and creation of mourning rituals. The cemetery was the focus of memorialization. With little money available, remembrance often took a modest, local form, such as small shafts or obelisks in graveyards. A Confederate decoration day soon was celebrated each spring, during which women and children spread flowers on graves and townspeople gathered to hear speeches praising the dead.[2]

The national government built cemeteries for the burial of Union soldiers, but it excluded the Confederate dead from these Federal graveyards, considering them to have been treasonous rebels. The creation of the National Cemetery System was a bitter pill to the South, which was left to depend on diminished private resources. And it was a tremendous source of pride that southerners rose to the challenge. Thus each stone laid was significant—an act of survival and continued genteel resistance.

White women took on these early chores and by diligent organization and fund-raising became the most important keepers of war memory in the coming decades. When the emphasis moved from mourning the dead to promoting the positive values of the Civil War effort at the end of the century, they persevered via changing organizational structures. Ladies' memorial societies formed in the 1860s and 1870s gave way in the 1890s to chapters of the regionwide United Daughters of the Confederacy. Through these groups, female members supported—and sometimes competed with—the goals of aging veterans and their sons about how to best justify the South's stubborn stand and stinging loss. Their activism, which carried women outside the limited sphere of the home, was an important and distinctive element of virtually all Confederate memorialization. It is the special topic of the essays by Catherine Bishir and Fitzhugh Brundage in part 1 of this book, but it is a thread that also is woven through the many episodes of monument building discussed elsewhere in this volume.

The death in 1870 of Gen. Robert E. Lee brought the early era of mourning for war casualties to a new stage. Virginia sculptor Edward Valentine designed the recumbent figure marking General Lee's final resting place in a special chapel at Washington and Lee University in Lexington, Virginia, where Lee had served as president after the war. As Pamela Simpson notes in her essay, the sculpture portrays Lee as a Christian knight, a warrior aristocrat who fought with valor and died with no shame. To this day, pilgrims approach it with hushed reverence.

Many other memorial drives, like the effort to erect a statue of Lee's popular lieutenant, Thomas "Stonewall" Jackson, on his Lexington grave site or the transformation of Old Blandford Church in Petersburg, Virginia, into one of the most beautiful shrines of the Confederacy, took decades to complete during these financially difficult times. Most came to completion in a new period of southern historical memory, which emerged in the decades following the end of Reconstruction. Reconstruction, which had been intended to protect newly freed blacks, officially came to a close in 1877 when all Federal troops were withdrawn from the South. With its eclipse, the immediate postwar era of grief and mourning in the cemetery began to give way to a regionwide celebration of the Confederate cause in public places.[3]

Even if the war was lost, many southerners now felt that tribute should be paid to the antebellum values shared by those who fought. From the late 1880s through the 1910s, hundreds of outdoor sculptures were installed across the South embracing what was called the Lost Cause. The Lost Cause is the name given to a whole body of writings, speeches, performances, prints, and other visual imagery that presented a certain version of Confederate history—as told from a southern white perspective (fig. 0.1). This sentimental narrative said the war was fought to defend states' rights and to protect a chivalrous antebellum way of life from northern aggression. It pictured an

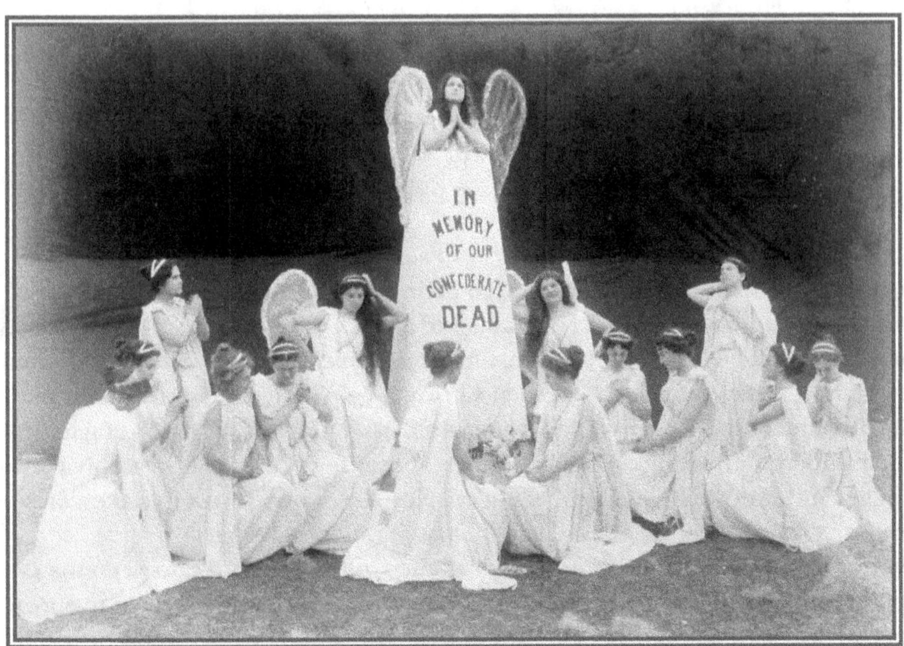



Fig. 0.1. "In Memory of Our Confederate Dead," circa 1885–90.
Collection of George S. Whiteley IV, Atlanta.

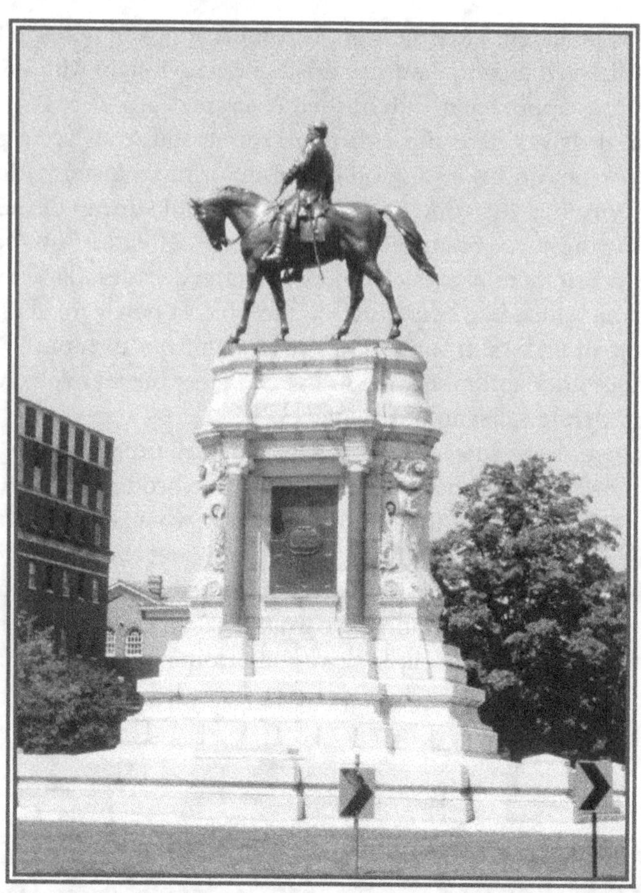

Fig. 0.2. Robert E. Lee Monument by Marius-Jean-Antonin Mercié,
dedicated May 29, 1890, on Monument Avenue,
Richmond, Virginia. Photograph by
Sean McCormally.

Old South in which genteel white men protected their beautiful and virtuous women and children, fighting with dignity and pride. While Lost Cause advocates did not seek to reinstate slavery, they often argued that it had been a benevolent institution in which southern whites gave guidance and nurture to a simple, dusky people who needed Christian help and were loyal to their masters. They emotionally contended that slavery was not the main reason for the war. According to this retelling, southern men suffered no shame in military defeat, because the war was lost only because of the industrial might and overwhelming numbers of the North, not because of mistakes, lack of bravery, or a false cause. Above all, the Lost Cause sought a restoration of respect.[4]

A number of regionwide organizations such as the United Confederate Veterans (founded in 1889) and United Daughters of the Confederacy (founded in 1894) were formed to spread this sanitized gospel. All had a common goal of controlling the revision of history; their programs included textbook and school curriculum campaigns as well as lectures, entertainments such as tableaux vivants, and veterans reunions. While the rhetoric of the Lost Cause has been well documented and much discussed in contemporary scholarship, this collection of essays seeks to shift the focus to the realm of the visual, including sculpture, architecture, and human performance on the landscape.

In the 1880s and later decades, some of the most costly, grand-scale memorials were erected to Confederate military and political heroes, primarily the big three: General Lee, Stonewall Jackson, and President Jefferson Davis. But Lee's image was paramount. In New Orleans, for example, Lee's form rose in 1884 atop a towering column. In Richmond, the heart of the Confederacy, a new street named Monument Avenue was created for an equestrian sculpture of Lee designed by the French artist Marius-Jean-Antonin Mercié (fig. 0.2). It was dedicated in 1890 during a major reunion of aging veterans with an audience surpassing 100,000. This colossal statue was to be the first in a line of five heroic memorials on the avenue—which became one of the most sacred spaces of Confederate memory—including one to Davis, whose death in 1889 set the whole South to mourning anew. In part 2 of this volume, Richard Guy Wilson describes the formation of Monument Avenue, analyzing it as a significant urban design and architectural phenomenon. M. Anna Fariello also writes of how "Winnie" Davis, the "first daughter of the Confederacy" born during the war, is remembered among a trilogy of monuments designed by sculptor George Julian Zolnay for the Davis family grave site in Richmond's Hollywood Cemetery.

Certain sculptors became key image makers of Confederate memory: Edward V. Valentine, Frederick W. Sievers, and Moses Ezekiel in Virginia; Pompeo Coppini and Frank Teich in Texas; and Zolnay, Frederick Cleveland Hibbard, and F. Wellington Ruckstull in a variety of locales. Some were native sons, some northerners, and others immigrants from Europe. Most were not of the same artistic rank as Augustus Saint-Gaudens and Daniel Chester French, who created the best-known northern Civil War monuments. And the bulk of Confederate monuments were modest affairs, often purchased for a price between $1,500 and $3,000 directly from a commercial monument-making firm, such as the McNeel Marble Company in Marietta, Georgia, or the Muldoon Monument Company in Louisville, Kentucky (fig. 0.3). A number were imported from Italy. The majority were carved of stone, often marble, but a good many are bronze, zinc, copper, granite, and even concrete. Most represent a single soldier, usually standing at parade rest on a high pedestal decorated with a variety of motifs, such as the letters CSA, a Confederate flag, cannonballs, crossed swords, or reliefs of Lee and Jackson or local heroes.

In his essay in this anthology, David Currey examines how the image of the virtuous Confederate common soldier functioned in Franklin, Tennessee, not just as a solace but also as a model for southerners to mold the individual character of a new generation. Hundreds of sentinel monuments were dedicated in town squares and on courthouse and state capitol lawns, as well as in parks and cemeteries. They were similar to many erected in the North, sometimes even commissioned from the same sculptors or firms, but often distinguished by the uniform and hat with broad brim. The facial features range from those of a mature white infantryman with mustache to a beardless youth. An analysis of survey statistics in the Inventory of American Sculpture shows that dedications of these soldier monuments peaked between 1903 and 1914, with a number being unveiled during World War I. The majority of southern soldier monuments were made possible by local chapters of the United Daughters of the Confederacy.[5] The stories told of fundraising and rituals around these seemingly mundane monuments confirm they had tremendous meaning in town after town, where people raised money for them with dances, dinners, stamp sales, all the strategies of the human imagination. The monuments seem to have represented an important confirmation of mutual respect and shared values and experiences.

# 50 Confederate Monuments Sold By
# The McNeel Marble Company   -   -

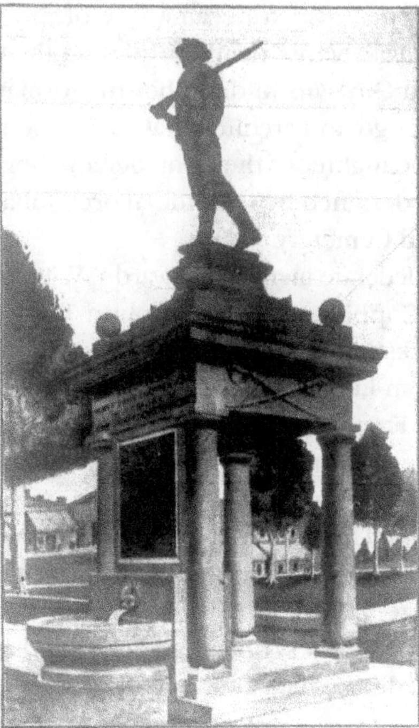

IN the April issue of the VETERAN we announced that we had sold monuments to 37 U. D. C. Chapters, and called the attention of the Daughters to our proposition to furnish the different Chapters with our plans for raising funds for Confederate monuments.

In response to this advertisement we have received numerous requests from Chapters throughout the South, each of whom we have gladly furnished with plans. These Chapters are now on the high road to success, and several of them have already placed their orders with us.

Since our last advertisement our list of Chapters sold has been increased from 37 to 50, the following Chapters having been added: Franklin, N. C., El Dorado, Ark., Monticello, Ga., McDonough, Ga., Jacksonville, Ala., Dresden, Tenn., Ozark, Ala., Union City, Tenn., Tifton, Ga., Eastman, Ga., Lakeland, Fla., Griffin, Ga., and a $10,000.00 monument to be erected to Hood's Texas Brigade, State Capitol Grounds, Austin, Tex.

Our plans for raising funds, our liberal terms, and reasonable prices have made it easy for the U. D. C. Chapters that have dealt with us to secure handsome monuments, and, best of all, to secure them *now*, before the Confederate Veterans and the good women of the sixties have passed away.

Our plans are yours for the asking. ¶ A letter from your Chapter will be given careful consideration and will receive a prompt reply.

## THE McNEEL MARBLE COMPANY
### MARIETTA, GA.

The largest monumental dealers in the South.     Branch House, Columbia, Tenn.

Fig. 0.3. Advertisement by the McNeel Marble Company, Marietta, Georgia, published in *Confederate Veteran* 17, no. 10 (October 1909): 528.

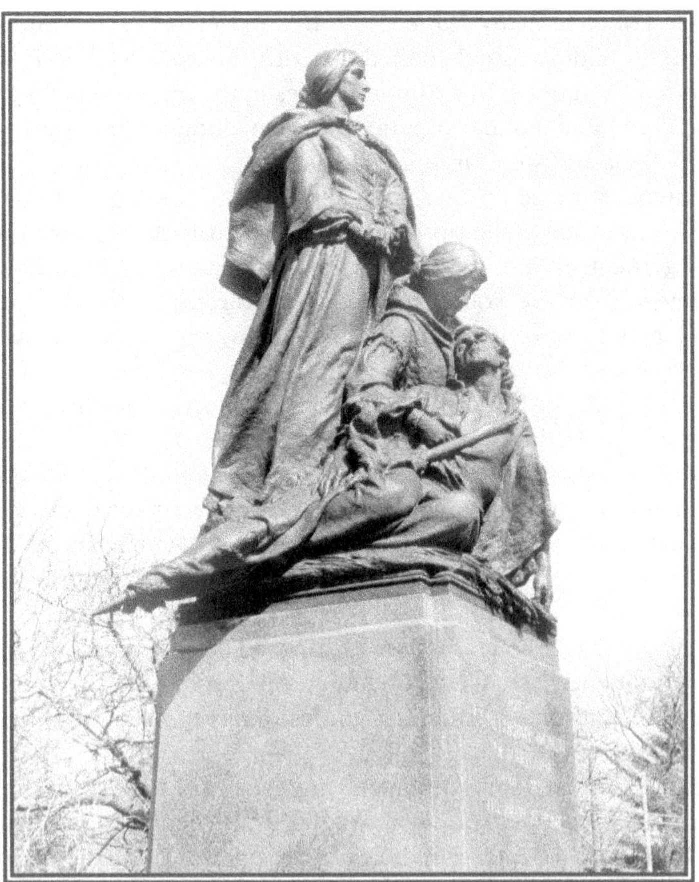

Fig. 0.4. Monument to Confederate Women, Baltimore, Maryland,
designed by J. Maxwell Miller and unveiled November 2, 1918.
Photograph by Sean McCormally.

Later a number of monuments were built by veterans to honor women's role in the war. Often they showed the idealized figure of woman as queen of the domestic space, someone worth fighting for. At other times Southern Woman was portrayed as a mother who read the story of the war to the next generation, training her sons to fight the next battle for southern honor, or she was shown ministering to fallen soldiers (fig. 0.4).

A clear, narrative style with carefully described figures was chosen for all of the Confederate sculptures, including the less common allegorical or male-female groupings, as the best way to relay their message of southern pride. Great attention was paid to inscriptions, which distinguished each town's monument, and featured Lost Cause ideology and such common refrains as "Lest We Forget" and citations from the poem "The Bivouac of the Dead" by Theodore O'Hara as well as quotations from Jefferson Davis. Unveilings sometimes took place on important historical dates, such as Confederate Memorial Days celebrated on April 26 in the Deep South, the day of Gen. Joseph Johnston's surrender; May 10 in the Carolinas, the anniversary of the death of Stonewall Jackson; or on various dates between May 10 and mid-June in parts of Virginia.[6] The unveiling ritual—described in many of the essays that follow—always included an elaborate procession and speeches. Children usually pulled the cord, a potent symbol of the monument's role of speaking to future generations. In addition to sites in the eleven seceding states, Confederate memorials may be found in a number of other places, including Illinois, Kansas, Kentucky, Maryland, Missouri, New York, and West Virginia.

While African Americans made up a substantial portion of the population, they expressed their different view of the Civil War in the postwar South primarily through means other than monument building.[7] Digging deep into newspaper archives, Kathleen Clark shows us how they performed their memories on the southern landscape through annual group observances on occasions such as Lincoln Day or Emancipation Day. Using the example of Augusta, Georgia, she describes African Americans' celebrations not only of the anniversary of emancipation but also other dates associated with the birth of freedom, such as July 4 and the passage of the Fifteenth Amendment. As years went by, however, their commemorations faced mounting obstacles, ranging from increasing white resistance to organizational rivalries, and the exuberant demonstrations of the Reconstruction era gave way to tamer events by the early 1900s. If African Americans did not have the wherewithal, or did not wish to build their own monuments to the Lost Cause, what did they think of those built by whites? That is another area of research that remains for the next generation of scholars.

Catherine Zipf argues that Union officials also imposed their "countermemories" in the heart of the South through alternate means—the architectural design of the Federal cemeteries spread throughout the region. She contends that design decisions represent a deliberate embodiment of Federal authority and conquest.

Obviously all of the Confederate monuments are backward-looking in the sense that they are tributes to the dead or ask people to honor a nostalgic constructed vision of the past. But historian Gaines Foster, in his influential interpretation of the stages of Confederate memory, has persuasively argued that they were not entirely regressive. He says they served a useful function at the turn of the century in helping southerners come to terms with the vast social and economic change their region was experiencing. The sculptures seemed to provide solid reference points about a common heritage in a confusing new world in which the South was reuniting economically with the North, women's roles were changing, the class system dissolving.[8]

The end of the century saw a growing reconciliation between North and South, especially as both sides joined in 1898 in fighting on a common front in the Spanish-American War. After that, the Federal government took a number of conciliatory steps, such as returning captured flags to southern states. In other expressions of respect, some Confederate bodies for the first time also were moved into Arlington National Cemetery near Washington, D.C., and the United Daughters of the Confederacy were permitted to erect a huge monument there, which they called a gift to the nation. In part 3, Karen Cox describes this unusual national memorial and interprets the resulting bronze as still shielding a desire for vindication. While Lost Cause sculpture did not generally directly refer to slavery, this monument does show a figure that becomes an icon in the Lost Cause mythology—the black female household slave who was said to have happily cared for southern white children and families. Supporting the notion that blacks were content in their servitude, the "mammy" was another of the tropes of historical amnesia promoted at a time when white supremacy ideas were strong in the North and South after separate-but-equal court rulings in the 1890s. In part 4, Micki McElya explains how a drive to build a monument to the "black mammy" in Washington, D.C., was nearly successful in the early 1920s, a period of especially rampant racism throughout the nation.

The Confederate Memorial Institute, better known as the South's "Battle Abbey," was built in Richmond as a response to the construction of Grant's Tomb in New York and the planned Lincoln Memorial in Washington. William Rasmussen describes the 1910 competition for the design of this "temple of the Lost Cause," a response to the North that also attracted national attention.

A few monuments continued to rise in the 1920s and 1930s and later decades. Some, like the Battle of Nashville Monument in Tennessee, originally dedicated on Armistice Day in 1927, honored the Blue and the Gray, the memory of both the Union and Confederate dead, as well as the soldiers who fought in World War I.[9] But after the end of the war generation many of the Confederate memorials that once had been unveiled to tears and acclaim were neglected and left in poor condition. As populations changed, Confederate parks in some cases became dilapidated inner-city sites. For many southerners, the monuments became nearly invisible, relics of a past they would rather forget than revere.

A new tide of interest in these monuments peaked in the 1960s, however, with the centennial of the Civil War. The 100-year celebration happened to fall amid the civil rights era in the United States, when African Americans were aggressively claiming a fuller equality and women, too, were starting to assert increased independence. African Americans and civil rights activists of all backgrounds joined to seek an end to segregation and to win access to economic and political power. A landmark Supreme Court ruling *(Brown* vs. *Board of Education)* in 1954 had declared that racially segregated schools were a violation of the U.S. Constitution, but federal efforts to desegregate schools met with resistance in the South for many years. A decade of black-led protests finally compelled Congress to pass the 1964 Civil Rights Act and 1965 Voting Rights Act. From some southerners' perspective, these actions represented another imposition of northern control on the former states of the Confederacy.

It was amid the turbulence of the 1950s and 1960s that a number of southern state legislatures voted to raise the Confederate flag again atop the domes of their capitol buildings in a new act of defiance. (In 1956, for example, Georgia redesigned its flag to include the "starry cross" of the Confederate battle flag. Alabama and South Carolina put a battle flag atop their capitols in the early 1960s.) In some towns, monuments also were cleaned and rededicated. Campaigns were begun to add more southern monuments to battlefield parks such as Gettysburg. The flags and monuments were symbols, in some part at least, of a revived southern streak of resistance and defiance.

Over the 1970s, 1980s, and 1990s, blacks did gain increased voting power, and governance of many southern towns slowly changed. With political leadership also came increasing black economic power. This has brought a new kind of attention in recent years to monuments and other symbols of the Lost Cause as the multiple perspectives of our new society have given voice to alternative views.

Some feel deeply that the monuments, flags, and other Confederate symbols place a stigma on the South, that they offend or, at the least, represent an indifference to the oppression of blacks in antebellum years. Now blacks with political muscle, and many whites supporting their views, have gained a say over the narrative of memory. To date, the most attention has been given to battle flags. Court suits were filed by critics charging that the flags are racist symbols and that governments have no right to display them. African American protesters marched, carrying signs such as

"Your Heritage Is My Slavery." Slowly, some of the state flags have come down, primarily through economic pressure and legislative action. Calls for South Carolina to take down the battle flag flying over its statehouse dome became an issue in the 2000 national elections as President Clinton and candidates for president entered the debate (fig. 0.5). In South Carolina, business groups applied strong pressure to move the flag, and the NAACP launched a boycott that reduced tourism in the state. Critics said the South must put behind itself the tokens of its earlier, isolated era if it wishes to join a global economic market.[10]

In the case of Lost Cause monuments, similar criticisms have been expressed. To the descendants of former slaves, these sculptures appear to be hurtful remnants of a biased history, not appropriate models for emulation. The veterans who originally erected the monuments hoped they would wipe clean the South's shame at military defeat. As Sanford Levinson has written: "All monuments are efforts, in their own way, to stop time," but history mocks such efforts. Statues can later generate discomfort or be used for new ideological purposes.[11]

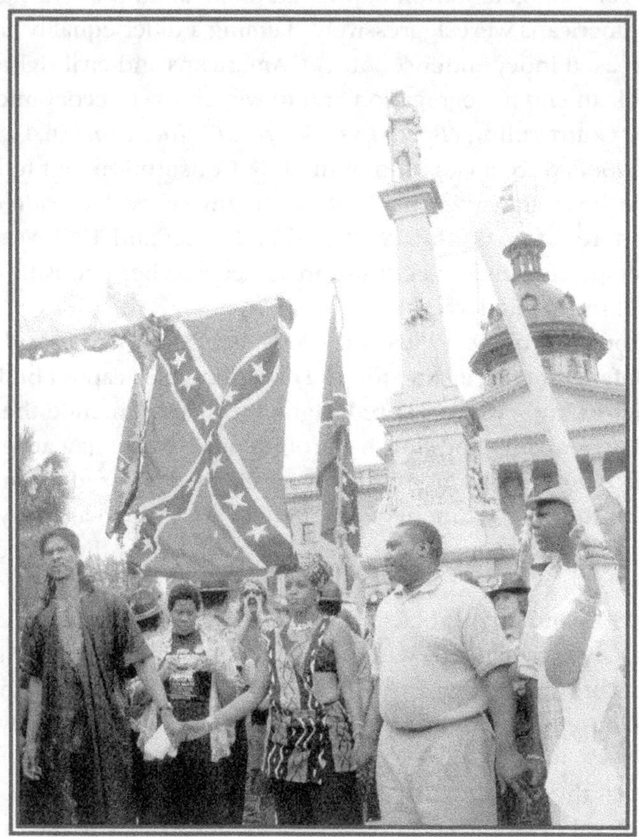

Fig. 0.5. Demonstrators watch a Confederate battle flag burn
during a May 10, 2000, protest against the flying of the
battle flag over the South Carolina statehouse.
Associated Press/Wide World photograph.

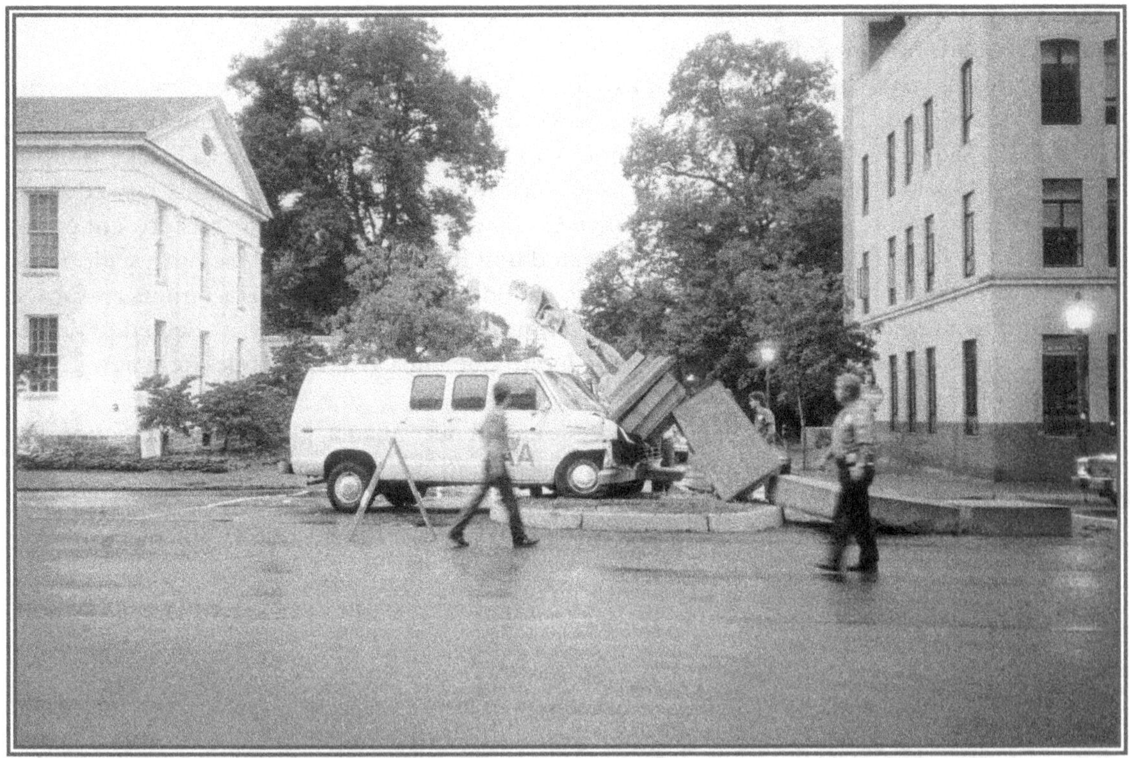

Fig. 0.6. Alexandria, Virginia, soldiers' monument, designed by Caspar Buberl and dedicated in 1889, was toppled when a van struck it in 1988. It has since been returned to its former position. Photograph by Claude W. Dean.

Now that new forces have the power to shape the narrative of memory, there have been a number of lawsuits and some monuments have been relocated—usually in connection with accidents or adjacent construction or roadway projects—but there has been no systematic effort to remove statues. In modern America there is, after all, a strong government-supported desire to provide space for groups of many different identities, origins, and ethnicities. Even when damaged (like the 1889 bronze Confederate soldier monument in Alexandria, Virginia, designed by Caspar Buberl, that was struck by a van in 1988, fig. 0.6), Civil War monuments generally are repaired if possible and reinstalled, often with rededication ceremonies. The bitter criticism of the Confederate memorials has been countered by the region's wish to preserve its distinctive heritage. The goals of the post-1960s historic preservation movement have come face to face with questions about how these monuments can continue to exist in a multicultural society.

With preservation has come the opportunity to reinterpret the monuments and make decisions about how they can continue to function. In general, this has been done by seeing them as slates, or palimpsests, on which history can be layered. The old message is not erased, but new language is written over it or beside it. In some cases plaques have been added to monuments or buildings explaining them in a new way, citing a more neutral history instead of the rhetoric of the Lost Cause. Some sculptures have been relocated to less visible or potent spots.[12] A final option in areas of sacred space, such as Monument Avenue, has been to leave the public sculptures in place but to add others honoring different kinds of leaders.

In the closing essay in this anthology, Brian Black and Bryn Varley discuss how Monument Avenue, with its representations of Lee, Davis, Jackson, and J. E. B. Stuart, has remained a distinctive space in Richmond's urban landscape. But by the early 1990s, Virginia had a black governor and Richmond had a black mayor as well as an African American majority on its city council. Names of streets and schools were being changed and holidays added to reflect its present population and provide different heroes. Few suggested bulldozing Monument Avenue's sculptures, but many felt something needed to be done there to address today's truths. For various reasons, a monument to an African American sports hero, tennis player Arthur Ashe, was selected to desegregate the avenue. It stands in the row of Confederate chieftains as a role model for a new generation in a New South.

Another interesting sign of the times is Stone Mountain near Atlanta, Georgia, where equestrian figures of the South's Civil War heroes have been carved into the mountain face. Grace Hale describes how this southern Mount Rushmore, decades in the making, is today a vast recreation area, described as a park for all. In another form of layering of southern history, the image of civil

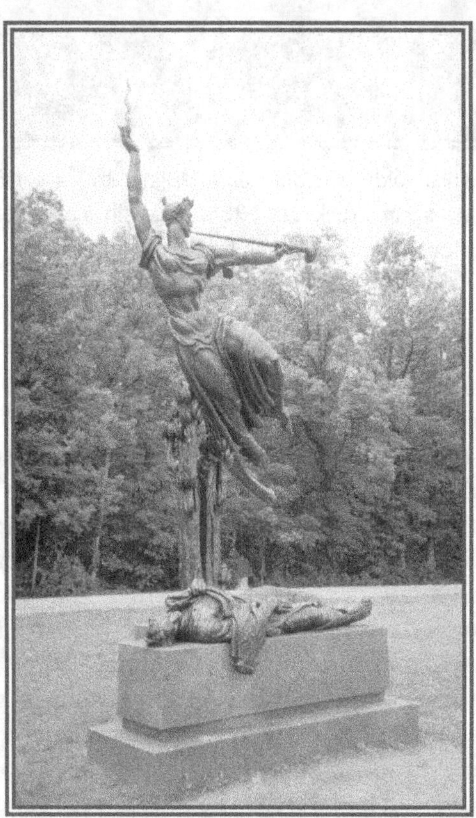

Fig. 0.7. Louisiana State Monument, designed by Donald DeLue. Dedicated June 11, 1971, on Confederate Row, Gettysburg National Military Park, Pennsylvania. Photograph by Cynthia Mills.

rights leader Martin Luther King Jr. has been projected over those of Lee, Jackson, and Davis in light shows upon the face of the mountain.

A small minority with extremist causes, generally reactionary, continue, however, to latch on to Confederate symbols as symbols of resistance and defiance. Pulitzer Prize–winning author Tony Horwitz, in his book *Confederates in the Attic,* discusses some of these antigovernment, antitax protestors and white supremacists, among others. Horwitz also describes in a gripping way the obsession with Civil War reenactment that has been growing in recent decades. This phenomenon demonstrates a genuine passion for reconsidering the Civil War today through individual and collective performance of memory.[13]

The story of the southern Civil War monuments is an ongoing one. Lost Cause groups, such as the United Daughters of Confederacy (UDC) and Sons of Confederate Veterans, still exist, and Confederate monuments are still being put up, especially now in battlefields, a less controversial site than statehouses. In 1917, the UDC raised $50,000 for completion of Frederick Hibbard's elaborate Confederate memorial at the national military park at Shiloh, Tennessee, with seven bronze allegorical figures and two stylized marble friezes of soldier's heads, in silent tribute to all Confederate soldiers but especially those who fought in the bloody battle at Shiloh. In 1971, Donald DeLue's spectacular Louisiana State Monument (fig. 0.7) was dedicated on Confederate Row in Gettysburg National Military Park in Pennsylvania, a project initiated by the Louisiana State UDC, which won $100,000 in state appropriations to see it completed. This colossal sculpture, one of three DeLue designed for Gettysburg in the 1960s and 1970s, shows the Spirit of the Confederacy blowing a clarion and holding a flaming cannonball in her other hand, with the figure of a fallen soldier below clutching the Confederate flag to his chest. Additional monuments were installed at Gettysburg in the 1980s and 1990s.[14]

Obviously, there are more chapters to be written in the story of Confederate collective memory, and the meaning of the monuments will continue to be reconsidered in a new millennium. Your editors believe the essays that follow will help to reshape our thinking about the Lost Cause by detailing the experiences of a variety of people in the postwar era as well as the ways in which their viewpoints changed over time. The essays grouped together in part 1 demonstrate the differing perspectives held by white southerners, male and female, Union supporters, and African Americans as they established the rites of memory following the Civil War. Part 2 recounts some of the debates that took place about how certain larger-than-life heroes and heroines of the South and the common soldier should be remembered. Part 3 focuses on southerners' continued desire to respond to the North in a period of Confederate celebration and reconciliation at the turn of the century; and in part 4 we witness the uneasy ways in which memories at times were reconstructed or adjusted as the twentieth century advanced. Together the essays highlight some of the key themes about how southerners expressed their hopes and aspirations in art, architecture, and performance on the southern landscape.

This book would not have been possible without the work of a handful of pioneering scholars whose research many of our authors relied on. First and foremost is Gaines Foster, whose *Ghosts of the Confederacy: Defeat, the Lost Cause, and the Emergence of the New South* (1987) remains essential reading for students of this subject. Kirk Savage's *Standing Soldiers, Kneeling Slaves: Race, War, and Monument in Nineteenth-Century America* (1997) and Kurt Piehler's *Remembering War the American Way* (1995) have laid the ground for all future discussions of Civil War and

Lost Cause memorialization. David W. Blight's fine book *Race and Reunion: The Civil War in American Memory* was not published until after our essays were completed, but it is another useful and important resource for future scholars. The task of identifying the breadth of Confederate monuments continues, now with new resources available from the Smithsonian American Art Museum's Inventory of American Sculpture, which has recorded the results of a comprehensive survey of public sculpture nationwide undertaken by the Save Outdoor Sculpture project. Indispensable still are Ralph Widener Jr.'s *Confederate Monuments: Enduring Symbols of the South and the War between the States* (1982) and Bettie Alder Calhoun's *Historic Southern Monuments: Representative Memorials of the Heroic Dead of the Southern Confederacy* (1911). Many monuments were discussed or pictured in *Confederate Veteran* (1893–1932), the official organ of the United Confederate Veterans, which later also represented the United Daughters of the Confederacy and Confederated State Monument Association; it was a crucial voice of the Lost Cause.[15]

Organizing this anthology and bringing it to publication has been a five-year process, and many individuals helped us immeasurably along the way. Catherine Bishir and Fitzhugh Brundage contributed much more than their individual essays. John Coski, Gaines Foster, Kirk Savage, Anastatia Sims, and two anonymous readers generously evaluated our proposal or our manuscript at different stages of peer review and provided comments that greatly improved this book. Acquisitions editor Joyce Harrison at the University of Tennessee Press had confidence in our proposal from the start and Scot Danforth made the editing and production process a smooth one. We also thank Monica Phillips, the editor of the manuscript, and Bill Adams, designer at the press. Stephen Gapps, Michael Anne Lynn, Dennis Montagna, Ann Hunter McLean, Michael Panhorst, and Pamela Potter-Hennessey ultimately did not contribute essays to this volume, but their ongoing work and our discussions with them helped us frame our thinking during early stages of the project. Potter-Hennessey, in particular, was a key player in our earliest brainstorming sessions and helped us select the initial essays before she was sidelined by a busy academic schedule. Thanks, too, to Civil War buff Robert Killian for reading our completed manuscript. On the home front, the editors thank Sean McCormally and Henry Simpson, as always, for their support, as well as Brenda, Joe, Peter, and Laura.

A concluding note about usage in this anthology: In public forums, most members of Ladies' Memorial Societies or the United Daughters of the Confederacy identified themselves and other women through their husbands' names. Where possible, we have used the women's full names to better identify them in the style of our time, but in many cases their first names are unknown.

## Notes

1. William R. Ferris, "'The War That Never Goes Away': A Conversation with Civil War Historian James M. McPherson," *Humanities* 21, no. 2 (Mar./Apr. 2000): 4–9, quotation on p. 2. The opening quotation for this essay is from David Lowenthal, *The Past Is a Foreign Country* (Cambridge: Cambridge Univ. Press, 1985), 26.

2. A major exception to the modest size of early markers was the ninety-foot stone pyramid constructed by the community in Richmond's Hollywood Cemetery in 1869 near Confederate graves.

3. Thanks to Michael Anne Lynn, executive director of the Stonewall Jackson Foundation and house, Lexington, Virginia, for sharing the text of her lecture "Making a Fitting Memorial: The Edward V. Valentine Statue of Thomas J. 'Stonewall' Jackson in the Stonewall Jackson Memorial Cemetery, Lexington, Va." On the

Petersburg church, which features Tiffany windows installed between 1904 and 1912 and was dedicated to the seceding states, see Ann Hunter McLean, "Unveiling the Lost Cause: A Study of Monuments to the Civil War Memory in Richmond, Virginia, and Vicinity" (Ph.D. diss., Univ. of Virginia, 1998), 162–71.

4. Gaines Foster discusses the terms *Lost Cause* and *Confederate Tradition* in *Ghosts of the Confederacy: Defeat, the Lost Cause, and the Emergence of the New South* (New York: Oxford Univ. Press, 1987), 4–5. Also see, among other possible sources, Charles Regan Wilson, *Baptized in Blood: The Religion of the Lost Cause, 1865–1920* (Athens: Univ. of Georgia Press, 1980); David Blight, *Race and Reunion: The Civil War in American Memory* (Cambridge, Mass.: Harvard Univ. Press, 2001); and Gary W. Gallagher and Alan T. Nolan, eds., *The Myth of the Lost Cause and Civil War History* (Bloomington: Indiana Univ. Press, 2000). Women often represented states in tableaux vivants. There may be fifteen women at the shrine in fig. 0.1 because border states Kentucky, Maryland, Missouri, and West Virginia were sometimes counted as well as the eleven seceding states in Lost Cause iconography.

5. See Michael Wilson Panhorst, "Lest We Forget: Monuments and Memorial Sculpture in National Military Parks on Civil War Battlefields, 1861–1917" (Ph.D. diss., Univ. of Delaware, 1988), 210–24. Panhorst notes that a more active pose outnumbers the "sentinel" figures in battlefield parks (222–24). Also see Lewis Waldron Williams, "Commercially Produced Forms of American Civil War Monuments" (master's thesis, Univ. of Illinois, 1948). A more recent discussion is Kirk Savage, *Standing Soldiers, Kneeling Slaves: Race, War, and Monument in Nineteenth-Century America* (Princeton: Princeton Univ. Press, 1997), chap. 6. Catalogs include W. H. Mullins Co., "The Blue and the Gray, Statues in Stamped Copper and Bronze" (Cleveland: Caxton Co., 1913). A greater understanding of the types and dates of Confederate monuments, their inscriptions, and their patronage is now possible through the Inventory of American Sculpture at the Smithsonian American Art Museum, which includes documentation on hundreds of Confederate monuments surveyed by the museum's Save Outdoor Sculpture program in the 1990s. Gaines Foster, in his *Ghosts of the Confederacy*, includes a chart of 544 Confederate monuments erected in the South, 1865–1912, in appendix 1, p. 273.

6. On Confederate memorial days, see Foster, *Ghosts of the Confederacy*, 42.

7. A monument representing a black Union soldier was completed in 1920 in a Norfolk, Virginia, cemetery. It grew out of the efforts of James Fuller, a former slave and Union veteran, to set aside a section of the cemetery for blacks who had served in the war and to raise a monument to their memory there. See Savage, *Standing Soldiers, Kneeling Slaves*, 187–88.

8. These ideas are discussed throughout part 2 of Foster, *Ghosts of the Confederacy*.

9. After extensive conservation, the Battle of Nashville Monument, sculpted by Giuseppe Moretti, was rededicated in a new location on June 26, 1999, with a speech by the governor and a free concert. Portions had been destroyed in a tornado in 1974, and construction of an interstate highway interchange had obstructed public view of the monument in the 1980s.

10. These flag disputes have been widely covered in the news media. Mississippi residents in 2001 voted overwhelmingly to keep a 107-year-old state flag that contains the Confederate battle cross in its upper corner. The South Carolina Legislature decided to move the battle flag from the statehouse dome to a Confederate soldier monument in front of the statehouse, sparking continued protests. A book that gives insight into the legal considerations in such cases is George Schedler's *Racist Symbols and Reparations: Philosophical Reflections on the Vestiges of the American Civil War* (Lanham, Md.: Rowman and Littlefield Publishers, 1998). See also J. Michael Martinez, William D. Richardson, and Ron McNinch-Su, eds., *Confederate Symbols in the Contemporary South* (Gainesville: Univ. Press of Florida, 2000). During the lengthy debate over what to do with the Confederate flag, the South Carolina legislature commissioned a $1.1 million granite and bronze monument to African Americans by sculptor Ed Dwight, depicting historical scenes and notable contemporary

figures. It was unveiled at the state capitol in Columbia in March 2001. See "Columbia, S.C.: Monument to African-Americans Unveiled," *New York Times,* Mar. 30, 2001.

11. Sanford Levinson, *Written in Stone: Public Monuments in Changing Societies* (Durham, N.C.: Duke Univ. Press, 1998), 7–8.

12. For example, Texas Gov. George W. Bush's administration removed two Confederate memorial plaques from the state supreme court building, including one bearing the image of the battle flag. They had adorned the lobby since 1955, after the building was constructed with money once set aside in a Confederate widows' pension fund. The plaques were replaced with two new ones, one of which says, "Because this building was built with monies from the Confederate pension fund, it was, at that time, designated as a memorial to the Texans who served the Confederacy." The other extols the principle of equal justice for all citizens. Paul Duggan, "Texas Removes Confederate Symbols from Court," *Washington Post,* June 13, 2000.

13. Australian scholar Stephen Gapps of the University of Technology, Sydney, has discussed the body of the reenactor as a mobile monument, the ultimate site for memory. We thank him for sharing with us his unpublished manuscript, "Mobile Monuments in Cemeteries without Headstones: Southern Civil War Reenactors and the Possibility of Winning the Lost Cause." Tony Horwitz, *Confederates in the Attic: Dispatches from the Unfinished Civil War* (New York: Random House, 1999).

14. Michael Panhorst and Dennis Montagna drew my attention to these monuments. Sadly, time did not permit either to participate in this anthology, which does not otherwise address the vast field of battlefield monuments, another area that awaits future scholarship. See Panhorst, "Lest We Forget," 30–38, on Shiloh, and David G. Martin, *Confederate Monuments at Gettysburg: The Gettysburg Battle Monuments* (Hightstown, N.J.: Longstreet House, 1986), 1:40–42. In 1999, Maryland millionaire William F. Chaney announced plans to build thirty-foot-high equestrian sculptures of Lee, Jackson, and Stuart on a privately purchased parcel of Antietam battlefield in Sharpsburg, Maryland. Matthew Mosk, "Southern Heroes to Rise at Antietam," *Washington Post,* Dec. 26, 1999.

15. In addition to Savage, *Standing Soldiers, Kneeling Slaves,* and Blight, *Race and Reunion,* see Kurt Piehler's *Remembering War the American Way* (Washington, D.C.: Smithsonian Institution Press, 1995); Ralph Widener Jr., *Confederate Monuments: Enduring Symbols of the South and the War between the States* (Washington, D.C.: Andromeda Press, 1982); and Bettie Alder Calhoun, *Historic Southern Monuments: Representative Memorials of the Heroic Dead of the Southern Confederacy* (New York: Neale Publishing Co., 1911).

# Part I

## THE RITES OF MEMORY: DIFFERING PERSPECTIVES

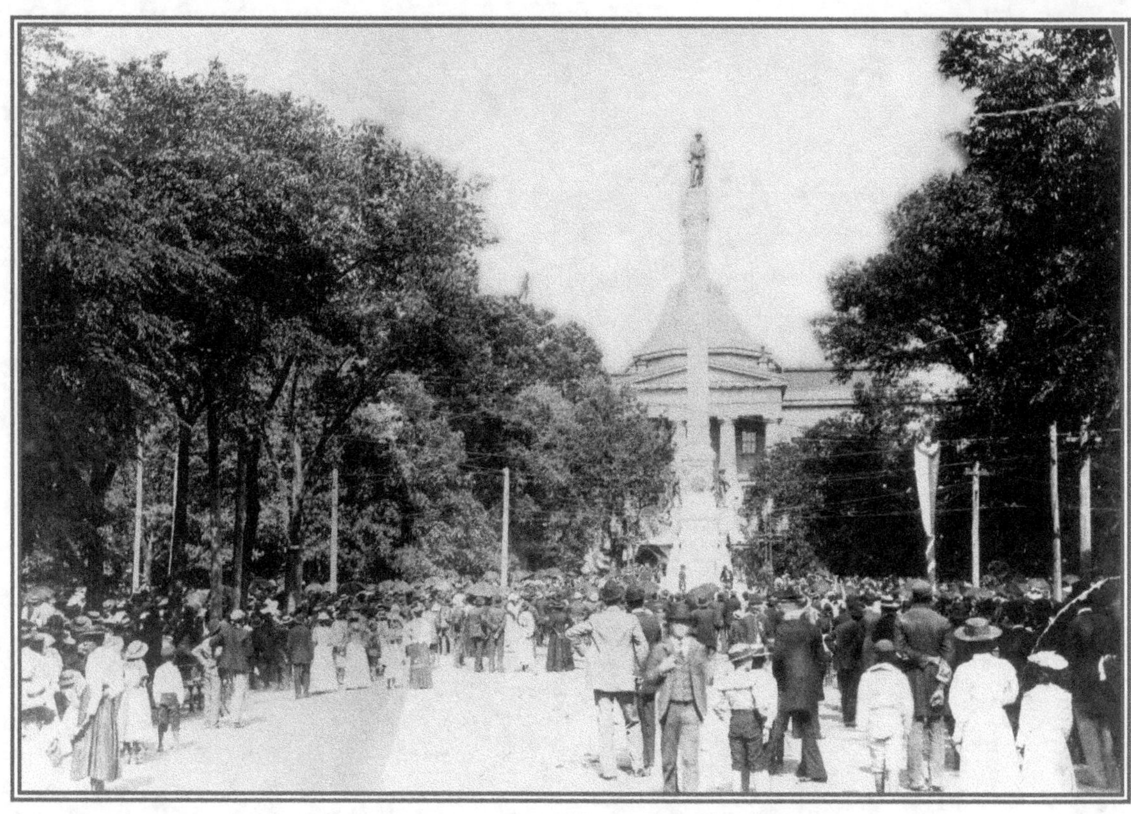

Fig. 1.1. Onlookers view Confederate Monument, Raleigh, North Carolina, on day of unveiling, May 20, 1895. Photograph by J. A. Anderson, courtesy of James Bundy, Raleigh. North Carolina Division of Archives and History.

# 1

# "A Strong Force of Ladies"

Women, Politics, and Confederate Memorial Associations in Nineteenth-Century Raleigh

*Catherine W. Bishir*

ON A FINE DAY IN MAY 1895 at the state capitol in Raleigh, North Carolina, Nancy Haywood Blount Branch surveyed the scene around her. Wearing her customary black and seated on a grandstand among other dignitaries, the seventy-seven-year-old widow gazed across a crowd of thousands that extended as far as the eye could see. Confederate flags, some bright and new, others faded to pale pink and blue, fluttered throughout the gathering of men and women, young and old. Line after line of aging veterans stood in wait for the occasion—the unveiling of the state's Confederate Monument (fig. 1.1). Near Mrs. Gen. Lawrence O'Bryan Branch, as she was known, sat a few other women, including her daughter, Nancy Branch Jones, and two other Confederate widows, Mrs. Gen. D. H. Hill and Mrs. Gen. "Stonewall" Jackson. Julia Jackson Christian, Jackson's seven-year-old granddaughter, clad in white organdy and with pink ribbons in her golden hair, sat in readiness to unveil the seventy-five-foot granite monument.

For Nancy Branch, as for many others, the occasion evoked memories that reached back three decades. In May 1866 she had moved into a position of leadership as the founding president of Raleigh's first organization to assure the proper burial and commemoration of the Confederate dead. The following year, in a turbulent period of military occupation, she and the Ladies' Memorial Association (LMA) of Wake County established one of the first Confederate cemeteries in the South and held their first memorial ceremonies on May 10, 1867. Since that time, the association had erected a monument at the cemetery and sponsored ever more elaborate memorial events in a changing political landscape. Most recently, Branch's daughter had led the North Carolina Monumental Association, formed in 1892 as an outgrowth of the LMA, in producing this public monument and event, whose scale and proud assertion of the Confederate cause would have been unimaginable in 1866.

These women and the organizations they led in the decades following the Civil War assumed important new roles in southern life. As historian Gaines Foster has shown in his *Ghosts of the Confederacy,* Ladies' Memorial Associations formed throughout the South in the 1860s played a crucial part in easing white southerners' adjustment to loss and helping them regain hope for the future. By sponsoring memorial events that were for the South "virtually the only cultural expression concerned with the meaning of the war," LMAs took an early and defining role in shaping public memory of the Lost Cause. Creating a widely accepted vision of the meaning of the Confederacy, they contributed to national reunification on largely southern terms. In North Carolina, their work also undergirded the reclamation of elite leadership in a social hierarchy disturbed by war and Reconstruction. Moreover, as scholars Anne Firor Scott, Anastatia Sims, and others have demonstrated, it was through these memorial associations that southern white women began to participate in organizational leadership in their communities. In such associations, whose purpose served the goals and had the approval of southern white men, women were encouraged to assume semipublic leadership roles hitherto unfamiliar in most of the South. Avowedly apolitical yet politically shrewd in their strategies, they used gender conventions to accomplish goals that would have been difficult or impossible for their male compatriots.[1]

The story of the Ladies' Memorial Association of Wake County and the North Carolina Monumental Association illuminates several interlocking themes: the roles of the women and men who worked together in these organizations, as elite women tempered by war stepped readily into leadership positions where they combined feminine deference with executive and persuasive skills; the sometimes dramatic interaction of memorial pursuits with political events from the first years of Reconstruction through the 1890s; and the ways in which these history-minded women retold the saga of their own accomplishments to suit changing times.

## *"A Labor of Love"*

In May 1866 a small group of Raleigh citizens met to organize the Ladies' Memorial Association of Wake County. Several participants had recently sought out the graves of Confederate soldiers throughout the town and county and found them in sadly neglected condition. To remedy this situation, the object of the association was a simple one: to "protect and care for the graves of our Confederate soldiers." Despite the name, the organization, like many LMAs, included men as well as women. At its initial meeting, on May 23, the group heard a prayer and a brief address by a Presbyterian minister, then elected officers, all women. The founders recalled that they had been inspired by the example of similar associations across the region. After the first LMA formed four months earlier in Columbus, Georgia, to plan spring memorial services, it had sent an appeal to "the ladies throughout the South" for a Confederate decoration day to be "handed down as a religious custom of the South."[2]

In 1866 Raleigh was under Federal occupation, as it had been since city leaders peacefully surrendered to Gen. William Tecumseh Sherman's troops on April 13, 1865. The military presence, however, had been reduced to a skeleton force, and under presidential Reconstruction a provisional state government was in effect, if not yet a return to the Union. The revised state constitution eliminated slavery but did not permit suffrage for blacks. Despite bitter political conflict, former Confederates and former Unionists were working to rebuild the economy. To a considerable degree the antebellum elite had resumed its accustomed dominance if not regained its wealth.

Like most LMAs, the Wake County organization was led by women associated with the antebellum upper classes and closely involved with the Confederate cause. By all accounts, the moving spirit behind the group was Sophia Partridge (1817–1881), its first secretary. A native of Vienna,

New York, she came to North Carolina as a child and in 1846 established Miss Partridge's Select School for Young Ladies in Raleigh, where she taught academic subjects, arts, and deportment. Keeping her school open through the war, this adopted southerner had her students make bandages and dressings for the men who filled the city's Confederate hospitals. "Until the close of the war, she was found in the hospitals, cheering and comforting the sick and wounded, and when these died, she saw that boards with their names were placed at the heads of their graves, and thus were the names of many preserved."[3]

After the war, according to Peter Pescud, a leading member and supporter of the LMA, it was Partridge who conceived the idea of an association "for the re-interment and future care of our dead braves." She brought to the endeavor a strong sense of order and system, as shown in her determination to mark and re-mark soldiers' graves and keep records of their names and regiments. Pescud asserted that it was due "to *her* influence and persistent exertions, that the *first* Confederate cemetery in the late Confederacy . . . was organized."[4]

The group selected as president Nancy Branch (1817–1903) who, like many LMA presidents, was the socially prominent widow of a Confederate officer. Her husband, Lawrence O'Bryan Branch, a Princeton-educated attorney, president of the Raleigh and Gaston Railroad, and U.S. congressman from 1855 to 1861, had enlisted in 1861 and become a brigadier general; he was killed by a sharpshooter in 1862 while serving under "Stonewall" Jackson. Nancy Branch, a well-educated member of a leading planter family, donned black for the rest of her life (as did many Confederate widows) and gained a reputation as "one of the best informed students of war history in the South." She brought to the LMA presidency not only her status as a general's widow and her political and social connections but also, as the LMA minutes suggest, the administrative skills, diplomacy, and firmness needed to pursue the association's goals in perilous times.[5]

The men and women of the LMA worked together to accomplish their mission but adhered to a traditional gender division of labor. President Branch regularly called upon the men to carry out such tasks as property negotiations, organizing heavy labor, and public speaking. She had the women focus on planning and persuasion, fund-raising, and social and ceremonial events. Men and women sometimes worked independently but often in cooperation, and Branch appointed key committees with equal numbers of men and women. At the first meeting on May 23, 1866, for example, she appointed a "Ways and Means" committee of ten ladies and ten gentlemen, plus twenty young ladies to solicit subscriptions among the public. She asked three men to explore suitable locations for a Confederate cemetery, and three women, aided by a male attorney, to draft a constitution.[6]

The committees reported promptly at the June 16, 1866, meeting. The women began the constitution with a statement that conveyed a spirit of undefeated gentility: "We may be poor, but enough is left to prove our hearts to be still rich in the treasures of gratitude and affection." Although they could not adorn their cemetery with "storied urn or sculptured pillar," its hallowed grounds would "by the strength of patriotism and love, loom up as the loftiest obelisks, on which are inscribed, the deeds of a hundred hard fought fields." During the war, the southern woman had nursed the dying soldier; now, "let her last labor of love be, to collect his remains within the sacred enclosure." The constitution went on to define the duties of the officers and board of managers (all women) and authorized the board to appoint six men to meet with them as "the President's Council."

The men of the cemetery committee reported on their visit to the burial ground near the Rock Quarry, where they found 400 to 500 Confederate graves. Located near a former Confederate hospital taken over by Union troops at the end of the war, the grounds lay neglected, with the inscriptions on headboards defaced and nearly effaced. The committee recommended immediate action lest the names fade away entirely. The cemetery site itself would have been suitable had it not been used as well for the burial of Union soldiers, whose graves now surrounded the Confederate dead. After considering the notion of planting hedges to separate the Confederates and Federals, the committee recommended establishing a new cemetery.

Branch appointed a committee of three women and three men, who asked civic leader Henry Mordecai to donate land for the Confederate graves. They promised to form a company later to purchase and develop his adjoining property as a cemetery and park, but Mordecai responded, "The Ladies' Memorial Association are welcome to as many acres of my land as they need for such a sacred purpose, without any consideration."[7]

By autumn 1866 work was proceeding apace. The women had set about raising money, selling life subscriptions of $100 each and many small annual subscriptions, organizing a sewing circle, and planning a winter bazaar. On November 17 the LMA published an appeal for help in clearing and leveling the forested and irregular terrain. Volunteers were asked to meet Monday morning at the Memorial Cemetery, with each "requested to bring either an axe, pick, or spade, and come prepared to remain all day." Meanwhile, Capt. George Mordecai Whiting took charge of transferring Confederate remains from the Rock Quarry cemetery and elsewhere. He and three young women re-marked the headboards in pencil and made a list of names before the graves were opened. Plans were sketched for the layout of the cemetery, and a stone monument there was discussed. By the beginning of 1867 preparation of the grounds had progressed substantially, but the cost of removing trees, grading and terracing, clearing walkways, and digging graves had used up all the funds.[8]

The LMA members mounted a carefully orchestrated, suitably feminine appeal to the state legislature for help. They had a friendly lawmaker introduce a request for $1,500, hopeful that the legislature, which included many former Confederates, would support their cause. On February 14, the day of the vote, they published in the *Raleigh Sentinel* a report aimed at the hearts as well as the heads of the legislators.

"Friends of the Ladies' Memorial Association," the report began reassuringly, would be "pleased to learn" that the cemetery was nearly prepared and would be ready for reburials within eight to ten days. Claiming broad public support, the LMA hoped that "every lady in Raleigh and Wake County, will feel it to be a sacred pleasure . . . to aid in decorating the Cemetery" and, along with hundreds of little girls, would be represented by a shrub or flower "planted by their own hands." The association leaders would "*expect,* and *will rely* upon the young men . . . to assist in the disinterment and burial of their late comrades in arms." Only because of widespread poverty of the times and unexpectedly high costs of grading and draining were they "constrained to appeal . . . to their friends in the Legislature" for $1,500 to complete their "labor of love."

Demonstrating their systematic approach to an immense task, the LMA explained that 750 to 800 men had to be reburied: "Their names and register will be alphabetically arranged and numbered, and corresponding numbers will be placed on a square capped post to be placed at the head of each grave," while the remains of 170 whose names were unknown would be buried under two or more mounds "surmounted with a cannon reversed, *if allowed.*" Softening the impact of this mass burial, the LMA envisioned a design that met the picturesque ideals of the era:

"At each angle of the cemetery will be a thatched summer house, of hexagon or octagon shape, arranged with seats, of gothic finish, and surmounted with a cross. An osage orange hedge will be planted next the fence, and a flower bed along the borders. The monument, mounds, graves and summer houses will be approached by winding gravel walks."

That same day, as the bill came before the legislature, the women left nothing to chance. When the House of Commons took up the LMA petition, the request was, as the *Sentinel* reported, "backed up by a strong force of ladies in the gallery." Under the eyes of the women, the House passed the bill without opposition and sped it to the Senate, where "the rules were suspended and the resolution passed its several readings unanimously." The LMA had used womanly persuasion without overstepping gender conventions. Although women were precluded from speaking before the general assembly, LMA leaders had arranged to have the bill introduced, quietly lobbied their friends, and then arrived to support the legislation. This may well have been the first time North Carolina women had filled the galleries of the capitol to encourage passage of a bill; after their success in 1866, women repeatedly used this acceptably feminine form of political expression.[9]

Events soon took an unexpected turn. In everyone's mind in mid-February was the congressional Reconstruction bill, which was opposed by President Andrew Johnson but supported by the radical Republican majority. In response to southern states' 1866 rejection of the Fourteenth Amendment and black suffrage, along with conservatives' success in regaining power under presidential Reconstruction, the congressional plan imposed stiffer voting and office-holding restrictions on former Confederates and required ratification of the Fourteenth Amendment and new state constitutions allowing suffrage for blacks. To enforce these policies, Congress placed the southern states under newly organized military rule, which had authority over state governments.[10]

In Raleigh, tensions ran high as each day brought news of developments in Washington. The *Raleigh Sentinel* counseled calm and introduced a humor column, commenting, "In these gloomy times, when men born free in a free Republic . . . are threatened with political slavery by a despotic majority, we may as well laugh as cry, since there is no help for it, but quiet submission or removal." Viewing passage of the bill as inevitable, the editor only hoped that under the new military occupation the Union officer assigned to Raleigh would be "a sensible, discreet man, and a thorough gentleman."[11]

The local situation soon shifted dramatically. On February 20, the LMA Board of Managers called a special meeting: "Ways and means were discussed for the removal of the Confederate Dead, the Association having been notified that Confederate soldiers buried at the Rock Quarry Cemetery must be removed immediately to make room for the Federal Dead."[12] Spurred by the order, the association adopted final plans for the cemetery, using a simpler scheme than originally envisioned and deferring hopes for a monument there.

LMA members and Captain Whiting quickly organized the onerous task of moving the graves. On February 22, they urgently requested the help of "the Young, Middle-Aged, and Old Men of Wake" on the next Monday and Tuesday "and longer if necessary" to begin to remove the Confederate remains. Gentlemen "who cannot personally attend . . . can assist very much by hiring a hand or two, or sending a waggon or cart."[13]

The response was heartening, but the work proceeded slowly. On February 28 the LMA encouraged the "gallant boys," declaring: "Your brows are already crowned with wreaths of laurel, on each field from Bethel to Bentonsville, and you are now linking your names, in the memories of the fairer sex, with those martyred ones who never flinched, when duty called." By March 6 the remains of 269 men had been moved, and it was predicted that the rest would be moved within ten days.[14]

As the workers labored against the Federal deadline, national events continued to unfold. After the Reconstruction bill passed on March 2 over Johnson's veto, the *Sentinel* editor advised on March 6, "It is the duty of all citizens of the Southern States, who remain in them, to obey the law and conform peaceably to the requirements of those who rule over us." Defense of heritage took on new meaning: though "the 'old North State' [was] legislated out of political vitality on the 2nd day of March 1867," certain comforts remained: "We still have the prestige of a right noble old Commonwealth *that was*. We may still tell our children of the erewhile goodly old state."

In the midst of all this, LMA secretary Sophia Partridge wrote to a friend:

> I have to go over to the Cemetery quite often. We have moved 447, all out of the Yankee line, and another week or ten days will I expect complete the work of removing all the bodies, then we will begin to set out evergreens and flowers and make improvements. Did I tell you in my last that the Yankees notified us that we must remove our dead *immediately* to make room for theirs? We felt insulted. They are making a National Cem. here and moving all their dead from other parts of the state here. Load after load of pine box coffins pass by here every day, and a great many of them are not more than 2 or three ft long, short Yankees they. I suppose though they are only pieces of them.[15]

The drama and unpleasantness of the removal etched the event into participants' memories and made it a central theme in the creation history of the association. In 1882 Pescud bitterly recalled the "heartlessness of the wretch sent by the authorities at Washington City to prepare a cemetery for the Federal dead, in which confiscated ground were interred most of our dead. The said *Nero* sent insulting messages to the Memorial Association, insisting on the removal of the Confederate dead before the cemetery was in readiness for the graves to be opened, and finally threatened that if our dead were not removed by a given day, their remains would be placed in the public road."[16]

The gruesome nature of the work left the strongest memory. Years later, Pescud remembered that many of the coffins were "half full of most offensive fluid and . . . leaked badly," so that "in removing them from the wagons to the graves the persons and clothing of those thus employed were thoroughly saturated." David Whiting, the younger brother of Capt. George Whiting, who was directing the removal, also recalled the events:

> There were about 15 of the Raleigh boys helping and some just looking on. The negroes were free and the whites had to work. As the wagons would come in with the boxes containing the remains of some Confederate soldier we would take it out of the wagon carry it to a grave and let it in with ropes. . . . Some of the boxes were decaying and the bottoms would drop out and sometimes the foot end would give way but it was on the bill and to be done now we commenced it. Bill Pell put his hands under a box at the head end and I was lifting the foot end and it was lower on account of my height. When the lid slid off and the foot board came with it and the body . . . started toward me, I dropped my end because the man in it scared me. His hair had grown all around his body to his feet and it was thick and as coarse as horse hair and he had a sword buckled to his waist. . . . I ran for home with Bill Pell trying to catch me but a flying machine could not have done it that day.[17]

By the end of March, the transfer from the Rock Quarry cemetery was finished, along with the reburial of nearly all the Confederate remains found elsewhere in the county. More than five hundred graves were filled, more than half with North Carolinians.

As spring arrived and the landscaping and "ornamenting" of the grounds proceeded, resilient gentility and optimism rendered the grim removal of late winter a thing of the past. By early May the Memorial Cemetery had become "the resort, every afternoon, of numbers of our townspeople." "Under the assiduous culture of our ladies, the grounds are daily becoming more and more beautiful and attractive. In twelve months from this time, when the flower-plants, mosses and shrubbery shall have fully developed, it will be one of the loveliest spots in all the land. . . . Most of our young ladies have selected two or three mounds, the preservation and decoration of which are to constitute their peculiar 'labor of love.'"[18]

At the LMA meeting May 3, President Branch's first annual report related the year's accomplishments with little hint of the tensions involved. A more pressing topic occupied the gathering—that of ceremonies to honor the Confederate dead. Throughout the South that spring, LMAs were sponsoring memorial events at which they decorated Confederate graves with flowers. In Raleigh in 1867, the LMA carefully negotiated the limits of its capacity to honor the war dead under the newly imposed Union military presence. Setting the stage, the *Sentinel* carried reports—probably supplied by the LMA—of recent observances in Georgia and other states, where businesses closed in honor of the day and "the ladies formed in procession, each bearing a floral offering, and marched to the cemetery, where memorial wreaths were deposited on the graves." Closer to home, however, it reported, "The military authorities at Newbern prohibited the procession contemplated by the ladies of the Memorial Association of that City, on the occasion of laying the corner-stone of the Confederate mausoleum, in Cedar Grove Cemetery, on yesterday."[19]

When they met on April 24, 1867, members of the Wake County LMA had considered carefully whether to hold any "*public* demonstration in honor of the Confederate Dead." On May 3 they determined that their ceremonies should be public "so far as to meet on the capitol square . . . and proceed from thence in procession to the cemetery." The event was planned for May 10, the anniversary of the death of Stonewall Jackson and of the association's formation.[20]

The decision to stage a procession and public ceremony was a politically charged one under the terms of military rule, and the LMA publicized its plans with care. On May 4, the *Sentinel* reported on the previous day's LMA meeting and announced, "It was decided to commemorate the 10th. of May . . . by becoming memorial observances. There will be no attempt at formal display." The *Sentinel* confirmed on May 10, "The ladies will assemble at the Capitol *at half past 3 o'clock* with their votive offerings of flowers and evergreens, whence they will quietly proceed to the Cemetery, for the purpose of decoration and other observances."[21]

On the appointed day, as the newspaper reported, "hundreds of persons wended their way to the Cemetery—many in vehicles, but most on foot.—fair women, little children and even many of our most prominent and venerable citizens,—so that [when] the ceremonies commenced, there was probably assembled a concourse of between five and six hundred deeply moved and interested spectators." The cemetery observance proceeded with a prayer by a former chaplain of North Carolina troops, a hymn, and a brief oration by Seaton Gales (veteran and editor of the *Sentinel*). Gales recalled that, a year ago to the day, the women had met at the capitol and "in detached and mournful groups" placed flowers on the "dispersed and isolated" sites of Confederate graves. After that "pilgrimage of love," they had decided to gather all the remains "in one consecrated spot."

Now, he proclaimed, "looking around you, this bright and balmy afternoon," upon the carefully maintained cemetery, "you may well feel a grateful pride, a holy satisfaction, in the consummation of your labors and your hopes."

Probably with an eye to the Federal presence, Gales spoke with resignation of the defeated cause, which "whether right or wrong, was inexpressibly dear to our hearts" as were those who had defended it. "The cause is gone;—the flag which symbolized it, is folded up and laid aside forever. We bow before the decree of that Providence." He acknowledged, "We may not build for them lofty monuments of marble or of bronze—for we are poor; we may not celebrate their prowess with pomp, with procession and with pageantry, for we are vanquished; we may not make public demonstration of our sorrow or our gratitude—for that, perhaps, would be unbecoming," but he assured listeners that their devotion and floral tributes were sufficient to hallow the graves. With that he invited the ladies to begin their "holy task"—"Go scatter those flowers, which so aptly prefigure the brightness of the resurrection morn!"[22]

In the *Sentinel* report of a large ceremony on a beautiful day in May, only Gales's references to the lack of a public demonstration hinted at the political issues the participants faced. Yet the decision to have a procession, the formality of the event, and the glowing newspaper report constituted a genteel but unmistakable defiance of any sense of subjugation to the occupying force. In other cities such as New Bern, Federal officers forbade "formation of processions." Possibly Branch and her colleagues devised a ceremony that both obeyed and flouted such regulations. Union officers in Raleigh also may have been more tolerant than in some other cities. A key figure was probably Col. James V. Bomford, the Raleigh post commandant, who earned the respect of Raleigh citizens for his "gentlemanly bearing" and fair administration of "delicate and responsible duties." Indeed, the chivalrous commander, according to Pescud, had come with his family to the ceremony, brought with him "a large quantity of rare flowers . . . stood uncovered in front of the orator during the delivery of his address, and then placed the flowers over the graves of our dead." It is not hard to imagine that LMA leaders and Colonel Bomford arrived at a mutually satisfactory agreement about honoring the dead, but there is no evidence of any negotiations.[23] Peaceful at the time, this event, like the transfer of graves, gained drama as its story was retold over the decades.

With the cemetery established, the LMA continued to make improvements. In the summer of 1867 members renewed efforts to erect a permanent monument there, but by 1869 they had raised only part of the funds. President Branch advised, before resigning her office in August, that the money was "inadequate to the erection of a monument yet not to its commencement, which in my humble opinion would be judicious, as it would have a tendency to stimulate and arouse persons to action." Her method worked, for in 1870 the monument, a simple stone obelisk (fig. 1.2), was dedicated. It was inscribed with a poem by Capt. George Whiting, who had died that February and was buried nearby.[24]

In the ensuing decades, the LMA members participated in various endeavors: the publication in 1882 of their own history by Peter Pescud; the reburial of North Carolina soldiers' remains from Gettysburg (1871) and Arlington (1883) in their cemetery; contributions to a local Confederate soldiers' home and to Confederate cemeteries in Virginia and elsewhere; and ceremonies honoring Jefferson Davis, whose casket lay in state in the capitol en route from New Orleans to Richmond in 1893. They also continued improvement of their cemetery and in the mid-1870s replaced the decaying headboards with granite markers, numbered to correspond to a list Sophia Partridge prepared in triplicate, depositing copies with county and state officials.[25]

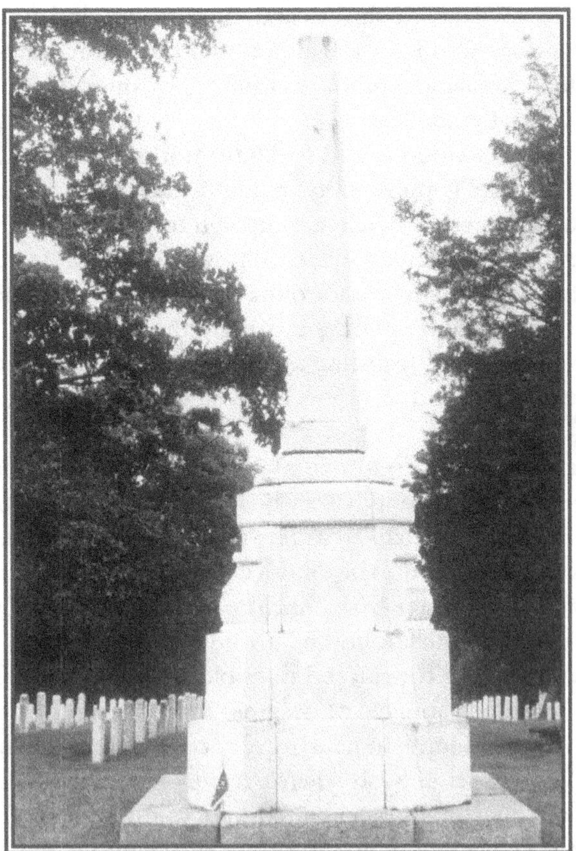

Fig. 1.2. Obelisk erected in Confederate Cemetery, Raleigh,
North Carolina, 1870. Photograph by Anne Miller.

Each year the LMA sponsored the May 10 ceremony, which grew more elaborate following the return to political power of former Confederate leaders. These men had organized as Conservatives to oppose the Republicans in 1867. They took the name of the national Democratic Party in 1876, the election that brought an end to Reconstruction and withdrawal of troops in 1877. In 1883 the LMA instituted a practice of having each Memorial Day speaker treat a North Carolina Confederate officer and publishing the lectures as a historical record. In time, the tenor of the memorial addresses shifted from simply honoring the dead to a broader vindication of North Carolinians' valor and the rightness of the Confederate cause.

### *"A Land without Monuments Is a Land without Memories"*

In the 1890s the memorial movement took a new turn as its leaders began the effort to raise a state Confederate monument. By this time a trend had begun throughout the South of erecting memorials on civic sites as well as in burial grounds. In the mid-1880s Confederate veterans in North Carolina had raised the idea. Samuel A'Court Ashe printed several articles in his *Raleigh*

*News and Observer* promoting patriotic shrines and monuments, and at the LMA's 1885 Memorial Day oration Col. Alfred Moore Waddell proclaimed that the Confederate dead deserved "to be perpetuated otherwise than by such memorial marbles as private affection may erect." No action was taken, however, for several years.[26]

In 1892, as the nation faced economic and social turmoil and North Carolina Democrats worried that a "third party" (later the Populist Party) might divide the loyalties of the white electorate, a few prominent Democratic veterans began a campaign for a state Confederate memorial. They included *News and Observer* publisher Ashe; Col. Edward D. Hall, state veterans organization leader; and Capt. Octavius Coke, the North Carolina secretary of state. Soon realizing that a monument drive required women's involvement, they sought the LMA's help. In June the LMA called a public meeting at the supreme court, featuring a speech by Coke, to which it invited all wives and daughters of Confederate soldiers and all others interested in "preserving the glorious memory of the dead."[27]

By July 1892 the North Carolina Monumental Association (NCMA) had been formed with a female "board of management," a male "advisory board" including Ashe and Coke, Nancy Branch Jones as president, and Donald W. Bain as treasurer (Bain also was state treasurer, as was his successor, Col. Samuel M. Tate). The election of Jones cemented the link with the LMA, since she was not only a "leader of society" whose husband, Armistead, was prominent in the Democratic Party but also the daughter of Nancy Branch, founding president of the LMA.[28]

In their first year NCMA leaders considered possible sites, including Nash Square, a Raleigh civic park, and explored potential sources of designs. To boost statewide enthusiasm, President Jones recruited female vice presidents in nearly every county. In Raleigh the ladies organized a September "lawn party" fund-raiser at Nash Square, featuring a Confederate concert, a tent full of Confederate relics, and a reenactment of a Confederate camp scene complete with some of the "best known citizens of the city" in their old uniforms. The event proved such a hit that it ran several days longer than planned and brought in substantial contributions.[29]

By the end of 1892, however, it was clear that private fund-raising was inadequate, and the NCMA turned to the predominantly Democratic legislature for an appropriation of $10,000. As in 1866, the women focused full attention on the legislators as they convened early in 1893. "The ladies" joined the committee on appropriation before the bill was presented, and when the bill came up they "took the House by storm"—crowding the galleries, filling the lobbies and aisles of the chamber, and even sitting on the steps of the speaker's stand, all to the immense approval of the *News and Observer:* "In the presence of so many fair patriots . . . there was no disposition manifested to antagonize the Monument bill." With little dissent, the appropriation was approved in both houses, with the added provisions that the monument be built of North Carolina stone and stand on the capitol square. The mandated position on the prime public site in the state confirmed the official identification of the state with the NCMA's cause.[30]

Within the Monumental Association men exerted more authority than in the LMA, but the women's prominence increased after their success with the legislature. The association maintained a genteel image of harmony and deference along traditional gender lines; only occasionally did any hint of tension enter the record. On October 26, 1893—eight long months after the appropriation passed—President Jones and the Lady Managers met to receive a committee's recommendation of the site and to consider selection of the design; the minutes noted that "a number of gentlemen, members of the Association, were also present." The committee recommended the south side of the capitol square, but a long debate ensued as other men refused to give up on Nash Square. Finally, and perhaps with some impatience, the Lady Managers settled the issue by accepting the legislated capitol site, with the exact spot still to be determined.[31]

The next topic was the choice of the design. Upon motion of one of the women, a "special committee of five of the Lady Managers was appointed to select a design." But the treasurer, Colonel Tate, swiftly suggested that a committee of "three experienced gentlemen" be appointed to "serve with" the women as "consulting members, in relation to the details of the plan." Jones acceded and appointed Tate, Gen. R. F. Hoke, and Col. W. J. Hicks, an architect-builder.

The eight committee members promptly met and recommended a design from the Muldoon Monument Company of Louisville, Kentucky. They "invited" Colonel Hicks "as an architect to supervise the whole" and, after "close inspection and inquiry on the part of Gen. Hoke and Col. Tate," settled on the design. A contract was drawn up and signed by Jones. With key decisions made, though with less than half of the $25,000 cost in hand and fund-raising curtailed by the

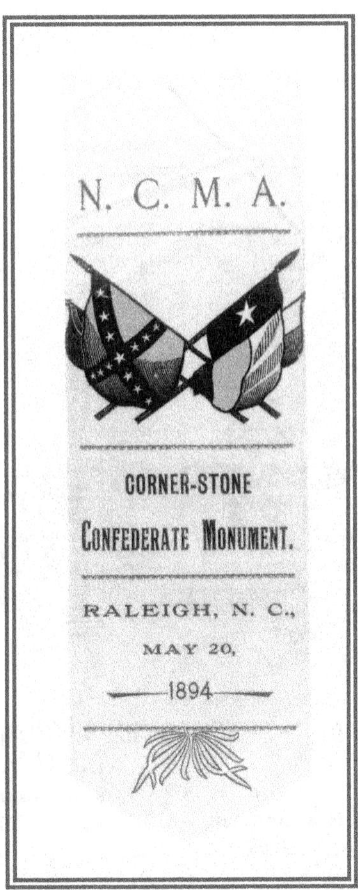


Fig. 1.3. North Carolina Monumental Association ribbon for cornerstone laying, Confederate Monument, 1894. Photograph courtesy of North Carolina Division of Archives and History.

national economic depression of 1893, the NCMA followed a strategy proposed by Jones's mother nearly twenty-five years earlier: "It was believed wisest to lay the corner stone, believing this would encourage the progress of the work."[32]

The cornerstone laying (fig. 1.3) on May 22, 1894, proved a "great event," with a procession of dignitaries, eloquent oratory, and military features. The women of the statewide NCMA filled half the grandstand. Confederate veterans leader E. D. Hall laid the cornerstone, which the women had made into a reliquary of the Lost Cause, filling it with mementos ranging from Confederate troop rosters to a strand plucked from the tail of Robert E. Lee's horse Traveller to a piece of the apple tree at Appomattox. After the event, fund-raising continued, fueled as predicted by the cornerstone laying and led by President Jones, who took an ever more public role, sending out appeals statewide and publishing letters above her name in the newspapers.[33]

But the NCMA soon faced unprecedented challenges in the face of a rapidly changing political landscape. For years Republicans, including many black voters, had regularly opposed the Democrats in North Carolina with little success, as Democrats used racial fears and the specter of a return to Reconstruction to win often narrow victories. Amid the hard times of the early 1890s, however, the third-party Populist movement gained strength among whites, including longtime Democrats and especially farmers, frustrated by entrenched "Bourbon" Democrats who favored big business and opposed progressive reforms. In 1894 the Republicans and Populists joined

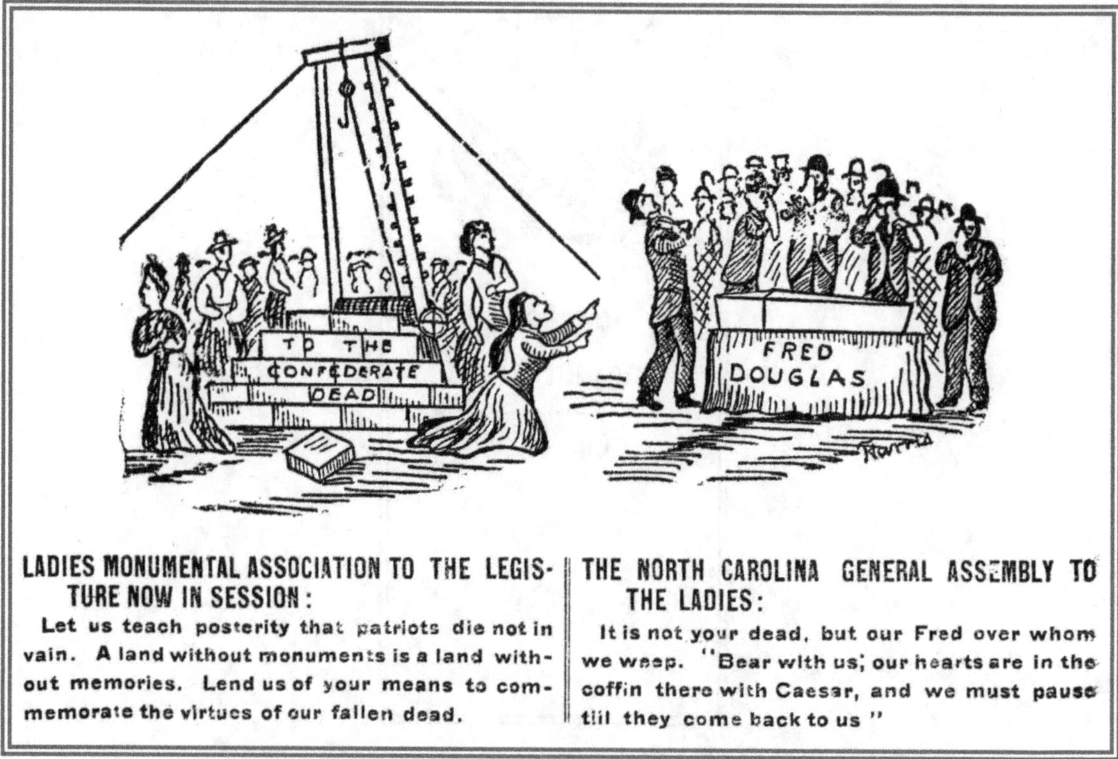


LADIES MONUMENTAL ASSOCIATION TO THE LEGIS-
TURE NOW IN SESSION:
Let us teach posterity that patriots die not in vain. A land without monuments is a land without memories. Lend us of your means to commemorate the virtues of our fallen dead.

THE NORTH CAROLINA GENERAL ASSEMBLY TO THE LADIES:
It is not your dead, but our Fred over whom we weep. "Bear with us; our hearts are in the coffin there with Caesar, and we must pause till they come back to us"

Fig. 1.4. Cartoon, *Raleigh News and Observer,* February 24, 1895.

forces as "Fusionists" and defeated the Democrats. The general assembly that took office in 1895 was "overwhelmingly Fusionist" and included five blacks among the Republicans.[34]

For the heavily Democratic NCMA, this startling defeat put the monument project in a different position. The 1893 legislature had "enthusiastically" appropriated $10,000, and by the end of 1894 private fund-raising had yielded an additional $5,000. But the monument construction was proceeding, with a projected completion date in April 1895, at which time full payment of the $25,000 contract was expected. The NCMA turned again to the legislature for aid, seeking a $10,000 loan.

This time the bill faced strong opposition. "Do Not Pass It," urged the Populist newspaper the *Caucasian.* The editor suggested that public money would be better spent on the common schools and asserted, "It is not at all certain that any monuments ought to be built on either side to perpetuate the memories of our unnatural civil war. The sooner the rancors and hates of that unhappy struggle are forgotten by both North and South, the better it will be for the whole country." He declared, "There has not been one of these monuments inaugurated, either North or South, that has not been the occasion of stirring up sectional bitterness that would better be left to quietly perish."[35]

The women of the NCMA seized the challenge. As the bill came up for debate, they again packed the capitol. When the Senate took up the topic on February 23, 1895, "the galleries were crowded to their utmost capacity with the ladies," who filled the lobbies on the floor of the Senate. Despite the women's presence, after long and impassioned debate, the measure was defeated 28 to 8.[36]

As luck would have it, an unrelated controversy had arisen a few days earlier that altered the fate of the monument bill. By tradition, legislators sometimes proposed that the body adjourn for the day in honor of notable public figures. On February 21, a black legislator had offered a resolution to adjourn in honor of Frederick Douglass, the African American leader who had died February 20, and the House passed it. Democrats and the *News and Observer* pounced on the unexpected opportunity. "Miscegenation Legislature Adjourns in Loving Memory of Fred Douglass," the newspaper crowed; "The affair . . . will be a vital blow in the State at the Fusionists." The *News and Observer,* recently acquired by Democratic partisan Josephus Daniels, accused legislators of honoring an "apostle of miscegenation"—a reference to Douglass's marriage to a white woman—and of thereby promoting "social equality" with its implication of interracial sexual relationships. The paper also drew patriotism into the brew, claiming (inaccurately) that the legislators had honored Douglass while refusing similar tributes to the birthdays of Lee and Washington. Other state newspapers joined the attack, and soon the national press was covering the story. The *News and Observer* relentlessly fanned the flames—"Shame, Shame, Shame" at the "General Assembly's Infamy"—and insisted, "All patriotic men must stand together to preserve the Anglo Saxon civilization."[37]

The *News and Observer* then devised the strategy of linking the February 21 Douglass resolution with the defeat of the Confederate monument bill on February 23—at once intensifying public outrage at the Fusionists and infusing new life into the monument campaign. Although there was no inherent connection between the two events, on February 24 the newspaper ran a cartoon (fig. 1.4) that tied them visually, an image that juxtaposed white female purity and male blackness and miscegenation, with not so subtle hints of black dominance and white subjugation. It showed the white women kneeling beside their uncompleted monument, with one woman pleading with the racially mixed legislators, who were weeping over Douglass's coffin: "A land without monuments is a land without memories."

The plight of the "noble women" ill treated by the "miscegenist legislature" captured popular attention as part of the larger fracas. Legislators struggled to defend themselves in the firestorm of public opinion. Some insisted they had not voted for the Douglass resolution. Others defended their votes as innocent gestures of courtesy. One cited an old story that George Washington had doffed his hat and bowed to a black man "because he did not want to be outdone in polite manners by a negro," and said, "I felt that as the negroes in this House . . . have for decades been pulling off their hats to my ideals, that it was not too much for me to doff mine once to theirs."[38]

Within days many legislators came to see support for the monument as an antidote to the Douglass problem. On February 28 a new bill, this time for an appropriation rather than a loan, was placed before the Senate by a leading Republican who was a former Union officer. Speaker after speaker—including former opponents—lined up in support of the appropriation, while others still staunchly assailed it. One opponent insisted that "to build a monument to the Confederate dead could not rectify the mistake of that adjournment," but finally, after one senator changed his vote, the bill passed, 21 to 20. "Glory to God and the Confederate dead," cried a supporter, and "there was prolonged cheering." The *News and Observer* rejoiced, "Blue and gray join in honoring Confederate dead."[39]

In the House, still raw from the Douglass furor, debate was emotional. Proponents waxed eloquent, some moving themselves and their audience to tears, another threatening that no one "would ever be re-elected . . . who dared to vote against this bill." One representative still opposed the bill, saying "our duty was to the living and not to the dead." Another said "the memories of the war should be buried out of sight, he was in favor of digging a hole and burying all monuments."

The women had again arrived in force and were not shy in making their feelings known. One speech brought loud approbation "from the galleries full of ladies, which the Speaker rapped down, saying he would allow reasonable applause, but not uproarious applause." At one point, opponents moved to table the bill, and when it was defeated "there was a flood of applause . . . and tears burst from the faces of some of the older mother-women while a smile swept over the faces of the gayly dressed younger women like light." Eventually the bill passed 60 to 38. Reflecting on a triumph gained by the combined efforts of Democratic leaders, a relentless newspaper campaign, and the ladies' ostensibly apolitical appeals, the *News and Observer* exulted: "And the Women Win."[40]

With state funds obtained, the NCMA moved to complete the monument, which was rising on the west side of the capitol square and scheduled for unveiling on May 20, 1895. Political tensions intensified the meaning of the upcoming celebration: it not only symbolized shared reverence for the Confederate cause but also demonstrated Democrats' success in snatching victory from the Fusionists using the twin appeals of southern patriotism and white southern womanhood. The women's leadership in the memorial project perfectly suited the Democrats' need to undercut Fusionism. The women rose to the occasion, following their legislative victory, with plans for a patriotic extravaganza.

Reports building up to the unveiling shared the newspaper pages with news of heated political struggles. The Fusionist legislature had authorized new charters in several cities, including Raleigh, which provided for direct local elections. As Raleigh's vote of May 6 neared, the *News and Observer* urged citizens to "leave no stone unturned to elect the Democratic ticket," unless they

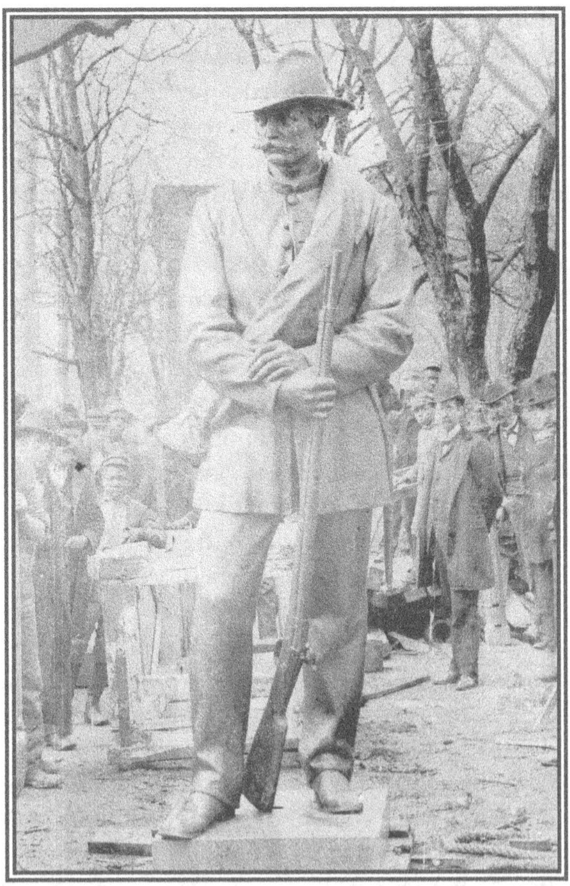

Fig. 1.5. Raleigh residents admire ten-foot-high sculpture of soldier after it is uncrated in 1895. The soldier would soon be hoisted atop their new Confederate monument. Photograph, North Carolina Museum of History, Raleigh.

wished to return to the Reconstruction era's Republican rule. On May 7 the paper announced the triumph of "pure white Democracy"—"The City Still Ours . . . No Negro Rule in Raleigh."

Meanwhile, crowds visited the monument site to watch the "dangerous and difficult work" as each section was put into place (fig. 1.5). President Jones appointed and published lists of committees, chaired by men, to handle reception, military, veterans, ways and means, transportation, entertainment, decorations, music, and more. Immense crowds were predicted, including hundreds expected to arrive by rail (reduced rates had been arranged with the railroad companies). The "order of the march of procession" was published to encourage citizens along the route to decorate their homes and businesses.[41]

An ongoing theme was that of broad unity. "Everybody and his wife coming," ran one headline. Announcements reminded Raleigh citizens to make every veteran and visitor welcome. The message of unanimity underscored the notion that the Confederate cause enjoyed the full support of the southern people, dismissing from public memory both the resistance to the war, which had been bitter and strong in the state, and the more recent conflict over public support for the monument.

By attracting thousands of people from across the state and widespread public attention to the unveiling, the sponsors affirmed social stability and race loyalty despite widening class divisions. The emphasis on the shared Confederate tradition carried a powerful appeal to Populists to return to the Democratic fold. Thus did Julian S. Carr—Durham tobacco magnate, veterans' association leader, and Democratic supporter—publish an open invitation to "every Confederate soldier" in Durham County to join him in the procession in Raleigh, "without regard to creed or party," and he offered free transportation.[42]

Enticing notices of social events—luncheons, afternoon receptions where the leading Confederate generals' widows would greet hundreds of veterans, a late-night ball after the unveiling— also whetted public interest. The NCMA planned a "Confederate Concert" to follow the unveiling, with a program of war songs and hymns. It was to include a special "old camp scene" feature: "as the soldiers lying around on the ground, talk over the day's battle," a soloist sings "Tenting to Night," and then as reveille is heard, Miss Carrie Young "rushes into camp with a Confederate cap, singing a most enthusiastic war song," including the "Rebel yell."[43]

At the "Great Event" of May 20, 1895, the women of the NCMA took a visible but silent ceremonial role. At the front of the mile-long procession to the capitol square came carriages with the speakers and honored officials, including the officers of the Monumental Association. Behind them marched the chief marshal, contingents of military groups, local light infantry organizations, and ordered ranks of Confederate veterans, many flying the faded and battle-scarred flags of their units. "Conspicuous among those first to be escorted to the grand stand were Mrs. Armistead Jones, Mrs. Gen. W. L. O'B. Branch, Mrs. Gen. Stonewall Jackson and granddaughter Julia Jackson Christian, and Mrs. Gen. D. H. Hill and little granddaughter."

Prominently positioned on the grandstand among male dignitaries, the women sat quietly during the long ceremony, continuing their custom of having the men speak for them. Captain Ashe welcomed the crowd on behalf of the "ladies who undertook this work and whose devoted labor accomplished its completion." Another speaker saluted the women's decisive role with the legislature, providing as well a classic stereotype of woman's ideal qualities and role in public life. Though "always modest, amiable and true," the daughters of the state "never retreat or surrender when once they unfurl their banner in a campaign of mercy or of love. 'Forward' is their command, and victory their goal," he said. It was woman's "low sweet voice, as enrapturing as the song of the Sirens, and as mighty as the thunders of Jupiter" that made the monument possible.[44]

After more speeches, most expounding on the valor of North Carolina's fighting men and the patriotism of the Confederate cause, finally came the unveiling. Little Julia Jackson Christian pulled the cord and the veil dropped from the monument like "the garments of Elijah." Visible to the public at last, the monument of Mount Airy granite stood seventy-five feet tall (fig. 1.6). Resting upon a stepped base, a large block featured seals of the state and the Confederacy, flanked by dynamic, life-size bronze figures of an artilleryman and a cavalryman. From the block, a tall shaft rose to a Corinthian capital, upon which stood a ten-foot bronze figure of an infantryman. Realistically modeled by "Prof. [Ferdinand] Von Miller, the finest sculptor in bronze living," and cast at the Royal Foundry in Munich, these figures, like most Civil War monuments, honored the common soldier rather than high-ranking officers. The symbolic reversal of hierarchy stressed the shared experience of war and served the purposes of the organizers by promoting social unity across all classes. When darkness came, the spectacle increased as the monument was illuminated by a halo of electric lights.[45]

The "Great Event" grandly fulfilled the NCMA's hopes. It attracted an estimated thirty thousand people and the attention of the entire state. Even the Populist newspaper lent its enthusiastic support to the event. A visiting northern officer praised the monument and commented that the South "would lose the respect of the world" if it did not thus honor its soldiers. Predictably, there was little mention of the black citizenry but for a report that the northern officer saw "no notable difference between such a gathering here and in New England, except that the absence of the negroes would be marked in a New England procession." Outside the official stance of universal welcome and at odds with the rhetoric seeking northern respect for southern valor, one Confederate veteran found that the ceremonies "were sadly marred, in the opinion of every ex-Confederate soldier with whom I have spoken, by a want of due consideration shown to ex-Federal soldiers, who were present for the purpose of uniting with us in doing honor to the bravest men that ever followed standard into action." For the sponsors, however, it was, as the *News and Observer* proclaimed, "a perfect success."[46]

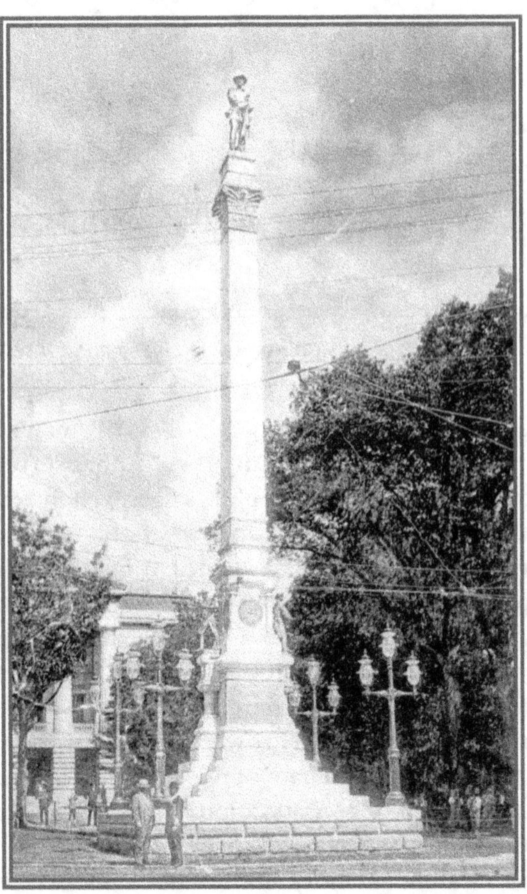

Fig. 1.6. Confederate Monument, Raleigh, North Carolina. Photograph, Wharton, 1895. North Carolina Division of Archives and History.

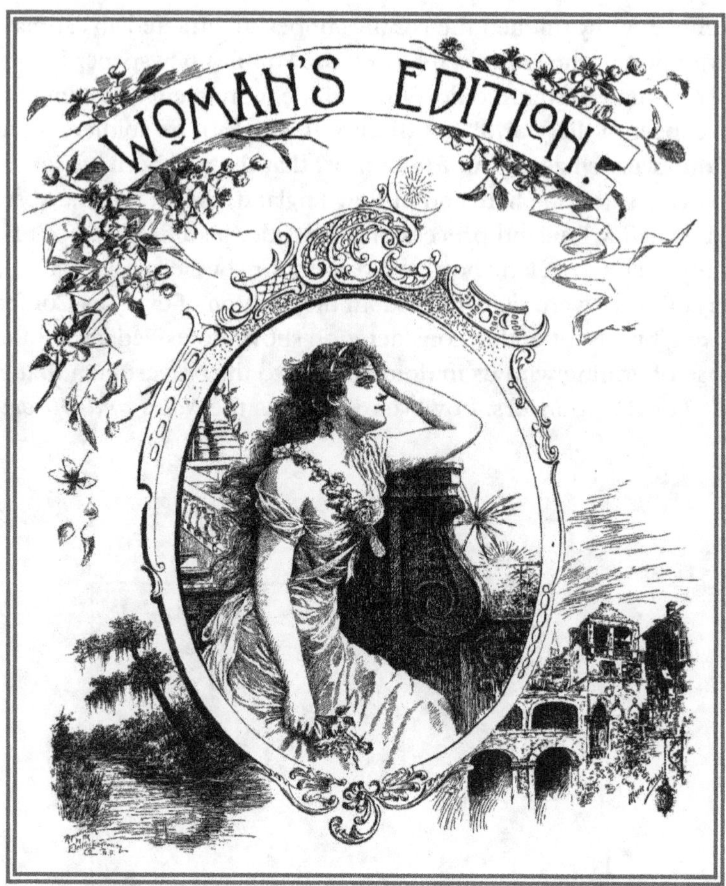


Fig. 1.7. "Woman's Edition" cover illustration, *Raleigh News and Observer*, May 20, 1895.

A unique and lasting contribution was the May 20, 1895, "Woman's Edition" of the *News and Observer* (fig. 1.7), which gave the women a printed voice that served as a socially acceptable counterpoint to their customary silence on the public stage. Well in advance, the newspaper had announced that the "Monumental Issue" of the paper was to be "gotten out by the Ladies' Monumental Association, under the supervision of Mesdames Armistead Jones, John W. Hinsdale, and Garland Jones." The title page assured readers: "A woman's noblest station is retreat, / Her fairest virtues fly from public sight." Within, the women assembled a twelve-page publication that provided an early and widely popular codification of the Lost Cause, with articles covering every aspect of the war and emphasizing elite female heroism.[47]

The women also set forth the history of their own memorial work, writing narratives that tailored events of the 1860s to the political climate of the 1890s. "How the Work Began, the Formation of the Wake County Ladies' Memorial Association," probably written by Mrs. Garland Jones, and "The Wake County Memorial Association," by Mrs. M. L. Shipp, constitute a remarkable example of the adjustment of public memory. At the same time that their politically active husbands and other Democratic friends were raising the specter of Reconstruction to discredit Republican foes, the women were recasting the saga of their founding in similar terms.

"It was a very short while after the federal soldiers took possession of our town," their story began, that Raleigh's mayor was informed that the Confederate dead must be "moved at once, [so] that the Yankee dead might be placed there." At a town meeting, the Ladies' Memorial Association was formed, and its president received a message the next day that unless the remains "were removed at once, they would be thrown in the county road." Encouraged by the women, the young men of the city, "rolling wheelbarrows through the scorching summer sun," moved the remains to the Confederate cemetery, where they were "safe from Sherman's bummers, as there was scarcely a new made grave anywhere, but what was opened in search of treasures by these men." Thus the LMA founding of 1866 and the grave-moving of February and March 1867—long after Sherman's "bummers" had left the city—were all shifted back to a single hot summer of 1865.

In the 1860s the LMA meetings and the transfer of remains were publicly announced and highly visible, but the 1895 version further villainized the Yankees and blacks while highlighting the women's courage: "This was a more perilous undertaking than can now be imagined. Everybody was under strict surveillance—the former slaves made spies upon the actions of their owners, as well as the vigilance of the troops to find any offence, however slight, against the military laws, kept the people from expressing openly their sympathy with the Confederates, as they would be put under arrest, not even ladies being exempt from this insult, and carried before the military court."

At the initial May 10 Memorial Day observation in 1867, the LMA had devised a quiet procession and a large gathering at a formal service at the cemetery. The 1895 version acknowledged that there had been a prayer, a hymn, and a short address, but (perhaps influenced by oft-told tales of events in New Bern and elsewhere), emphasized, "No procession was allowed, unless the United States flag was carried, and as it was several years before the ladies were so much 'reconstructed' as to march under this flag, the gathering of the people was without special order or ceremony." Dramatizing the tyranny of Reconstruction and the contrast with the proud, flag-fluttering procession of the present day, the 1895 narrative formed the LMA's standard origin story and the basis of further tellings over the years.[48]

With the monument completed and unveiled, and the "Woman's Edition" published, President Jones paid the final bills and sent to each of the vice presidents across the state an elegant packet of mementos—a photograph of the monument, an "authorized badge" of the association, and a copy of the "Woman's Edition" of the *News and Observer.* With that she bid "adieu" to the North Carolina Monumental Association.[49]

The Ladies' Memorial Association continued its activities, adding a stop at the Confederate Monument to its annual May 10 procession to the Confederate Cemetery. Gradually, however, the LMA's visibility waned as the fast-growing United Daughters of the Confederacy (UDC), which began a chapter in Raleigh in 1896 and included many LMA members, assumed guardianship of the Confederate tradition. In 1897 it was announced that the UDC would join the LMA in the May 10 ceremonies, and before long the Daughters dominated the event.[50]

The Memorial Day tradition endured and even intensified amid the political strife at the end of the century. National reunion on southern terms and vindication of the southern soldier were solidified by the Spanish-American War in 1898 as northern and southern men fought under the same flag. In North Carolina, following a second Fusionist victory in 1896, Democrats in 1898 and 1900 resorted to a violent "white supremacy crusade," which recaptured white voters by pulling out all the stops on the old themes of "Negro domination," interracial sex, and Reconstruction horrors. In 1900, Memorial Day, an official state holiday held shortly before the election, was an occasion to emphasize shared values in the white populace: "the people of Raleigh of all classes and creeds, all of these will join hands and hearts tomorrow in a common cause and will decorate with the purest flowers the last resting places of the fallen soldiers."[51]

It was in this context that the origin story of the LMA gained its definitive retelling, provided by the new LMA president, Mrs. Garland Jones, to the *News and Observer* early in the 1900 election year. She stuck close to the version prepared for the 1895 "Woman's Edition" but amended the chronology and added some new flourishes. The time grew more specific: "It was hardly more than a month after Sherman's army entered the City of Raleigh," she wrote, that the women had organized the LMA, and the Federal deadline for removal grew tighter: after taking possession of Pettigrew Hospital, the Federal officer threatened to throw the bodies in the road if they were not "removed in two days." The transfer under "scorching, summer sun" gained a "touching little incident" considerably softened by memory: "one of the coffins had been a little strained . . . allowing a long, half-curled lock of fair hair to escape, which hung down as the coffin was lifted from the wagon. This lock of hair is now in the possession of one of the ladies."

Mrs. Jones also updated the account of the first memorial ceremonies by intensifying Federal officers' tyranny and again changing the weather, from a sunny day to a dreary one:

> [On] the first Memorial Day, May 10, 1867 . . . the writer well remembers the meeting in the rain at the capitol square of a number of faithful men and women, who walked to the cemetery, carrying their garlands and crosses and flowers, and closely followed by several Federal officers, detailed by the military authority, who then governed the State, to see that "no procession was formed." It was believed at the time, and it has never been contradicted, that the threat was made that if the L.M.A., chiefly women and children, did form a procession, it would be fired on without further warning. On this day there were no exercises of any kind, not even a prayer, and it demanded some courage and some independence from those who walked under the dripping skies through the ankle-deep mud of the country . . . to fulfill this poor duty to the dead.

Mrs. Jones's 1900 rendition, reprinted by the UDC in 1938, became the most widely accepted version of the LMA history.[52]


## *Coda*

By 1919 the days of the LMA were over. In that year, its officers asked the local chapter of the UDC to "accept our membership as its own and to take over and carry on the work in which we are now and have so long been engaged," especially the care of the Confederate cemetery. The UDC chapter maintained the cemetery until 1998, when it was deeded to the Oakwood Cemetery management. The UDC also fended off in 1934 a proposal to remove the Confederate Monument from Union Square, claiming state legislative authority and the memory of the women who weathered "those long dark days of the Sixties, and the dreadful reconstruction times"—"To tear down their labor of love and sacrifice which was the work of many long years will be an insult to their memory, and breaking faith with the dead—we cannot do it."[53]

Within the span of half a century after the Civil War, the Lost Cause had been transformed and so had the South. Through their use of symbols, ceremonies, and feminine appeals, the LMA and the NCMA played key roles in advancing and refining the Confederate tradition and reinforcing the social and political hierarchy they believed in. Ostensibly apolitical, these women accomplished what their overtly partisan men could not. Remaining above the political fray yet skillfully navigating difficult political situations, they repeatedly gained state support in establishing their version of history as the official public memory.

Women's public roles had been likewise redefined by the turn of the century, as women assumed leadership in myriad causes from educational reform to both sides of the woman suffrage issue; many women pursued these along with continued participation in the UDC and other patriotic organizations. It was the women of the LMA, girded by their experience in war and working in tandem with male friends and relatives, who had in the 1860s first stepped competently and discreetly into the unfamiliar territory of public leadership. If their cause was one that honored dead heroes and reinforced a social structure rooted in the past, they themselves were pioneers in the public realm, effectively combining feminine deference and strategic public actions in pursuit of their goals and thereby shaping the direction of the future.

## *Notes*

Research for this article was supported by an Archie K. Davis Research Fellowship from the North Caroliniana Society. For assistance in locating information, I thank Elizabeth Reid Murray, John C. Williams, George Stevenson, and Michael Hill; and for readings of drafts, I am grateful to John Bishir, Jerry Cashion, Jeffrey Crow, Michael Hill, Kate Hutchins, and Anastatia Sims. A longer version of this essay appeared in the *North Carolina Historical Review* 77 (Oct. 2000): 455–91.

1. Gaines M. Foster, *Ghosts of the Confederacy* (New York: Oxford Univ. Press, 1987), 4–8, 38–45, 127–35; quotation 43. In North Carolina, evidence indicates the activities of the LMA and the NCMA were more closely related to partisan politics and the reclamation of political power than Foster sees in the movement in general. See discussion of this process in memorials and architecture in Catherine W. Bishir, "Landmarks of Power: Building a Southern Past, 1885–1915," *Southern Cultures,* inaugural issue (1993): 5–46, republished in Fitzhugh Brundage, ed., *Where These Memories Grow* (Chapel Hill: Univ. of North Carolina Press, 2000), 139–68. Details of the dedication ceremony are drawn from accounts in the *Raleigh News and Observer,* May 20–22, 1895.

On Southern women's public roles see Anastatia Sims, *The Power of Femininity in the New South: Women's Organizations and Politics in North Carolina, 1880–1930* (Columbia: Univ. of South Carolina Press, 1997); Anne Firor Scott, *The Southern Lady: From Pedestal to Politics, 1830–1930* (Chicago: Univ. of Chicago Press, 1970); Margaret Supplee Smith and Emily Herring Wilson, *North Carolina Women Making History* (Chapel Hill: Univ. of North Carolina Press, 1999). Sims points out that even in the antebellum era, "southerners applied the taboo against public activity for women selectively," and North Carolina women took a role in "benevolence, reform, and patriotism" (15). While Drew Gilpin Faust in *Mothers of Invention: Women of the Slaveholding South in the American Civil War* (Chapel Hill: Univ. of North Carolina Press, 1996), 251–53, depicts women's memorial work as focused on restoring their men's shattered morale, evidence from the Raleigh groups suggests joint work among men and women to accomplish mutual goals.

2. Ladies' Memorial Association Minutes (Ladies' Memorial Association Papers, privately held, Raleigh), May 1866. *Raleigh Sentinel,* May 13, 1867. Last quotation (Mar. 12, 1866, letter) in Mrs. Bryan Wells Collier, *Biographies of Representative Women of the South, 1861–1929* (n.p.: privately printed, 1929), 5:233; Collier relates that the Columbus association planned its first memorial day for Apr. 26, 1866, the anniversary of General Johnston's surrender to General Sherman in North Carolina. See also Foster, *Ghosts of the Confederacy,* 38.

3. Peter F. Pescud, *A Sketch of the Ladies' Memorial Association of Raleigh, N.C., Its Origin and History* (Raleigh: privately printed, 1882), 2; Grady Lee Ernest Carroll Sr., *They Lived in Raleigh* (Raleigh: privately printed, 1977), 1:166–67.

4. Pescud, *Ladies' Memorial Association,* 2. It is difficult to ascertain the accuracy of Pescud's claim that Raleigh's Confederate Cemetery was the first in the South. Most of the other early Confederate burial grounds were in existing cemeteries or extensions of those. During the war, marking of soldiers' graves had been funded by the state legislature, which authorized headboards marked "with their names, States, and regiments, as far as practicable" (*Public Laws of North Carolina, 1862–63,* 73, courtesy of Elizabeth Reid Murray).

5. Collier, *Representative Women of the South,* 5:175–78. Branch Family Papers, North Carolina State Archives, Division of Archives and History (henceforth NCDAH), Raleigh. See entry on Lawrence O'B. Branch in William S. Powell, ed., *Dictionary of North Carolina Biography* (Chapel Hill: Univ. of North Carolina Press, 1979–1996), hereafter cited as *DNCB.*

6. These actions and those described below are reported in the Minutes of the LMA, 1866–67, Ladies' Memorial Association Papers, Raleigh.

7. Pescud, *Ladies' Memorial Association,* 3. As promised, additional Mordecai land was subsequently acquired and developed as Oakwood Cemetery, a parklike burial ground chartered in 1869 by the Raleigh Cemetery Association and still in use. Elizabeth Reid Murray, *Wake: Capital County of North Carolina* (Raleigh: privately printed, 1983), 112, 506, 567, 589.

8. *Raleigh Daily Sentinel,* Nov. 17, 1866, hereafter cited as *Sentinel.* There are no LMA minutes between August 1866 and January 1867.

9. *Sentinel,* Feb. 14, 1867. I have been unable to identify an earlier time that women filled the Capitol to lobby the legislators, though as early as the 1840s politicians who rejected participation by women nevertheless appealed to them to use their influence in politics, and many political events were "cheered by the 'approving smiles of the fair.'" Guion Griffis Johnson, *Ante-Bellum North Carolina* (Chapel Hill: Univ. of North Carolina Press, 1937), 249, quoting *North Carolina Standard,* Oct. 28, 1840.

10. *Sentinel,* Feb.–Mar. 1867; William S. Powell, *North Carolina through Four Centuries* (Univ. of North Carolina Press, 1989), 380–95; and Allen W. Trelease, "Reconstruction: The Halfway Revolution," in Lindley S. Butler and Alan D. Watson, *The North Carolina Experience: An Interpretive and Documentary History* (Chapel Hill: Univ. of North Carolina Press, 1984), 286–94.

11. *Sentinel,* Feb. 16, 18, 1867. The newspaper identified Col. James V. Bomford as such a gentleman.

12. LMA Minutes, Feb. 20, 1867. Perhaps the order was an unexpected and unreasonable demand, as LMA members' memoirs suggest, but it is also possible that the officer in charge of the National Cemetery, facing the prospect of new shipments of Union dead, had been urging the LMA for some time to complete the move.

13. LMA Minutes, Feb. 24, 1867; *Sentinel,* Feb. 22, 1867; Pescud, *Ladies' Memorial Association,* 8.

14. *Sentinel,* Feb. 28, Mar. 6, 1867.

15. [Sophia Partridge] to Fanny Lewis, Mar. 10, 1867, Ladies' Memorial Association of Wake County Papers, NCDAH. The last page(s) of the letter being lost, it is unsigned, but internal evidence and handwriting indicate that it is from Partridge.

16. Pescud, *Ladies' Memorial Association,* 4–5.

17. Ibid. David B. Whiting, "Some Things That Happened in My Life," early twentieth-century typescript, 40–41, David Brainard Whiting Papers, NCDAH. Thanks to George Stevenson for calling my attention to this account.

18. *Sentinel,* May 3, 1867.

19. LMA minutes, May 3, 1867. *Sentinel,* May 3, 1867. The New Bern exercises at the local cemetery were to be allowed, according to the newspaper; only the procession was barred. While ceremonies in Georgia were held on April 26, North Carolina selected May 10 and other states chose other days. Foster, *Ghosts of the Confederacy,* 42–44.

20. LMA minutes, Apr. 24, May 3, 1867. The April 24 minutes ambiguously state that the LMA considered whether to have an address at the Capitol and a procession from there to the cemetery and decided "*not* to have no *public* demonstration." The double negative could be interpreted as expressing either an intent not to have a public demonstration or a determination to have one.

21. *Sentinel,* May 4, 10, 1867.

22. Ibid., May 13, 1867.

23. Pescud, *Ladies' Memorial Association,* 5. See Murray, *Wake,* 593, for Raleigh leaders' praise of Bomford, a West Point graduate and career officer, and regret at his departure in 1868. Pescud also stated that the post commandant had "severely rebuked" the cemetery official for his threats in February.

24. LMA minutes, Aug. 10, 1869, Mar. 21, 1870; marker, Confederate Cemetery. George Mordecai Whiting (1842–1870) died of tuberculosis contracted during the war. Carroll, *They Lived in Raleigh,* 1:149.

25. Pescud, *Ladies' Memorial Association,* 5, 8.

26. LMA papers, 1885.

27. *News and Observer* (henceforth *N&O*), Mar. 24, June 15, 19, 1892, and May 20, 1895. On March 24, the *News and Observer* published a letter from "Rebel" proposing a Confederate monument at the capitol square, but nothing concrete occurred until summer. The idea for the organizing meeting was initially credited (*N&O*, Feb. 2, 1893) to Col. Edward Dudley Hall (1823–1896) of Wilmington, elderly leader of the North Carolina Division of the United Confederate Veterans, but in subsequent accounts the younger Democratic stalwarts Octavius Coke (1840–1895) and Samuel Ashe (1840–1938) were identified as having called it (*N&O*, May 24, 1894, and others).

28. *N&O,* July 16, 1892. The women were variously referred to as officers of the "Board of Lady Managers" and of the organization itself.

29. Ibid., Sept., 1–10, 1892.

30. Ibid., Feb. 16–24, 1893. Undated clippings, Branch Papers, NCDAH. While the square is commonly known as the capitol square, the proper name is Union Square, the site of the state capitol, positioned at the meeting point of four axial streets. Four secondary squares, including Nash, mark the quadrants of the grid plan.

31. NCMA minutes, Oct. 26, 1893, Branch Papers, NCDAH.

32. Branch Papers, NCDAH. *N&O,* May 24, 1894. Last quotation, *N&O,* May 20, 1895.

33. NCMA minutes, Nov. 2, 8, 1893. *Raleigh Daily Press,* May 22, 1894. The event was actually held on May 22 because May 20 was a Sunday.

34. Helen G. Edmonds, *The Negro and Fusion Politics in North Carolina, 1894–1901* (Chapel Hill: Univ. of North Carolina Press, 1951), 37–38, and Allen Trelease, "The Fusionist Legislatures of 1895 and 1897: A Roll-Call Analysis of the North Carolina House of Representatives," *North Carolina Historical Review* 57, no. 3 (July 1980): 280–309.

35. *Caucasian,* Feb. 21, 1895. Marion Butler was editor of the Populist newspaper.

36. *N&O,* Feb. 24, 1895.

37. Edmonds, *The Negro and Fusion Politics,* 41–43. *N&O,* Feb. 22, 24, 1895, and afterward.

38. *N&O,* Feb. 27, 1895.

39. Ibid., Mar. 1–2, 1895. Republican state Sen. Hiram Grant, who had previously abstained from voting on the NCMA loan, introduced the bill; a native of Connecticut, he was a Union officer who served in North Carolina and settled in Goldsboro after the war (see Hiram Grant entry, *DNCB*). Upon passage of the bill, Senator White, a Confederate veteran, crossed the aisle and shook Grant's hand, thanking God "the time had come when there was no North, no South, no East, no West, but one common country of brothers in peace." *N&O*, Mar. 2, 1895.

40. *N&O*, Mar. 8, 1895.

41. Ibid., Apr.–May 1895 as cited; May 9, 1865.

42. Ibid., May 14, 1895, for quotation; May 3, 1895. See Julian S. Carr entry, *DNCB*.

43. Ibid., May 16, 1895.

44. Ibid., May 20, 1895.

45. Ibid., May 20, 1895. Foster, *Ghosts of the Confederacy*, 127–44, explains how Confederate unveilings and other celebrations "ritually aligned the common man with the social order" and fostered social unity and deference to leadership (131). This purpose was especially important for North Carolina Democrats hoping to recapture white voters from the Populists. See Kirk Savage, *Standing Soldiers, Kneeling Slaves* (Princeton: Princeton Univ. Press, 1997), 162–208, on meanings of common soldier sculptures on northern and southern memorials. The sculptor was Ferdinand von Miller II (1842–1929).

46. *N&O*, May 20–21, 1895; *Caucasian*, May 23, 1895; Fabius Busbee to *N&O*, May 14, 1896.

47. *N&O*, May 5, 1895; May 20, 1895, copy in Hinsdale Papers, Duke Univ. Library, Special Collections. Subsequent quotations are from this issue.

48. *N&O*, May 20, 1895. This and the subsequent retelling, while tailored to political circumstances, also share characteristics of traditional stories in general: dramatic emphasis and exaggeration; compression of similar events into a single incident; and attachment of many incidents to a single main figure, such as Sherman and his troops.

49. Bills in Treasurer's and Comptroller's Papers, Capitol Buildings (Confederate Monument), NCDAH. One souvenir packet is in the Hinsdale Papers, Duke Univ. Library.

50. *N&O*, Apr. 8, 1897.

51. Ibid., May 9, 1900. The 1900 election also resulted in the effective disfranchisement of black North Carolinians.

52. Ibid., Mar. 25, 1900. Charlotte Bryan Grimes Williams, ed., *History of the Wake County Ladies' Memorial Association* (Raleigh: James Johnston Pettigrew Chapter, UDC, 1938), 7–10. Mrs. Garland Jones was evidently not kin to Nancy Branch Jones.

53. Williams, *History of the Wake County Ladies' Memorial Association*, 22–23.

# 2

# Marking Union Victory in the South

## The Construction of the National Cemetery System

*Catherine W. Zipf*

These [Federal] cemeteries are scattered throughout the South, and their
green, regularly-shaped graves, with the country's flag waving over
them, are always in the vicinity of the rude resting-places of the
Confederate dead, who, by law, are damned irretrievably.

Richmond Daily Dispatch, *May 24, 1872*

IN THE YEARS DURING and immediately following the Civil War, the Federal government established a new and highly visible presence in the South through development of the National Cemetery System. These cemeteries not only honored the fallen dead of the Union army but also served an ideological agenda as a permanent, systematic embodiment of Federal authority within the former Confederacy—an agenda easily understood by northern and southern audiences. Amid the punishing policies of Reconstruction and a continued spirit of rivalry, careful consideration was given to these cemeteries' design and decoration. The standardized architectural form chosen for the National Cemetery lodges provides an important visual cue of officials' intentions, signaling clear connections with other contemporary Federal construction projects, such as the State, War and Navy Building in Washington, D.C. In the case of the national cemeteries, Reconstruction took form through the built environment. They must be viewed, therefore, as architectural monuments to the Union cause.

In 1861 the War Department issued General Order 75, which set up procedures for the proper and permanent burial of Union casualties. This initial order required the army's quartermaster general to distribute forms to generals and post hospitals for recording deaths and to provide headboards for each grave. Soldiers were to be buried by army commanders or hospital staff within preexisting local cemeteries or on new cemeteries set up on donated land. The following year, Congress appropriated money to buy property for military burial grounds, embarking with the War Department on the first stage of what would become the National Cemetery System.

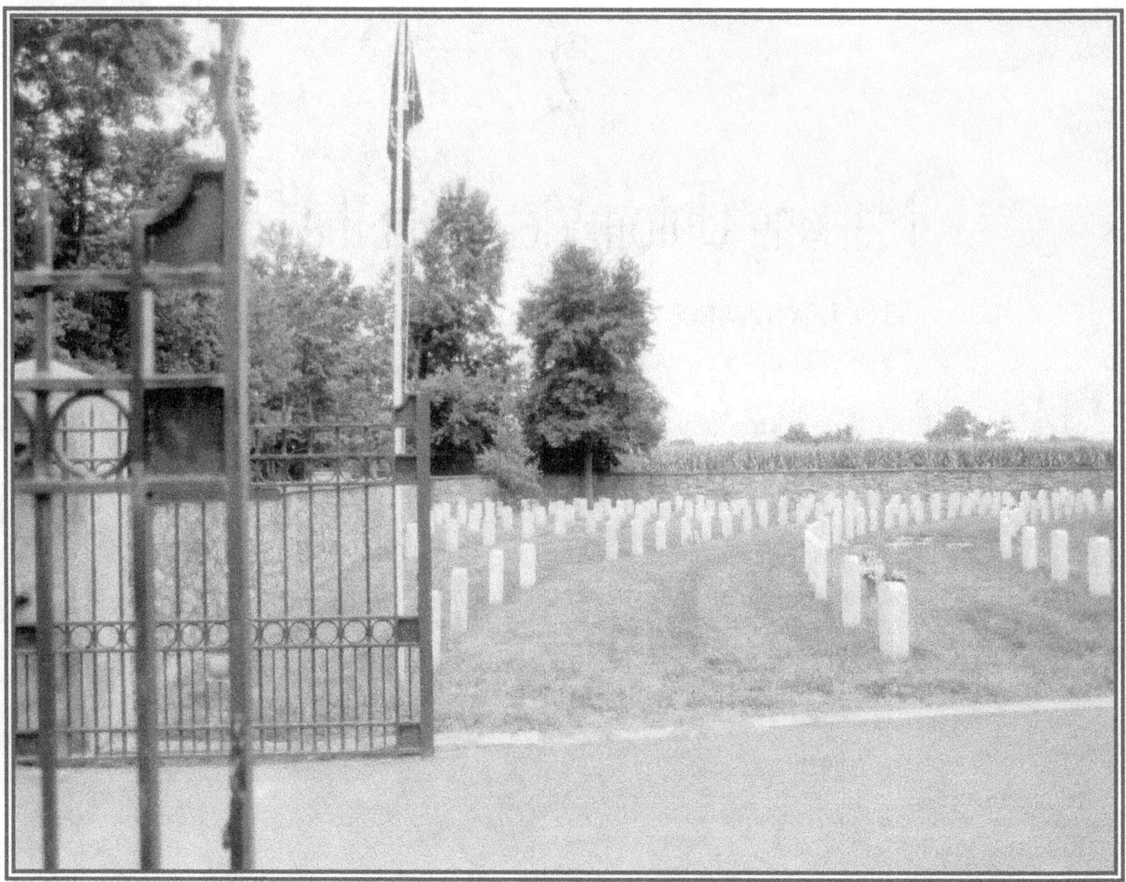

Fig. 2.1. General view of Glendale National Cemetery, Richmond, Virginia, 1873. Photograph by Catherine Zipf.

Events in the southern and western theaters moved too swiftly, however, for these early plans to be effective. Generals on the move to the next front could not wait for the quartermaster to provide land for a cemetery, nor could they take time to legally acquire burial land. On April 3, 1862, the War Department issued a new order directing commanding generals to "lay off lots of ground in some suitable spot near every battlefield . . . and to cause the remains of those killed to be interred, with headboards to the graves bearing numbers, and when practicable, the names of the persons buried in them. A register of each burial ground will be preserved, in which will be noted the marks corresponding with the headboards."[1] Field generals no longer had to wait for the quartermaster but could designate a section of the battlefield themselves, in effect seizing the land. As the responsibility for choosing a site shifted to the field, the quartermaster general's office functioned as a central repository for records of burials and cemetery locations and handled such follow-up issues as compensating owners for their loss.

Between 1862 and 1863, thirteen national cemeteries were laid out, usually within a proximate distance to a major battlefield or, in the North, a hospital. Some cemeteries in the western theater, such as the Chattanooga National Cemetery in Tennessee, were situated with exquisite care, following the natural grade of the land. Graves were arranged in geometric patterns, usually in concentric circles facing a central point. Cemetery plans varied greatly from place to place, however, as generals had different ideas about appropriate arrangements and tried to incorporate native landscapes. Size also varied, as corpses might be collected from many nearby battlefields or just one.

The escalation of the war in late 1863 forced further changes. As action in the southern theater, particularly near Washington, grew heavier, it became impossible for generals to follow the outlined procedures for proper burial. By the time fighting had ceased on a battlefield, the area might be strewn with half-buried bodies, the dead outnumbering the living. Faster mobility forced generals to create makeshift cemeteries or to simply leave bodies where they fell. Fatally wounded soldiers who had moved with the troops were buried by the roadside, while procedures for recording graves were largely ignored.[2] The rising death toll crowded older cemeteries, leaving little room for additional burials.

By the close of the war in 1865, only 101,736 of 359,520 total Union dead had been placed in permanent recorded graves according to the outlined wartime procedures, and only twenty-seven new national cemeteries had been founded, a little over half of what was needed.[3] In the Washington area, most of the bodies were collected in cemeteries either appropriated for military use, such as the Soldier's Home in Washington (1862), or constructed anew for military burials, as at Alexandria, Virginia (1862). Sites were founded near Antietam Creek in Maryland (1862) and Gettysburg, Pennsylvania (1863), for the dead from those battles, while cemeteries in Knoxville, Tennessee (1863), and Fort Scott, Kansas (1862), served the western theaters. Many others were established to serve hospitals behind the lines and in the North; some, such as Lexington, Kentucky (1863), occupied parts of existing church or town cemeteries. Others were built on confiscated lands in areas where Union support was thin or nonexistent, such as Beaufort, South Carolina (1863). With the exception of Antietam and Arlington, most lacked infrastructure such as gates and walls, and all were in varying states of disrepair.[4]

Responding to a public outcry, the War Department in June 1865 began compiling an inventory of the locations and names of the more than 250,000 bodies still unburied or buried in substandard graves. Battlefields were searched in an attempt to find and identify all Union bodies and move them to reburial areas a manageable distance away. By 1866 fifteen additional cemeteries were founded in Virginia alone, such as the Fredericksburg National Cemetery (1865), which housed remains collected from the Wilderness, Chancellorsville, and Fredericksburg battlefields. In the West, new cemeteries followed the path of the northern offensive, from Shiloh, Tennessee (1867), to Vicksburg, Mississippi (1866), and from Chattanooga, Tennessee (1863), to Andersonville, Georgia (1865). In the first year of the program 87,664 bodies were reburied in forty-one different cemeteries at a cost estimated at $9.75 per body. Efforts were renewed each year until 1870.[5]

## *The Building Blocks of Federal Authority*

By 1867 the work of identifying and reburying the dead had progressed enough for the quartermaster general's attentions to turn toward alleviating the desperate condition of the cemeteries. The overall size and shape of each cemetery varied greatly. Most graves needed headstones, and there were few fences cordoning off the cemeteries from surrounding fields. In accordance with a

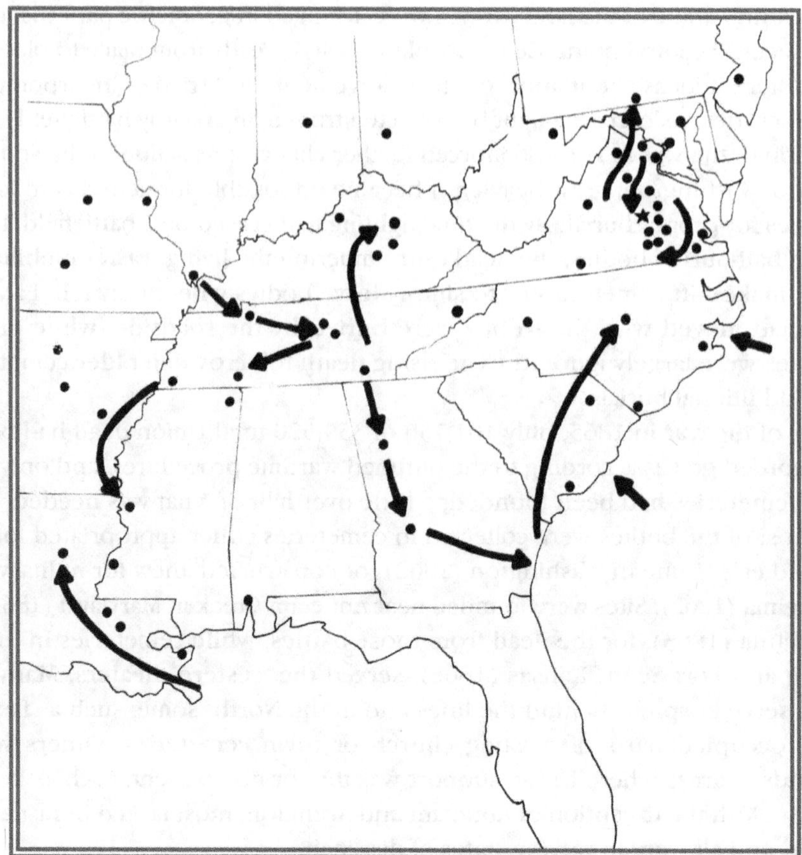

Fig. 2.2. Locations of U.S. National Cemeteries established between 1865
and 1873 and the offensive route of the Union army, 1861–65.

congressional act of February 22, 1867, the quartermaster's office began efforts to enclose, landscape, and beautify the cemeteries. In this phase of its development, the National Cemetery System presented Federal officials with an opportunity to render the government's Reconstruction outlook in architectural form through maintenance and added infrastructure.

Early beautification efforts resulted from the government's decision to employ former Union soldiers as superintendents at each cemetery, to be on the grounds at all times. To house these men, the War Department first built large stone walls around each cemetery and then equipped each with a lodge of approximately six rooms. The lodges served not only as living quarters but also functioned as centers for welcoming visitors, maintaining records of the dead, holding funerals, and organizing Decoration Day festivities. Commemoration was critical to the function of the national cemeteries. In assuming that a full-time, live-in superintendent was needed, government officials expressed their expectation that the cemeteries would serve as shrines and pilgrimage sites within the South.[6] From their perspective, southerners could easily see the cemeteries as small plots of Federal land within the former Confederacy, walled off from the surrounding territory and guarded by former Union soldiers.

Responsibility for designing and overseeing the beautification measures fell to Q.M. Gen. Montgomery C. Meigs. Meigs was in charge of the entire process of identifying and relocating the Union bodies; he supplied provisions for the search, lobbied for employment of superintendents, and produced the schematics for all the architectural accessories built under the beautification act. From 1867 to 1877, he created designs for cemetery walls, gates, rostrums, and, most notably, the cemetery lodge.

Each of these design elements recalled the image of Federal authority. Since the graves were generally organized in concentric circles, Meigs placed a flagstaff at the center of the motif, ensuring that the Union soldiers' allegiance, loyalty, and service to the United States was marked in death as it had been in life. Nearby, usually located outside of the circle, Meigs designed a rostrum, which could be used for ceremonies of remembrance or for funeral services. Standing on the rostrum, a speaker would be raised about three feet high on a podium of approximately ten by twenty feet. On each end of the rostrum, brick columns supported a wooden scaffolding, likely intended to hold a canopy of flowering vines. Surrounding it were the soldiers' marble

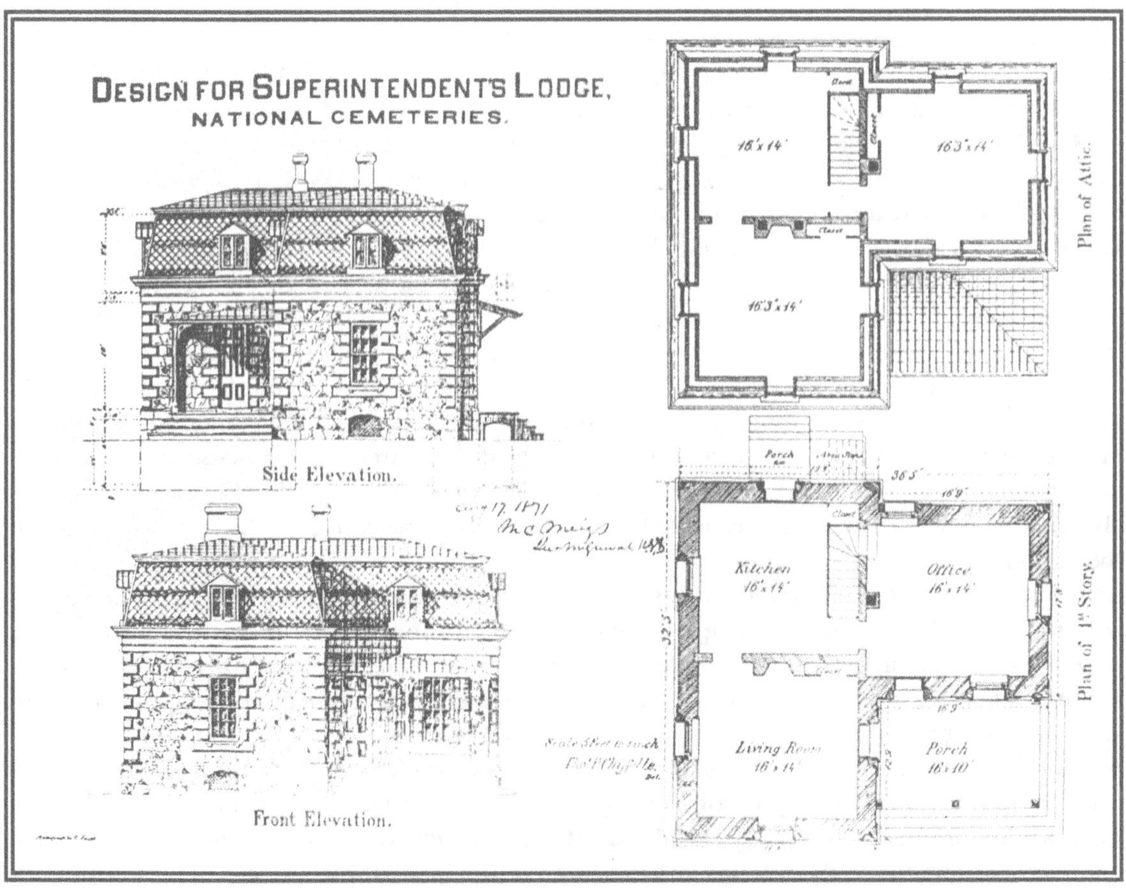


Fig. 2.3. Design by Montgomery C. Meigs for Superintendent's Lodge, National Cemeteries, 1871. National Archives, Washington, D.C.

headstones, each identical in size and shape and engraved with name and regiment. A heavy stone or brick wall with an elaborate entrance gate separated the cemetery from surrounding fields.

Taken together, each part—governmental patronage, the flagstaff, rostrum, gates and lodge, the military supervision, and visitation—represented the government's assertion of the morality and righteousness of the Union victory. In the second stage of development, beautification efforts provided the primary means by which the government could express its strength and permanent presence.

## A Standardized National Identity

The beautification of more than forty-five cemeteries required great organization and ingenuity on Meigs's part. To complete this task quickly, he created a set of standardized designs. Along with a scheme for cemetery walls, gates, and the rostrum, Meigs's designs (fig. 2.3) created an aesthetic that could be applied to each cemetery without regard to landscape or native materials. His plans were specific enough to include appropriate detailing for each design, creating specifications, for example, for the lodge window and door moldings and for the roof structure. But they were flexible enough to be applicable to a variety of locations. In organizing all of the parts of the cemeteries, Meigs also specified that relationships exist—for example, that the lodge should be located near the gate at the edge of the cemetery or that the flagstaff should be at the center of the graves.

Meigs's designs had an immediate impact on the appearance of the national cemeteries. In the early phase, cemeteries were laid out in regular patterns on irregularly shaped plots. Each cemetery was highly individual, reflecting not only the local context but also the size of the battle in its layout. Meigs's plans introduced an element of regularity to each, ultimately tying them together into a single statement. All the cemeteries now had common parts: a lodge, a rostrum, a gate, and a flagstaff. Their common identity was highlighted by the uniformity of the white marble headstones, each engraved with the same motif and lettering for the name and regiment.

Faced with the sudden need to build multiple cemeteries at once, a standardized plan could accommodate regional differences in terrain and materials. Costly design competitions or commissions were avoided, and construction could occur rapidly. Meigs's idea made sense in a military environment, eliminating waste for a more efficient use of time and resources. His designs also ensured that the message of renewed Federal authority was conveyed uniformly throughout the region.

Although the army's experience with standardized plans had not been overly positive, Meigs's solution worked well. Earlier attempts at standardizing frontier forts and barracks had become mired in regional difficulties, lack of appropriate materials, and managerial problems.[7] Federal architects like Ammi B. Young had tried to standardize Federal customs houses, but the trend seems to have been abandoned by his successor, Alfred B. Mullett.[8] Meigs's operation was independent of most other contemporary Federal projects, as well as the traditional military structure: his office was the only point of contact. Though the War Department paid the bills, it did not question the merits of Meigs's designs. Mostly the projects were executed in the field; civilian contractors submitted bids to Meigs and procured local labor to work within the government's budget. Local contractors had regional reputations to uphold as well as access to local contacts and resources. This disconnection between the local contractors and the machine of the Federal

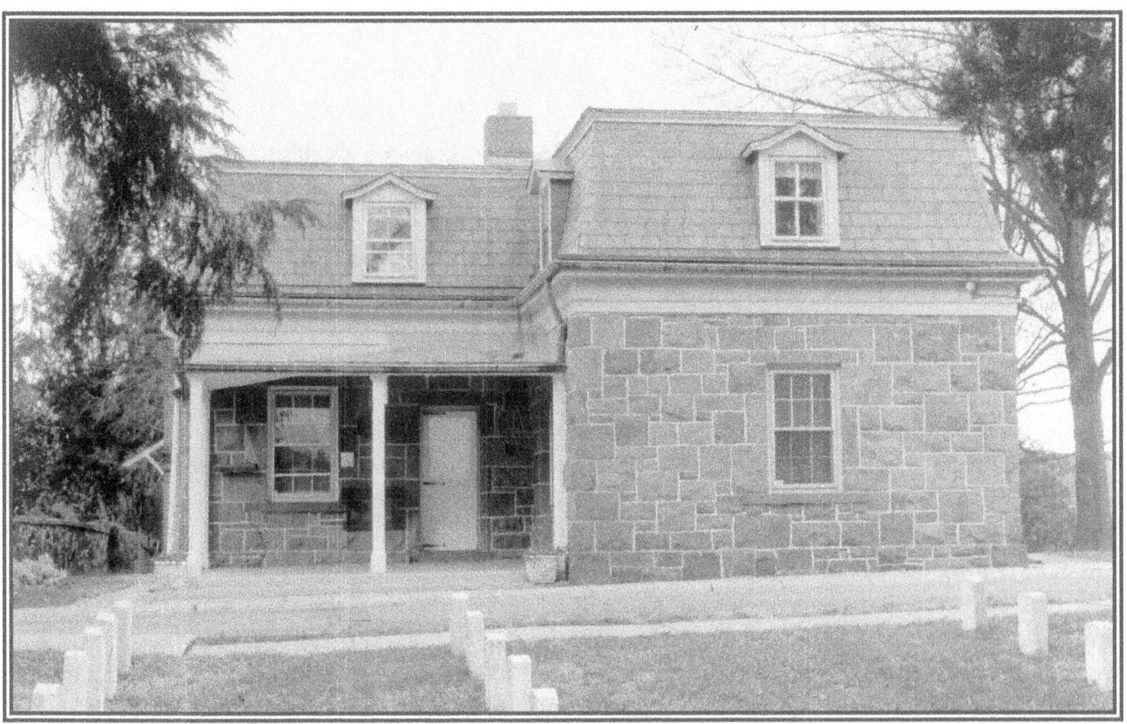

Fig. 2.4. Alexandria National Cemetery Lodge, Alexandria, Virginia, 1887. Design by Montgomery C. Meigs. Photograph by Catherine W. Zipf.

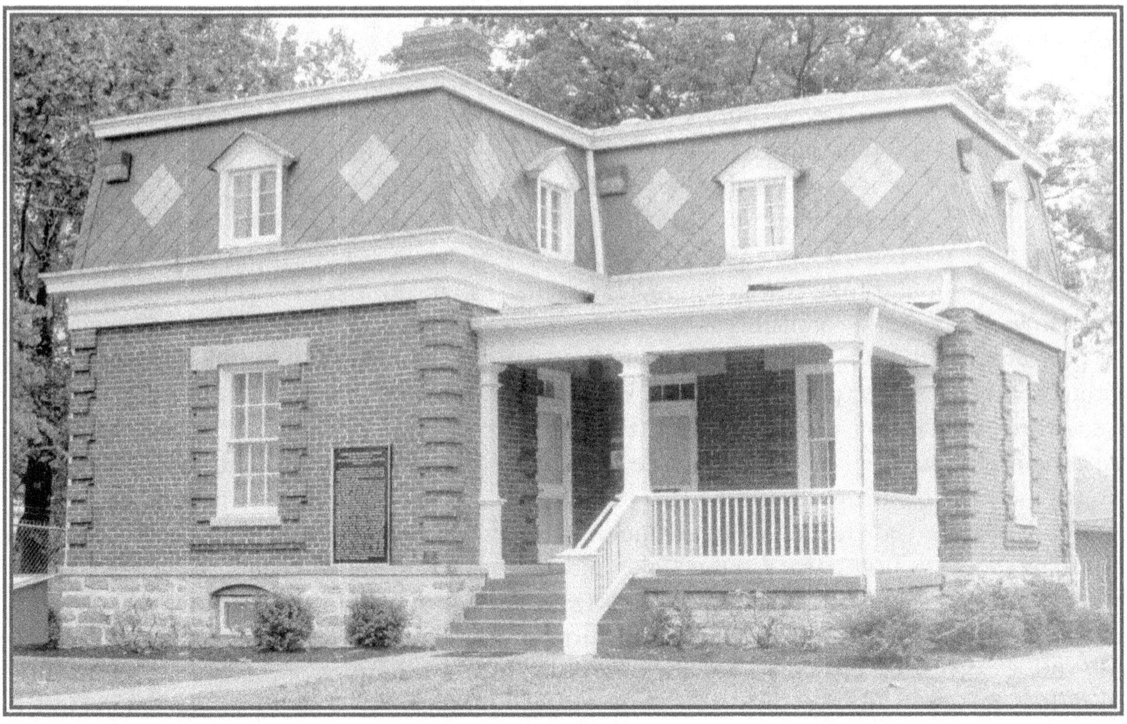

Fig. 2.5. Camp Nelson National Cemetery Lodge, Nicholasville, Kentucky, 1875. Design by Montgomery C. Meigs. Photograph by Catherine W. Zipf.

government had the added advantage of mitigating any issues of loyalty to the former Union or Confederacy.

The flexibility of Meigs's designs also accounted for the availability of materials from place to place. Although only those for brick have survived, Meigs wrote specifications and made drawings for stone and brick lodges.[9] The form and design of the building did not change, but with options granted for materials Meigs could account for differences in price and location. His office could bid out several lodges at a time, asking for proposals in both brick and stone and selecting the most cost effective. The advantage he gained through uniform designs also affected his message: if his design relied on a material that was not universally available or not cost effective, then his attempt to standardize the plans would not have functioned correctly and the universality of the meaning would have been lost. Meigs was rigorous in the overall appearance of his lodge house but flexible in its execution.[10]

There is little doubt that Meigs ran a tight ship. By taking advantage of a standardized design, he introduced a military approach that guaranteed efficient use of labor and materials. Standardization accounted for regional context in available materials and landscape. The lodges themselves were small and sturdy, specific enough to be seen as a cohesive set of buildings, yet general enough to apply to any situation. Meigs had responded to a clear need with a frugality that set him apart from the corrupt spending of the Grant administration and likely saved him from the impending scandals of the era.

## *Meigs at the Helm*

In Civil War scholarship, Meigs is a prolific yet puzzling figure, as famous for his role as Union quartermaster general as for the designs of the Washington Aqueduct and Pension Office building and supervision of the U.S. Capitol extension. Meigs was a career military engineer who was staunchly pro-Union but, perhaps due to familial ties to Georgia, initially believed the Confederates had a right to their cause. His brother fought for the Confederacy, and Meigs had worked with Robert E. Lee on a survey of the Mississippi River. But after the betrayal and killing of his son, who was shot after surrendering to a Confederate ambush, Meigs took a sour approach to the South, especially toward his brother, from whom he remained estranged, and toward Lee. Meigs's biographer, Russell F. Weigley, comments as follows on his sentiments toward Lee and the Confederacy: "'The murderer' [of John Rogers Meigs]—in these words was a sting that signified General Meigs could never again feel quite the same toward the South and his old friends of the South. . . . [Meigs] returned to the war [in the fall of 1864] with a cold anger."[11] If these feelings did not manifest themselves in his position on other Reconstruction policies, they may have colored his views on the message that the National Cemetery System should convey about the Union cause.

Historians have labeled Meigs an engineer, but he also studied a wide range of architectural styles, as shown by his sketches of the 1860s and 1870s. They include detailed studies of classical works such as the Arch of Titus, the Maison Carrée, and the Temple of Castor and Pollux, as well as German models such as Walhalla and the Wurtzburg Residence. His notes show Meigs calculating and recalculating the classical orders. He also studied examples of American architecture, including the Alamo and log cabins. In addition, his portfolio contained views of Italian hill towns and picturesque ruins, punctuated by vernacular and residential architecture. In 1868, before completing his design for the lodge, Meigs's study culminated in a tour of Europe, where he further examined the latest trends in French design. He knew his canon of architecture and seemed acutely aware of the differences in styles, nationalities, and the relationship between vernacular and high-style architecture. The idea of using architectural form to send a Federal message was well within his abilities and understanding.[12]

Meigs's architectural study suggests he had ambitions beyond that of army engineer. Since the close of the war, he had watched Federal construction reach new heights through the spoils system, in which local businesses were patronized in return for their loyalty and support of Federal policies. In Washington, the War Department, with Meigs's hearty support, lobbied successfully for a new building west of the White House. Outside of Washington, the Treasury Department was building thousands of mints, customhouses, banks, and post offices.[13] As Congress enthusiastically spent money on new buildings and Federal construction projects were easy to come by, Meigs, who had taken a backseat to prominent architects Thomas U. Walter and Alfred B. Mullet, might have been looking for an opportunity to publicize his thoughts on architecture.

Issues of national identity remained at the heart of the Federal construction boom. Like many others, Meigs believed the Greek Revival identity of the Federal government needed to be updated to better compare with the architecture of European capitals. A new American style of architecture was needed to reflect the reunited status of the United States and demonstrate the nation's modernity.[14] To advance this agenda, Meigs actively promoted use of a variation on the Italian Renaissance, the Germanic Rundbogenstil, for the State, War and Navy Building.[15] Of all the Federal projects, this building had the greatest possibility of generating an image specific to the War Department that would be recognizable on first sight. In Meigs's mind, a new Federal style had immediate ramifications for the design of the cemetery lodge, and he was eager to take a stand on the issue.

## Model Cemeteries

No direct precedent for large-scale burial of wartime casualties existed in the United States, so Meigs sought out examples from a variety of cemetery traditions. Nineteenth-century cemeteries generally were church cemeteries, country cemeteries, or nonprofit, nondenominational cemeteries. The oldest of these, church cemeteries, were usually located in or near a town, in lots adjacent to a house of worship. Country cemeteries also were small, supplementing town cemeteries by providing burial plots for the rural population. There was little uniformity to their designs, which had evolved over time. Most church and country cemeteries lacked infrastructure like flagstaffs and lodges, and many were not walled off.

Nonprofit, nondenominational cemeteries, such as Mount Auburn Cemetery in Cambridge, Massachusetts, served as the best civilian model for Meigs. Surrounded by a cast-iron fence, Mount Auburn Cemetery featured an Egyptian gateway leading to a Gothic-Revival chapel, complete with pinnacled buttresses and tracery windows. The chapel's Gothic design expressed the ideals of the picturesque landscape movement, while its religious and moral connotations were appropriate for a cemetery. Garden follies presented a theme of American history through their forms and connection to past events.[16]

As a career army officer, Meigs was also well versed in military burial practices. Since the Revolutionary War, the Federal government had undertaken responsibility to bury those who died in service, particularly in remote areas of the West. Most frontier posts had their own cemeteries marked off from territory allocated to the post reservation, and garrison commanders were responsible for burying those who died in government service. In general, graves were numbered and the names and positions recorded according to a fairly uniform system. Markers were usually temporary and made of hard wood, while the area around graves would be fenced or marked off from the landscape. As part of the post reservation, the cemetery did not require additional infrastructure, and, although such cemeteries might have a flagpole, they usually did not have lodges, gates, or rostrums.[17]

Of the military cemeteries in existence at the close of the Civil War, Arlington had the highest profile, and Meigs had been closely involved in its conversion to a cemetery when he was quartermaster general. The Greek Revival Arlington House was designed in 1804 by George Hadfield for George Washington Park Custis, Martha Washington's grandson who sought to build a museum for his collection of Washington memorabilia. Architecturally, the Greek Revival style was associated with the democracies of ancient Greece, thus presenting Arlington as a temple of American democracy. The Capitol building could be seen from its front porch, establishing a visual link and a sense of the shared use of classical elements in each structure's design. With all of these associations, Arlington seemed to be an architectural embodiment of the principles upon which the United States had been founded.[18]

During the Civil War, its architecture took on a different interpretation, however. The plantation had become the home of Robert E. Lee, whose wife, Mary, was George Washington Custis's only child. Ultimately, Lee's loyalty to the Confederacy—and disloyalty to the Union—carried over from the man to the architecture. Not only was Arlington now tied to the Confederacy, but its form embodied the southern plantation lifestyle, including the slaves who had formerly worked nearby lands. Greek Revival mansions dotted the southern landscape, and their shady porticoes had made living more comfortable for the antebellum elite. Throughout the Civil War and into the following decades, many Union officials, including Meigs, viewed Arlington as a symbol of the Confederacy, its economic system, and its treason.[19]

Some historians have attributed Arlington's conversion to a cemetery to Meigs's personal bitterness over the murder of his son and a vengeful determination to make Arlington uninhabitable for the Lee family. Perhaps this was partly true, but there were good reasons for choosing Arlington as a Union burial ground. Because of its proximity to Washington and its strategic military value as a promontory over the Potomac, Arlington had been seized and occupied by Gen. Winfield Scott in 1861. Since that time, the plantation had been stripped of its resources, logged for firewood, and used as a training ground for Union recruits. In the summer of 1864, when the Soldier's Home Cemetery could no longer accommodate the bodies arriving in Washington, Meigs requested permission to set aside part of the Arlington estate for burial purposes. Arlington's fields were not far from the city, but they were far enough to prevent the spread of disease. The part Meigs desired was located behind Arlington mansion but not so close to the house as to prevent its occupation by Union troops; today this is the site of the Civil War section.[20]

Thus, a site first linked with American nobility gained Confederate associations and then evolved into a place for commemorating fallen Union soldiers. The message of Arlington was clearly received by northerners, who commented that it was "a righteous use of the estate of the rebel General Lee," and by southerners, who said there was no "sadder walk than the visit to the heights of Arlington."[21] Although Arlington was one of the few national cemeteries to include Confederate graves, only Union soldiers were formally honored. The Confederate graves were marked as "REBEL" and were excluded from decoration and care. If many southern families chose to remove their sons from Arlington, it was perhaps because of this strenuous pro-Union agenda.

For Meigs, Arlington served as an important example of the power architecture held to commemorate the war's events. But he likely understood the advantages that other cemeteries offered as well. The regularity and efficiency of post cemeteries was critical to Meigs's institution of the National Cemetery System, as the uniform headstones derived from an older military and frontier tradition. The peaceful qualities of church cemeteries provided a vision of perpetual care, while park cemeteries, like Mount Auburn, constituted an example of active commemoration through visitation. Meigs combined aspects of each type of cemetery into a new creation, setting a high standard for cemetery design.

## *The Lodge Design*

The National Cemetery System entered a final phase of development with completion of the lodge design. Meigs ultimately chose a Second Empire French style, with each lodge consisting of six rooms, three up and three down, placed in an L-shape. In the corner of the L, Meigs set a porch, which squared out the building and provided a covered spot for reception and amusement. The lower story of the building was made either of rough or smooth cut stone or brick, usually with a window on each side opening into each room. Above was a slate-covered Mansard roof, with regularly spaced dormer windows covering a second story. The interior arrangement of rooms included a reception hall, which could be used for any necessary ceremonial function, while the upper rooms were reserved for the use of the keeper and his family. Meigs's lodge was considerably smaller and far less elaborate than most of the European Second Empire French models he had seen during his trip, but its style was clearly recognizable from its identifiably French parts, particularly the Mansard roof.[22]

Meigs had several major reasons for finally choosing the Second Empire French for the cemetery lodge. More so than either the Greek Revival or the Rundbogenstil he had promoted earlier, this style expressed the idea of modernity because it came from Paris, which set many standards in the late nineteenth century. In France, where architects were produced by the state-run École des Beaux-Arts, architecture and government were deeply interconnected. Not only was the Second Empire French style created by a government-controlled system of architectural training, but it also was used chiefly for governmental buildings.

By 1860, Federal architects had seized upon this connection and began promoting the Second Empire French style as the next national style. Before the war, the style had been mostly seen in collegiate and museum buildings in the United States. But after 1865 it was used for almost all Federal projects, to the extent that it was nicknamed the "General Grant" mode. For the South, the Second Empire French stood out as a noticeable change from the Greek Revival porticoes of large plantations.[23] Since tensions immediately following the war still ran high, it is unlikely that the importation of a style so closely associated with the Federal government and so contrary to its own native style could have been seen as a style intended to reunify the nation. Instead, with restrictive and punitive Reconstruction policies in place, the Second Empire French came to be associated with the patronage of the Federal government, to the exclusion of southern interests.

Thus Meigs chose to ally the cemetery lodges with the authority of the government through the forms and properties of style. Federal authority was further derived by looking at the relationships

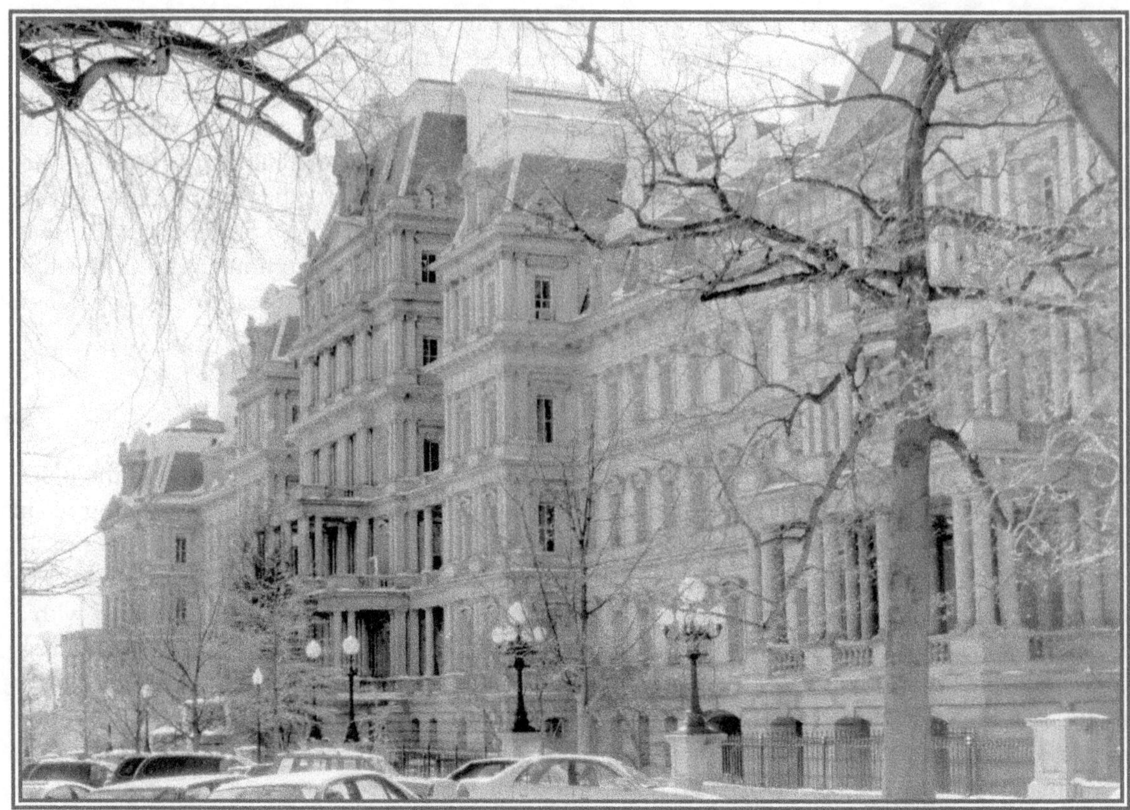

Fig. 2.6. State, War and Navy Building, Washington, D.C. 1869–75. Alfred B. Mullett, architect.
Photograph by Catherine W. Zipf.

between the cemetery lodge and its parent building, the State, War and Navy Building (today known as the Old Executive Office Building). In 1869 planning was begun on a massive new headquarters for the State, War, and Navy Departments, to be located west of the White House in complement to the Treasury Building. By late 1869 the Second Empire French style had been selected for this building designed by Mullett to contrast with the neoclassicism of earlier Federal buildings, particularly the White House and the Treasury Building. As quartermaster general, Meigs was involved in the planning of this building and accordingly viewed it as an appropriate Federal model for his lodge.[24]

Long before construction was complete, the State, War and Navy Building (fig. 2.6) rose to the top of the hierarchy of Federal buildings. Not only was it the largest Federal project Washington had seen since the Capitol extension, but its stylistic modernity was impressive. It was a notable change from earlier Federal projects, which consisted of smaller courthouses, banks, customhouses, post offices, and mints throughout the nation. Most prewar Federal buildings had been sponsored by the Treasury Department and designed by its supervising architect. Now the War Department's architectural identity gained a higher profile, dominating the Federal scene.[25]

Once the design of the State, War and Navy Building had been established, Meigs had an opportunity to create a relationship between the War Department and his cemetery lodges. Before and during the Civil War, the department had been housed in several buildings scattered around Washington, with no overarching architectural identity. The new headquarters gave the War Department a modern identity. The next logical step was to increase the department's profile through a series of subsidiary buildings that read as little war departments. The National Cemetery lodge provided the opportunity, with the bonus of extending War Department influence over the one area of the country that most needed its presence.[26]

In Meigs's hands, the department's new architectural identity proved useful in reminding the former Confederacy of the Union victory and allowing the War Department to spread its influence without employing troops. Not only did the cemeteries read as small enclaves guarded by Union soldiers, but the architecture directly connected the lodge with the War Department headquarters in Washington. Each of these aspects of the National Cemetery System attempted to deter further hostilities by creating tangible reminders of Federal authority. Those who did not understand the message had only to look at the slate roof of Richmond's Glendale National Cemetery lodge (fig. 2.7), on which was imprinted a massive "U.S."[27]

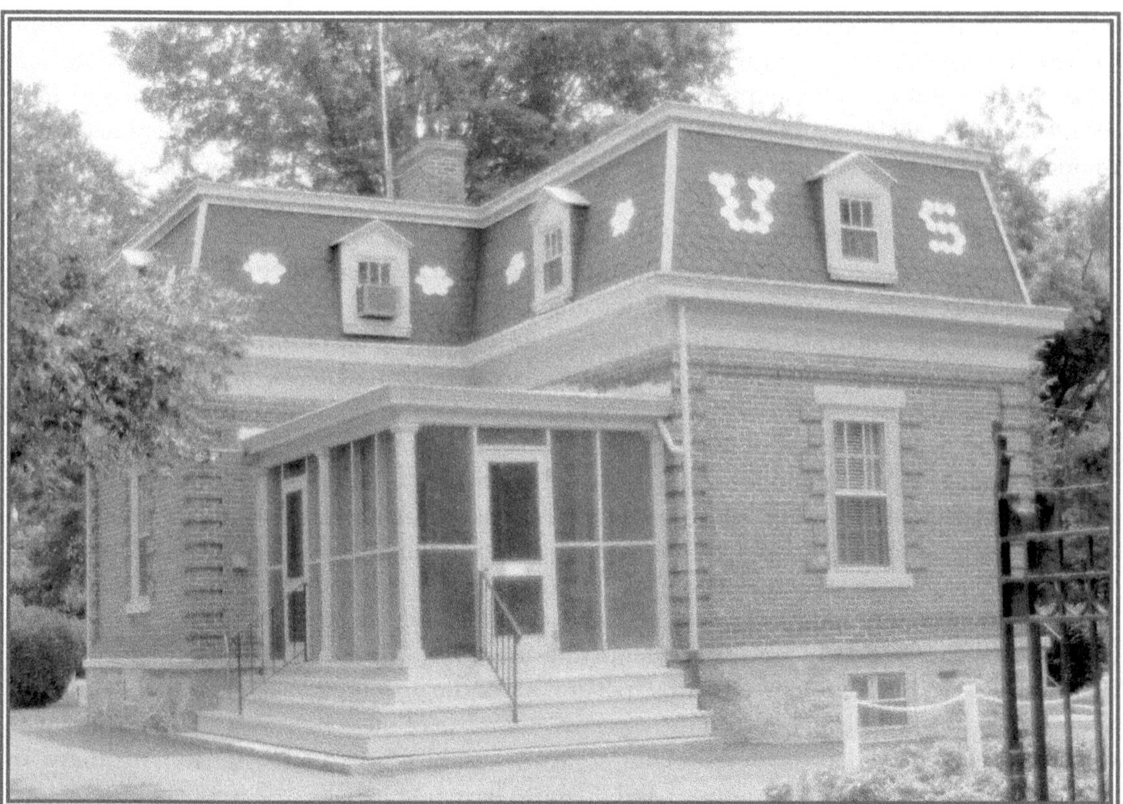

Fig. 2.7. Glendale National Cemetery Lodge, Richmond, Virginia, 1873. Design by Montgomery C. Meigs. Photograph by Catherine W. Zipf.

## Southern Perspectives

The National Cemetery System, as conceived by the War Department, provided only for Union soldiers. In the decade following the war, tensions between northerners and southerners prevented the existence of a single cemetery for both sides. On a few occasions, officials did propose measures to include Confederate soldiers in the Federal cemetery programs, but even as late as 1880 these had little popular support and were usually quietly dropped. As a result, only a handful of national cemeteries house Confederate as well as Union dead, and generally those were established in response to drastic need before the war's end.

Residents of the former Confederacy faced different challenges in caring for and removing their own dead due to limited resources. Attempts to identify and bury southern soldiers occurred on a local level, without benefit of government funding and direction. There were some Confederate cemeteries, for example Shepardstown in West Virginia, which housed the dead from Antietam, and Hollywood Cemetery, which was taken over to hold the graves of those killed in the battlefields surrounding Richmond. In general, however, there was no program comparable to the National Cemetery System instituted to care for the fallen of the now-dissolved Confederacy.[28]

The absence of an organized, regionwide system for managing the southern dead does not imply that southerners were disorganized about caring for their fallen soldiers; the contrary seems to have been true. Immediately after the war local residents, particularly women, formed groups to provide perpetual care for the Confederate dead by procuring land for cemeteries, locating and reburying the bodies and attempting to identify the dead. Not only could local efforts achieve results far more quickly than the slower processes of the Federal bureaucracy, but regional organizations could better capitalize on the sentiment and loyalty generated by the war to facilitate the fund-raising process.[29]

These efforts to preserve and care for the dead soldiers of the former Confederacy were monitored by the Federal government, especially the Office of the Quartermaster General. Government correspondence and publications document a long history of southern women caring for Confederate graves, as particularly noted in the *Report on the Reburial of the Confederate Dead in Arlington Cemetery* and the *Report of the Special Committee on the Graves of Southern Soldiers.*[30] These publications were included in the records of the quartermaster general, along with correspondence indicating the condition of the battlefields and of the cemeteries throughout the South.

The reports and correspondence suggest a rivalry between the North and the South in terms of caring for the dead and making a show of perpetual concern. One letter documents the condition of Union graves after the war but before the institution of the National Cemetery System as follows: "Their condition is extremely neglected; there are no regular cemeteries: the dead were buried where they fell, and scarcely covered; the graves are not enclosed; there are, generally, no headboards, and rarely any means of identifying the bodies. In many localities the ground is thickly strewn with bones; legs and arms sticking out of the ground and skulls rolling about. . . . The contrast now is striking between these graves and those of the rebels who fell there, and who were carefully removed to the nearest church yards, with headboards. The inhabitants there, or very many of them, glory in the contrast and ought to have no further cause to do so."[31]

Given this response, it might be argued that immediately following the war southern women provided more efficiently for the Confederate dead than the Federal government. To compete, the government implemented a comprehensive system for burials and provided architectural accessories arranged in an identifiable format to create a whole aesthetic for the national system. Meigs's elaborate schemes for the national cemeteries pushed the level of competition beyond the South's resources.

Almost every Union cemetery was located a short distance from a Confederate cemetery, inviting comparisons between the uniform look and feel of Union cemeteries and the less structured Confederate cemeteries. The National Cemetery at Antietam, for example, is located only about ten miles from the Confederate Cemetery at Shepardstown. Glendale National Cemetery in Richmond is less than twenty miles from Hollywood and Oakwood cemeteries. Oakwood originally contained casualties from both sides, until the Union bodies were removed to Glendale as part of the quartermaster general's reinterment program. Other sites, such as Lexington Cemetery and Danville National Cemetery, both in Kentucky, had separate sections—sometimes immediately adjacent—devoted to Union and Confederate soldiers.[32]

The National Cemetery System, in addition to caring for the dead with dignity, should be viewed as an intensely competitive propaganda for the perceived righteousness of the Union cause. By inviting comparison in cemetery design, the government reminded southerners again of its victory.

## *Getting the Message*

Even before the National Cemetery System was completed, southerners began to comment on its establishment within their territory. Southern communities resented the fact that tax dollars went to support not just construction of the cemeteries but beautification measures and keepers as well. As the *Richmond Daily Dispatch* commented in 1873:

> These legislators and political aspirants . . . commenced a partial and cruel system of pains, penalties, and humiliations for the South. They drew lines and distinctions for their own advantage, and to the lasting detriment of the State, carrying their discriminations to the very grave, and cursing the bones of the "rebel dead," as they were pleased to style them, with neglect and opprobrium, while the "Union dead" were gathered into so styled national cemeteries, which were placed under the flag of the Union and guarded and kept in order by a public officer. These cemeteries are scattered throughout the South, and their green, regularly-shaped graves, with the country's flag waving over them, are always in the vicinity of the rude resting-places of the Confederate dead, who, by law, are damned irretrievably.[33]

The difference between "us" and "them" was acutely felt within the former Confederacy, to the extent that it affected commemoration ceremonies through the 1890s. Differences over whether and how casualties from the former Confederacy would be commemorated persisted at cemeteries of both national and local prominence. The Executive Committee of the Grand Army of the Republic tried to settle the issue in 1873 through a formal resolution forbidding any decoration of the Confederate graves located in Arlington Cemetery on Decoration Day, May 30. The committee stated: "Any attempt by the friends of the rebel dead to strew flowers on their graves will be regarded as an interference with the programme of the day and will not be tolerated."[34] In response, southerners immediately complained of partisan tactics and discrimination against their dead. Richmond's *Daily Dispatch* said the resolution would only foster "the war of passion and prejudice" and "help all the more to keep alive the rancors and hates of war."[35] Despite conciliatory efforts by Meigs, the prohibition was upheld by Secretary of War William W. Belknap, confirming the continued divisions between North and South.[36]

Differences between Federal and Confederate commemoration ceremonies, often held within a few days or weeks of each other, further demonstrate how the National Cemetery System was viewed as a symbol of Federal authority. Southern newspaper accounts describe in detail the formal decoration ceremonies and speeches held in local Confederate cemeteries; memorial wreaths given by northerners were publicly cited as examples of how partisan feelings could be overcome and how inclusive the southern ceremonies were toward both sides of the war. By contrast, Decoration Day ceremonies at the national cemeteries were celebrated as a day off from Federal employment. The festivities began with a military parade out to the cemetery, where flowers also were strewn and planted. No speeches or formal program were presented, although the entire day was set aside for commemoration. The act of honoring the dead primarily consisted of a military salute and a holiday at the cemetery, in contrast to the organized ceremonies at the Confederate cemeteries. A further difference was that many of those participating in Federal Decoration Day festivities were African American.[37]

Despite the partisan nature of the national system, a few communities did manage to overcome their differences and hold communal ceremonies. At the Mound City National Cemetery in Illinois, which contained both Union and Confederate soldiers, both sides were commemorated on the same day and had been since the close of the war.[38] This example was rare but inspiring to those hopeful of ending Civil War tensions. It was not until two decades later that Decoration Day ceremonies were extended to include Confederate graves under the administration of President William McKinley. McKinley's 1898 decision began to close the gap between Federal and Confederate efforts to commemorate the war, finally allowing the healing process to begin.[39]

## *Notes*

The author is indebted to Katherine E. Comeau and Judith H. Robinson of Robinson and Associates, Inc., for their assistance with research on Antietam and Battleground National Cemeteries.

1. Both executive orders are reprinted in Edward Steere, "Origins of the National Cemetery System," *Quartermaster Review* 32 (Jan.–Feb. 1953): 12–15, 136–39. Steere's article is one of six he wrote on the history of the American military cemeteries; the others are found in vol. 32, nos. 4–6, and vol. 33, nos. 2–4.

2. One example of the neglect of fallen bodies is recorded in the *History of the Antietam National Cemetery* written by the Board of Trustees. RG 92, Entry 225, "Antietam National Cemetery," National Archives.

3. Records of the Quartermaster General, RG 91, National Archives. This information was compiled by Meigs under General Order No. 40, July 3, 1865, and does not include Confederate dead.

4. Founding dates and first burial dates often differ, especially for the earlier cemeteries. The Veterans Administration considers the date that a cemetery was marked off as the founding date. Dates and locations of all National Cemeteries are found on www.cem.va.gov/nmc.htm.

5. Steere, "Evolution of the National Cemetery System," *Quartermaster Review* 32 (May–June 1953): 22–24, 120–26 n. 2.

6. The requirements for the keeper are spelled out in "An Act to Establish and Protect National Cemeteries," Feb. 22, 1867, 39th Cong., sess. 2, chap. 61.

7. On the standardization of military architecture, see Alison K. Hoagland, "'The Invariable Model': Standardization and Military Architecture in Wyoming, 1860–1900," *Journal of the Society of Architectural Historians* 57 (Sept. 1998): 298–315.

8. See Daniel Bluestone, "Civic and Aesthetic Reserve: Ammi Burnham Young's 1850s Federal Customhouse Designs," *Winterthur Portfolio* 25 (summer/autumn 1990): 131–56.

9. Specifications and drawings for the National Cemetery Lodge are found in RG 92, Office of the Quartermaster General, Consolidated Correspondence File, 1794–1915, Entry 576, "Lodges," and in the Cartographic Division, RG 92, Entry 225, National Archives.

10. In response to requests for bids for cemeteries in Knoxville and Pittsburgh Landing, Tennessee, and Camp Nelson, Kentucky, Meigs's office received bids from five firms, three of them local to Kentucky. In all three instances, construction proposals for stone were 15 to 20 percent higher than for brick. See abstract of proposals for the erection of lodges at National Cemeteries, Aug. 28, 1872, in the files of Lt. Col. James A. Ekin, Deputy Quartermaster General, RG 92, Office of the Quartermaster General, Consolidated Correspondence File, 1794–1915, Entry No. 576, "Lodges," National Archives.

11. Russell F. Weigley, *Quartermaster General of the Union Army: A Biography of M. C. Meigs* (New York: Columbia Univ. Press, 1959), 32–34, 309–10. John Rogers Meigs followed in his father's footsteps by attending West Point. The Meigs family plot, which includes a recumbent memorial to John Rogers Meigs, is located near Arlington House at Arlington National Cemetery.

12. Montgomery C. Meigs papers, AC 18202.1, Miscellany, 1815–1971, Drawings and Sketches, folder 34, microfilm reel 20, Library of Congress Manuscripts Collection.

13. On the relationship between the Treasury Building and subordinate buildings outside of Washington, see Jennifer Laurie Ossman, "Reconstructing a National Image: The State, War and Navy Building and the Politics of Federal Design, 1866–90" (Ph.D. diss., Univ. of Virginia, 1996).

14. On national identity and the War Department, see Ossman, "Reconstructing a National Image," 27–31.

15. Ibid., 33.

16. Kenneth T. Jackson and Camilo José Vergara, *Silent Cities: The Evolution of the American Cemetery* (New York: Princeton Architectural Press, 1989); Blanche Linden-Ward, *Silent City on a Hill: Landscape of Memory and Boston's Mount Auburn Cemetery* (Columbus: Ohio State Univ. Press, 1989). Linden-Ward, chaps. 4–5, discuss "meaning" in Mount Auburn Cemetery and its significance to the construction of the identity of the early Republic.

17. On early burial practices of the Federal government, see Steere, "Origins of the National Cemetery System," 12–13.

18. See Philip Bigler, *In Honored Glory, Arlington National Cemetery: The Final Post* (Arlington, Va.: Vandemere Press, 1987), 11–22; and John Vincent Hinkel, *Arlington: Monument to Heroes* (Englewood Cliffs, N.J.: Prentice-Hall, 1970), chaps. 1–2. The connection between democratic ideals and Greek architecture is established in Talbot Hamlin, *Greek Revival Architecture in America* (London: Oxford Univ. Press, 1944), which mentions Arlington on page 91. Roger G. Kennedy, *Greek Revival America* (New York: Stewart Tabori and Chang, 1989), reexamines the meaning of Greek Revival architecture in the context of the early Republic.

19. Bigler, *In Honored Glory*, 27.

20. See ibid., 27–28, for the siting of the Civil War section and Hinkel, *Arlington: Monument to Heroes*, chaps. 1–2, for a record of correspondence regarding Arlington's conversion. Both sources argue that Meigs's location of the Civil War section was intended to render Arlington uninhabitable to the Lee family.

21. Bigler, *In Honored Glory,* 30–31. On Confederate graves at Arlington, see the essay by Karen Cox in this anthology.

22. On the spread of the Second Empire French style, see Henry-Russell Hitchcock, *Architecture: Nineteenth and Twentieth Centuries* (New Haven: Yale Univ. Press, 1977), chaps. 8–9.

23. On the architectural identity of the South, see Mills Lane, *The Architecture of the Old South* (New York: Abbeville Press, 1993).

24. Completion of the State, War and Navy Building (1871) postdates the design of the cemetery lodge, but planning for the big Washington, D.C., building began in 1869. Meigs had sufficient time to familiarize himself with Mullett's design before conceiving his cemetery lodge. As army quartermaster general, Meigs would have been involved in the planning process for the new War Department from the start. The idea that the State, War and Navy Building represented a new era in Federal management is documented in Elsa M. Santoyo, ed., *Architectural Drawings of the Old Executive Office Building, 1871–1888* (Washington, D.C.: American Institute of Architects Press, 1988), and Ossman, "Reconstruction a National Image," introduction and chap. 1.

25. On the relationship between the Treasury Building and subsidiary buildings, see Ossman, "Reconstructing a National Image," 52. Ossman mentions the relationships between Federal buildings in passing, and the idea merits further study.

26. An understanding of how remote government buildings appeared Federal can be gained from any state's survey of historic resources. In particular, Calder Loth, *The Virginia Landmark's Register* (Charlottesville: Univ. Press of Virginia, 1987), 327; Charles E. Brownell et al., *The Making of Virginia Architecture* (Charlottesville: Univ. Press of Virginia, 1993), 89, 165; and John O. and Margaret T. Peters, *Virginia's Historic Courthouses* (Charlottesville: Univ. Press of Virginia, 1995), chaps. 3–4.

27. On the founding of Glendale National Cemetery, see RG 92, Entry 576, Cemeterial, 1828–1919, General Correspondence relating to Post and National Cemeteries, "Glendale Cemetery," Box 3d, National Archives.

28. Information regarding the government's 1898–1902 efforts to ascertain the status of Confederate soldiers' grave sites is found in RG 92, Office of the Quartermaster General, Entry 585, Cemeterial, Papers relating to Confederate Cemeteries, Interment of Confederate Soldiers in National Cemeteries and Isolated Confederate Graves, 1898–99, National Archives. An undated article from this collection published in the *New York Sun* (probably Jan. 14, 1899), notes, "a few of [the southern] dead have been exhumed here and there and removed by their friends, but there has been no general care of the Confederate dead like that which characterized the Union policy, for the reason that there was no central authority to direct and no Government Treasury to pay the expense of such an undertaking."

29. For an example of local organizations' work at southern cemeteries, see Catherine Bishir's essay in this anthology.

30. Both of these documents are located in RG 92, Office of the Quartermaster General, Entry 585, Cemeterial, 1828–1929, Papers relating to Confederate Cemeteries, Interment of Confederate Soldiers in National Cemeteries and Isolated Confederate Graves, 1898–1999, National Archives. Both documents are dated in the 1899s but suggest a great familiarity with southern women's prominent role in caring for confederate cemeteries since the close of the war.

31. C. W. Folsom, Captain, USA, to Montgomery Meigs, Washington, D.C., Nov. 23, 1865, RG 92, Office of the Quartermaster General, Entry 576, Cemeterial, 1828–1919, General Correspondence relating to Post and National Cemeteries, "Glendale Cemetery," Box 3d, National Archives.

32. Danville National Cemetery, Kentucky, was founded as a church cemetery but later converted to a National Cemetery. This happened relatively late; consequently, there is a locally sponsored Confederate Section adjacent to the Union section. Federal funds were not used to bury the nearby Confederate dead.

33. "Patriotism and Partisanism," *Richmond Daily Dispatch,* May 24, 1873.

34. Ibid.

35. Ibid.

36. Meigs's response is found in "The Confederate Dead at Arlington," *Richmond Daily Dispatch,* May 26, 1873 (reprinted from the *Philadelphia Press*). For Belknap's final word in an untitled letter to all local newspapers, see *Richmond Daily Dispatch,* May 28, 1873.

37. "Oakwood Memorial Day," *Richmond Daily Dispatch,* May 15, 1873; "Honors to Federal Dead: Decoration Day at the National Cemetery," *Richmond Daily Dispatch,* May 31, 1873.

38. "Blue and Gray," *Richmond Daily Dispatch,* June 23, 1873.

39. Hinkel, *Arlington: Monument to Heroes,* 45–50.

# 3

# Making History

African American Commemorative Celebrations
in Augusta, Georgia, 1865–1913

*Kathleen Clark*

AFRICAN AMERICAN EDUCATOR John Hope bore witness to black commemorative celebrations in his hometown of Augusta, Georgia, from early Reconstruction to the turn of the century. Vividly recalling the celebrations he witnessed as a young boy during the years following emancipation, when massive parades clogged the streets and African Americans thronged the steps and park of the local city hall, Hope said: "No hall or church could hold that concourse. The city hall park for [the] multitude and the city hall porch for orators were none too roomy. Added to these were the military and civic organizations parading each to the triumphant music of the bands, nor did foul weather ever interfere with speakers' words, with flying banners, or with martial arts. We small boys wormed our way among the listening crowds mindful more of uniforms and drums than speakers' words. Yet every little while such words as emancipation, freedom, liberty would lodge in our ears."[1]

Hope (fig. 3.1) went on to describe alterations in Augusta ceremonies during and after Reconstruction. First, much of the oratory was given over to party politics. "A few years later," Hope recollected, "when I added inches to my stature, this immense multitude had shrunk into a hall and I heard not 'emancipation,' 'freedom,' 'liberty,' but these words: 'Cable versus Grady.'" Later, when Hope returned to the city as an adult after having been away for some time, he observed a further transformation in local celebrations: "[O]n my return [I] found that vast multitude of my boyhood years shriveled into a church. The orator was no longer on the courthouse porch . . . . He said not emancipation, freedom, liberty nor yet did he discuss the subject Cable versus Grady."[2]

To a certain extent, John Hope's narrative of decline aptly captures the evolution of African American commemorative celebrations in Augusta and other southern cities during the decades following the Civil War. African Americans in postwar Augusta vigorously celebrated not only the anniversary of emancipation but also other dates associated with the birth of freedom, such as July 4 and the passage of the Fifteenth Amendment. As years went by, however, their commemorations faced mounting obstacles, ranging from increasing white resistance to organizational rivalries, and the boisterous demonstrations of Reconstruction gave way to tamer events by the early 1900s.

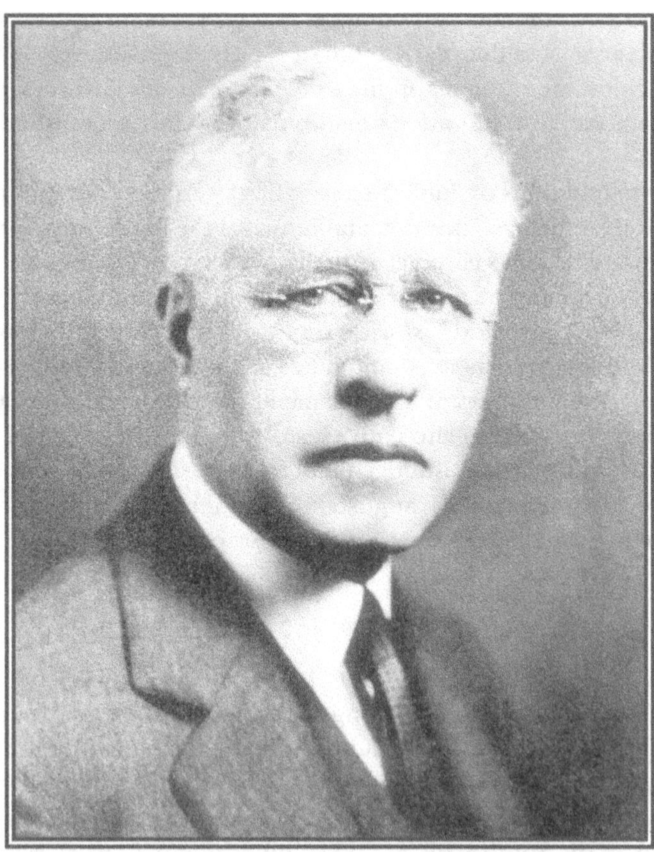

Fig. 3.1. John Hope, African American educator, circa 1920s. Atlanta University
Photographs, Atlanta University Center, Robert W. Woodruff Library.
Photograph by Blackstone Studios Inc.

Yet Hope's story of devitalized black ceremonies is only half the tale. Considering the challenges that confronted black Augustans during the decades following Reconstruction, African American celebrations actually represented the black commemorative traditions' remarkable persistence in the face of increasing hardship. Moreover, the endurance of African American traditions meant that whites in Augusta did not have a monopoly over public memory—not even during the grim Jim Crow era. The alterations observed by Hope provide important insight into the institutionalization of black public memory in the postbellum South and help to delineate shifting negotiations—and outright struggles—over the meaning of the region's past and the direction of its future.

Beginning with a massive July 4 celebration in 1865, this essay focuses on the development of African American commemoration in Augusta after the Civil War while also paying heed to white residents' considerable efforts to define public memory on their own terms. Unlike white Augustans, who devoted thousands of dollars to constructing a Confederate memorial, African American commemorative occasions did not produce physical manifestations of public memory in the form of ponderous statues or soaring monuments. Instead, African American women and men forged their own versions of southern, American, and black history through annual ceremonies that brought together hundreds, sometimes thousands, of local residents as well as African Americans from the surrounding area. Whether celebrating the passage of slavery, narrating traditions of black heroism and achievement, or mapping a racially inclusive future for the South and the nation, these commemorative celebrations made history—and established memories—in the post–Civil War era.

In building their own traditions of public memory, black residents persistently challenged white Augustans' efforts to define the past, present, and future of the South on their own terms. Even as they cast a wary eye toward history's chroniclers in the North, white citizens were forced to confront the disagreeable reality of competing memories and histories closer to home. Indeed, white Augustans forged their commemorative and historical traditions in a context of interracial conflict and negotiation, as did white southerners in communities throughout the South—a fact that has been obscured in much of the scholarly literature on the memorialization of the Lost Cause. By neglecting black southerners' efforts to create an alternative history, we have lost sight of a significant facet of African American culture and risked misunderstanding the formation of southern white historical memory as well. By reconstructing black Augustans' commemorative efforts and white residents' efforts to control them, we can help restore the full landscape of public memory.[3]

## *July 4, 1865*

When African Americans arrived in Augusta for an Independence Day celebration on the morning of July 4, 1865, they entered a city just beginning to recover from the hardships of war. White citizens, anyway, thanked God that the town had been spared the destruction wrought in nearby areas by Union Gen. William Tecumseh Sherman's march from Atlanta to Savannah. There had been no battle of Augusta, and the town escaped much of the physical ruination that the war brought to other parts of the South. Still, at mid-summer plenty of work remained to be done— local railways ran nowhere, the town's financial system was in disarray, and local industries languished. Under the direction of presidential Reconstruction, military and civil authorities shared responsibility for getting Augusta up and running again.[4]

The enormous influx of new residents during the past five years challenged available resources. In 1860 Augusta had stood as the state's second largest urban center, with eight thousand white and four thousand black residents. In the war years, thousands of refugees, white and black, poured in from the surrounding countryside. The town housed numerous government agencies and manufactories of vital importance to the South's military effort; this expansion of Augusta's industrial base also contributed to a surge in population. Surveying the changed landscape of the town in 1865, a local newspaper editor estimated that Augusta's African American population had tripled over the course of the war.[5]

As in other southern cities, the crowded streets of Augusta teemed with disorder and violence. With black and white refugees pouring into town toward the war's end, one observer complained that Augusta had become "the Eldorado of sutlers, cotton thieves . . . and other such riffraff." Hungry Confederate deserters had damaged local businesses when they rioted in January 1865, and several incidents involving black military regiments culminated in December of that year when a fight broke out between eight black soldiers and a local white family.[6] Officials of the local Freedmen's Bureau faced an uphill battle as they struggled to persuade black and white residents to cultivate more "friendly relations" with one another in the months following the war's end.

Amid these turbulent conditions, black Augustans set about creating a new life for themselves. Many freed people settled into two areas of Augusta, known as Campbell's Gully and Springfield Village. The latter was the site of the Springfield Baptist Church, established in 1793. The Springfield church, an important hub of organized community life for African Americans, was joined in the late antebellum period by four additional black churches, two Baptist and two Methodist. After emancipation, freed people extended this core of community life with the creation of numerous civic organizations. The Trinity Moral Society, the Brothers and Sisters of Love, the Lilies of the Valley, the Bonds of Hope, the Morning Stars of Benevolence, and the Sons and Daughters of Jerusalem were just a few of the associations black Augustans founded during the postwar years. Several freedmen's schools also opened in Augusta after the war. Together the churches, societies, and fledgling schools provided an important foundation for African American community life.[7]

Federal organizations and missionary societies also helped create institutional supports for black Augustans in the early postwar years. The Freedmen's Bureau established a school in a former shoe factory on the corner of Ellis and Campbell Streets, opened a hospital in east Augusta, and formed a bank on Broad Street, the town's main business district. Local Freedmen's Bureau official John Emory Bryant immersed himself in a broad range of public affairs and helped make Augusta a center for Republican Party organizing and black politics in the early years of Reconstruction. Both white and black missionaries representing a host of organizations, including the American Missionary Association and the African Methodist Episcopal Church, also settled into town and committed themselves to guiding the transition from slavery to freedom.[8]

The 1865 Independence Day celebration exemplified the development of a participatory and democratic African American public culture in post–Civil War Augusta. It is likely that black celebrants, whom newspapers estimated to number in the thousands, came not only from local neighborhoods but also from a broad expanse of the surrounding countryside. Augusta was set in the midst of a large area of farmland stretching out in all directions. Nearby counties consisted of a mix of small and large land holdings, with cotton growing alongside fields of corn, wheat, and other foodstuffs. The freed people who traveled to Augusta that day would have lived and worked on the farms that dotted the region.[9] Federal officials, visiting black luminaries, and northern missionaries also joined the multitudes thronging Augusta's streets on July 4.

By midmorning, crowds began to assemble in downtown Augusta in anticipation of the day's opening event—a massive parade. Ministers, tradesmen, field laborers, members of various societies, and local schoolchildren jostled to get in place for the procession. Just before these marchers got under way, a group of women unfurled three banners bearing inscriptions: "Abraham Lincoln the Father of Our Liberties and Savior of His Country"; "Slavery and Disunion Dead!"; and "Freedom and Equality Is Our Motto." Then a regiment of black troops marshaled the parade through downtown streets and out to a nearby parade ground, where an eager audience awaited speeches by black leaders and Federal officials.[10]

The Reverend James Lynch, a missionary for the African Methodist Episcopal Church, headed the bill that day; along with the other speakers, he mounted a platform "handsomely decorated with banners." The ceremonies opened with a prayer, which was followed by recitations of both the Declaration of Independence and the Emancipation Proclamation. At last Reverend Lynch rose to deliver his oration. Standing at a podium graced by a national flag, he quickly warmed to the enthusiastic audience of men, women, and children and launched into a detailed chronicle of the nation's past. For too long, Lynch thundered, the United States had failed to recognize her mission: "to scatter light where tyranny casts the blackest shades." The fate of the nation, he declared, had hung in the balance until the decisive moment when Lincoln issued the Emancipation Proclamation on January 1, 1863, signaling that the "destiny of both races" was united. Turning to the future, Lynch called upon his audience to swear upon Lincoln's grave to "maintain the honor of the starry standard . . . the liberty of all men—forever and forever."[11]

The audience went wild and Lynch sat down to a storm of applause. After the crowd settled, several more speakers set forth their vision of the nation's history and its future. At their conclusion, a local minister gave the benediction, and the participants dispersed. Everyone pronounced the day a success, and a Freedmen's Bureau official was pleased to report that although the celebrants' spirits were "jubilant with high and ardent expectation," no "disorder or unnecessary tumult marred the occasion—all passed off quietly."[12]

The July 4 celebration, replete with mass procession, prayer, recitations, extensive speech making, and general festivity, was typical of the largest African American commemorative celebrations during Reconstruction in the South. It was not uncommon for African Americans to travel long distances to participate in commemorative and patriotic celebrations in major towns and cities, and postwar ceremonies frequently incorporated a broad spectrum of participants, including Federal officials, African American leaders, and white missionaries, as well as local black citizens.[13]

The gendered organization of the Augusta ceremony was similarly representative of postwar celebrations. Throughout the postbellum period, men assumed the lead in most African American occasions, dominating both parades and speech making. Yet women clearly made their presence felt. Active behind the scenes, their labor was crucial to the success of black ceremonies as they frequently took charge of tasks such as fund-raising, decoration, and refreshment. Moreover, they had a formal role in many occasions, including some processions. Women's ceremonial functions often served to emphasize gender difference, as when "tastefully dressed ladies" presented the Augusta parade—led by male soldiers—with homemade banners. But African American women also came out in large numbers to cheer marchers, applaud speakers, and revel in the general merrymaking—all of which reflected the shared participation of men and women in public celebrations during Reconstruction.[14]

Black celebrants' occupation of Augusta's downtown streets also reflected broader trends in African American patriotic and commemorative celebrations. While some ceremonies took place within the confines of African American institutions, particularly churches and schools, many others spilled over into common public arenas such as town squares, city halls, downtown streets, town parks, and outlying parade grounds. Taking over significant public spaces—some of which had been off limits to blacks during slavery—African Americans forcefully altered the social geography of cities and towns across the postwar South. Where once the movements of black and white residents had articulated the inequalities of slavery, now African Americans gave concrete meaning to freedom. In large parades, freed people dominated thoroughfares where daily interactions had previously made manifest the boundaries between white and black, free and slave. It must have thrilled black marchers to hold their heads high and shout slogans of liberty in places where they had formerly been expected to demonstrate deference and humility. One can similarly imagine the joy and excitement of listening to dramatic oratory delivered by talented black leaders from atop the steps of a city hall or the center of a town square.[15]

## *Claiming Public Spaces*

In Augusta, elaborate parades demonstrated African Americans' determination to claim important public spaces as their own. Significantly, parade routes nearly always encompassed a march up Broad Street, Augusta's busiest thoroughfare and the very "soul" of the city (fig. 3.2). The majority of local businesses, including banks, dry goods stores, furniture dealers, hotels, boardinghouses, tailors, and grocers lined the street. As they marched along the avenue—one of the widest in the country—celebrants passed before such notable institutions as the Augusta Insurance and Banking Company, the Planters Hotel, and the offices of the *Constitutionalist,* a local Democratic newspaper. But African American marches along Broad Street held an additional meaning. Before the Civil War, slave trading took place in the market houses that lined the upper end of the street. By parading in celebration of freedom on the very street where they had once been led to auction, African Americans underscored the transformation of realities.[16]

From Broad, marchers made their way to Greene Street, home to many of Augusta's most prominent residents, including doctors, lawyers, and city officials. Proceeding up Greene, they not only passed through one of the city's most illustrious neighborhoods but also encountered time-hallowed symbols of the American Revolution. Many of the most highly prized historical markers in the city, including the Signers Monument, dedicated to the memory of Georgians who signed the Declaration of Independence, held pride of place on Greene.[17]

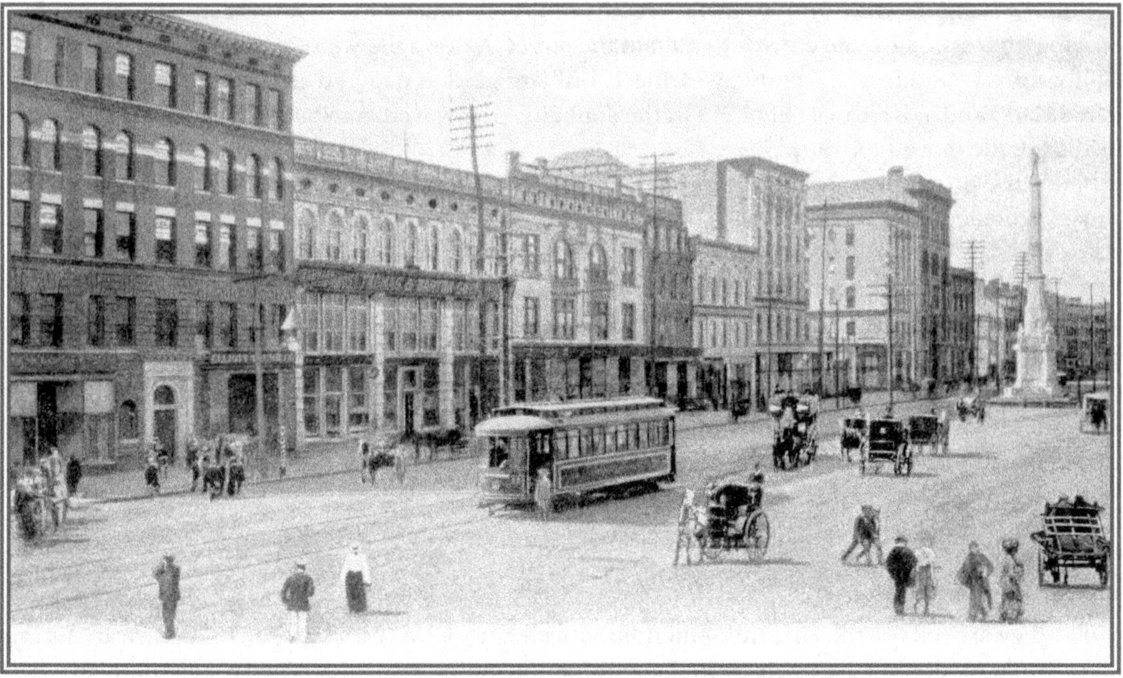

Fig. 3.2. View of Broad Street, where African Americans paraded on Emancipation Days over the years. Postcard collection, Hargrett Rare Book and Manuscript Library/University of Georgia Libraries.

By incorporating markers of the Revolution into their celebrations, African Americans in Augusta both legitimated emancipation and invested the birth of American freedom with deeper meaning. Elsewhere in the South, black processions similarly highlighted local symbols of the revolutionary period. In Richmond, Virginia, for instance, black marchers joyfully paraded through the capitol square and even decorated the monument to George Washington that presided there along with its accompanying figure of Thomas Jefferson. The significance of their appropriation of revolutionary icons was not lost on white observers; after black celebrants in Richmond decorated the sculpture with evergreens and flags, angry whites brooded over the matchless "liberty" that freed people had taken with "Virginia's great work of art."[18] After passing the Signers Monument on Greene, African American marchers in Augusta soon arrived at the Richmond County Courthouse. While crowds milled below, leading black orators mounted the steps of the building.

This was the scene that unfolded again on April 28, 1870, when African Americans joined together for an elaborate celebration marking the recent passage of the Fifteenth Amendment, which declared that no one's right to vote could be restricted "on account of race, color, or previous condition of servitude." Attracting a crowd of four thousand to Augusta, the ceremonies reminded observers of the massive July 4 celebration in 1865. Festivities began in the morning with a grand procession up Broad Street en route to Greene and City Hall. Accompanied by a band and waving banners reading "We Are Rising" and "Georgia, Our Native State, with All Thy Faults We Love Thee Still," legions of marchers made their way on foot. In their wake came several horse-drawn carriages as well as a decorated wagon bearing a banner labeled "Fifteenth Amendment." Atop this wagon sat an assemblage of elegantly clad women, representing the states of the Union. Dressed in white and wearing wreaths of green, these African American women made a striking impression on the crowds that lined the street. Among the women sat an even more beautifully attired "Goddess of Liberty." Wearing a "brilliant golden papered crown, studded with variegated stars" and a dress that "glittered in the sunlight," she waved graciously to cheering spectators as the parade moved forward.[19]

Once the procession arrived at city hall, men, women, and children milled about, enjoying the music provided by the band. Finally, however, the audience quieted down in anticipation of the day's oratory. William Jefferson White, a religious, educational, and political leader in the local black community, rose to deliver the keynote address. Men, women, and children expressed their hearty appreciation for White's speech, in which he heralded the Fifteenth Amendment as the crowning achievement of American freedom; white reporters, standing at a "remote location," could clearly hear their cheers and applause. After three hours the rally concluded, but the celebration lasted well into the night. At 9:30 P.M., participants gathered for a torch-light procession down Broad Street; the procession, accompanied by "an innumerable throng" along the sidewalks, continued until late in the evening.[20]

## How White Augustans Responded

When they arrived for the Fifteenth Amendment celebration in the spring of 1870, African Americans would no doubt have been excited about the upcoming festivities. They also would have had a pretty good idea of what to expect. Traditions of African American celebration already were being established in Augusta just five years after the end of the Civil War. Not only were events following an increasingly familiar pattern, but the organizers were becoming more recognizable. In particular, leaders in the Republican Party had assumed a heightened prominence in celebratory affairs as black men became involved in local and state politics. Men like White, who were active in the party and who also were linked to the local black community through their educational and religious leadership, held center stage at many events, along with members of black military companies and civic organizations.

Even as the course of black ceremonies became more familiar to African American participants, they became increasingly well known to local whites. Each year on New Year's Day and July 4, as well as on special occasions such as the Fifteenth Amendment celebration, local whites were forced to cede local streets to African Americans. The imposition of a black calendar of celebration was a travesty to some, a mere annoyance to others, but it could hardly be avoided altogether, as Ella Gertrude Clanton Thomas discovered one New Year's Day. The wife of a prominent planter who resided just outside of Augusta, Thomas came to town on business on the morning of January 2, 1871. Having left home reluctantly, she was relieved to finally make it to her destination—an office on Broad Street. No sooner was her business under way, however, than a parade of African Americans began to pass up the street. Only at that point did it dawn on Thomas that African Americans were out celebrating "their emancipation." Perhaps it was the evident joy of black celebrants that caused Thomas to reflect on her own, contrasting position, "[T]his is not a Happy New Year to me," she lamented. After waiting out the procession, Thomas made her way home, where she looked back on her day out on the streets of Augusta with evident regret: "I do not generally go on the street on New Years Day but have usually remained in doors to receive calls, but today I was not a fashionable lady but a business woman—I am afraid I am becoming cross when I remember how changed everything is."[21]

Thomas's response to the Emancipation Day ceremony corresponded with the actions of many whites in Augusta and elsewhere in the South who shut their doors and closed their shutters on black celebration days. Others preferred to leave town altogether. Country excursions became popular forms of white entertainment in Augusta and elsewhere in the South throughout the years of Reconstruction. The *Augusta Constitutionalist* underscored white residents' efforts to absent themselves from the city during African American holidays. "Many of our people left town" on July 4, 1866, the paper reported, including the staff of the *Constitutionalist:* "[A]s we went with a party of friends at an early hour . . . and enjoyed a fine time going up the canal . . . we are unable to inform our readers what the freedmen did." The editors could not resist trying to discredit the day's events, however, with a final, contemptuous comment: "We learn that the [celebration] was a highly colored affair," they concluded, *"Sic transit gloria mundi."*[22]

Implicit in white Augustans' actions was a reluctant recognition that African Americans had now laid claim to a share of public space where they enacted their own versions of the past, present, and future of the South and the nation. This realization did not come easily. Across the region there were numerous instances of white interference with African American ceremonies during the postwar years. In the most extreme cases, angry whites issued dire threats in the days leading up to a black celebration, and, in some instances, physically assaulted African American celebrants.[23]

In contrast to the threats and violence that marred African American celebrations in Norfolk and other southern towns, early black ceremonies in Augusta did not encounter physical abuse. White residents did succeed, however, in averting at least one memorial effort by local blacks. On an early morning in May 1866, white women assembled at a local cemetery to honor the Confederate dead. Some days later, students and teachers from a freedmen's school were attempting to ornament the graves of Union soldiers when armed men suddenly surrounded them. In the ensuing conflict, the mayor of Augusta justified the exclusion of African Americans from the cemetery by drawing upon a prewar ordinance; fearful of provoking local whites, the commander of the Georgia Freedmen's Bureau declined to support the efforts of the freed people to obtain access to the local graveyard, and the Union graves went unadorned.[24]

In spite of these and other victories, southern whites were unable to suppress the development of competing memories in the postwar South. With the onset of congressional Reconstruction in 1867 came tighter controls on southern society, and hostile whites were forced to seek new means for dealing with black commemorations. More modest forms of harassment, such as spraying parades with water from nearby fire plugs, took the place of earlier violence.[25] While certainly bothersome, such actions were sporadic and limited in effect; perpetrators were now subject to punishment from local authorities. For the most part, white residents refrained from directly confronting black celebrations, and African American commemorations prospered in the late 1860s and early 1870s.

Thwarted in their efforts to block the development of African American commemoration, Confederate sympathizers nevertheless maintained their battle for control over public memory. Shifting their lines of defense, white southerners labored simultaneously to undermine black accomplishments and to assert contrary historical ideologies. Democratic newspapers aimed to define the meaning of black events through extensive—and typically derisive—commentary. In the meantime, white memorialists endeavored to consecrate their own versions of southern history through the decoration of graves, establishment of new holidays, and construction of elaborate monuments—all dedicated to sanctifying the memory of the Lost Cause.

In an effort to distort the meaning of African American affairs, white newspapers persistently lampooned various aspects of black proceedings. Serious historical and political speech making were pronounced a ridiculous sham. Elaborate, well-ordered parades were described as vulgar and pretentious. A common strategy was to emphasize the presence of women at African American events, an attempt to undercut the legitimacy of historical and political oratory and to hint at the presence of sexual impropriety. Reporting on a July 4 celebration in Atlanta, a Democratic reporter took evident pleasure in pointing out that a "considerable portion" of the crowds were "females, who seemed to enjoy the thing amazingly." Refusing to credit the women with serious contemplation of the issues at hand, the writer mockingly opined, "Whenever anything was said by one of the speakers to tickle their fancy, these latter would demonstrate the fact by a waiving of handkerchiefs, the peculiar aroma from which the frequent breezes seemed to delight in disseminating."[26]

The Atlanta reporter's allusion to "peculiar aroma[s]" was another means of satirizing African American celebrations. Indeed, these allusions were so pervasive as to seem almost obligatory. Time and again, southern whites spoke of "rank" smells and offensive "perfumes" at black affairs. Following a July 4 celebration in Augusta, the *Constitutionalist* offered a "sanitary suggestion" typical of the commentary in white-authored reports. Alluding to the summertime warmth, the paper recommended that, in the future, city authorities be required to present every African American "man, woman, and child" participating in July 4 ceremonies with a bottle of perfume.[27]

Like their allusions to female participants, white observers' allegations of offensive smells were clearly intended to recast—and disempower—black ceremonies. At the moment when southern freed people lay claim to identities as full citizens of both the South and the nation, white detractors resolutely rejected black assertions of common humanity and shared citizenship. Drawing on longstanding traditions that ascribed subhuman characteristics to African Americans, southern whites alleged that freed people's essential incapacity for equality emanated from their very bodies.[28]

Even as they labored to refashion the historical and political ceremonies of African Americans as ludicrous, farcical affairs, however, white commentators let slip an underlying anxiety that black ceremonies were not as laughable—and unthreatening—as they wished. White apprehensions were evident in repeated assertions that southern society was giving way to an overwhelming black force. "This time honored day was surrendered to the colored people" and "Africa has had full sway" were typical of the sentiments expressed by whites in cities throughout the South as they contemplated African American celebrations on January 1 and July 4. Additionally, the graphic language employed by whites commonly invoked images of odious plagues and pestilence. On a day of African American celebration in Norfolk, Virginia, white observers reported that a "black pall appeared to hang over the city—it was negro everywhere." They went on to liken the crowds of freed people to a scourge from God, exclaiming, "The excursionists spread over the town like locusts in Egypt." Clearly white observers went to such lengths to denigrate black ceremonies because they viewed them as a potentially powerful force. The apocalyptic imagery was not a mere rhetorical device; it reflected whites' profound belief that they resided in a world turned upside down. What else could explain African American demonstrations on behalf of equality on the same streets where they had once dutifully enacted the rituals of their subordination?[29]

Faced with the immediate and all-too-tangible evidence of African American patriotic and commemorative organization in the present, southern whites fervently hoped that the future would somehow be different, that the "cloud" which had "o'erspread the bright sky" of white happiness would someday lift.[30] In the meantime, white memorialists countered the patriotic and commemorative pageantry of African Americans with equally elaborate public ceremonies of their own making, and "distinguished" citizens founded the Southern Historical Society, an organization dedicated to maintaining "a true history of the facts of the past."[31] Just as Democrats and Republicans competed for political control in the Reconstruction South, so too did black and white southerners vie for cultural authority over the region's history.

In Augusta, members of the Ladies' Memorial Association took the lead for local whites, making it their job both to grieve the Confederate dead and to construct historical narratives that neatly excised slavery as a cause of the Civil War, replacing that explanation with stories that insisted upon southern soldiers' worthy—and manly—defense of the "life, honor and happiness" of white women and children. Women also took charge of local efforts to erect a monument to the Lost Cause, a goal finally achieved with the erection of a Confederate Monument at the center of Broad Street (see fig. 3.2). Costing more than twenty thousand dollars, the monument featured the marble image of a lone Confederate soldier atop a tall shaft, with figures—all carved in Italy—of four Confederate generals below. It was unveiled with great fanfare before an estimated crowd of ten thousand in 1878.[32] From that point onward, marchers occupying Broad Street on days of black celebration would have to thread their way around the soaring monument.

The imposition of a Confederate monument onto the path of black commemorations stood as indelible evidence of white residents' determination—and capacity—to shape the historical landscape of the city with substantial, not to mention costly, physical markers. African Americans did not have access to the resources needed to erect competing statues. Still the regular presence of African American celebrants—many of them former slaves—filling the area around the monument was testimony to the ongoing elaboration of both black and white memories on the streets of postwar Augusta.

### *After Reconstruction*

The end of Reconstruction did not fundamentally alter the commemorative practices of either black or white residents in Augusta. In the following decades, African Americans continued to hold public ceremonies hailing the end of slavery, memorializing black achievements, and celebrating the expansion of American freedom. In particular, New Year's Day was designated as a day of black celebration; each year, African Americans persisted in the tradition, begun in the 1860s, of congregating in large numbers to celebrate the anniversary of their freedom. While the size and makeup of Emancipation Day celebrations varied from year to year, the fundamentals—a procession followed by prayer and speech making—remained constant. For their part, white residents elaborated a panoply of events and institutions to embody their own memories of the Lost Cause.[33]

Two separate ceremonies in 1913 epitomized the evolution of distinct historical practices enacted by black and white commemorators in Augusta nearly half a century after the Civil War. On New Year's Day, African Americans assembled for a celebration of the fiftieth anniversary of the Emancipation Proclamation, perpetuating a tradition handed down from one generation to the next. Later that year white Augustans gathered for an equally momentous occasion: the dedication of the "Four Poets" monument commemorating four Augusta writers on a green in downtown Augusta. The monument's organizers, motivated by a fear of northern bias in cultural distinction, were determined to ensure the recognition of white southern writers.[34]

Even as black and white Augustans elaborated commemorative patterns that had been initiated during the early postwar period, however, there were changes in African American commemoration and in the relationship between black and white memory during the decades following Reconstruction. In the 1870s and 1880s the decline of the Republican Party in Georgia, coupled with rising themes of "national reunion" among northern and southern whites, altered the context in which African American celebrations took place. Then in the 1890s and early 1900s, the insidious advance of Jim Crow placed significant constraints on public demonstrations by African Americans, including commemorative ceremonies. While African Americans continued to assert their visions of the past and hopes for the future on the streets of Augusta, they negotiated an increasingly perilous terrain.[35]

An enormous celebration by white Augustans on July 4, 1875, signaled the shifts in political and cultural authority that accompanied the end of Reconstruction in the South. This was the first such occasion in the city since the Civil War; in previous years, white officials had scorned the notion of celebrating the anniversary of American freedom, insisting that northern actions had profoundly compromised the principles for which the Revolution had been fought.[36] Now, however, white Augustans had good reason to celebrate. Not only had Democrats succeeded in seizing power in Georgia, they also were rapidly assuming control of governments elsewhere in the South; additionally, northern weariness of intervening in "southern affairs" increased white residents' confidence that Reconstruction would soon end. While the political outlook seemed promising, cultural developments also were hopeful. Amid preparations for a centennial celebration in

Philadelphia in the coming year, northern whites had made overtures to their former adversaries in the South while scorning African American bids for equal representation. The centennial developments reflected and reinforced an emerging trend in historical memory. In striking contrast to the immediate postwar years, northern and southern whites were moving, tentatively but unmistakably, toward re-creating a common understanding of history—one that rested, first and foremost, on the exclusion of African Americans from the "imagined community" of the nation.[37]

In the weeks leading up to July 4, 1875, local newspapers were awash with anticipation. Augusta residents were excited to be hosting large numbers of visitors from Charleston for what promised to be a "historical event." When the big day arrived, white military companies in Augusta were joined by eight battalions from South Carolina. With "guns glittering in the sunlight, banners flying, and bands playing," the lengthy procession marched through town and out to the nearby Schutzenplatz, where the attendant crowds enjoyed an afternoon of music, dancing, and barbecue. Throughout the afternoon and into the evening, militias engaged in several rounds of competitive marksmanship, and former Confederate officials delivered congratulatory speeches filled with the particular admixture of conciliation and defiance that would characterize white southerners' political rhetoric for years to come. One speaker looked forward to the day when men would "strike a blow to resurrect . . . Southern liberty . . . from the grave of oblivion," while the next emphasized the special martial brotherhood of Georgia and South Carolina but took pains to express his happiness that representatives of the Federal navy and army had attended the day's festivities. The orator who best summed up the day's themes spoke eloquently of peace but concluded: "[W]hile we have shaken hands with Massachusetts, we shall never forget that . . . God has bound Carolina heart and soul . . . together, and may we ever so remain."[38]

Where were African Americans during these festivities? Many had traveled by train to Charleston (see fig. 3.3), reversing the journey made by white South Carolinians. In effect, black and white residents traded cities for the day, a development that reflected the contrasting political situations in Georgia and South Carolina in 1875: whereas Georgia Democrats had successfully gained control of the state government in 1870, South Carolina was still held by Republicans. Even before the white-led ceremonies of 1875, black celebrations of July 4 had declined in Augusta as a consequence of diminished Republican organization. It is not surprising, then, that many African Americans looked to nearby South Carolina, where Republican-supported July 4 celebrations endured, as an attractive alternative.[39] Still, it must have been disconcerting for African Americans to give way to white celebrants altogether in Augusta. Just a few years before, black southerners had heralded emancipation and the Fifteenth Amendment as the "finish of our national fabric"; now northern and southern whites were busily shaping revolutionary rhetoric and symbolism into a foundation for a renewed national community of white "brothers." Indeed the past year's festivities in Charleston, which black Augustans had also attended, had been marred by the ugly outburst of a white speaker who strode to the podium to mock the very idea of African Americans celebrating the Fourth of July. "The day," he reportedly insisted, "did not belong to them. They had nothing to do with it."[40]

While July 4 celebrations reflected the devolution of the Republican Party as well as the cultural labors of white reunionists, annual Emancipation Day ceremonies remained significant in Augusta throughout the 1870s and in following decades. There were shifts, however, in the form and content of Emancipation Day events. As Republican organizations faltered, religious and educational institutions, which had always played a key role, stepped up their involvement. More and more,

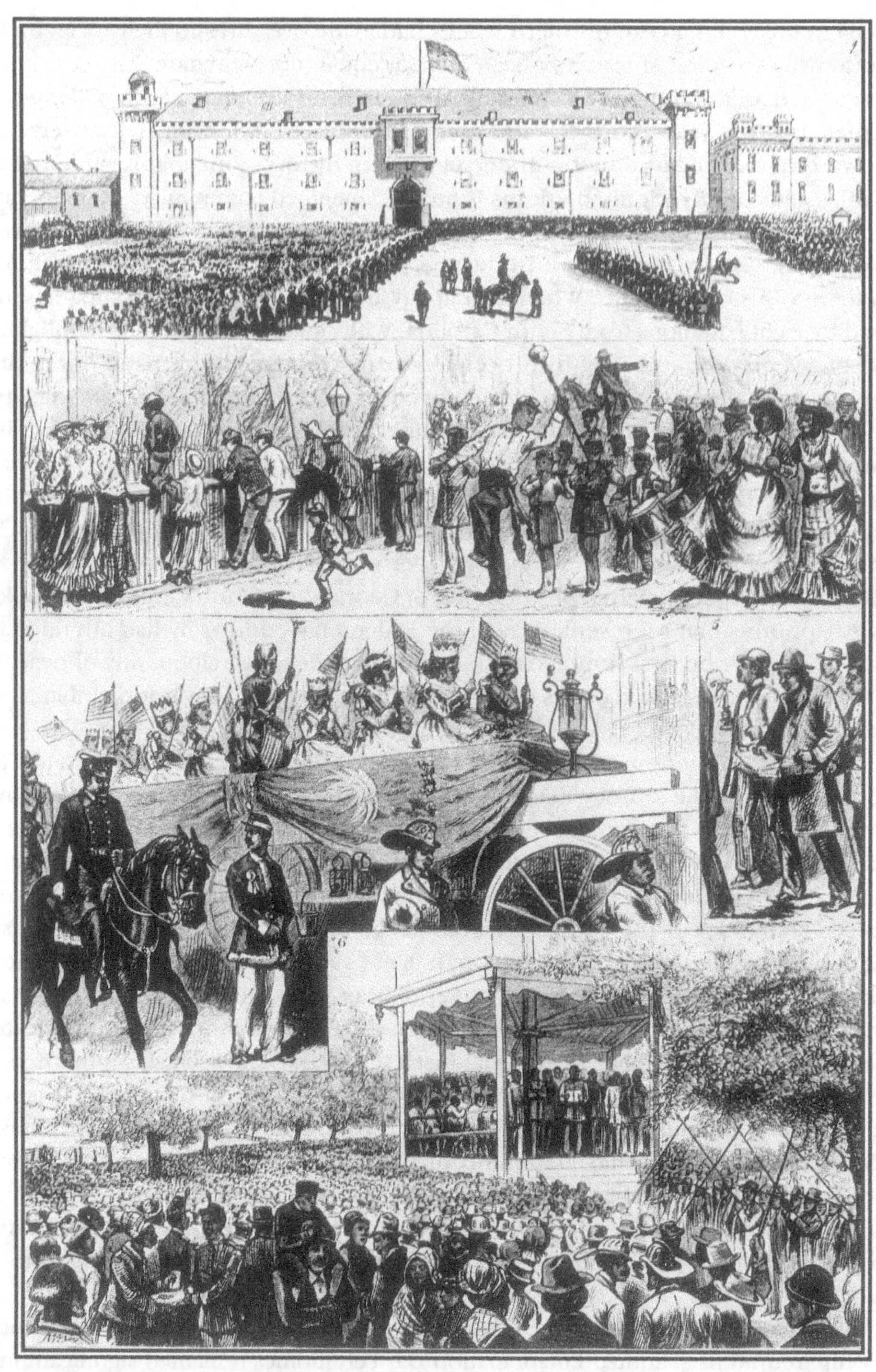

Fig. 3.3. Scenes from the Emancipation Day parade and celebration in Charleston, South Carolina. *Frank Leslie's Illustrated Newspaper*, February 10, 1877. Photograph courtesy of the Avery Research Center, College of Charleston—Black Charleston in Slavery and Freedom Collection.

educators and ministers presided over local ceremonies, and educational and religious themes dominated representations of historical progress. The shift toward educational and religious institutions was similarly reflected in the site of African American celebrations. While Emancipation Day parades continued to occupy the main streets of town each year on January 1, they reversed their direction in the 1880s, concluding not on the steps of city hall but at local black churches, where ceremonies continued indoors.[41]

The expansion of educational and religious themes did not mean that Emancipation Day ceremonies were emptied of political content—far from it. Particularly in the 1880s and 1890s, African Americans used the annual celebrations not only to honor the passing of slavery and pay homage to black achievements but also to assert black interests. Speeches and collective resolutions, for instance, emphasized the legitimacy of black men's right to vote and called repeatedly for monuments to honor black men's service in American wars. Moreover, the leadership of black militias in Emancipation Day parades forcefully depicted African Americans' ongoing determination to defend their rights.[42] Gradually, however, a note of compromise crept into many black speeches and resolutions, beginning in the late 1890s and continuing into the early 1900s. Echoing the themes expounded by Booker T. Washington, African American orators increasingly avoided contemporary controversies and instead urged their audiences to be more industrious and sober, to "dignify labor" and avoid crime, and to earn reputations for "truthfulness and honesty."[43]

Such conciliatory themes brought high praise from white observers, who also were quick to condemn individuals who challenged white opinions of appropriately "conservative" oratory. When Professor John W. Gilbert of Paine College, a prominent African American institution in Augusta, delivered an Emancipation Day speech in Macon, Georgia, in 1906, he was castigated by the white press for insisting on African Americans' right to equal treatment before the law as well as for allegedly characterizing African Americans' rapid progress since emancipation as evidence of black superiority. "'[Blacks] will [someday] be on top,' were the words that fell from the speaker," reported an outraged writer in the *Augusta Chronicle*. The newspaper implied that Emancipation Day ceremonies were a dangerous practice, with the power to grip black participants with false beliefs and aspirations.[44]

With whites warning that the Macon speech could "breed mischief," Gilbert rushed to issue a retraction. White newspaper editors made a great show of accepting Gilbert's statement that he had been misunderstood and seized the opportunity to reinforce earlier warnings of the dangers African Americans would face if they kept pressing for black rights. At the same time, white officials pointedly praised more cautious speeches delivered by African Americans elsewhere in the state. "How much better it would be if these Emancipation Day orators would follow the very sensible and conservative lines laid down in [other orations] last Monday," one said.[45]

By drawing a sharp line between "incendiary" and "conservative" black speeches, white Augustans aimed to narrow the parameters of African American oratory and control the meaning of Emancipation Day celebrations. Their message could hardly have been clearer: local whites would accept the perpetuation of black ceremonies, but only within limits. Given the current racial climate in Georgia, African Americans would have been hard pressed—if not foolish—to ignore white warnings. Indeed, the attention to Gilbert's speech was part of a growing campaign to stir up white animosity and curtail black power in the state. Just eight months later these efforts bore bitter fruit when white mobs attacked black neighborhoods in Atlanta, killing at least ten African

American residents and causing countless injuries. The Atlanta riots were a prelude to effective black male disfranchisement in Georgia, which was accomplished by an amendment to the state constitution in 1908.[46]

White Georgians were unable to assert complete control over black celebrations in the early 1900s, but they did succeed in considerably narrowing the parameters of much African American political and historical oratory. Having gained a near monopoly on political power in the state, white Georgians also banned the participation of black militias in African American parades, stripping processions of one of their most salient features—not to mention protection against white abuse.[47] No wonder John Hope viewed later celebrations as a mere shadow of the ceremonies he had witnessed in his youth. Still, it would be a mistake to assume that African American commemoration ceased to propel black memory—or challenge white authority—in early twentieth-century Augusta. However constrained the circumstances, African Americans continued to gather in large numbers both to honor their history and to envision a better future for themselves and their children. They did so openly and dramatically, occupying downtown streets with "monster" processions, such as the mile-long parade that accompanied the semicentennial celebration on January 1, 1913.[48] Nurturing their own visions of the past and the future, African Americans' annual celebrations were a crucial reminder, to themselves and to white Augustans, that white southerners' power was immense but not complete and that African Americans would persist in pressing forward to a truly new South.

## *Notes*

1. John Hope, quoted in Ridgely Torrence, *The Story of John Hope* (New York: Macmillan, 1948), 56–60.

2. Ibid.

3. Until recently the proliferation of African American celebrations in the postwar South had garnered little attention from historians. An important early study is William H. Wiggins, "'Lift Every Voice': A Study of Afro-American Emancipation Celebrations," in *Discovering Afro-America,* ed. Roger D. Abrahams and John F. Szwed (Leiden, The Netherlands: E. J. Brill, 1975). Elsa Barkley Brown and Gregg D. Kimball examine black public ceremony in post-emancipation Richmond, Virginia, in "Mapping the Terrain of Black Richmond," in *The New African American Urban History,* ed. Kenneth W. Goings and Raymond A. Mohl (Thousand Oaks, Calif.: Sage Publications, 1996), 309. See also Kathleen Clark, "History Is No Fossil Remains: Race, Gender, and the Politics of Memory in the American South, 1863–1913" (Ph.D. diss., Yale Univ., 1999) and "Celebrating Freedom: Emancipation Day Celebrations and African American Memory in the Early Reconstruction South," in *Where These Memories Grow,* ed. W. Fitzhugh Brundage (Chapel Hill: Univ. of North Carolina Press, 2000). The practice of Juneteenth in Texas has been more closely examined. See Dorris Hollis Pemberton, *Juneteenth at Comanche Crossing* (Austin: Eakin Publications, 1983).

4. Richard H. L. German, "The Economic Development of Augusta in the Gilded Age, 1860–1900," *Richmond County History* 3, no. 1 (winter 1971): 5–20; Charles D. Saggus, "1865—Year of Despair, Year of Hope: Augusta Recovers from the War," *Richmond County History* 7 (summer 1975): 21–41.

5. Howard N. Rabinowitz, *Race Relations in the Urban South, 1865–1890* (Athens: Univ. of Georgia Press, 1978), 3–30; Clarence L. Mohr, *On the Threshold of Freedom: Masters and Slaves in Civil War Georgia* (Athens: Univ. of Georgia Press, 1986).

6. Edward J. Cashin, *Old Springfield: Race and Religion in Augusta, Georgia* (Augusta: Springfield Village Park Foundation, 1995), 43–46.

7. Cashin, *Old Springfield;* Diane Harvey, "The Terri, Augusta's Black Enclave," *Richmond County History* 5 (summer 1973): 60–75; Lloyd P. Terrell and Marguerite S. C. Terrell, *Blacks in Augusta: A Chronology, 1741–1977* (Augusta: Preston Publications, 1977).

8. Edmund L. Drago, *Black Politicians and Reconstruction in Georgia: A Splendid Failure* (Baton Rouge: Louisiana State Univ. Press, 1982), 28–30; Carl Lavert McCoy, "A Historical Sketch of Black Augusta, Georgia from Emancipation to the *Brown* Decision: 1865–1954" (master's thesis, Univ. of Georgia, 1984).

9. J. William Harris, *Plain Folk and Gentry in a Slave Society: White Liberty and Black Slavery in Augusta's Hinterlands* (Middletown, Conn.: Wesleyan Univ. Press, 1985).

10. *National Freedman* 1 (Aug. 1865): 230–31; *Christian Recorder,* July 29, 1865.

11. James Lynch, *The Mission of the United States Republic: An Oration, Delivered by Rev. James Lynch at the Parade Ground, Augusta, GA., July 4, 1865* (Augusta: Steam Power Press Chronicle and Sentinel Office, 1865).

12. *National Freedman* 1 (Aug. 1865): 230–31; Letter of John Emory Bryant, Sub-Commissioner of the Freedman's Bureau, printed in Lynch, *The Mission of the United States Republic,* 2.

13. For examples of celebrations elsewhere in the early post-emancipation South, consult "New Years Day in Port Royal, South Carolina," *Christian Recorder,* Jan. 10, 1863; Elizabeth Hyde Botume, *First Days among the Contrabands* (1893; reprint, New York: Arno Press, 1968), 75–78; letter of Bessie L. Canedy to the *Freedmen's Record* 2 (June 1866): 116; J. W. Alvord, *Letters from the South, Relating to the Condition of the Freedmen, Addressed to Major General O. O. Howard* (Washington D.C.: Howard Univ. Press, 1870), 7; and Ray Allen Billington, ed., *The Journal of Charlotte L. Forten* (1953; reprint, London: Collier Books, 1961), 171–75, 212–22.

14. For insights into the range of women's participation in black celebrations, see "Negro Demonstration on the 'Glorious Fourth' at Capital Square," *Atlanta Constitution,* July 5, 1868; "Department of the South," *New York Times,* Apr. 4, 1865; Hamilton W. Pierson, *A Letter to Hon. Charles Sumner with "Statements" of Outrages upon Freedmen in Georgia, and an Account of My Expulsion from Andersonville, Ga., by the Ku Klux Klan* (Washington, D.C.: Chronicle Print, 1870), 23–28; "School Exhibition" and "From a Superintendent," *American Missionary Magazine* (July 1868): 151–53; John F. Marszalek, ed., *The Diary of Miss Emma Holmes* (Baton Rouge: Louisiana State Univ. Press, 1979).

15. For an insightful discussion of black and white negotiations of public spaces in the postwar South, see Jane Dailey, "Deference and Violence in the Postbellum Urban South: Manners and Massacres in Danville, Virginia," *Journal of Southern History* 63 (Aug. 1997): 553–90.

16. *Pughe's City Directory of Augusta, GA 1865–66;* Joseph M. Lee III, *Augusta: A Postcard History* (Dover, N.H.: Arcadia, 1997); A. Ray Rowland and Helen Callahan, *Yesterday's Augusta* (Miami: E. A. Seamann, Pub., 1976).

17. Junior League of Augusta, Georgia, Arts Committee, *Augusta—Yesterday and Today* (Augusta: Cornelison Printing Co., 1951), 27–29 .

18. *Richmond Dispatch,* July 6, 1866.

19. *Augusta Constitutionalist,* Apr. 28, 1870.

20. Ibid.

21. Virginia Ingraham Burr, ed., *The Secret Eye: The Journal of Ella Gertrude Clanton Thomas, 1848–1889* (Chapel Hill: Univ. of North Carolina Press, 1990), 357–58.

22. *Augusta Constitutionalist,* July 6, 1866.

23. On white hostility in Richmond, see letter of Bessie L. Canedy to the *Freedmen's Record* 2 (June 1866): 116; and letter from Rev. W. D. Harris to the *American Missionary Magazine* (May 1866): 105. Whites

attacked an emancipation celebration in Norfolk, Virginia, and threatened to do the same the following year. *Norfolk True Southerner,* Apr. 19, 1866; *Norfolk Virginian,* Apr. 17–21, 1866; H. C. Percy, Norfolk, to Rev. Edward P. Smith, Jan. 9, 1867, American Missionary Assoc. Manuscripts, Amistad Research Center, Tulane Univ., New Orleans; E. F. Campbell, Norfolk, to Rev. Edward P. Smith, Jan. 9, 1867, AMA MS.

24. Editorial by John Emory Bryant in the *Loyal Georgian,* reprinted in the *American Missionary Magazine* (June 1866): 134–35; also consult Paul A. Cimbala, *Under the Guardianship of the Nation: The Freedmen's Bureau and the Reconstruction of Georgia, 1865–1870* (Athens: Univ. of Georgia Press, 1997), 12–20; Jacqueline Jones, *Soldiers of Light and Love: Northern Teachers and Georgia Blacks, 1865–1873* (Chapel Hill: Univ. of North Carolina Press, 1980), 28–29.

25. *Augusta Constitutionalist,* Apr. 28, 1870. On the development of Reconstruction, see Eric Foner, *Reconstruction: America's Unfinished Revolution, 1863–1877* (New York: Harper and Row, 1988).

26. *Atlanta Constitution,* July 5, 1868.

27. *Augusta Constitutionalist,* Aug. 4, 1869.

28. George Frederickson, *The Black Image in the White Mind: The Debate on Afro-American Character and Destiny, 1817–1914* (New York: Harper and Row, 1971).

29. *Augusta Constitutionalist,* July 7, 1867; *Charleston Daily Courier,* July 6, 1869; *Norfolk Virginian,* Jan. 2, 1867.

30. *Charleston Daily Courier,* July 6, 1867.

31. *Atlanta Daily Constitution,* Jan. 16, Feb. 14, 15, 17, 18, Apr. 3, 1874, Box 11, Scrapbooks 1861–1875, John Emory Bryant Papers, Manuscript Collection, Perkins Library, Duke University.

32. LeeAnn Whites, "'Stand by Your Man': The Ladies' Memorial Association and the Reconstruction of Southern White Manhood," in *Women of the American South: A Multicultural Reader,* ed. Christie Anne Farnham (New York: New York Univ. Press, 1992), 133–49; Junior League of Augusta, *Augusta—Yesterday and Today,* 26–27.

33. *Augusta Chronicle,* Jan. 2, 1885; Jan. 3, 1888; Jan. 2, 1892; Jan. 1, 1899; Jan. 2, 1900; Jan. 2, 1902; Jan. 2, 1904; Jan. 3, 1905; Jan. 2, 1906.

34. Junior League of Augusta, *Augusta—Yesterday and Today,* 27.

35. *Augusta Chronicle,* Jan. 2, 1885; Jan. 3, 1888; Jan. 2, 1892; Jan. 1, 1899; Jan. 2, 1900; Jan. 2, 1902; Jan. 2, 1904; Jan. 3, 1905; Jan. 2, 1906.

36. *Augusta Constitutionalist,* July 4, 1866; July 4, 1867; July 6, 1869. On a similar note, see editorials in the *New Orleans Daily Picayune,* July 4–6, 1867; July 4, 6, 1869; the *Norfolk Virginian,* July 4, 1868; *Tarboro (N.C.) Southerner,* July 14, 1866; July 4, 1867; July 1, 1869. Anne Sarah Rubin explores Confederate claims on the imagery and rhetoric of the American Revolution in "Seventy-Six and Sixty-One: Confederates Remember the American Revolution," in Brundage, *Where These Memories Grow.*

37. Philip S. Foner, "Black Participation in the Centennial of 1876," *Phylon* 36, no. 4 (winter 1978): 283–84; on black representation at the Centennial in Philadelphia, consult Kirk Savage, *Standing Soldiers, Kneeling Slaves* (Princeton: Princeton Univ. Press, 1997), 87; and Robert W. Rydell, *All the World's a Fair: Visions of Empire at American International Expositions, 1876–1916* (Chicago: Univ. of Chicago Press, 1984). Peter Novick emphasizes the role of history in promoting a vision of national reconciliation premised on a shared (North and South) notion of black inferiority. See Peter Novick, *That Noble Dream: The "Objectivity Question" and the American Historical Profession* (Cambridge: Cambridge Univ. Press, 1988), 77; also see Nina Silber on the growing "culture of conciliation" in the late nineteenth-century in *The Romance of Reunion* (Chapel Hill: Univ. of North Carolina Press, 1993), chap. 4.

38. *Augusta Constitutionalist,* July 4, 6, 1875; *Charleston News and Courier,* Jan. 3, 1875.

39. *Augusta Constitutionalist,* July 6, 1870; July 6, 1872; and July 4, 7, 1874; *Charleston Daily News and Courier,* July 6, 1875.

40. *Charleston Daily News and Courier,* July 6, 1874.

41. *Augusta Chronicle,* Jan. 3, 1888; Jan. 2, 1892; Jan. 1, 1899; Jan. 2, 1900; Jan. 2, 1904; Jan. 3, 1905; Jan. 2, 1906; Jan. 2, 1908; Jan. 2, 1909; Jan. 3, 1911.

42. Ibid., Jan. 2, 1885; Jan. 3, 1904.

43. Ibid., Jan. 3, 1899; Jan. 2, 1900; Jan. 2, 1902.

44. Ibid., Jan. 2–3, 1906.

45. Ibid., Jan. 3, 1906.

46. Kevin Gaines, *Uplifting the Race: Black Leadership, Politics, and Culture in the Twentieth Century* (Chapel Hill: Univ. of North Carolina Press, 1996), 48–51. While Democratic efforts to curtail African American votes had had a clear impact on black male voter turnout by the late 1890s, the codification of exclusionary principles in the constitutional amendment of 1908 extended and reinforced black men's political marginalization in Georgia. See J. Morgan Kousser, *The Shaping of Southern Politics: Suffrage Restriction and the Establishment of the One-Party South, 1880–1910* (New Haven: Yale Univ. Press, 1974), 209–23.

47. An altercation between whites and blacks broke out during an Emancipation Day celebration in Savannah, Georgia, in the first year (1906) that the black parade proceeded without militia protection. *Augusta Chronicle,* Jan. 2, 1906.

48. *Augusta Chronicle,* Jan. 2, 1913.

# 4

# "Woman's Hand and Heart and Deathless Love"

## White Women and the Commemorative Impulse in the New South

*W. Fitzhugh Brundage*

ON JUNE 17, 1891, more than three thousand visitors from across Florida joined with more than seven thousand residents of Pensacola to witness "the most glorious day that the old city has ever seen," the highlight of which was the unveiling of a thirty-four-foot shaft, crowned with an eight-foot musket-bearing Confederate soldier (fig. 4.1). Engraved on the four faces of the Virginia granite column were inscriptions immortalizing the recently deceased Jefferson Davis, two prominent local Confederates, and the "Unknown Heroes of the Southern Confederacy." The day's ceremonies had begun with a parade of thousands led by city officials, the state's governor, the day's orator, a float festooned with fifteen young women representing the states of the Confederacy, and carriages bearing the women of the Ladies' Confederate Monument Association, who had raised the money for both the ceremonies and the monument. Following behind in order were state militia companies, members of the United Confederate Veterans, the rank and file of myriad voluntary associations, local fire companies, and white schoolchildren. If news accounts may be trusted, the occasion was "a grand scene—grander by far indeed, than pen might adequately picture."[1]

The unveiling of the monument concluded a year-long campaign by the Ladies' Confederate Monument Association. An earlier appeal in 1881 for the construction of a memorial had floundered after raising less than half of the necessary sum. Nine years later a local notable, Col. William D. Chipley, took up the cause again and published a circular in which he entreated Pensacola white women to lead a new campaign. In short order, Chipley's wife joined with several other prominent women to organize the Ladies' Confederate Monument Association, and by November 1890 they had awarded the contract for the monument to sculptor J. F. Manning of Washington, D.C. Once the fabrication of the monument was under way, the association tirelessly solicited contributions by hosting benefit suppers, auctions, musical shows, "elocution" performances, lectures, and sporting events. In April 1891, with less than two months to spare before the planned unveiling, the association raised the final $1,300 needed to pay for the $5,000 monument. The unveiling ceremonies provided an opportunity to celebrate the collective sacrifice not only of Confederates, living and dead, but also of those who had made the monument possible.

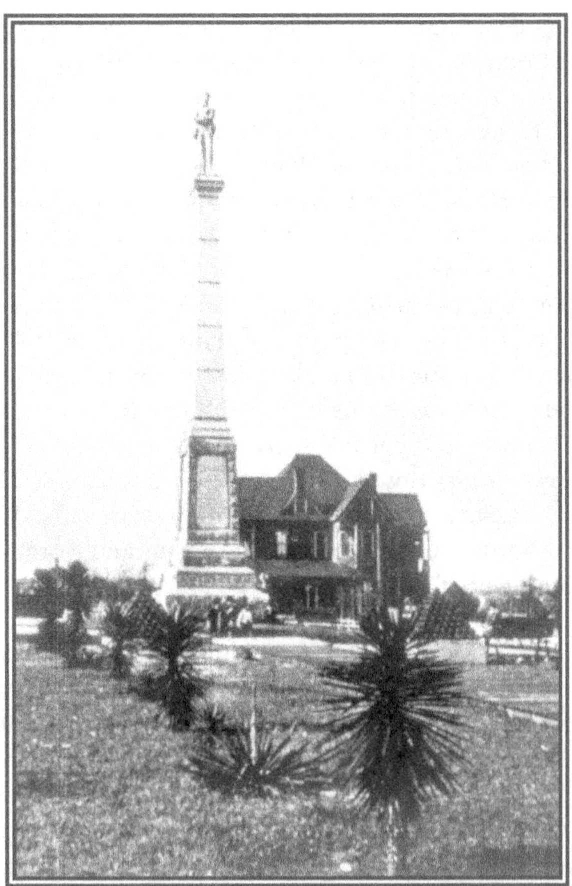

Fig. 4.1. Confederate Monument, Pensacola, Florida, designed by sculptor J. F. Manning
and unveiled June 17, 1891. Photograph circa 1900. Special Collections,
John C. Pace Library, University of West Florida.

The privileged position of the members of the Ladies' Confederate Memorial Association in the procession and during the unveiling made manifest the prestige accorded them. With good cause, accounts of the monument's origins stressed that "woman's hand and heart and deathless love" had "raised this object lesson in stone."[2]

The Confederate tradition, as these events in Pensacola indicate, was never primarily a private matter. It was deliberately and self-consciously identified with public life. Of course, the quotidian private acts of countless white southerners who placed flowers on graves, preserved the tattered uniforms worn by loved ones, and nurtured wartime memories contributed mightily to the cult of the Lost Cause. But the quality of being public, with all it implies, was inescapable and fundamental to the historical memory of the Confederacy celebrated in Pensacola and elsewhere in the New South.[3]

Manifestations of these commemorative crusades were rife across the South during the late nineteenth and early twentieth centuries. Hundreds of monuments were erected, parades organized, streets named, plaques unveiled, and parks established in a good-natured competition among white southerners to revere the Confederacy. In time this memorial zeal literally altered the landscape of the South by imposing the Confederate tradition onto it, bequeathing a legacy of courthouse squares guarded by Confederate monuments, battlefields preserved as hallowed shrines, and highways lined with historic markers that trace wartime heroics.[4]

By no means, however, were white southerners the only people besotted with the past at the close of the nineteenth century. However much the distinctive experience of loss and military defeat informed the commemorative impulse that gripped the South, it was but one manifestation of a larger mania for remembrance that swept the industrialized world during the era. When John Stuart Mill chided his contemporaries in Britain for being so fixated upon the past that they carried "their eyes in the back of their heads," he might just as well as have been describing Germans, Canadians, or southerners. The conditions in the industrialized world—wrenching economic transformation, political turmoil, and chronic social tensions—seemed to demand new means to create social cohesion, express identity, and structure social relations. The acceleration of social change and the perceived chasm between the past and present caused by headlong innovation inspired contemporaries to obsess upon the past. Europeans and North Americans responded to the challenge of modernity with a frenzy of "invented" tradition. The romance with all things medieval in Britain, for *heimat* in Germany, and for the national patrimony in France were expressions of a transnational urge to fashion relevant traditions and representations of the past. This recalled past in turn encouraged and justified social action by offering a framework of sorts and an inspiration for contending groups as they asserted new sources of cultural authority.[5]

The commemorative impulse of the era took diverse forms. All manner of ostentatious rituals, ranging from parades to festivals, filled the calendar with opportunities to celebrate collective identities and remembered pasts. At the same time, prompted by the transitory nature of memories, commemorators labored to make them permanent by rendering them in physical form. Expressing attitudes that seemingly were ubiquitous among the era's architects of collective memory, Dolly Blount Lamar, president of the United Daughters of the Confederacy's Georgia Division, explained that memorials expressed "in permanent physical form the historical truth and spiritual and political ideals we would perpetuate." By erecting monuments or marking off hallowed places, memory was anchored in space and time. Objects became infused with commemorative qualities and thereby served as physical markers of memory that preserved the past in the present, underscoring the connectedness of the past and present. Social memory throughout Europe and North America accordingly became associated as much with material culture as with intangible and rhetorical images of the past.[6]

Yet, if the commemorative impulse was by no means singular to the United States or the American South, it nevertheless acquired some singular qualities there. In contrast to many other contemporary societies, matters past in the United States, and in the South specifically, were not primary concerns of governmental authorities. Instead, voluntary associations assumed the task of crafting and disseminating public memory. This salient feature of the commemorative process in the United States is crucial to any understanding of how and why white women exerted profound influence over many manifestations of the cult of the Lost Cause in Pensacola and elsewhere. Indeed, to explain commemorative activities in the fin de siècle South is necessarily to answer the question of why white women *could* assume such conspicuous roles, not just why they *chose* to do so.

## *Contrast and Context*

When, three years after the erection of the Pensacola monument, the Virginia novelist Thomas Nelson Page complained that white southerners were "so indifferent to all transmission of their memorial," he contrasted them unfavorably with their contemporaries elsewhere, especially in Europe.[7] Page did not deny the laudable activism of historical enthusiasts like those in Pensacola, but he lamented the comparative paucity of their accomplishments. Who, by way of contrast, could gainsay the effectiveness of the propagation of historical memory and adoption of "invented" traditions in Europe? What Page failed to acknowledge in his lament, however, was that the intensity of commemorative activity in Europe reflected to a considerable extent the active participation of European governments in the production of historical memory.

Even a cursory comparison reveals the divergence of American commemorative traditions, and southern practices especially, from commemorative conventions that prevailed elsewhere. To consider, if only briefly, the larger national and international context for the Confederate tradition is to throw into high relief the different agents who were responsible for the production of historical memory in different parts of the Western world. In France, for example, the national state used its administrative apparatus to affect everything from the market for art to museum holdings and civic rituals. The agents of the national state failed in many instances to impose their dictates, but their influence, felt through patronage and funding, swayed the strategies of cultural arbiters in the French hinterland. Whatever the limits of the powers of the national bureaucracy, any consideration of public culture in nineteenth-century France nevertheless must begin with the state. To a lesser degree, the same was true in Britain, where the handiwork of the state in promoting historical consciousness was pervasive. The monarchies of Queen Victoria, Edward VII, and George V assiduously crafted "invented, ceremonial splendor" with the aim of inspiring allegiance to the Crown and the empire even at a time when royal power was declining. And although regional identities endured and even appeared to strengthen in late-nineteenth-century Britain, both state aid and royal patronage served to tether these indigenous expressions of memory to a larger national and imperial historical project. Even in Germany, where civic associations remained instrumental in promoting national monuments and celebrations through the 1870s, the reign of William II at the end of the century was marked by ostentatious public works, monuments, and rituals in which the emperor himself played a prominent role. Private organizations retained a place in articulating images of the German past, but the active role of the imperial state in selecting, popularizing, and institutionalizing a particular fund of historical knowledge between 1880 and 1914 was unmistakable. By actively influencing, directing, or subsuming most campaigns to define public memory by the bourgeoisie and others, European states pursued a much larger and urgent quest to organize their citizenries into unitary and cohesive "modern" societies.[8]

That a small circle of white women raised money and approved the design for the most impressive monument erected in nineteenth-century Pensacola is a telling example of the tradition of historical voluntarism that prevailed in the United States. The ambitious cultural policies in France and elsewhere in Europe had no parallel in the United States. With no meaningful tradition of royal cultural patronage inherited from the colonial era, Americans during the nineteenth century established only the weakest link between the national government and national culture. Here, the tradition of limited government extended to the realm of public culture, where cultural voluntarism, rather than state intervention, prevailed. The skeletal administrative structure of the national government and the dispersed authority inherent in American Federalism offered few resources with which to craft a national cultural policy, much less national historical memory.[9] Campaigns to shape public memory, even by the most elastic definition of the term, rarely were topics of discussion within American administrative corridors and legislative chambers. For instance, one of the most striking and enduring invented traditions of the 1890s—the Pledge of Allegiance—was instigated by impressive grassroots activism; the Federal government gave nothing more than its tacit approval to the campaign to promote this nationalist anthem.[10] Likewise, none of the administrators of the nation's museums (excluding the Smithsonian) dared to or could rely on the generosity of government officials to fund their activities. The condition of state records was just one especially glaring example of officialdom's apathetic attitudes about the preservation of the past. John Hugh Reynolds, a crusader for the creation of a state archive in Arkansas, complained in 1905 that state records and historical collections were scattered in "damp, dismal, and disagreeable" catacombs beneath the old statehouse, where finding a book or document was "very much like the process of exhuming a mummy."[11] And usually only persistent pestering could pry funds from state coffers sufficient to subsidize even partially the myriad monuments, statues, and other physical manifestations of memory that began to clutter the American landscape in the late nineteenth century. In Florida, for instance, at a time when state disbursements grew from $1.5 million to nearly $4 million per annum, the largest single appropriation for historical commemoration between 1900 and 1915 was $14,654 for the Women of the Confederacy monument in Jacksonville. The sum total of state contributions for this as well as similar projects during this period totaled less than $50,000.[12]

It is tempting to conclude that the absence of cultural activism by the state in the South was simply a reflection of the inherent weakness of constituted authority in the region. White southerners, after all, had a reputation for being wary of the establishment of any powerful state institutions that might challenge private autonomy. They, Wilbur J. Cash observed in an oft-quoted passage, harbored "an intense distrust of, and, indeed, downright aversion to, any actual exercise of authority beyond the barest minimum essential to the existence of the social organism." Yet it is important to recall that southern states enforced Jim Crow laws that comprised some of the most extensive and intrusive state-imposed prescriptions on public and private behavior adopted anywhere in the nation. State authority in the South, simply put, was not uniformly weak, only selectively so.[13]

## *Representing the "Public"*

Throughout the nineteenth century state governments abjured responsibility over historical memory because it fell within that area of the public realm, where their authority ended and the traditional authority of home and church began. It was precisely in this cultural space that voluntary associations held sway. Well before midcentury, the tradition of private citizens mingling independently from the state in an amorphous public space to discuss public matters had given way to public voices and activism that were mediated by voluntary societies. These organizations, by claiming a mandate to place their private concerns before the public and the state as issues of general concern, served as self-proclaimed intermediaries between the state and a broader and ill-defined constituency, the so-called public. Because public authorities and ruling elites embraced a classically liberal conception of state obligations, citizens necessarily looked to voluntary associations to meet needs that public officials were either incapable or indisposed to address. These conditions inspired increasingly ambitious voluntary organizations to shoulder ever larger roles within the public realm in the late nineteenth century.[14]

A glaring illustration of the limited initiative of southern states and the contrasting hustle of voluntary groups was the spotty participation of southerners in the much-anticipated World's Columbian Exposition in Chicago in 1893. While northern states had long since reconciled the tradition of limited government with public funding for elaborate industrial and historical exhibits at expositions, most southern legislatures were so parsimonious that they allotted no funds for exhibits of any kind. Five southern states had no state buildings whatsoever. That Texas, Louisiana, and Arkansas had historical exhibits and state buildings at all was, according to the official history of the exposition, due to private efforts and especially "the assistance rendered by women." It was the white clubwomen of the South, not southern public officials, who were responsible for the faux-antebellum slave cabins, staffed by elderly former slaves, and the southern reliquaries that intrigued crowds at the fair. In this and other instances, the absence of any tangible reality to the southern states' cultural ambitions encouraged voluntary associations to assume a role in the late nineteenth century that elsewhere public officials began to claim exclusively or share grudgingly.[15]

These characteristics of nineteenth-century American public culture placed a premium on the ability to manufacture or harness "public" support for any would-be custodians of collective memory. Demonstrations of public support, however crudely generated and staged, established the authority of voluntary associations to speak for the "public." Consequently, voluntary organizations were keen to represent their campaigns as spontaneous expressions of popular enthusiasm and reverence. Any organized group that could summon sufficient support and funds might influence public representations of the past, and even place demands on the state to recognize that memory. Indeed, to the extent that southern state and local governments acknowledged any obligation to sponsor public memory, it was as a consequence of lobbying by voluntary societies.

The innumerable drives to erect commemorative monuments and statues in the late nineteenth-century South (and elsewhere in the nation) are illustrative. The reality was that the "public" that mobilized to commemorate a local hero or hallowed cause typically was in fact, as in Pensacola, a self-appointed committee of local notables who summoned the citizenry to contribute funds and provide support for their preconceived projects. Eventually, after months, even years, of fund-raising, sculptors were hired, designs approved, and then the preserved shrines or completed monuments were unveiled before the gathered public. The monuments and sites that emerged from this process frequently were testimonials to popular interest, but neither was that enthusiasm spontaneous nor the "public" necessarily united by shared sentiments. Yet once the monuments were unveiled, their particular origins receded into the background and they became sacrosanct, even to the point of defining the enduring image of the communities that purportedly erected them.[16]

However much voluntary associations proclaimed their inclusiveness and breadth of support, the crafting of historical memory took place in a less-than-democratic public arena where those groups with the deepest pockets and the closest ties to elites had the greatest likelihood of imposing their sense of the past on the civic landscape. The officers of the Ladies' Confederate Monument Association of Pensacola, for example, included Angela S. Mallory (fig. 4.2), whose husband was memorialized on the monument; Ann Elizabeth Billups Chipley, whose husband had originally proposed the monument; and the wives of several leading businessmen. By organizing into voluntary associations, these elite historical enthusiasts presumed to speak for a broader "public"

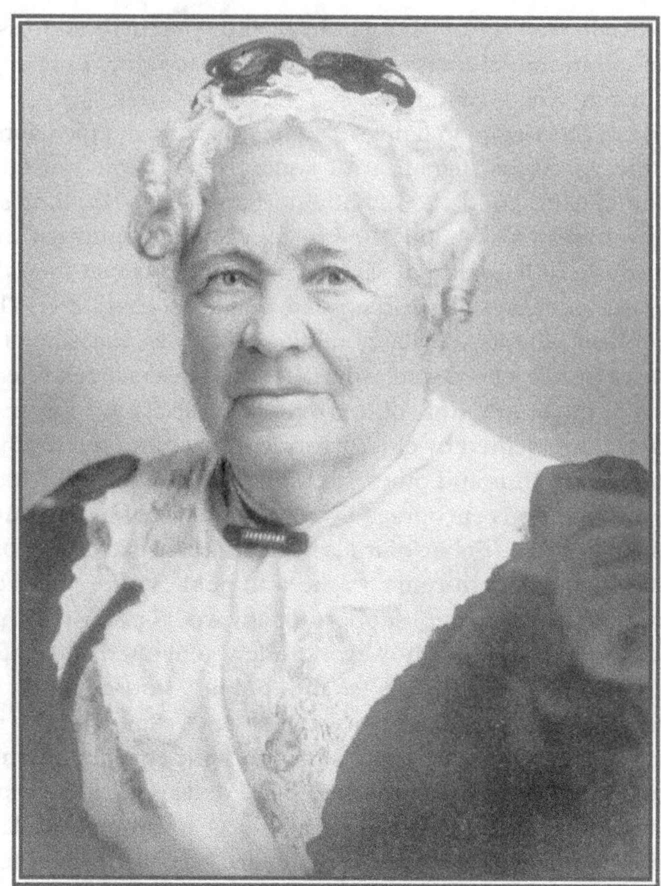

Fig. 4.2. Angela S. Mallory, president of the Ladies Confederate Memorial Association of Pensacola, Florida, circa 1900. Special Collections, John C. Pace Library, University of West Florida.

in Pensacola, even though the membership of that public, as these representatives conceived of it, was unmistakably limited to whites, and better-off whites at that. Armed with the privileges of whiteness and affluence, commemorative activists employed the full array of cultural resources at their disposal—scholarly monographs, mawkish stage dramas, romantic poetry, atmospheric local-color fiction, heroic public sculpture, and pious public commemorations—to insinuate their memory into the public realm.

Southern African Americans, too, yearned to make their recalled past permanent by anchoring it in space and time. Despite the oppressive conditions that blacks faced in the South, the public sphere there remained sufficiently porous and open to voluntary, collective action that they could not be entirely excluded from it. They made creative use of the resources at their command and defiantly gave public expression to their collective memory, thereby offering a countermemory to that of southern whites. Their diverse public ceremonies, which became the preeminent forum in which they displayed their recalled past, enabled vast numbers of blacks to learn, invent, and practice a common language of memory. As the Memorial Day ceremonies for the Union dead across the

South vividly demonstrated, blacks endowed cemeteries with enduring commemorative significance. And wherever a tradition of commemorative processions existed, urban streetscapes and rural byways, if only temporarily, also became sites of memory. But poverty and oppression sharply circumscribed these efforts. More important, southern whites diligently strengthened their grip over the public realm in the late nineteenth century until some expressions of black memory eventually were marginalized or altogether suppressed.[17] This competition between white and black southerners over the meaning of the past was never equal; whereas white southerners created a landscape dense with totemic relics, southern blacks could never fix their memory in public spaces in the same manner or to the same extent. Not only did whites enjoy an advantage in establishing the materiality of their memory, but they also possessed the power to silence parts of the past; they, for instance, reverently erected monuments to "faithful" slaves but raised no statues of black Civil War soldiers. Thus, over the course of the late nineteenth century, southern whites, with the complicity of white northerners, secured the cultural resources necessary to make their particular memories authoritative while rendering those of blacks illegitimate or imperceptible to whites.[18]

If class and race dictated who could participate in the crafting of public memory, gender did so to a far lesser degree. Although white elites and their allies inherently had undue influence over public representations of the past, they were the exclusive domain of neither men in general nor public officials in particular. Admittedly, the voluntary organizations that exerted the greatest influence over public culture cleaved along the fault line of gender that was so conspicuous in Gilded Age America. Southern white men manifested their own keen interest in the presentation of their region's past and joined together in various historically oriented all-male groups. The founding of Confederate veterans' organizations, culminating in the United Confederate Veterans (UCV) in 1889, the growth of chapters of patriotic and hereditary organizations such as the Sons of the American Revolution, and the burgeoning state and local historical societies underscored the ambition of southern white men to shape the public memory of the region. But by the close of the nineteenth century an increasing number of observers, especially male observers, conceded that women had emerged as the preeminent custodians of "liberal culture," including especially "the preservation of links with the past." Indeed, it was the presumption that women were peculiarly adept custodians of the past that prompted Colonel Chipley's appeal to the white women of Pensacola to assume the leadership of the Confederate monument campaign in the first place.[19]

The emerging recognition of white women's claim to custodianship of memory in part was a consequence of the organizational revolution under way among southern women during the late nineteenth century. Just as voting and participation in the rituals of partisan politics were an essential part of contemporary male public identity, club activities had become for many women an equally important component of their public identity. So ubiquitous was the tireless and invasive clubwoman that she became a popular figure of ridicule. But the dismissive stereotype of armies of busybody women who demanded deference from men bespoke a real fear on the part of many contemporaries about the expansion of white women's cultural influence within the public sphere.

Evidence of women's advancing organizational might included the dramatic proliferation of women's literary associations, social reform groups, and such hereditary and patriotic organizations as the Association for the Preservation of Virginia Antiquities (APVA), the Daughters of the American Revolution (DAR), and the United Daughters of the Confederacy (UDC). Organized like corporations, with boards of directors and trustees who supervised squads of members, these voluntary associations exerted influence out of proportion to their size. Moreover, the overlapping memberships that were routine among women in civic, philanthropic, and hereditary associations facilitated the pursuit of missions that extended well beyond the fields of activity implied by the names of many women's organizations. Women's clubs, ranging from the Caxtons Club of Pensacola to the Every Saturday History Class in Atlanta, maintained an active interest in local history, and virtually all state federations of women's clubs took up historical issues. The rapidly swelling ranks of these societies, which could muster impressive organized might, were ideally positioned to be artisans of public culture and collective memory in particular.[20]

Women's circumstances could discourage their participation in voluntary activism, which characteristically ranged from petitioning and letter-writing to fund-raising. More than coincidence, for instance, explains the pronounced influence that clubwomen exercised in Pensacola and the New South's other burgeoning towns and cities. There the convergence of resources and needs was most pronounced; the comparative wealth of townspeople, the concentration of women eager to assume larger roles in public affairs, as well as the perceived urgent need for civic culture and identity in the New South's rough and ragged cities all urged women's activism. In contrast, distance and the burdens of heavy domestic responsibilities often discouraged participation in women's organizations in the rural hinterland. Voluntary associations, then, much as they had a generation earlier in the North, occupied an especially important place in the lives of the better-off urban dwellers of the New South.[21]

The earnestness and stamina displayed by white women's associations in southern city centers demonstrated the potency of the ideology of public service that many women embraced. Inherited ideals of "republican motherhood" and the cult of domesticity had long given women an important role in the transmission of culture within the home and had even encouraged them to assume an ever-widening range of public responsibilities. Now an increasingly complex society, confronted by urbanization and industrialization, demanded broader forms of feminine public influence. Arguably, women's "patriotic" activities in the seven decades after the Civil War were a logical extension of their traditional role as educators and moral stewards of the nation's children. Women's historical organizations and activism, then, were just another manifestation of moral housekeeping writ large.[22]

The fervor of white women historical activists also bespoke deeper anxieties about contemporary debates over the role of white women as agents of civilization. The logic of some contemporary ideas of civilization, reflecting the influence of Darwinism and romantic nationalism, suggested that Anglo-Saxon men alone had the racial genius for self-government and the manly capacity of self-control that made the highest levels of social development possible. Accordingly, the story of human progress was a record of the power and beneficence of white men. What, if any, contribution white women had made to the advancement of civilization was open to debate. Merely vessels of civilization, women arguably furthered human evolution chiefly as wives and mothers. Many white middle-class and elite women found in history an antidote to these exaggerated assertions of men's roles in human progress. History, for a substantial number of white women who refused to surrender either the field of history or the realm of public culture to men, became an instrument of self-definition. They insisted that women of culture were integral to human progress. The field of history provided one opening through which they could revise the link between manliness and civilization. By giving meaning to the past, by crafting public memory, white women claimed for themselves the work of recording and narrating the progress of civilization, thereby laying claim to a new source of cultural authority.[23]

## *Organizational Might*

Whatever the personal and social inspirations for women's activism, the influence that women sought might have remained beyond their reach had they not possessed the organizational fortitude to wield power in the public sphere. Above all, organized white women in the South possessed impressive fund-raising acumen. As long as voluntary contributions, in lieu of state subsidies, were essential to the funding of collective memory, the influence of women's organizations was secure. Few voluntary societies by themselves possessed the resources to sustain grandiose and unending projects, but by the mid-nineteenth century women's groups had devised all manner of fund-raising techniques, such as charitable balls, fairs, and bazaars, that lightened the collective purses of their communities and raised prodigious sums of money. Clubwomen harnessed their own increasingly important role as consumers to philanthropic ends by fashioning crafts and other goods for sale to other public-spirited women. They also tapped the wealth of their husbands and any likely male contributors. (We can only speculate about why men were such willing contributors to such campaigns, but perhaps male donors looked to these causes as an opportunity to cleanse wealth acquired in the hurly-burly world of commerce by associating it with the unsullied public service of women.) During the fund-raising campaign in Pensacola, for example, women secured the local opera house and a public dining room for free, then hosted a public lecture for one thousand and organized a dinner for five hundred. A fund-raising extravaganza of this scale required formidable organizational and publicity skills. Moreover, this and similar fund-raising events demonstrated financial competency and commercial prowess requisite for the increasingly ambitious philanthropic activities undertaken by women.[24]

Male voluntary organizations, in contrast, were often less energetic and successful at fund-raising. In this regard, the success of the UDC and the comparative failure of the UCV in raising money for the Jefferson Davis Monument (fig. 4.3) in Richmond, Virginia, is telling. Calls for a memorial to the Confederate president rang out almost immediately after his death in 1889. In 1896 the UCV launched a campaign to build an elaborate and costly marble shrine in the Confederate capital. But as of 1899 they had raised only $20,000 of the $210,000 their plans required. With fund-raising stalled, the veterans grudgingly turned the project over to the UDC. During the following eight years the UDC revised the plans in favor of a more inexpensive and less grandiose monument and methodically raised money. Eventually the women's group collected $70,000, a sum sufficient to complete the monument that now stands. The unveiling in 1907 was glaring testimony to the capabilities of the UDC and unintentional confirmation of the organizational limits of the UCV.[25]

Women's voluntary associations employed their equally well-honed skills at using suasion to influence public debate, an essential attribute in campaigns that relied upon voluntarism. Women had since the early nineteenth century used associations to exert power lodged not in legal or religious institutions but in the mandate of "public opinion."[26] The commemoration of past valor and sacrifice meshed easily with the belief held by many women that public life should be conducted according to moral convictions. Women, to a greater degree than men in the nineteenth century, endorsed the idea that popular suasion and, when appropriate, government influence could and should be used to shape citizens' behavior. For these clubwomen, circumstances demanded stronger forms of suasion than the state possessed. They crusaded for the teaching of the "true history" of the South, especially with regard to slavery and the sectional strife of the nineteenth

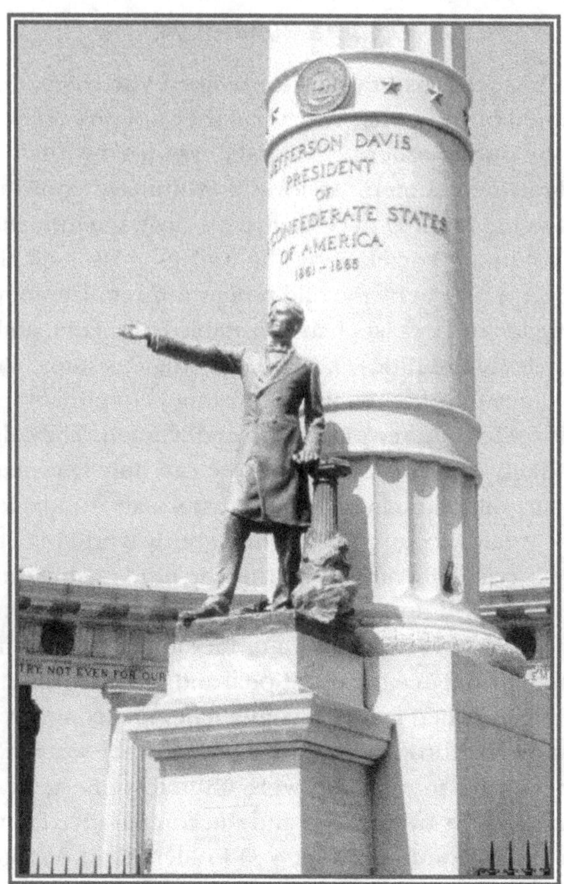

Fig. 4.3. Jefferson Davis Monument on Monument Avenue in Richmond, Virginia, designed by William C. Noland and Edward V. Valentine and dedicated June 3, 1907. Photograph by Sean McCormally.

century, by censoring school texts and intimidating textbook publishers. Mrs. W. C. H. Merchant bragged to the 1904 meeting of the UDC that "owing to the efforts and influence of the United Daughters" every state of the former Confederacy had adopted texts sympathetic to the Lost Cause. Likewise, women's organizations supplied classroom materials, awarded cash prizes for student essays on topics dear to the organizations, and funded college scholarships. As these examples suggest, voluntary associations in the New South often became the fulcrum of public opinion, especially with regard to the Confederate tradition.[27]

This power became evident in 1911, for example, when Enoch M. Banks, a young history professor at the University of Florida, six years out of graduate school at Columbia University, recklessly announced that, "in the calm light of history," secession was contrary to the national interest and that "the North was relatively in the right while the South was relatively in the wrong."[28] Ever vigilant to defend the legitimacy of secession, members of the UDC, reinforced by members of the UCV, berated the university for employing a historian who was "not fitted to teach true and unprejudiced history." In little more than a month the uproar compelled Banks to resign. Eager to

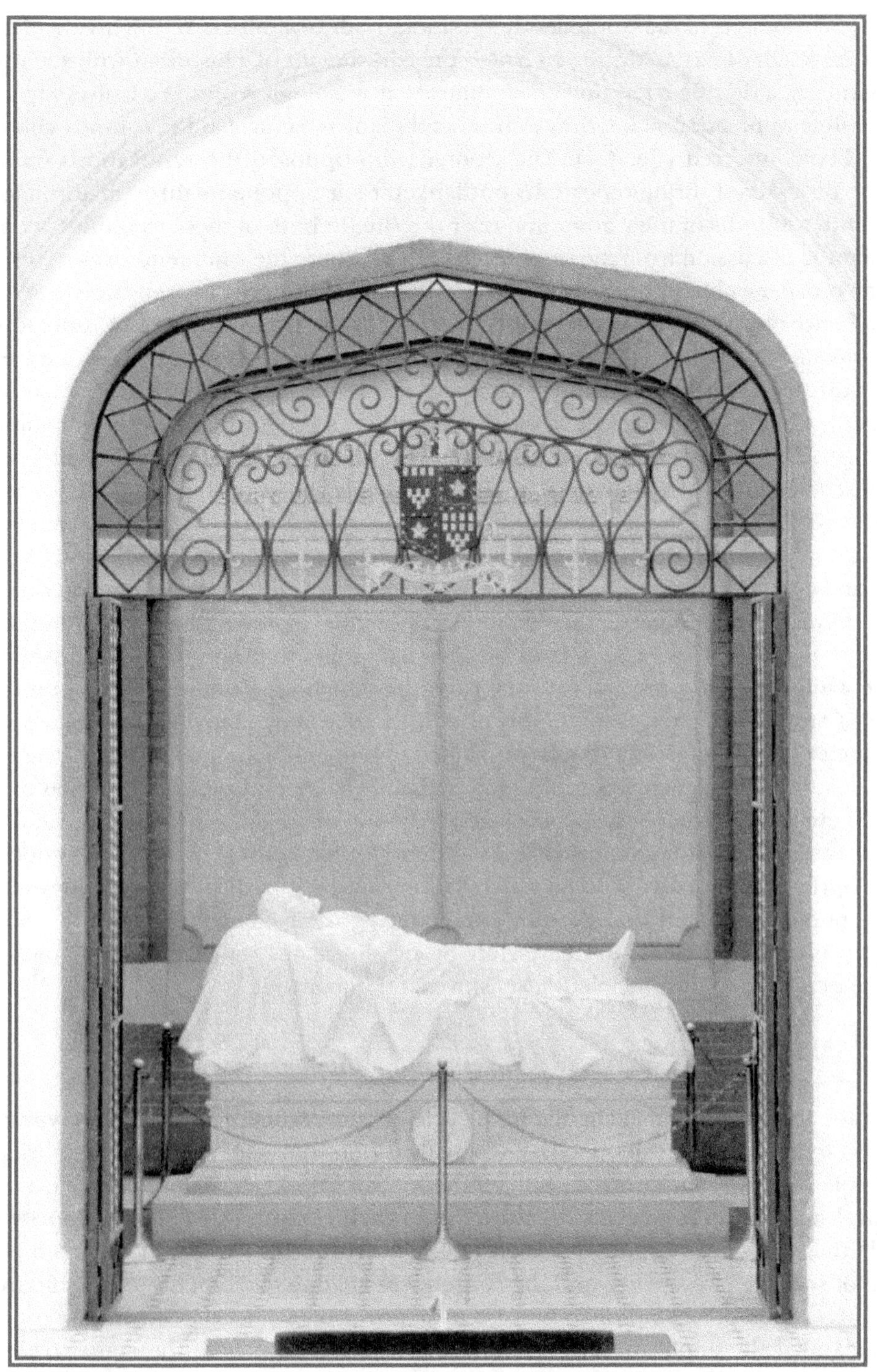

Fig. 4.4. Recumbent sculpture of Robert E. Lee, Washington and Lee University chapel, Lexington, Virginia, designed by Edward V. Valentine and dedicated June 1883. Photograph by W. Patrick Hinely, Washington and Lee University. Special Collections, Washington and Lee University.

appease the custodians of the Confederate tradition, both Gov. Albert W. Gilchrist and University of Florida President Albert A. Murphree hailed the banishment of a historian with such "unsound views." Similarly, a decade later, university officials at Washington and Lee University underestimated possible opposition when they announced plans to refurbish the campus chapel where Robert E. Lee is interred (fig. 4.4). The women who opposed the renovations of what they believed to be a sacred shrine repeatedly outflanked their opponents through adroit appeals to tradition and assertions of their dominion over the site. In both of these examples, women skillfully shifted the discussion from the campus chambers, where their influence was necessarily limited, to the broader public sphere, where their artful use of publicity proved decisive.[29]

The influence of white women over public memory, as the controversies at Washington and Lee suggest, was not unchallenged. But unlike other contemporary and divisive issues, especially those that directly threatened male privilege and economic interests (such as prostitution and temperance), white women's attentive commemoration of the Lost Cause was not vulnerable to easy criticism. The small cadre of women-led activists in Charleston, South Carolina, who mobilized against adaptations of the cityscape to the automobile age—construction of gasoline stations, street improvements, and the razing of old buildings—warned that the "modern commercial age can ill afford to dispense with" ancient buildings possessed of a "certain stability and nobility of character and taste."[30] City officials and businessmen initially belittled their preservationist crusade but eventually came to appreciate the commercial potential of "Charleston's greatest attraction," its historic architecture.[31] Likewise, Atlanta businessmen eager to promote local tourism refused to stand idle while the UDC presided over the carving of the huge Confederate monument on the rock face of Stone Mountain, Georgia. Eventually in 1924 they elbowed the women aside and assumed control over the project (but in turn failed to bring it to completion). In Stone Mountain, as in Charleston, women activists fought indefatigably to defend their jurisdiction over public memory. There and elsewhere, the broad goal of revering the region's white heroes and all things Confederate was as safe and unimpeachable a ground for women's activism as was conceivable in the New South. Consequently, women's associations engaged in disputes without undue risk of alienating public sentiment and thereby surrendering their claim to speak for "the public." Instead, it was their opponents in Charleston, Stone Mountain, and elsewhere who often found themselves perceived as unprincipled, insensitive, and unpatriotic.[32]

## *"Success" and Waning Influence*

Ironically, the most profound challenge to the role of white women as arbiters of white memory came not so much from opposition to their campaigns but from their success. The erosion of their influence followed from the efforts of women themselves to coax the state to assume a larger role in historical matters. In important regards, the gradual expansion of state authority over the region's heritage, and the resulting waning of women's authority, mirrored the contemporaneous extension of state welfare services and the consequent abating of women's leadership over social welfare.[33] Many women championed more activist government because myriad pressing public issues demanded the application of resources and power that only the state possessed. For example, by the turn of the century white clubwomen in the South were anxious to ensure that state governments properly represented the region in the seemingly unremitting cycle of international expositions that characterized the age. Never again, they insisted, should women have to assume, as they had during the 1893 world's fair, a burden that state governments should at least partially bear. Yet, at the same time, clubwomen were eager to retain their influence over public history. To the satisfaction of many women activists, effective partnerships between the state and private women's organizations emerged during the early twentieth century. For example, a committee of three North Carolina women, underwritten by both state and private funds, organized and oversaw the installation of one of the earliest public (if temporary) displays of state historical artifacts at the 1907 Jamestown Exposition. Similarly, women's organizations entered into agreements with state governments to assume responsibility for maintaining and operating hallowed state historic sites from Nashville, Tennessee, and Charleston, South Carolina, to San Antonio, Texas, to name only a few examples.[34]

Women's associations also threw their organizational brawn behind campaigns to create a state-subsidized infrastructure of archives and museums in the region. Hereditary and patriotic women's groups, such the UDC, looked upon archives as long-needed shrines of public memory. They anticipated using the archives for genealogical research, which, in addition to being a turn-of-the-century fad, was essential to substantiate their membership applications to most patriotic and hereditary societies.[35] More important, women, who had resolutely insisted upon the relevance of a historical awareness for civic life, were eager to insinuate historical activities into the business of the state. They well recognized the innovation that state-funded archives and museums represented. Such institutions offered an opportunity to promote narratives of the past that carried the imprimatur of the state. And with each appropriation of funds for archives and museums, southern state legislatures acknowledged that the preservation and interpretation of the past, which previously had been almost exclusively the preserve of voluntary associations, was now a matter of state government policy.

The struggle to establish a state historical commission in Texas underscored the effectiveness of women's voluntary associations in rousing the state to assume new responsibilities over public culture. The Texas State Historical Association had suffered repeated frustrations after three consecutive sessions of the legislature rejected bills to establish such a commission. Each time, the legislation failed "for want of energetic support." Simultaneously the newly founded State Federation of Women's Clubs, which promoted public libraries throughout the state, failed to secure legislation to establish a state library commission. Finally in 1909, the Historical Association and the State Federation joined forces and cajoled the legislature to create the Texas Library and Historical Commission.[36]

In the wake of the accelerating institutionalization of public history in the South came professional opportunities and authority attractive to the young professional historians who began to join the faculties of southern universities during the 1890s. Intent on establishing respectable professional institutions across the region and eager to enhance their insecure status, these scholars labored to create institutions that would cultivate competence and consolidate their professional authority over the past.[37] Initially, these professional historians desperately needed allies to support their ambitious programs to create public institutions that would occupy a central role in the formation of a modern civic culture in the South.[38] As the success in Texas demonstrated, the support of the women's organizations at least made plausible claims that public constituencies beyond the tiny academic community in the South had an interest in archives and museums. But given the aims of professional historians and the prestige they hoped to garner, they could not easily tolerate competitors who made false claims of expertise. Like other professional men of the late nineteenth century, southern historians and archivists set out to establish communities of specialists and standards of competence. In the process, the claims of other practitioners, especially those of white women activists, demanded challenge. Telling and insidious metaphors of gender in public addresses and condescending dismissals of the competence of women as students of history behind closed doors were all evidence of the disposition of many male professionals to make the interpretation of the past an overwhelmingly male and professional enterprise.[39] Women's voluntary associations (and other nonspecialists) had a place in the professional enterprise of recalling the southern past as long as they remained adjuncts who deferred to trained (male) specialists. They were welcome to contribute as fund-raisers, to provide essential secretarial skills, and to direct the social activities of historical societies. But women enthusiasts who displayed unwelcome ambition to participate in the serious business of crafting history were politely reprimanded.

Yet even after the commemorative impulse in the South waned and the energy of organized women was directed elsewhere, the legacy of white women's half-century guardianship of public memory in the South remained. On a scale that should have impressed even Thomas Nelson Page, white women had succeeded in their goal of filling the civic spaces of the South with monuments glorifying the Confederacy for "unborn generations." Indeed, with school texts parroting a pro-Confederate rendering of the past and with monuments in every town square, we might well ask what more white women's groups in the South could have achieved. For good and ill, their accomplishments, from the modest monument in Pensacola to the enormous Jefferson Davis statue in Richmond, from historical markers on the Natchez Trace in Mississippi to the UDC shrine in Charleston, South Carolina, linger as an indelible fixture of the southern landscape.

## Notes

1. *Pensacola Daily News,* June 18, 1891.

2. Confederated Southern Memorial Association, *History of the Confederated Memorial Association of the South* (New Orleans: Graham Press, 1904), 74. The fund-raising campaign may be traced in the *Pensacola Daily News* as follows: Mar. 15, 20, 22, 29, 1891; Apr. 4, 12, 15, 16, 1891; May 13, 1891; and June 14, 16, 18, 1891. See also *Bliss' Quarterly* (Pensacola) 3 (Jan. 1897): 121–23; and W. Stuart Towns, "Honoring the Confederacy in Northwest Florida: The Confederate Monument Ritual," *Florida Historical Quarterly* 57 (Oct. 1978): 205–10; Edward C. Williamson, "W. D. Chipley, West Florida's Mr. Railroad," *Florida Historical Quarterly* 25 (Apr. 1947): 333–55.

3. The terms *historical, social, public,* and *collective* memory elude precise definition. While some scholars have expressed concerns about their expansive and vague meaning, I believe these terms can apply to any organized, explicitly public, socially constructed representation of the past. See W. Fitzhugh Brundage, "No Deed but Memory," in *Where These Memories Grow,* ed. W. Fitzhugh Brundage (Chapel Hill: Univ. of North Carolina Press, 2000), 1–28; N. Gedi and Y. Elam, "Collective Memory—What Is It?" *History and Memory* 8 (1996): 30–50; Jeffrey K. Olick and Joyce Robbins, "Social Memory Studies: From 'Collective Memory' to the Historical Sociology of Mnemonic Practices," *Annual Review of Sociology* 24 (1998); and Barbie Zelizer, "Reading Against the Grain: The Shape of Memory Studies," *Critical Studies in Mass Communications* 12 (June 1995): 234–35.

4. In addition to the essays in this book, other valuable discussions of the "monumentalization" of the Confederacy are E. Merton Coulter, "The Confederate Monument in Athens, Georgia," *Georgia Historical*

*Quarterly* 40 (Sept. 1956): 230–47; Stephen Davis, "Empty Eyes, Marble Hand: The Confederate Monument and the South," *Journal of Popular Culture* 16 (winter 1982): 2–21; Gaines M. Foster, *Ghosts of the Confederacy* (New York: Oxford Univ. Press, 1987), esp. chap. 3; H. E. Gulley, "Women and the Lost Cause: Preserving a Confederate Identity in the American Deep South," *Journal of Historical Geography* 19 (1993): 125–41; James W. Loewen, *Lies Across America: What Our Historic Sites Get Wrong* (New York: New Press, 1999); and John J. Winberry, "Lest We Forget: The Confederate Monument and the Southern Townscape," *Southeastern Geographer* 23 (Nov. 1983): 107–21.

5. John Stuart Mill, cited in David Lowenthal, *The Past Is a Foreign Country* (New York: Cambridge Univ. Press, 1985), 97.

6. Dolly Blount Lamar, *When All Is Said and Done* (Athens: Univ. of Georgia Press, 1952), 135. Pierre Nora explains that memory "relies on the materiality of the trace, the immediacy of the recording, the visibility of the image." Pierre Nora, "Between Memory and History: Les Lieux de Memoire," *Representations* 26 (spring 1989): 13. See also Nathan Wachtel, "Memory and History: Introduction," *History and Anthropology* 12 (Oct. 1986): 212; and L. S. Vygotsky, *Mind in Society: The Development of Higher Psychological Processes* (Cambridge: Harvard Univ. Press, 1978), 51.

7. Thomas Nelson Page, *The Old South: Essays Social and Political* (New York: Scribner's, 1894), 253, 256, 258.

8. Alain Touraine, *Critique of Modernity,* trans. David Macey (Oxford: Blackwell, 1995), 10. Another instance of the power of the state is the example of the Portuguese monarchy, which had transferred its seat to Brazil during the Napoleonic era. There "the national culture," "including epic poems celebrating the 'classic' Brazilian past and paintings of a historical or allegorical sort," was "defined, produced, and effectively imposed by the sovereign and his creatures." See Jeffrey D. Needell, "The Domestic Civilizing Mission: The Cultural Role of the State in Brazil, 1808–1930," *Luso-Brazilian Review* 36 (summer 1999): 1–18. For the international context, see David Cannadine, "The Context, Performance and Meaning of Ritual: The British Monarchy and the 'Invention of Tradition,' c. 1820–1977," in *The Invention of Tradition,* ed. Eric Hobsbawm and Terence Ranger (New York: Cambridge Univ. Press, 1983); Alon Confino, *The Nation as a Local Metaphor: Wurttemberg, Imperial Germany, and National Memory, 1871–1918* (Chapel Hill: Univ. of North Carolina Press, 1997), esp. pt. 1; Charles Dellheim, *The Face of the Past: The Preservation of the Medieval Inheritance in Victorian England* (New York: Cambridge Univ. Press, 1982), esp. chaps. 2–3; Eric Hobsbawm, "Inventing Tradition," in Hobsbawm and Ranger, *The Invention of Tradition;* Ian McKay, *The Quest of the Folk: Antimodernism and Cultural Selection in Twentieth-Century Nova Scotia* (Kingston, Ontario: McGill Queens Univ. Press, 1994), esp. chap. 1; Daniel J. Sherman, *Worthy Monuments: Art Museums and the Politics of Culture in Nineteenth-Century France* (Cambridge: Harvard Univ. Press, 1989), esp. pt. 1.

9. On the limits of the nineteenth-century American state, see Alan Dawley, *Struggles for Justice: Social Responsibility and the Liberal State* (Cambridge: Harvard Univ. Press 1991), pt. 1; and Stephen Skowronek, *Building a New American State: The Expansion of National Administrative Capacities, 1877–1920* (Cambridge Univ. Press: Cambridge, 1982), esp. pt. 2.

10. Cecilia Elizabeth O'Leary, *To Die For: The Paradox of American Patriotism* (Princeton: Princeton Univ. Press, 1999), chap. 9.

11. John Hugh Reynolds, "Public Archives of Arkansas," *Annual Report of the American Historical Association, 1906* (1908), 2: 28.

12. This information is compiled from the *Annual Report of the State Comptroller* (Tallahassee: Florida Comptroller's Office, 1900–15).

13. W. J. Cash, *The Mind of the South* (New York: Knopf, 1941), 35. For a discussion of the administrative capacities of southern states, see William A. Link, *The Paradox of Southern Progressivism, 1880–1930* (Chapel Hill: Univ. of North Carolina Press, 1992), esp. pt. 3.

14. My ideas about the cultural space assumed by voluntary associations reflect the influence of Jürgen Habermas, *The Structural Transformation of the Public Sphere: An Inquiry into a Category of Bourgeois Societies,* trans. Thomas Burger with the assistance of Frederick Lawrence (Cambridge: MIT Press, 1989), esp. 43–67, 232; and Harold Mah, "Phantasies of the Public Sphere: Rethinking the Habermas of Historians," *Journal of Modern History* 72 (Mar. 2000): 153–82. In this essay, my use of the term *public sphere* is informed by Habermas's concept, not to be mistaken with the notions of public and private spheres associated with the nineteenth-century ideology of "separate spheres" governing gender roles.

15. Rossiter Johnson, ed., *A History of the World's Columbian Exposition* (New York: Appleton, 1898), 3:433, 478.

16. This process of "public" mobilization is best described in Kirk Savage, *Standing Soldiers, Kneeling Slaves* (Princeton: Princeton Univ. Press, 1997).

17. On black commemorative traditions, see David W. Blight, *Race and Reunion* (Cambridge: Harvard Univ. Press, 2001), chap. 9; W. Fitzhugh Brundage, "Race, Memory, and Masculinity: Black Veterans Recall the Civil War, 1865–1915," in *The War Was You and Me: Civilians and the American Civil War,* ed. Joan Cashin (Princeton: Princeton Univ. Press, 2002), 136–56; Kathleen Clark, "Celebrating Freedom: Emancipation Day Celebrations and African American Memory in the Reconstruction South," in Brundage, *Where These Memories Grow,* and in her essay in this anthology; Mitchell A. Kachun, "The Faith that the Dark Past Has Taught Us: African-American Commemorations in the North and West and the Construction of a Useable Past, 1808–1915" (Ph.D. diss., Cornell Univ., 1997), chaps. 5–7; William H. Wiggins Jr. and Douglas DeNatale, *Jubilation! African American Celebration in the Southeast* (Columbia: McKissick Museum, 1993); David A. Williams, *Juneteenth: The Unique Heritage* (Austin: n.p., 1992).

18. This process is traced in Catherine W. Bishir, "Landmarks of Power: Building a Southern Past, 1855–1915," *Southern Cultures,* inaugural issue (1994): 5–46; Foster, *Ghosts of the Confederacy;* Savage, *Standing Soldiers, Kneeling Slaves,* chap. 5; and Nina Silber, *The Romance of Reunion: Northerners and the South, 1865–1900* (Chapel Hill: Univ. of North Carolina Press, 1993), chaps. 4–5. On the importance of physical manifestations of memory, see Michel-Rolph Trouillot, *Silencing the Past: Power and the Production of History* (Boston: Beacon Press, 1995), esp. 28–30.

19. Earl Barnes, "The Feminizing of Culture," *Atlantic Monthly* 109 (June 1912): 770; "Critic," Letter to the Editor, *New York Times,* Mar. 2, 1902. See also Michael Kammen, *Mystic Chords of Memory: The Transformation of Tradition in American Culture* (New York: Knopf, 1991), 266–69.

20. Darlene R. Roth, *Matronage: Patterns of Women's Organizations, Atlanta, Georgia, 1890–1940* (Brooklyn: Carlson, 1994), 17–72; and Sims, *The Power of Femininity in the New South,* 128–54.

21. Paula Baker, *The Moral Frameworks of Public Life: Gender, Politics and the State in Rural New York, 1870–1930* (New York: Oxford Univ. Press, 1991), chap. 3; Janette Thomas Greenwood, *Bittersweet Legacy: The Black and White "Better Classes" in Charlotte, 1850–1910* (Chapel Hill: Univ. of North Carolina Press, 1994), 68–69, 110–13; and Mary Ryan, *Cradle of the Middle Class: The Family in Oneida County, New York, 1790–1865* (New York: Cambridge Univ. Press, 1981), chaps. 3 and 5.

22. For accounts that emphasize the importance of "republican motherhood" as a pretext for women's historical activism, see Joan Marie Johnson, "'This Wonderful Dream Nation!': Black and White South Carolina Women and the Creation of the New South, 1898–1930" (Ph.D. diss., Univ. of California, Los Angeles, 1997), esp. chap. 2; Sims, *The Power of Femininity,* 128–54.

23. For a fuller discussion of this theme, see W. Fitzhugh Brundage, "White Women and the Politics of Historical Memory in the South, 1880–1920," in *Jumpin' Jim Crow: Southern Politics from Civil War to Civil Rights*, ed. Jane Dailey, Glenda Gilmore, and Bryant Simon (Princeton: Princeton Univ. Press, 2000).

24. On women's fund-raising techniques in the nineteenth century, see Beverly Gordon, *Bazaars and Fair Ladies: The History of the American Fundraising Fair* (Knoxville: Univ. of Tennessee Press, 1998), chaps. 4–5; F. K. Prochaska, *Women and Philanthropy in Nineteenth-Century England* (New York: Oxford Univ. Press, 1980), pt. 1.

25. Catherine Clinton, *Tara Revisited: Women, War and the Plantation Legend* (New York: Abbeville Press, 1995), 184–85; and Angie Parrott, "Love Makes Memory Eternal": The United Daughters of the Confederacy in Richmond, Virginia, 1897–1920," in *The Edge of the South: Life in Nineteenth-Century Virginia*, ed. Edward L. Ayers and John C. Willis (Charlottesville: Univ. Press of Virginia, 1991), 219–20.

26. Elizabeth Varon, *We Mean to Be Counted: White Women and Politics in Antebellum Virginia* (Chapel Hill: Univ. of North Carolina Press, 1998), esp. chap. 1 and epilogue.

27. Mrs. W. C. H. Merchant, "Report of the Historical Committees, UDC," *Confederate Veteran* 12 (Feb. 1904): 64. On the campaigns of white women's organizations to influence "public opinion," see Fred. A. Bailey, "The Textbooks of the 'Lost Cause': Censorship and the Creation of Southern State Histories," *Georgia Historical Quarterly* 75 (fall 1991): 507–33; idem, "Free Speech and the 'Lost Cause' in Texas: A Study of Social Control in the New South," *Southwestern Historical Quarterly* 97 (Jan. 1994): 453–77; idem, "Mildred Lewis Rutherford and the Patrician Cult of the Old South," *Georgia Historical Quarterly* 78 (fall 1994): 523–30; Karen L. Cox, "Women, the Lost Cause, and the New South: The United Daughters of the Confederacy and the Transmission of Confederate Culture, 1894–1919" (Ph.D. diss., Univ. of Southern Mississippi, 1997); Foster, *Ghosts of the Confederacy*, 163–79; Johnson, "This Wonderful Dream Nation!" chap. 2; and Sims, *Power of Femininity*, chap. 6.

28. Enoch Marvin Banks, "A Semi-Centennial View of Secession," *Independent* 70 (Feb. 9, 1911): 302–3.

29. The Banks case is ably chronicled in Fred A. Bailey, "Free Speech at the University of Florida: The Enoch Marvin Banks Case," *Florida Historical Quarterly* 71 (July 1992): 1–17. On the controversy over the Lee Chapel, see Pamela Simpson's essay in this collection.

30. Susan Pringle Frost, Apr. 12, 1920[?], Manigault House Papers, 11-278B-3, South Carolina Historical Society.

31. *(Charleston) News and Courier,* Dec. 30, 1937.

32. On women and the preservation crusade in Charleston, see Stephanie E. Yuhl, "High Culture in the Low Country: Arts, Identity, and Tourism in Charleston, South Carolina, 1920–1940" (Ph.D. diss., Duke Univ., 1998), chap. 1; on the Stone Mountain controversy, see David B. Freeman, *Carved in Stone: The History of Stone Mountain* (Macon, Ga.: Mercer Univ. Press, 1997), chap. 4; and Elizabeth Grace Hale's essay in this collection.

33. For an interesting comparison of the simultaneous transformation of women's role in social work, see Robyn Muncy, *Creating a Female Dominion in American Reform, 1890–1935* (New York: Oxford Univ. Press, 1991), esp. chaps. 2 and 5.

34. Mary Hilliard Hinton, "North Carolina's Historical Exhibit at Jamestown Exposition," *North Carolina Booklet* 7 (Oct. 1907): 138–44. On women and other historic preservation campaigns, see Holly Beachley Brear, *Inherit the Alamo: Myth and Ritual at an American Shrine* (Austin: Univ. of Texas Press, 1995); Mary C. Dorris, *Preservation of the Hermitage, 1889–1915* ([Nashville, Smith and Lamar, c. 1915] ); Lewis F. Fisher, *Saving San Antonio: The Precarious Preservation of a Heritage* (Lubbock, Tex.: Texas Tech Univ. Press, 1996); Charles B. Hosmer Jr., *Presence of the Past: A History of the Preservation Movement in the United*

*States before Williamsburg* (New York: G. P. Putnam's, 1965), 69–72; and Mollie Somerville, *Historic and Memorial Buildings of the Daughters of the American Revolution* (Washington: National Society, Daughters of the American Revolution, 1979), 190, 200.

35. On the relationship between the genealogical fad and hereditary and patriotic societies, see Kammen, *Mystic Chords of Memory,* 220–22, 249–50.

36. Charles W. Ramsdell, "The Preservation of Texas History," *North Carolina Historical Review* 6 (Jan. 1929): 6; E. W. Winkler, "Some Historical Activities of the Texas Library and Historical Commission," *Quarterly of the Texas State Historical Association* 14 (1910–11): 294–304.

37. On the rise of professional historians, see Mary O. Furner, *Advocacy and Objectivity: A Crisis in the Professionalization of American Social Science, 1865–1905* (Lexington: Univ. Press of Kentucky, 1975); Thomas L. Haskell, *The Emergence of Professional Social Science* (Urbana: Univ. of Illinois Press, 1977), esp. chaps. 7–10; Peter Novick, *That Noble Dream: The 'Objectivity' Question and the American Historical Profession* (Cambridge: Cambridge Univ. Press, 1988), esp. chaps. 1–2. On the rise of professional historians in the South, see especially Robert B. Simpson, "The Origin of State Departments of Archives and History in the South" (Ph.D. diss., Univ. of Mississippi, 1971), 127–31, and Wendell H. Stephenson, "A Half Century of Southern Historical Scholarship," in *The Pursuit of Southern History: Presidential Addresses of the Southern Historical Association, 1935–1963,* ed. George B. Tindall (Baton Rouge: Louisiana Univ. Press, 1964).

38. Professional/amateur tensions are discussed in R. D. W. Connor, "Lessons from North Carolina," *Annual Report of the American Historical Association, 1922* (1926): 125; North Carolina Historical Commission, *Report of the Historical Commission to Governor Charles B. Aycock* (Raleigh: E. M. Uzzell and Co., 1904), 1; Franklin L. Riley, "The Work of the Mississippi Historical Society," *Publications of the Mississippi Historical Society* 10 (1910): 42; *Report of the Alabama History Commission to the Governor of Alabama* (Montgomery: Brown Printing Co., 1901), 1:38; John Hugh Reynolds, "A Comprehensive Historical Policy for Arkansas," Arkansas Historical Commission, Circular No. 3 (1905), 11.

39. For a cogent discussion of the marginalization of women by professional historians, see Bonnie G. Smith, *The Gender of History: Men, Women, and Historical Practice* (Cambridge: Harvard Univ. Press, 1998), esp. chaps. 4 and 6.

# Part II

## Heroes and Heroines of the South

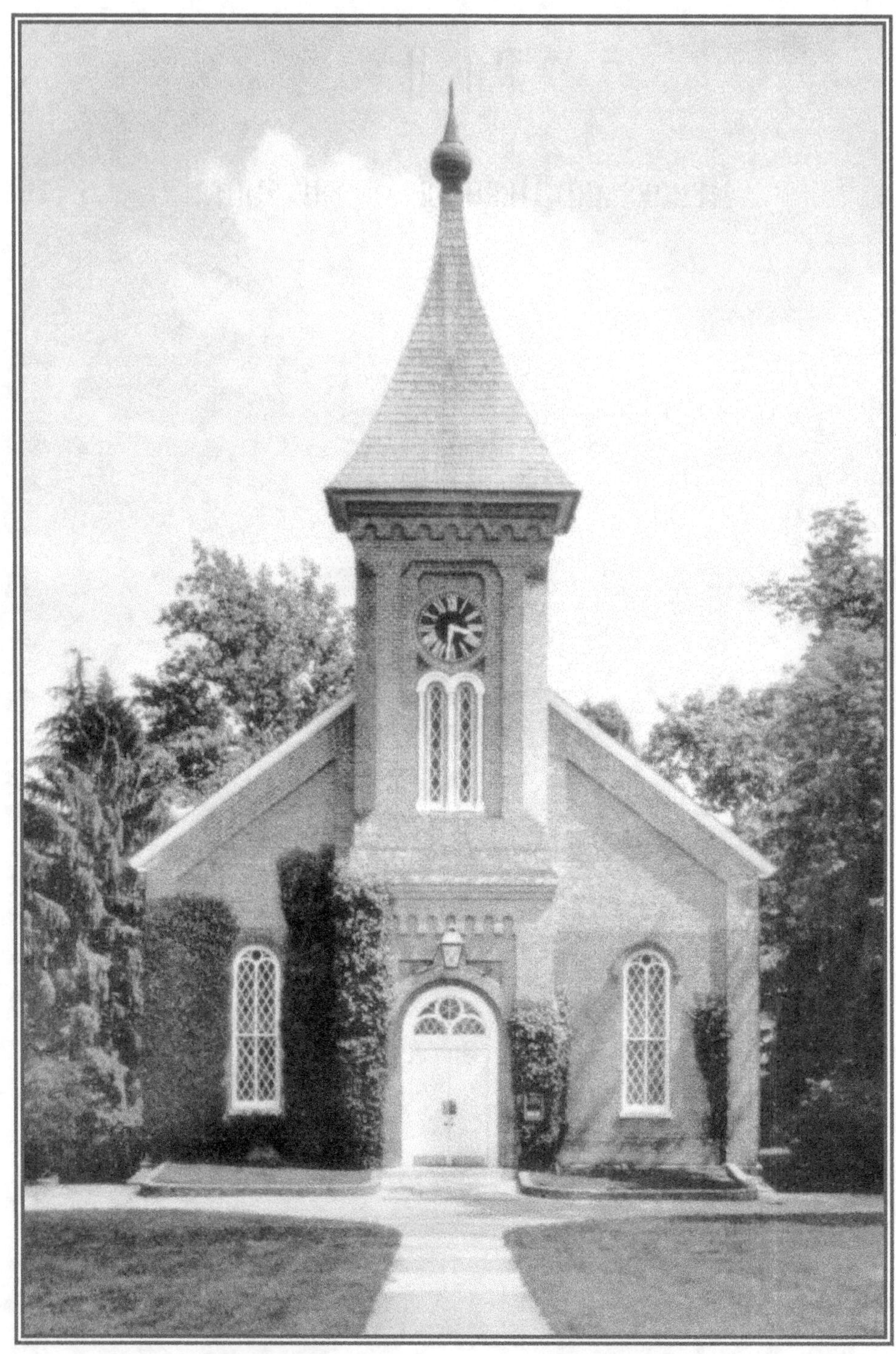

Fig. 5.1. Lee Chapel, Washington and Lee University, Lexington, Virginia. Photograph by Sally Mann, courtesy of Historic Lexington Foundation.

# 5

# The Great Lee Chapel Controversy and the "Little Group of Willful Women" Who Saved the Shrine of the South

*Pamela H. Simpson*

A 1922 EDITORIAL in the *Norfolk Virginia Pilot* declared, "The South has but one Lee and that Lee has but one tomb—that enclosed in the small brick mausoleum constructed against the rear wall of the Washington and Lee Chapel."[1] The editorial went on to criticize the university's plans for enlarging the chapel, but in that simple combination of Lee/tomb/chapel, it had identified the essential elements for the making of a shrine.

Ironically, in the name of preserving that shrine, Washington and Lee University officials proposed tearing down the chapel and replacing it with a larger, grander building deemed more fitting as a memorial to house the Lee tomb. The proposal unleashed a storm of protest that has since become known as the "Great Lee Chapel Controversy."[2] For nearly two years, concerned parties debated the meaning of commemoration and how a building might or might not embody historical memory. An analysis of that debate reveals much about the memorialization process, about early efforts at historic preservation, about differences between early-twentieth-century "progressive" and "conservative" views, and about the differences in male and female approaches to power. This essay attempts to explain how Lee Chapel (fig. 5.1) came to be identified as the Shrine of the South and how a small group of local women preservationists managed to save it.

There were many buildings associated with Lee. His home at Arlington, Virginia, was still standing, though now part of a national cemetery. His family home at Stratford was an important historical landmark that linked Lee family prominence with both the Revolutionary and the Civil Wars. The house where Lee lived the last two years of his life and where he died was still an important part of the Washington and Lee campus. Why did the university chapel become the center of attention, the Shrine of the South?

An obvious answer is because Lee was buried there. The burial sites of saints and the places where their relics remain often become shrines. Evidence emerging from the 1922 controversy suggests that for most of the late nineteenth and early twentieth centuries the general's tomb was venerated but the chapel building itself was not. This was to change as a result of the debate over the university's plans for "reconstruction" of the building.

## A History of Lee Chapel

Washington and Lee University traces its origins to Augusta Academy, a small preparatory school founded by Scotch-Irish Presbyterians in 1749. During the Revolution it renamed itself Liberty Hall Academy. After the war, when George Washington endowed it with a generous gift of canal stock, the grateful school changed its name again, to Washington College. By 1783 it was granting baccalaureate degrees, and in the early nineteenth century it developed an impressive Greek Revival campus on the edge of the small Valley of Virginia town of Lexington.[3]

In 1865 the college's board of trustees elected defeated Confederate Gen. Robert E. Lee to be the school's president—apparently without consulting him as to whether he would consider the job. To the trustees' surprise and delight, Lee accepted. He later commented that it was the only offer he had received that allowed him to serve his country rather than exploit his name. In his acceptance letter, Lee said it was "the duty of every citizen to do all in his power to aid in the restoration of peace and harmony."[4] During his five years as president of Washington College (1865–70), Lee helped change the once-sectarian classical academy into a modern and innovative university.

The school was no longer associated with the Presbyterian church, but the Christian faith was still held basic and chapel attendance was an essential part of college life. The institution urgently needed a new chapel building. So many young men had enrolled in "General Lee's College," as it came to be called in the postwar years, that the old chapel room on the colonnade could no longer accommodate them. Thus early in 1866 Lee recommended to the board of trustees that a new chapel be built. By the following year construction was completed.[5]

The question of who actually designed the chapel has been long debated. The board of trustees' minutes refer to a "plan prepared by President Lee." A retired professor at the school claimed in 1922 that it had been designed and supervised by George Washington Custis Lee, Lee's son who was teaching at the nearby Virginia Military Institute (VMI). In 1909 Custis Lee wrote a friend that the design for the chapel had come "out of a book" and had been used because it was "simple and comparatively inexpensive."[6] Against all this is a letter from Thomas H. Williamson, an engineering professor at VMI who wrote to his daughter in 1866, "I have been thrown a good deal with General Lee lately. The buildings Committee at the College got me to design the new chapel . . . and I have made all the working drawings and written all the specifications all of which I had to confer with the General and explain to him."[7]

Lee, his son Custis, and Williamson were all trained engineers and were probably all involved in the planning for the chapel, but the Williamson letter leaves little doubt that he should be credited with the design. Williamson had introduced a course on architecture at VMI in 1848 and had even written a textbook for it.[8] The chapel he designed draws heavily from the Romanesque style and was probably influenced by James Renwick's 1849 Smithsonian Institution building in Washington, D.C. The Smithsonian had been the focus of an 1849 book by Robert Dale Owen called *Hints on Public Architecture, Containing, among Illustrations, Views and Plans of the Smithsonian Institution.* Williamson was well aware of the book, which included numerous plates of the Smithsonian and its details; it was in the VMI library and he quoted from it in his own text. It may have been *Hints on Public Architecture* that Custis Lee referred to when he said the design came from a book. While the letter from Williamson to his daughter clearly establishes him as the architect, it was not discovered until 1941, so the debate about the identity of the chapel's architect continued for a large portion of this century, with many seeking to credit Robert E. Lee or Custis Lee for the project's design.[9]

## *The Lee Memorial*

Lee also was responsible for another addition to the campus during his tenure as president. This was his own house, designed by another VMI professor who used an architectural pattern book as a source. It was finished in 1868, and Lee died in the house in October 1870.

The university mounted a grand funeral (fig. 5.2), and Lee's body lay in state guarded by students before he was laid to rest in the basement of the chapel. Even while the ceremonies were under way, officials began planning a suitable memorial. The newly created Lee Memorial Association commissioned a life-size marble statue of Lee from Richmond sculptor Edward V. Valentine in 1871.[10] Valentine (fig. 5.3) was a natural choice since he had done a life portrait of Lee less than a year earlier. During a week-long visit to Lexington in May 1870, Valentine had modeled a bust and taken detailed measurements of Lee's head. The sculptor also measured Lee's horse, Traveller, indicating that he anticipated doing an equestrian statue as well. The image he created for the Memorial Association, however, was of Lee asleep on his camp bed. The monument to Queen Louisa of Prussia in the Charlottenburg Palace park, completed in 1815 by the German sculptor Christian Daniel Rauch, apparently served as a model for the idea of a recumbent, sleeping figure. A much-fingered photograph of that mausoleum sculpture survives in the Valentine papers. According to Valentine, it was Mary Custis Lee herself who suggested the idea of presenting Lee asleep, not in death.[11]

Five months after receiving the commission, Valentine presented the plaster model for approval. The finished stone carving, made from a five-ton piece of Vermont marble, drew admiring crowds to Valentine's Richmond studio in April 1875. The statue was crated and shipped to Lexington on April 13. The Memorial Association, however, had great difficulty raising the $15,000 for the statue and the $12,000 needed for the mausoleum addition. In 1877 the effort was greatly aided when Baltimore architect J. Crawford Neilson offered his services to design the chapel addition free of charge, but it still took another six years to raise the money to build it.

Dignitaries from all over the South came to Lexington for the dedication of the Lee Mausoleum (fig. 5.4) in June 1883. The gleaming white marble statue dominated a memorial room on the main level (figs. 4.4 and 5.5). The mausoleum lay below this; Lee's office was preserved as he had left it in the chapel basement. Students from the college and VMI cadets took turns guarding the statue and welcoming a growing number of visitors.

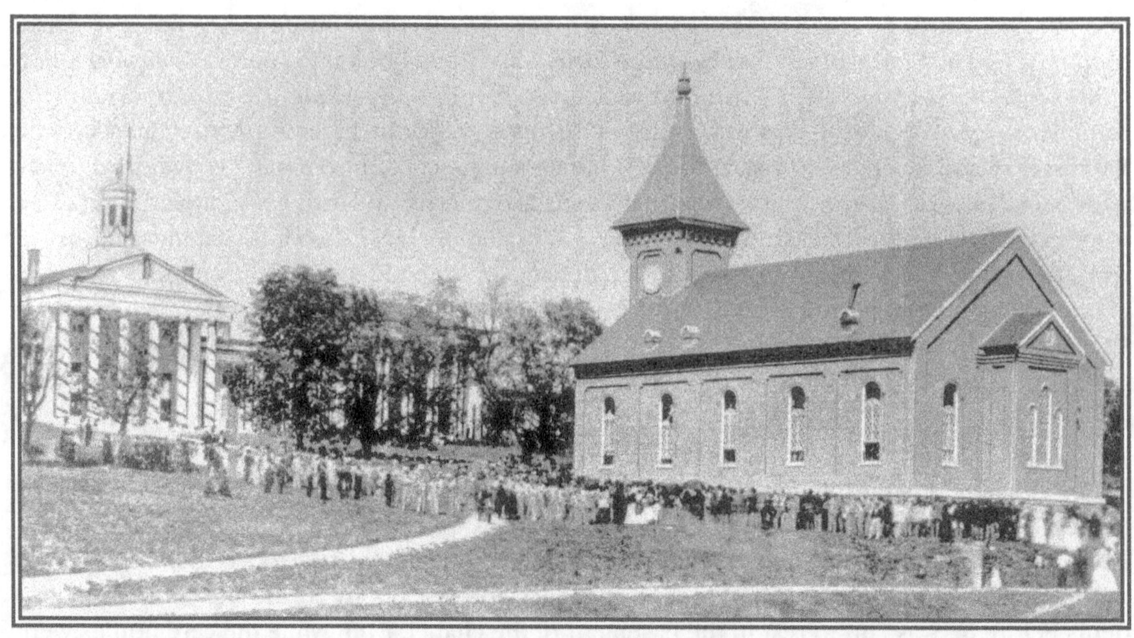

Fig. 5.2. Robert E. Lee's funeral, October 1870. Virginia Historical Society, Michael Miley photograph, courtesy of Special Collections, Washington and Lee University.

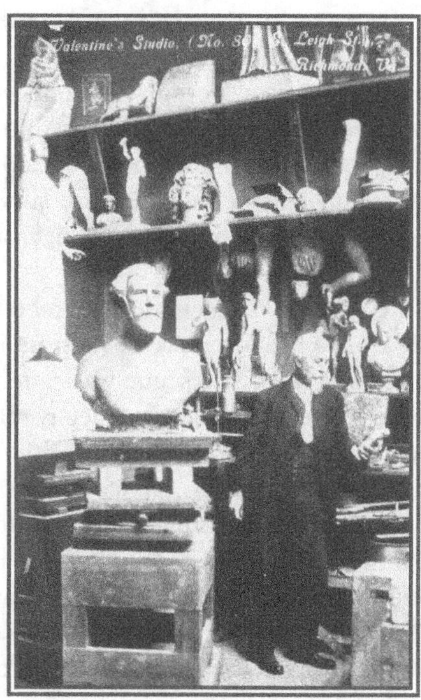

Fig. 5.3. Edward V. Valentine in his Richmond, Virginia, studio, circa 1906–10. Valentine Museum/Richmond History Center.

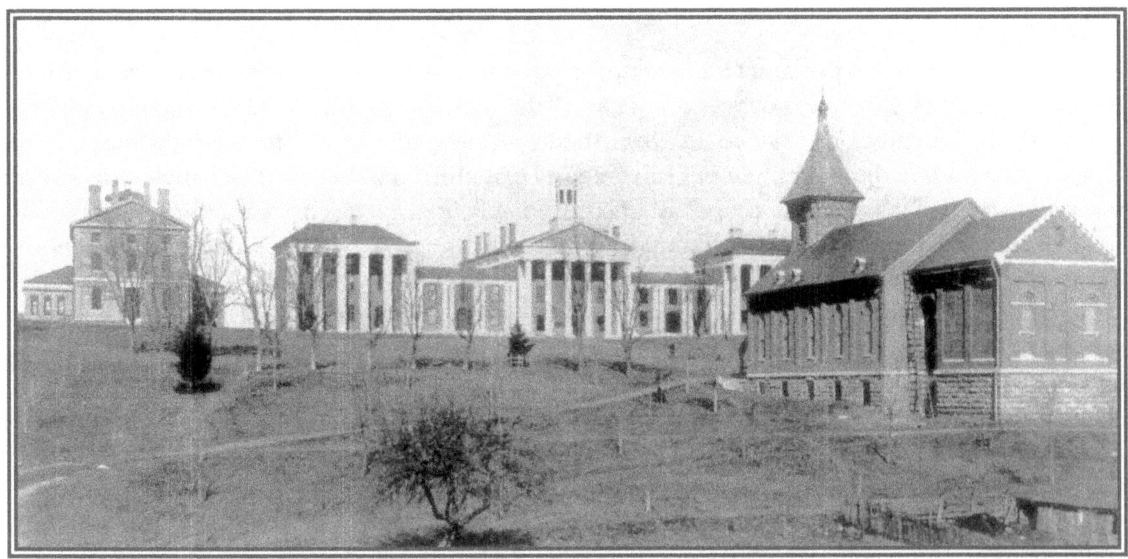

Fig. 5.4. The Mausoleum addition to Lee Chapel in Lexington, 1883. Virginia Historical Society, Michael Miley photograph, courtesy of Special Collections, Washington and Lee University.

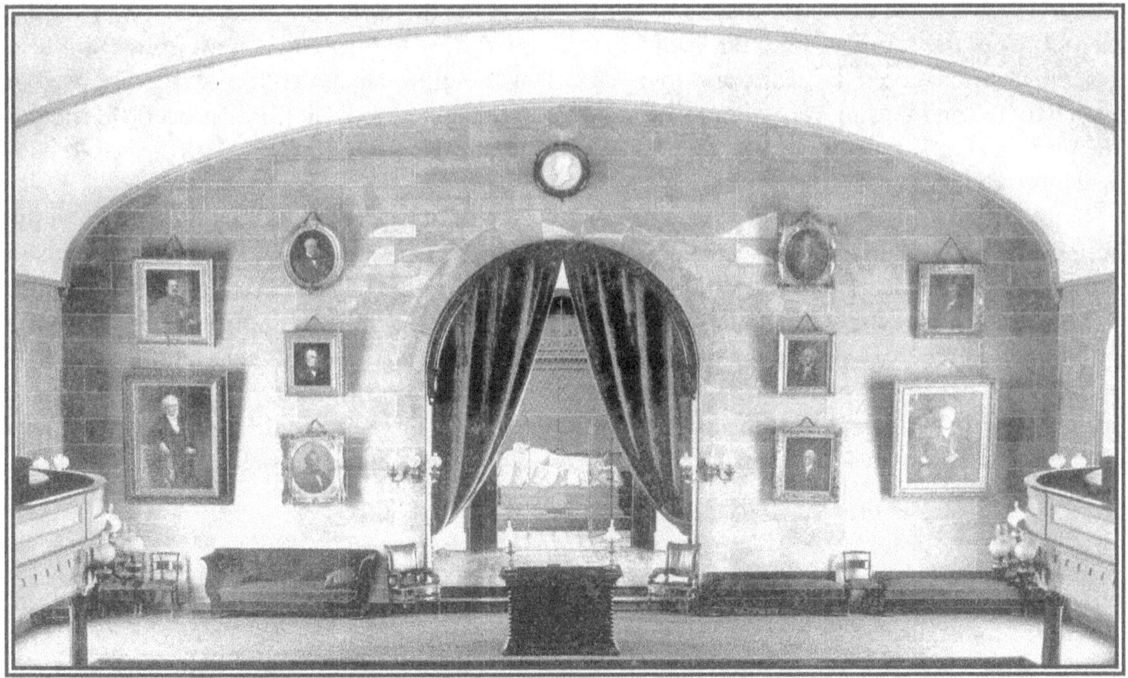

Fig. 5.5. Interior of Lee Chapel, circa 1890, showing marble sculpture of Robert E. Lee designed by sculptor Edward V. Valentine. Virginia Historical Society, Michael Miley photograph, courtesy Special Collections, Washington and Lee University.

## *Plans for a New Chapel*

During the later years of the nineteenth century, the statue and tomb were objects of veneration, but there is evidence that the chapel building itself was not cherished. In 1922 a student who had attended the college from 1877 to 1879 recalled that no one referred to the building as "Lee Chapel" and said he did not remember "anyone in Lexington" looking on the chapel with special reverence. He remembered the chapel as an "exceedingly unattractive brick building," which was "entirely out of harmony with the old buildings of the University." He concluded, "There is nothing about the building to make it a worthy memorial."[12]

At the centennial celebration of Lee's birth in 1907, the Lee Memorial Association broached the subject of improving the building. It was reported that visiting dignitary Charles Francis Adams had said to a companion upon leaving it, "The only reproach to General Lee's memory is this chapel which he allowed to deface his campus."[13] When Custis Lee was consulted about the family's feelings in the matter, he replied, "There will be no objection, I am sure, on the part of any member of General Lee's family to anything the authorities may decide to do to the chapel."[14] Because of a financial panic, however, nothing came of the Memorial Association's plans.

Thirteen years later, in 1920, the United Daughters of the Confederacy entered into a contract with the university to provide a custodian for the chapel and an endowment for her wages. With about 1,500 annual visitors by this time, the student/cadet guardianship was unable to accommodate the demand. This agreement would be significant for the future, because it brought the Daughters into a direct role in the care of the chapel.

In 1921 Washington and Lee President Henry Louis Smith gave an impassioned address to the General Convention of the UDC in Saint Louis, calling for the complete "reconstruction" of the chapel "from the foundation to the roof."[15] He claimed the old building was an unsafe fire hazard, which endangered the statue and tomb as well as the university art collection then housed in the chapel. The building was so unattractive, he also complained, that it disgraced the sacred memory of Lee. The national UDC responded, voting to raise $100,000 for the project to reconstruct the chapel.

Smith already had the approval of the university's board of trustees, and he thought he had the support of the Lee family as well, though subsequent events would prove him wrong. Smith asked the university architects, Flournoy and Flournoy of Washington, D.C., to prepare several schemes that would preserve the statue, tomb, and office but would also more than double the size of the building, essentially replacing it with a grand Neo-Georgian structure with a 1,200-seat auditorium.[16] One of the university's pressing needs, according to Smith, was a place large enough to seat the entire student body. He also felt the new design (fig. 5.6) would be more fitting as a memorial and more in sympathy with the classical architecture of the campus.

## *The Great Lee Chapel Controversy*

Smith announced the new plans as the great event of 1922 and launched a fund-raising campaign. But much to his dismay, he met with a steadily rising tide of opposition. Smith wrote to Mary Lee, wife of trustee Robert E. Lee III, Lee's grandson, in hurt bewilderment: "A few daughters of the Confederacy in Lexington have suddenly determined to block the plans of the Trustees and the UDC to reconstruct and fireproof the chapel. They have called a meeting in the absence of their two chief

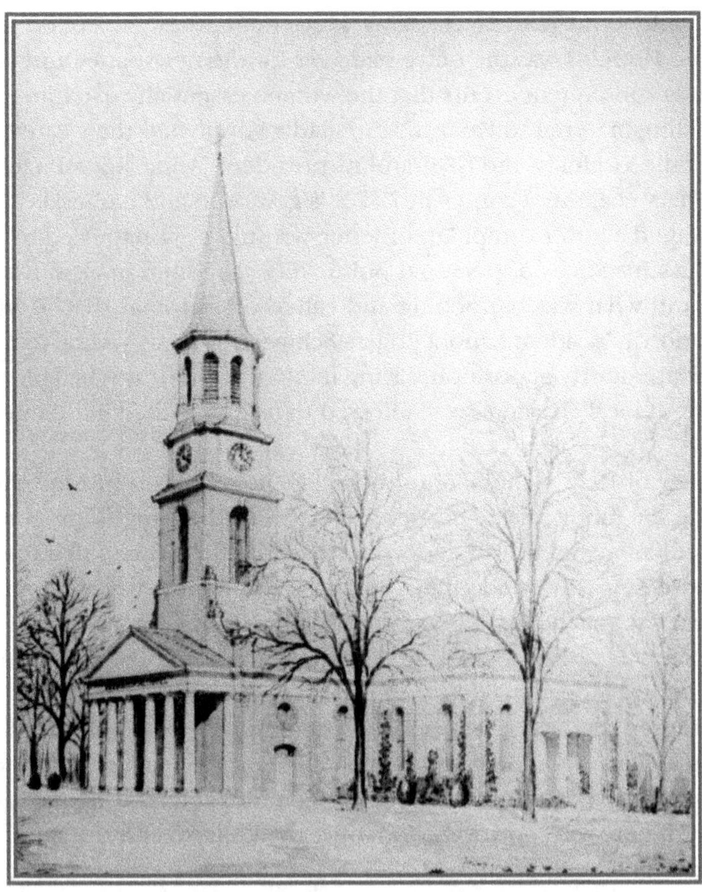

Fig. 5.6. Flournoy and Flournoy's proposal for Lee Chapel reconstruction, 1922. Courtesy of Special Collections, Leyburn Library, Washington and Lee University.

officers, have passed urgent resolutions against touching this historic building, have gotten the ultra conservative editor of one of the town papers to take the leadership in the movement, and have sent his editorial and their resolutions to every chapter of the UDC in the United States."[17]

The rector of the board, William A. Anderson, a Civil War veteran and noted Virginia politician, also expressed surprise at the sudden insurrection when he wrote a friend that, acting on some "hallucination," a few local women were making a "commotion," but that he could not "give a satisfactory diagnosis" or explanation consistent with what he knew to be the ladies' "lovely character and recognized intelligence and good sense."[18]

The Lexington Mary Custis Lee Chapter of the United Daughters of the Confederacy had indeed organized to oppose the university's plans. The chapter, founded in 1895, had more than one hundred members by 1922, including some of the most prominent women in Lexington. Alice Marian Miller White led the opposition effort and organized the letter-writing campaign.[19] President Smith claimed that she had done so "in the absence" of the local chapter's officers, but in reality there was little dissent within the group.

Another of the leaders was Jeannie Hopkins, niece of Matthew W. Paxton, editor of the *Rockbridge County News.* Hopkins was the office manager for the newspaper and enlisted her uncle's aid. It is evident from subsequent events that the women essentially used the newspaper as their public voice, funneling material to Paxton, who gladly supported their cause. The chapter also won the support of the Virginia State UDC and its president, Anne Norvell Otey Scott, and, most important, that of Mary Lee, the second wife of Lee's grandson and namesake.

The two sides waged a bitter campaign of letter writing, newspaper editorials, printed pamphlets, and countless instances of personal politicking. The men in authority at the university could not understand what was happening and called on national UDC leaders to bring their troops into line. National President Lenora Rogers Schuyler tried. In several letters she scolded the Mary Custis Lee Chapter for its opposition, saying the UDC would "not be able to accomplish anything of importance" if local chapters were allowed to take this unorthodox method of opposing the national group.[20]

In the late summer of 1922, Schuyler and Bessie C. Rogers, who headed the UDC committee charged with raising the funds for the chapel project, visited Lexington to confer with President Smith and Rector Anderson. Smith and Anderson reassured the women that there were only a few dissenters, who could be easily quelled, but Schuyler and Rogers were not so sure. Rogers later wrote the rector that she was heartsick over the problems and concluded, "so you see that 'little group of willful women' . . . have held up the work and are making no end of trouble."[21]

The local women were indeed making trouble. They instituted an extensive letter-writing campaign full of impassioned rhetoric. The chapel was "a most holy procession" whose "sacred atmosphere" had been created by tradition. "Spare, keep and guard the chapel," wrote Mary Lee, "for in spite of Dr. Smith, the chapel is the shrine and not the tomb and mausoleum alone."[22]

Here was the key. Before the controversy, attention had focused on the statue, mausoleum, and office; now that the chapel was threatened with destruction, the associations were transferred to it. "This little chapel represents a period in which General Lee lived in Lexington," wrote one defender. "It represents the courage, fortitude, endurance of the South's great hero, General Lee who was the designer and practically the builder!"[23]

The persistent belief that Lee actually designed the chapel seems to arise from these 1922 arguments, which tried to associate him with the building in every way possible. Anne Scott, president of the Virginia UDC, asserted that "Lee Chapel is more identified with General Lee than any other building in the world. It was built through his efforts, under his supervision, with the gifts of an impoverished people. Lee worshipped there daily."[24]

President Smith and the trustees countered the women's arguments with their own, evoking Lee's name to defend their plans. They called on the "sacred trust" to create a building that would have architectural dignity worthy of Lee's memory and of his tomb. They declared that Lee's spirit was present in the university he had created and not in the actual bricks of what was clearly an ugly building. In their propaganda they also stated that the chapel was "erected during a period when American architecture had reached its lowest ebb."[25]

The chapel's defenders countered that telling them the building was ugly had as much effect as "criticism made to a man about his mother's countenance."[26] It did not matter to him if she lacked beauty; he loved her anyway. The chapel, however humble, was filled with hallowed memories and should be left untouched, they argued.

At the UDC general convention in Birmingham, Alabama, in November 1922, the leaders of the Lexington chapter and the Virginia state delegation introduced a resolution to preserve the chapel. But the national UDC was still behind President Smith, and Lenora Schuyler ruled the convention with a determined hand. The convention defeated the Virginia resolution. A Birmingham newspaper reported that when the vote was counted, some of the Virginia delegates wept while others leapt to their feet and cried, "We have not yet begun to fight!"[27]

Smith's victory in Birmingham was a hollow one, and he knew it. After a year of rising controversy and a debate that he characterized as having "depths of falsehood and personal hostility," the college president concluded that compromise was necessary if the project was to go ahead.[28] So early in 1923 he went to Boston to consult with famed architect Ralph Adams Cram. The two men conceived a plan for leaving the chapel intact, adding a new building at its rear, and taking down the back wall of the mausoleum to open the statue vault to view in the new structure. Smith quickly had his architects develop the scheme and then further consulted with Fisk Kimball, noted restoration architect and head of the Architecture School at the University of Virginia. The National

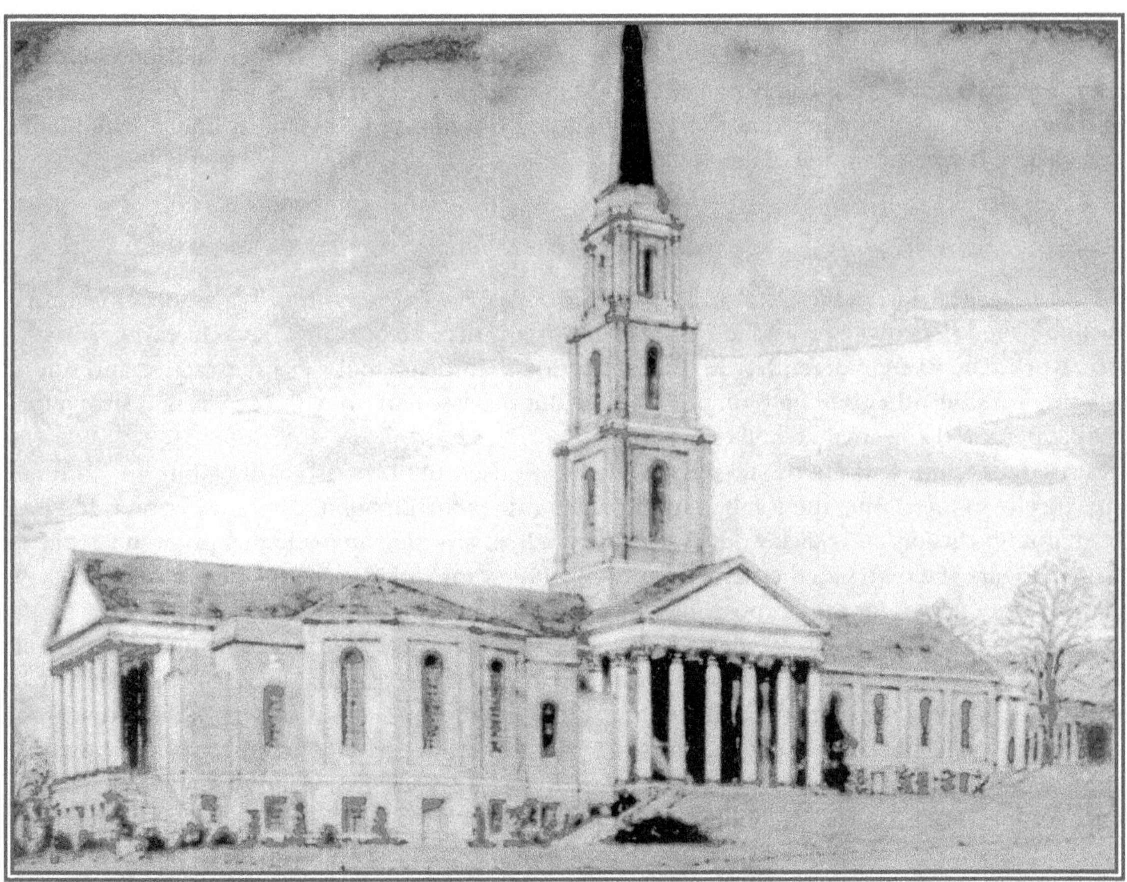

Fig. 5.7. "Final Solution" Proposal for Lee Chapel, 1923. Courtesy of Special Collections, Leyburn Library, Washington and Lee University.

Commission of Fine Arts also gave its nod to the plan. Smith proudly presented the compromise in a news release that was published in newspapers across the eastern United States, including the March 23, 1923, *New York Times* as "The Final Solution of the Lee Chapel Problem" (fig. 5.7).

But while Smith had secured the approval of the national UDC executive committee and of Mary Lee, he had not won over the Mary Custis Lee Chapter or the Virginia State UDC. Its leaders reiterated their demand that the chapel not be changed in any way. The proposed addition, they insisted, would "mar the dignity and tragically impair the historic and inspirational service of the chapel as it is and as it was when General Lee worshiped and presided within its sacred precinct."[29]

The women launched a renewed letter-writing campaign that gained the backing of a number of national and international dignitaries. "[A] building like the Lee Chapel has really become the property of the American race and whatever you think of the fitness of the building, it really ought to be beyond our power to touch it," declared British dramatist John Drinkwater.[30] Letters of opposition also came from Congressman Henry St. George Tucker, Lady Nancy Astor (the Virginia-born member of Parliament), the Colonial Dames, the Sons of the Confederacy, and, finally, from former President and Mrs. Woodrow Wilson.[31]

In January of 1924, Smith and his trustees admitted defeat. They spent the $6,000 that had been raised on fireproofing the building and left Lee Chapel unchanged. But it had gained something in the controversy. It had become the focal point of Lee veneration. Not the house where he lived and died, nor any other Lee-associated building would ever be as closely linked with him as this chapel. It was the Shrine of the South.

## Analysis of the Debate

What can we learn from the Great Lee Chapel Controversy? One lesson is that association with a distinguished personage proved to be more important than architectural style in early preservation work. The women defenders readily conceded that the chapel was unattractive and out of keeping with the other buildings on the campus. But the associations with Lee were so strong that they superceded any architectural criticism.

President Smith and the trustees also valued and used the Lee associations but linked them specifically to the statue, the tomb, and the office rather than to a building they contended had been put up cheaply and quickly out of expediency. Rector Anderson made that point in a letter to Bessie Rogers when he said the chapel was built with "scant and inadequate means" and was now "utterly inadequate" for the purpose for which it had been designed.[32]

Smith and the trustees also argued for a more abstract ideal: Lee's legacy as living on in the university he once led. The tomb and the statue represented the spiritual force of Lee's presence, wrote Smith. It was imperative that the entire student body be able to see them. "Since we cannot possibly preserve both [the spirit and the too small chapel], we have concluded that the hovering spirit is of more value than brick and mortar and that it is greater to conserve General Lee's influence for the future than this building which represents the past."[33]

The "innovators" asserted that Lee had been a forward-thinking educational leader who would have embraced the opportunity to improve campus buildings. Trustee John W. Davis wrote, "Those who would leave the chapel unchanged are influenced by their reverence for the traditions clustered around it . . . . Those who think a change imperative are thinking of the spiritual influence on the students yet to come. One view looks to the past, the other to the future." He concluded, "I cannot help feeling that if Lee himself could speak in the matter he would say, 'I choose to stay with the boys.'"[34]

President Smith, Lenora Schuyler, the trustees, and their supporters thought they were offering a "more fitting" memorial, one that was grander and more architecturally attractive. Its Beaux-Arts inspired, Neo-Georgian forms were the dominant style of the period for college campuses. Ralph Adams Cram had created a central campus in the style for nearby Sweet Briar College only a few years before. The style also was popular at Harvard and Princeton. There were ample precedents for the Neo-Georgian as the contemporary mode for college architecture. By this standard, Smith and his friends represented progressive, modern thinking, while the local women seemed senti-mental, nostalgic, and conservatively rooted in the past.

The controversy is equally revealing for what it demonstrates about gender roles and approaches to power. Smith and his colleagues epitomized the white male elite. They were accustomed to power and to manipulating organizational structures to achieve their goals. Smith enlisted the sup-port of the UDC's national leadership as well as recognized authorities in architecture and art. He repeatedly cited their professional expertise to legitimize the project. In contrast, the ladies formed a grassroots network, turning to sympathetic men who could help make their protest heard.

Smith and his backers were clearly surprised by what had happened. Within their inner circles they belittled the women, privately dismissing their opposition as stemming from "hallucinations" and "willfulness." The rector of the board, trying to be generous in his reading of the situation, supposed that the women were acting inconsistently with what he knew to be their true character —such "lovely, intelligent, sensible" women were not expected to behave this way, though he could not "diagnose" why they were. The implication was that they were ill, and the references to "delusions" and "hysteria" were frequent. Meanwhile, Anderson praised President Smith for hav-ing "borne himself manfully."[35]

According to the view of Smith and Anderson, the women were subversive. Not only did they challenge the male authorities in their community, they even started a mini–civil war within the UDC. Historian W. Fitzhugh Brundage has described how groups such as the UDC took leadership as the keepers of southern memory in the period between 1900 and 1920. At a time when women were given little opportunity for public roles, such groups gave them a voice. In preserving the monuments to male leaders of the past such as Lee, they could uphold traditional patriarchy even while challenging the tradition of female subservience.[36] The women of the Mary Custis Lee Chap-ter did just that. They believed so strongly in their ideal that they were willing to ignore the elite pronouncements of distinguished architects, powerful men, and their own national organization. In the end they won because they refused to give up.

One more point should be made in this analysis. It is tempting to use modern ideas about "uppity women" refusing to bend to male power structures to cast these women as feminist hero-ines. The idea would have shocked them. These were not feminists. Many of them even held a deep ambivalence about female suffrage. What they defended was not their right to challenge authority but instead the conservative position we have come to know as the Lost Cause. As James Lindgren and other scholars have observed, in the face of modernist change, white, Anglo-Saxon Americans such as the Mary Custis Lee Chapter used history and its monuments as a means of asserting their control over the past. Lindgren called it the "Gospel of Preservation."[37] In Lost Cause rhetoric, Robert E. Lee became a saintlike hero. The warrior-knight effigy of Valentine's reclining statue and the sacred reliquary of the chapel building were the visual embodiment of this hagiography.

George Orwell once observed that he who controls the past controls the future. The women of the Mary Custis Lee Chapter did that by making themselves the guardians of Lee Chapel. President Smith's abstract ideas about Lee's spirit living on in his university may have made for some fine speeches, but it was intellectual and sterile compared with the emotional appeal of an actual building that Lee had built, had used daily, and had been buried in. Thus the women who controlled the past did indeed control the future. They galvanized feelings about the importance of the structure. They successfully transferred the Lee associations to it, even perpetuating the myth that he was the architect. They made the chapel itself the shrine.

## *1924 to the Present*

In the end the defenders prevailed; the chapel remained, and Smith and the trustees were left merely to do some repairs. The new attention brought to the chapel, however, inspired the creation of a more formal museum display in the basement in 1927. Working with the UDC, which continued to serve as the building's guardians, the university officials placed various pieces of Lee memorabilia on display, including the bones of his horse Traveller.[38] The steed that had carried Lee through the Civil War had outlived him by only a year and had been buried in the ravine behind the campus. In 1875 the bones were dug up, probably in anticipation of putting them on display at the Centennial Exposition, but they were never sent to Philadelphia. In 1907 they were mounted and put on display in the campus natural history museum, where they remained until they were moved to the new Lee Museum in the chapel basement.

A more ambitious restoration of the chapel took place in 1960. This time the idea was not to tear it down but to preserve it. With a $376,000 grant from the Ford Motor Company Fund, university officials completely refurbished the building. The well-known Boston firm of Perry, Hepburn, Shaw and Dean, which had supervised the restoration of Colonial Williamsburg, served as consultants.[39] Applying contemporary standards of restoration, the workmen replaced most of the structural elements with modern materials, the old wooden rafters with steel, and the wooden basement floor with concrete, reinforcing the columns with steel, rebuilding the walls to make them true, and adding air-conditioning, a sprinkler system, and modern wiring. They did it all without visible changes to the surfaces. The museum display in the basement was completely refurbished, and Traveller's bones, which had been put in storage during the restoration, were given a dignified reburial outside the mausoleum walls in 1971.

As extensive as the 1960s renovations were, no restoration lasts forever. In 1997 the university raised $1 million to update the heating, ventilation, and electrical systems, to make the building handicapped accessible, and to modernize the basement museum display. Traveller's grave site also was landscaped and refurbished. The renovated chapel opened again in May 1999 in time for the school's 250th anniversary celebrations.

Lee Chapel continues to be a place of pilgrimage and a site for certain rituals. VMI cadets approaching the building are required to salute, signaling their continued homage to the Confederate general. In October the chapel bells ring out on the anniversary of Lee's death. In January, on Lee's birthday, the university community takes time out to gather in the chapel for a Founders'

Day ceremony.[40] Inaugurations and graduations take place on the lawn in front of the building. Every year some fifty thousand visitors still come to see this Shrine of the South. Few may realize it, but they can see the chapel today because of the determined efforts of a "little group of willful women" who in 1922 fought to save it.

## *Notes*

The author would like to acknowledge the previous work on this subject by Oliver Crenshaw, *General Lee's College* (New York: Random House, 1969), and Winifred Hadsel, "How Mary Custis Lee Chapter Saved Lee Chapel," *UDC Magazine* 61 (Apr. 1999): 11–15. Parts of this story also were published in Royster Lyle and Pamela H. Simpson, *The Architecture of Historic Lexington* (Charlottesville: Univ. Press of Virginia, 1977), and in idem, "The Lee Chapel Wars," *Washington and Lee Alumni Magazine* 61 (Jan. 1986): 8–11.

1. *Norfolk Virginia Pilot,* 1922 clipping in Chapel Controversy Folder, Washington and Lee University, Leyburn Library Special Collections (henceforth WLLSC).

2. Referred to as such in an unpublished paper by Matthew W. Paxton Jr., "The Great Lee Chapel Debate," given to the Fortnightly Club in Lexington, Va., 1961. The manuscript is in WLLSC.

3. Crenshaw, *General Lee's College* is the best history of the school. Lyle and Simpson, *The Architecture of Historic Lexington* has a section on its architecture.

4. Lee, acceptance letter, Trustees' Papers, WLLSC.

5. Board of Trustees' Records, Jan. 1866, WLLSC.

6. G. W. C. Lee to D. C. Humphreys, 1909, Trustees' Papers, WLLSC.

7. On January 4, 1943, John A. Graham, Williamson's great-grandson, sent a copy of this letter to Col. William Couper, historian at the Virginia Military Institute. A copy of the letter, dated October 12, 1866, is in the VMI Museum.

8. Thomas H. Williamson, *An Elementary Course on Architecture and Civil Engineering* (Lexington, Va.: Samuel Gillock, 1850).

9. Lyle and Simpson, *The Architecture of Historic Lexington,* 158–62.

10. Gerard M. Doyon, "The Recumbent Lee Statue in the Lee Chapel," *Washington and Lee Alumni Magazine* 58 (Mar. 1983): 3–6. Pamela H. Simpson, *American Sculpture in Lexington* (exhibition catalog, duPont Gallery) (Lexington, Va.: Washington and Lee Univ., 1977), 32–33. Christopher R. Lawton, "Myth and Monument: The Sculptural Image of Robert E. Lee and the Ideology of the Lost Cause" (master's thesis, Univ. of Georgia, 2000). Valentine (1838–1930) was the South's foremost sculptor after the Civil War. A Richmond native, he studied with Thomas Couture and François Jouffroy in Paris and August Kiss in Berlin before returning to Richmond in 1865. In May 1870 he asked Lee, who was visiting in Richmond, if he could take measurements for a portrait bust. Lee agreed and offered to sit for Valentine in Lexington. Valentine did the portrait study during his visit, June 7–11, 1870.

11. Doyon, "The Recumbent Lee," 5.

12. John M. Glenn to *Baltimore Sun,* Sept. 30, 1922, clipping and letter in Chapel Controversy Files, WLLSC. He also mentioned that a VMI professor designed the chapel, indicating that some contemporaries knew of Williamson's role. Glenn cited it, however, as further evidence of the building's unimportance.

13. Quoted in pamphlet published by Washington and Lee Univ., 1922, Chapel Controversy Files, WLLSC.

14. Custis Lee to D. C. Humphreys, 1909, Trustees' Papers, WLLSC.

15. Henry Louis Smith, speech to the UDC National Convention, St. Louis, Mo., 1922, Anne Norvell Otey Scott Papers, WLLSC.

16. The plans are in WLLSC. See Simpson, *Architectural Drawing*, 32.

17. Smith to Mary Lee, Aug. 21, 1922, Anne Norvell Otey Scott Papers, WLLSC.

18. Anderson to Mrs. G. Tracey Rogers, Oct. 5, 1922, copy. See also Anderson to Joseph John Allen, Sept. 20, 1922, for similar statement. Chapel Controversy Files, WLLSC.

19. While this essay uses the women's first names when they are known, most of them normally went by their husband's names. Alice White was married to a prominent local doctor and always signed her letters as "Mrs. Reid White." Both her husband and son were Washington and Lee alumni, and her husband's grandfather was on the board of trustees.

20. Lenora Rogers Schuyler usually identified herself as "Mrs. Livingston Rowe Schuyler." She wrote to the Mary Custis Lee Chapter, Aug. 28, 1922, "I did not suppose when receiving Mrs. White's letter that any act would be taken by any chapter contrary to the prescribed method [for appeal] . . . . Without full knowledge of the situation, a chapter has placed itself in opposition to the expressed will of an entire organization; this action gives me much pain, for anyone can see if chapters pursued this method with the work undertaken by the organization, we could not be able to accomplish anything of importance." Anne Norvell Otey Scott Papers, WLLSC.

21. Rogers to Anderson, Sept. 27, 1922. Her quotation was a paraphrase in reference to Woodrow Wilson's famous characterization of Henry Cabot Lodge and his Senate cohorts as a "little group of willful men" who opposed his policies. She signed this letter Bessie C. Rogers, although she used "Mrs. G. Tracey Rogers" on the letterhead. Chapel Controversy File WLLSC.

22. Mary Lee to Mrs. Scott, Nov. 10, 1922, Anne Norvell Otey Scott Papers, WLLSC

23. Mrs. J. Taylor Ellyson to Smith, Nov. 14, 1922, Trustees' Papers, WLLSC.

24. Scott speech to Virginia UDC, 1922, Ann Norvell Otey Scott Papers, WLLSC.

25. Pamphlet published by Washington and Lee Univ., 1922, Chapel Controversy Files, WLLSC.

26. Marietta Minnegerode Andrews, *Rockbridge County News*, Apr. 5, 12, 1923.

27. Quoted in Winifred Hadsel, "How Mary Custis Lee Chapter of the UDC Saved Lee Chapel in 1922–1923," paper presented to Virginia Division of UDC, Staunton, Va., Sept. 1997. Copy of paper supplied to the author.

28. Smith to Anderson, Oct. 1922, Trustees' Papers, WLLSC.

29. Scott to Smith, Oct. 17, 1923, Anne Norvell Otey Scott Papers, WLLSC. The Virginia Division had voted its opposition to the plan on October 4, 1923.

30. Drinkwater to Mrs. Moore, Nov. 7, 1923, in Chapel Controversy Files, WLLSC.

31. Crenshaw, *General Lee's College*, 303.

32. Anderson to Rogers, Oct. 5, 1922, Chapel Controversy Files, WLLSC.

33. Smith to Wilmer, Nov. 20, 1922, Anne Novell Otey Scott Papers, WLLSC.

34. Davis to John H. Latane, Nov. 10, 1922, Chapel Controversy Files, WLLSC.

35. Anderson to Rogers, Oct. 5, 1922, Chapel Controversy Files, WLLSC.

36. W. Fitzhugh Brundage, "White Women and the Creation of a Southern Public Memory, 1865–1920," paper presented to Women in Preservation Conference, Mesa Verde, Ariz., Mar. 1997. Copy of paper supplied to the author.

37. James M. Lindgren, *Preserving the Old Dominion* (Charlottesville: Univ. Press of Virginia, 1992), 1–12. Lindgren's book is a history of the Association for the Preservation of Virginia Antiquities. He argues that the "Gospel of Preservation" was a means of asserting white, Anglo-Saxon, elite history as "the" history of Virginia. That sometimes meant the exclusion of African American history, as when the APVA refused to allow a plaque at Jamestown to mark the arrival of the first Africans to the country.

38. W. Donald Rhinesmith, "Traveller: 'Just the Horse for General Lee,'" *Virginia Cavalcade* (summer 1983): 38–39, and Stephanie E. Terwell, "Lee Chapel: Just One Symbol of Robert E. Lee," student paper prepared for Pamela H. Simpson, Apr. 1996, WLLSC.

39. Terwell, "Lee Chapel," 13. The Lynchburg firm of Clark, Nexsen, and Owen was in charge of the project.

40. The third week in January holds not only Robert E. Lee's birthday but also those of Stonewall Jackson and Martin Luther King Jr.—a juxtaposition that in Virginia, until the law was recently changed, resulted in the third Monday being named Robert E. Lee, Stonewall Jackson, and Martin Luther King Jr. Day— a joining that seems to reflect the sometimes uncomfortable ambiguity of the South's continued ties to traditionalism.

# 6

# Monument Avenue, Richmond

## A Unique American Boulevard

*Richard Guy Wilson*

MONUMENT AVENUE MARCHES OUT, a long cadence of homes, a progression of trees lining a boulevard interspersed with a rhythm of statues. In common with many of the other grand residential streets developed during the nineteenth and early twentieth centuries, Monument Avenue in Richmond, Virginia, became the preferred address for the wealthy and those who aspired to that status. It is lined with a mixture of dwellings, some large and impressive, others more modest, that represent the various fads and styles of American architecture from the 1890s to the 1920s.

Few of its 260 buildings, which include spacious apartment blocks and six churches, are architecturally distinguished by themselves. The avenue's impact comes instead from the overall harmony of scale, form, materials, and details of buildings and street that stretches for a mile and a half. This is a pattern repeated many times across the United States. What gives Monument Avenue a unique character and distinguishes it from other American avenues can be perceived in its name and defining feature—the monuments. Many other grand avenues have statues, but none contain a consistent iconographic program as does Monument Avenue. The program or narrative of Monument Avenue's statues is an homage by those who lost the Civil War to their leaders. On Monument Avenue stand Robert E. Lee, J. E. B. Stuart, Jefferson Davis, Thomas "Stonewall" Jackson, and Matthew Fontaine Maury, each a hero of the Lost Cause. The development of the avenue is intimately linked with these statues.

Monument Avenue (fig. 6.1) was laid out and built between the late 1880s and the 1920s; it is a divided boulevard, 140 feet wide, planted with parallel rows of maples and other trees along its center and a single row in front of the houses. The houses are set back an almost uniform fifteen feet from the street, and although they vary in size, style, and materials, there is an overall consistency. The core of the avenue that contains the five Confederate monuments is a fourteen-block section that stretches westward from Stuart Circle to Roseneath Road. Roseneath Road constituted Richmond's city limits for many years and also marks a boundary of Confederate earth works from the Civil War.

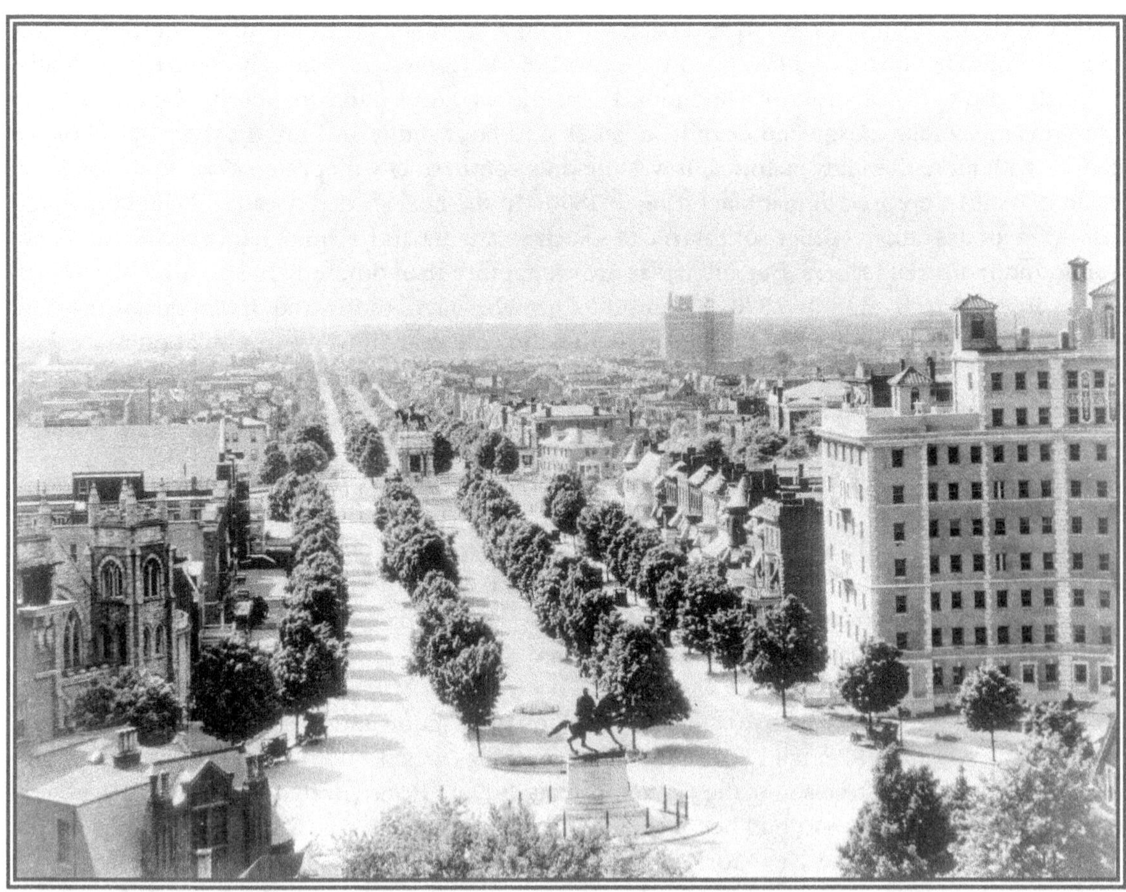

Fig. 6.1. Monument Avenue, Richmond, Virginia. View west from Stuart Circle, circa 1925, with Lee and Davis Monuments in the distance. Cook Collection, Valentine Museum / Richmond History Center.

## *Richmond and the New South*

The origins of Monument Avenue can be found in the diverse elements of Richmond's growing urban population, the need to express wealth in the form of residences, the concept of a New South, and the desire by many southerners to erect monuments to the recently vanquished. The Richmond that built the avenue thought of itself as the first city of the New South.[1] Beginning in the late 1880s and extending well into the early twentieth century, many southern leaders argued that the South could no longer be tied to its agrarian and hence poverty-stricken past; instead, the South had the possibility, with its resources both natural and physical, to establish a great industrial, commercial, and financial empire along with the requisite cultural emblems that would rival the North. According to these progressive leaders, the South should become modern. Urban rivalry with other southern cities and especially with northern cities was paramount. Nowhere was this attitude more prominent than Richmond.[2]

Before the Civil War, Richmond had been the industrial, financial, political, and cultural center of the South. That Richmond had been the capital of the Confederacy merely confirmed this fact. Since the end of Reconstruction, Richmond's business leaders had prospered. The city was the terminus of six railroads; a center of iron, steel, and flour mills; and the tobacco capital of the nation, with more than fifty factories. It was the only southern city that came close to the national mean of males employed in manufacturing in 1890.[3] In the next several decades Richmond would lose some of its status as other southern cities such as Atlanta and Birmingham eclipsed it as economic and industrial leaders. But still it was growing, more than doubling in size from 37,910 residents in 1860 to 81,338 in 1890. Richmond's growth stagnated in the 1890s because of the national depression of that decade, but in the next twenty years the city's population more than doubled to 171,667 in 1920. Both the established wealthy and the newly affluent who benefited from this growth needed an appropriate setting to illustrate their accomplishments, and Monument Avenue became a prime vehicle for this aspiration.

Richmond's natural growth, topographically and culturally, has always been toward the west. The James River to the south, uneven topography, and the expansion of the manufacturing and transportation belt in the other directions directed the growth of elite residential neighborhoods largely to the west of the commercial and governmental core.[4] Streetcar lines began to snake out to the west from the downtown in the 1870s, linking outlying parks and suburban developments. Monument Avenue is locally seen as an extension of the "Fan" or "West End," a group of streets that radiate out from the city at the western end beginning at Monroe Park. Although Monument Avenue formally begins at Lombardy Street, with the Stuart statue and circle at its eastern end, it is actually an extension of Franklin Street and hence provides an axis, both literally and symbolically, with the capitol square, the site of the Commonwealth's State House designed by Thomas Jefferson in the 1780s. Franklin Street had become since the 1830s the city's most prestigious residential address. In the 1890s the New York architectural firm of Carrère and Hastings designed on Franklin Street Richmond's great hotel, The Jefferson, and remodeled Richmond's elite club for men, the Commonwealth Club.

Three large undeveloped tracts of land, originally located just beyond the city line at the western end of Richmond and Franklin Street, made up the area in which Monument Avenue was constructed. This area was bisected by one road, Reservoir Avenue, which was renamed the Boulevard. The R. E. Lee Camp Soldier's Home, for Confederate veterans, was located on the Boulevard, and in the twentieth century that street would become the city's cultural acropolis. Monument Avenue was laid out, graded, and the surrounding land subdivided between 1889 and 1909. This was not done continuously but took place with starts and stops over the years as the city annexed the area and land was sold. Construction of houses, apartments, and churches followed the progression of the statues.

## *The Monuments*

The real beginning of Monument Avenue is 1870 and the death of Robert E. Lee. Immediately, two competitive Lee monument groups were born and began a series of unsuccessful campaigns to select a site and erect a monument to the former commander of the Army of Northern Virginia (fig. 6.2). In March 1886, under the leadership of the newly elected Gov. Fitzhugh Lee, a former Confederate general and also a nephew of R. E. Lee, the rivalrous groups were unified with him as

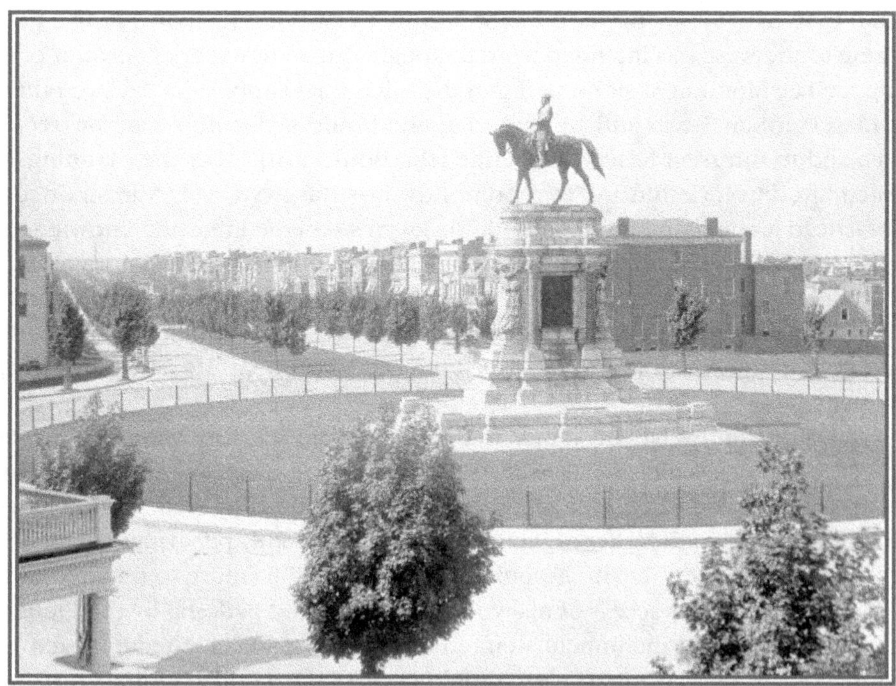

Fig. 6.2. The Lee Monument by Marius-Jean-Antonin Mercié, dedicated May 29, 1890. This 1925 picture also shows the new architecture and landscaping along Monument Avenue reaching to the Davis Monument in the distance. Cook Collection, Valentine Museum/Richmond History Center.

the chief officer. On June 18, 1887, the Lee Monument Commission selected a site just outside the western boundary, or West End, of Richmond. In October 1887 a sculptor was chosen, and the resultant statue was unveiled on May 29, 1890.[5]

The site of the Lee Monument lay within a tract of fifty-eight acres just beyond the western edge of the city owned by the heirs of William C. Allen who had died in 1874. Allen had been a very successful builder who had accumulated property. His son, Col. Otway S. Allen, was a socially prominent Richmond businessman, a friend of Governor Lee and later a member of Richmond's board of aldermen. He also had served in the war as commanding officer of Virginia's First Battalion. Allen offered to donate a site to the Lee Monument Commission and to build two broad intersecting boulevards around the monument and give them to the city. Although other sites around Richmond had been considered and this West End site was flat and bare, it had several possible advantages. The *Richmond Dispatch* described it as a broad open space on one of the "greatest elevations of the city . . . several feet above the Capitol site," which had earlier been proposed. Actually there were other higher sites, but they were discarded. The newspaper went on to explain: "A too close proximity of buildings has ruined some of the finest monuments in Europe."[6] Located at the end of prestigious Franklin Street, the site of the Lee Monument lay in a direct line with the capitol square. In 1892 the state legislature passed a law allowing the Allen tract, the Lee Monument, and another 292 acres in the area to be annexed by the city.[7]

Although it took many years for Monument Avenue to be built, the concept of a grand boulevard stretching to the west was intended from the beginning. A newspaper account of the debate surrounding the Lee Monument site stated that the Allen tract supporters declared that they proposed to widen Franklin Street and "to make a grand boulevard, with room for trees down the middle. & c., and to intersect Reservoir avenue [the Boulevard]."[8] For the planning of his tract Otway S. Allen hired Col. Collinson Pierrepoint Edwards Burgwyn, a Harvard-trained civil engineer who practiced architecture in Richmond. Burgwyn's scheme indicated knowledge of American and European boulevards such as Commonwealth Avenue in Boston, Monument Square in Baltimore, and Baron Georges Haussmann's transformations of Paris under Napoleon III. He laid out cross-axial boulevards with a fifty-foot-wide median and a round point of two hundred feet in diameter at the center of which would be placed the Lee Monument. He labeled the major boulevard "Monument Avenue."

While several competitions had been held in the past for the Lee statue, the new Lee Monument Commission chose French sculptor Marius-Jean-Antonin Mercié. Augustus Saint-Gaudens, the eminent American sculptor who had been a member of an earlier jury and a fellow student with Mercié at the École des Beaux-Arts and atelier of Jouffroy in Paris, apparently persuaded the new Lee Monument Board to select the Frenchman.[9] An outcry ensued over the failure to retain local talent, but the choice of Mercié and the success of his work, along with the pedestal by the French architect Paul Pujol, ultimately gave the monument an international flavor and elevated it far above parochial sentimentalism. This was no favorite-son sculptor but one of the world's leading artists who agreed to provide Richmond with a masterpiece. Lee, mounted on his horse Traveller, is presented as larger than life size, monumental, and impassive.[10]

The Lee Monument came at a critical juncture, for the war was now several decades in the past and memories of the grim carnage began to fade and be replaced with a romantic nostalgia. In the North the announcements and unveilings of major monuments and memorials gained momentum: Saint-Gaudens's Admiral Farragut Memorial, with the base by Stanford White, was unveiled on Madison Square in New York in 1881; the arch at the Grand Army of the Republic Plaza in Brooklyn was proposed in 1885 and completed in 1892; and the Grant Tomb in New York was announced in 1885, though not completed until 1897. All of this activity was part of a wider tendency by Americans to immortalize the American past, to create what was termed an American Renaissance.[11] In this context the monument to General Lee became part of the monumentalization of the War between the States. But Lee's reputation also underwent a substantial shift in meaning; he became not a rebel but a great American hero, a tragic personage of noble dimensions caught in an unsolvable conflict between his state (Virginia) and his nation.[12]

The Lee Monument (see fig. 0.2) was dedicated in May 1890 at a huge celebration whose audience was estimated at between 100,000 and 150,000, larger than the population of Richmond. A grand parade wound through the city so it would pass Lee's former home. At its head as chief marshal was former Gov. and Gen. Fitzhugh Lee, and more than forty other generals either marched or rode along with governors from the former Confederate states and 15,000 veterans. Especially honored were the widows of Stonewall Jackson and George Pickett.

Not every Richmonder hailed the occasion; the black councilman and owner of the *Planet* newspaper, John Mitchell Jr., argued vehemently against any city money spent on the occasion. His paper argued that the entire proceeding handed down a "legacy of treason and blood" to future generations. For the Lee Monument came at precisely the time when southern lynchings of blacks were increasing and Jim Crow laws were instated.[13] From the North also came a few expressions of outrage that a statue to Lee could be erected: a Philadelphia newspaper compared him to Benedict Arnold, while the *New York Mail and Express* proposed a congressional law that would ban monuments of Confederate heroes and displays of the Confederate flag. But other northerners saw it differently. For them the monument was not a rebellious act, for, as the *New York Times* editorialized, Lee was brave and honorable: "His memory is, therefore, a possession of the American people."[14]

The other monuments lining the avenue have similar stories of complicated and conflicted origins and elaborate dedications. Ideas for a monument to the Confederate cavalry leader J. E. B. Stuart had been announced as early as 1875 but not until 1903 was a competition held. Former Governor Lee chaired the competition committee and Richmond sculptor Edward V. Valentine served on it. Frederick Moynihan, a sculptor from New York who had worked on the monument for years, won the competition; he had worked for Valentine as a studio assistant. The selection of the site on Monument Avenue came in September 1904, and the statue (figs. 6.3 and 6.4) was unveiled on May 30, 1907, at the opening ceremony of the annual Confederate Reunion.[15] In addition to the proximity to Lee, the site further recommended itself as just a few miles from the site of Stuart's death in 1864 and close to the old church from which he was buried. Stuart is portrayed as a cavalry leader, twisting in his saddle.

A few days later, on June 3, the monument to Jefferson Davis (figs. 6.5 and 4.3) was unveiled on the ninety-ninth anniversary of his birth, to a crowd variously estimated between eighty thousand and two hundred thousand. The United Daughters of the Confederacy had sponsored the Davis memorial, and in July 1903 they had chosen Valentine as the sculptor and William C. Noland, also of Richmond, at the architect of the setting. After much controversy a site on Monument Avenue was selected because it was the location of the Star Fort, a piece of the Confederate defense line in the siege of Richmond. A cannon located just east of the Davis Monument further commemorates the site. Davis stands in front of a giant—sixty-foot-high—Doric column capped by Vindicatrix, a representation of the spirit of the South, with the inscription "Deo Vindice." Behind this is an exedra of thirteen Doric columns symbolizing the states that made up the Confederacy or sent troops in support.[16]

The cornerstone for the Stonewall Jackson Monument (fig. 6.6) was laid during the twenty-fifth Confederate Reunion of 1915, but a "penetrating misty rain" preempted the large parade of the by-now aging veterans.[17] The unveiling took place four years later on October 11, 1919, the fifty-sixth anniversary of Jackson's death at Chancellorsville. A parade of Virginia Military Institute students and other veterans marked the occasion, and Col. Robert E. Lee, the great general's grandson, gave the oration. The sculptor was F. William Sievers, who had studied in Italy and France. In 1910 Sievers won a competition for the grand-scale Virginia Monument at Gettysburg and moved to Richmond, where he remained for the rest of this life.[18]

Sievers also was the sculptor for the fifth and last Confederate monument, to Matthew Fontaine Maury. Interest in a monument to Maury began in 1912 when it was pointed out that while he was scarcely recognized at home he had an international reputation in navigation, meteorology, and oceanography, along with the invention of the electric torpedo and service as a Confederate diplomat. A Maury Committee formed by the Richmond Woman's Club along with the United Daughters of the Confederacy began to raise funds in 1916; the cornerstone was laid in June

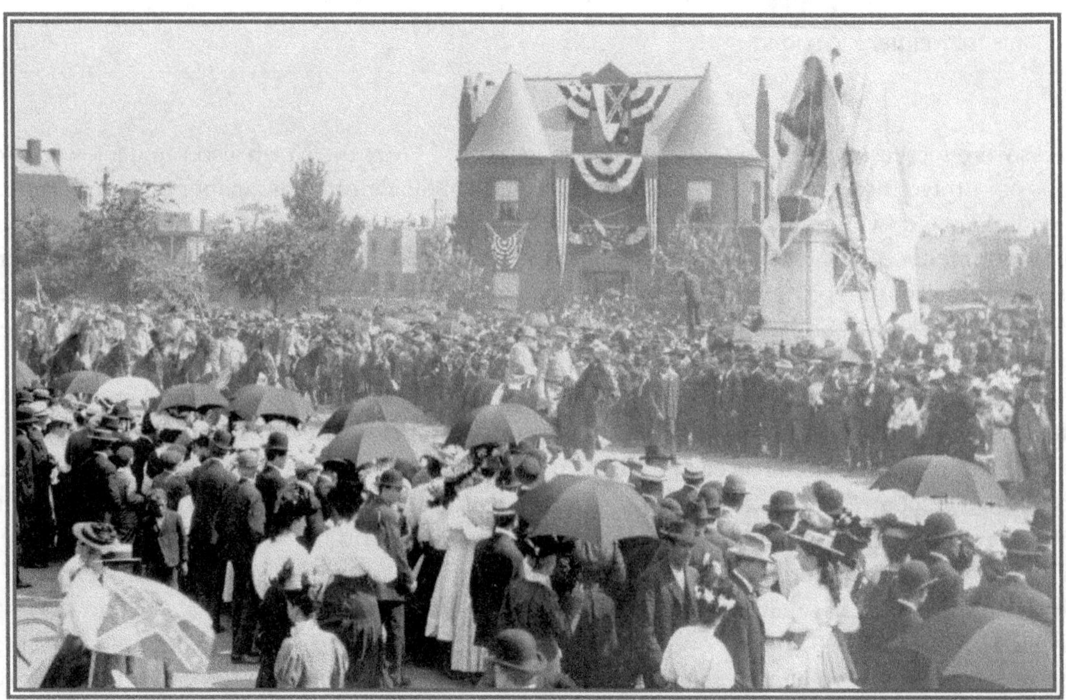

Fig. 6.3. Unveiling of the J. E. B. Stuart statue, designed by sculptor Frederick Moynihan, on Monument Avenue, May 30, 1907. Cook Collection, Valentine Museum/Richmond History Center.

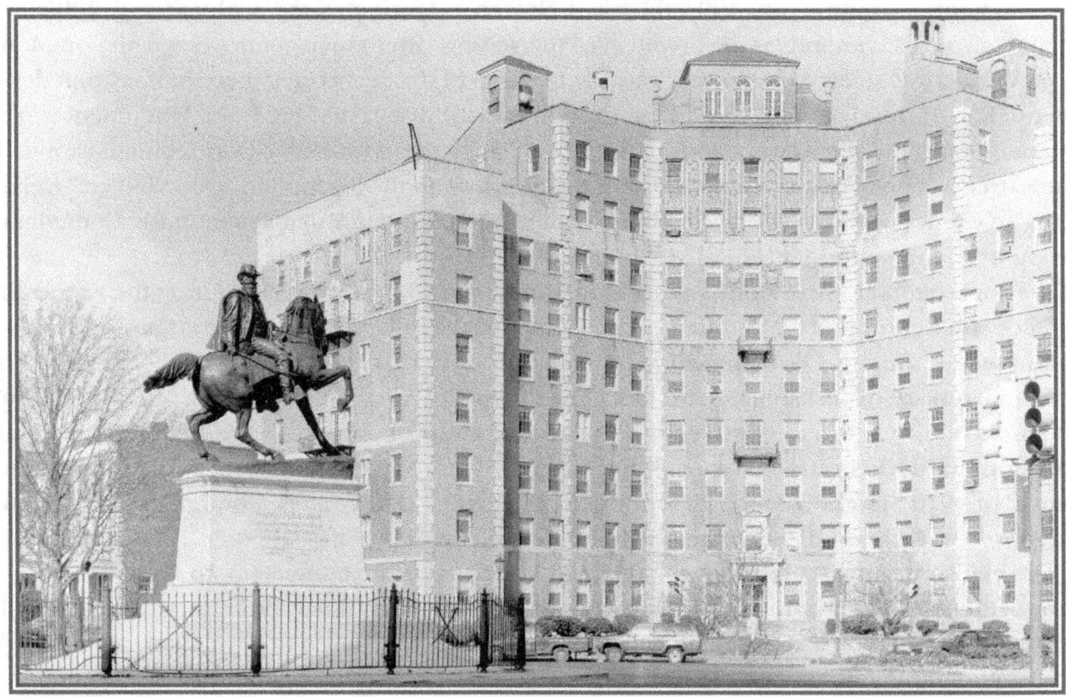

Fig. 6.4. J. E. B. Stuart statue and Stuart Circle Apartments, William Lawrence Bottomley, architect, on Monument Avenue, 1924. Historic American Buildings Survey, Library of Congress.

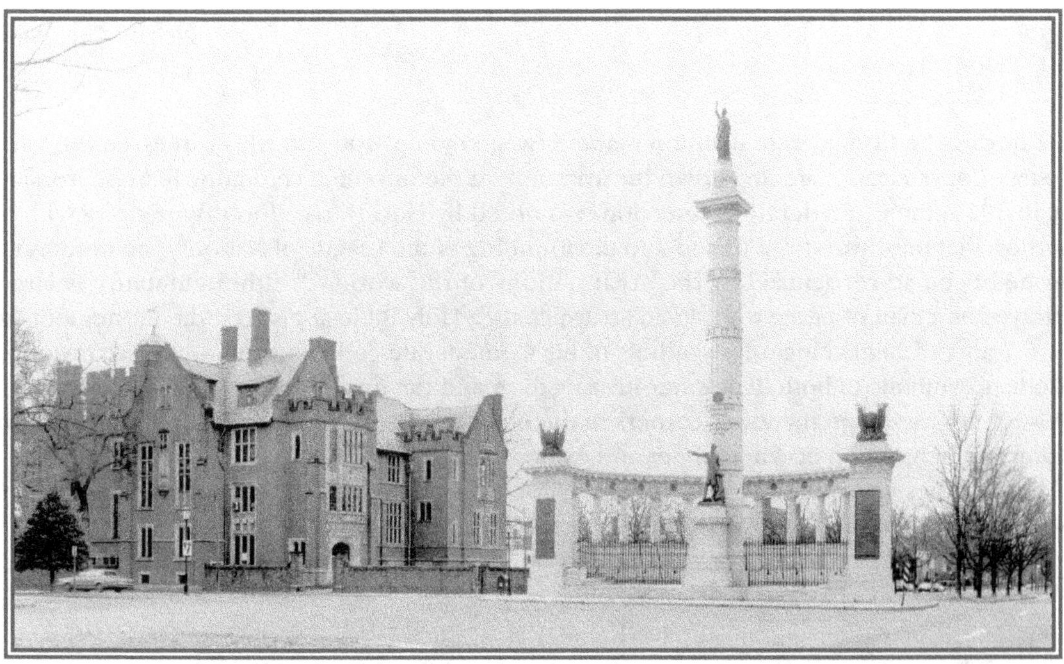

Fig. 6.5. Jefferson Davis memorial, designed by William C. Noland and Edward V. Valentine and dedicated June 3, 1907. John Kerr Branch house, 1917–19, John Russell Pope, architect. Monument Avenue. Historic American Buildings Survey, Library of Congress.

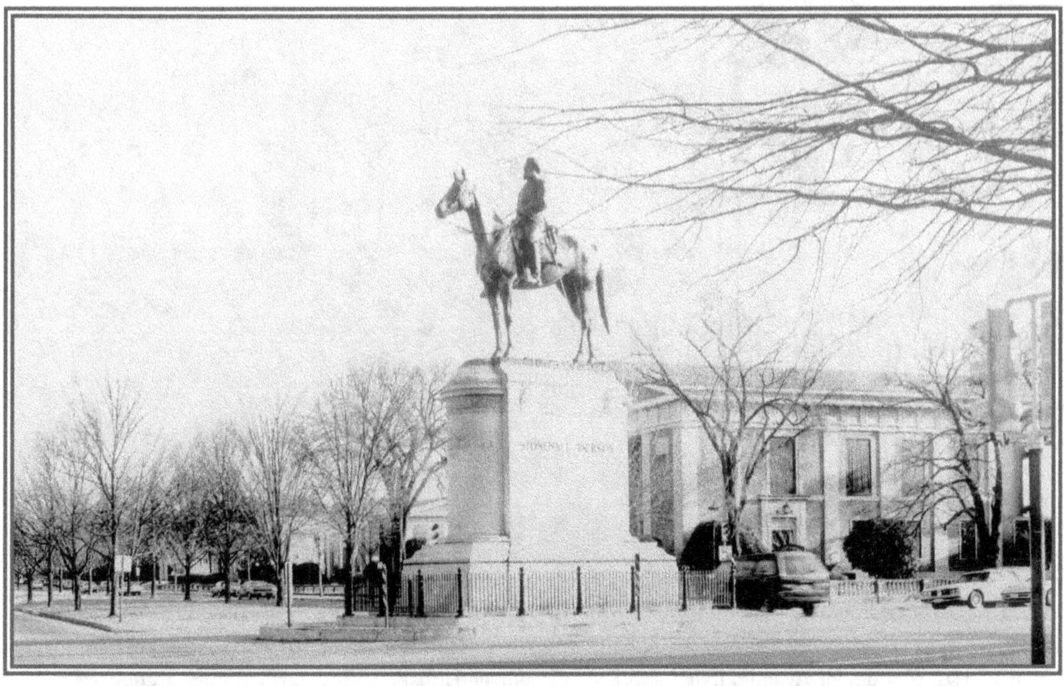

Fig. 6.6. Thomas "Stonewall" Jackson statue, designed by William F. Sievers and dedicated October 11, 1919. First Baptist Church, 1927–29, Herbert Levi Cain and Joseph P. Hudnut, architects. Monument Avenue. Historic American Buildings Survey, Library of Congress.

1922 during the Confederate Reunion marked by a crowd of 100,000 who witnessed the "slowing steps" of veterans marching down the avenue.[19] At the unveiling ceremony held on Armistice Day in 1929, the Confederate connection was noted by Gov. Harry Flood Byrd along with the assertion that until Woodrow Wilson and the founding of the League of Nations, "no other American had been so recognized by the great nations of the world."[20] Although Maury is largely portrayed as a man of peace who sits in an armchair, a Holy Bible at his feet, the monument (see figs. 6.7 and 14.2) also includes symbols of his Confederate contributions—electric ray or torpedo fish, symbolic of both deepwater investigation and the invention of the electric torpedo in 1861–62, are carved on the lower corners of the pedestal. The giant globe behind him recalls his accomplishments as an oceanographer and explorer.[21]

These statues give Monument Avenue much of its character and indeed its meaning. It is not just a street of memories, however, but also one where people lived.

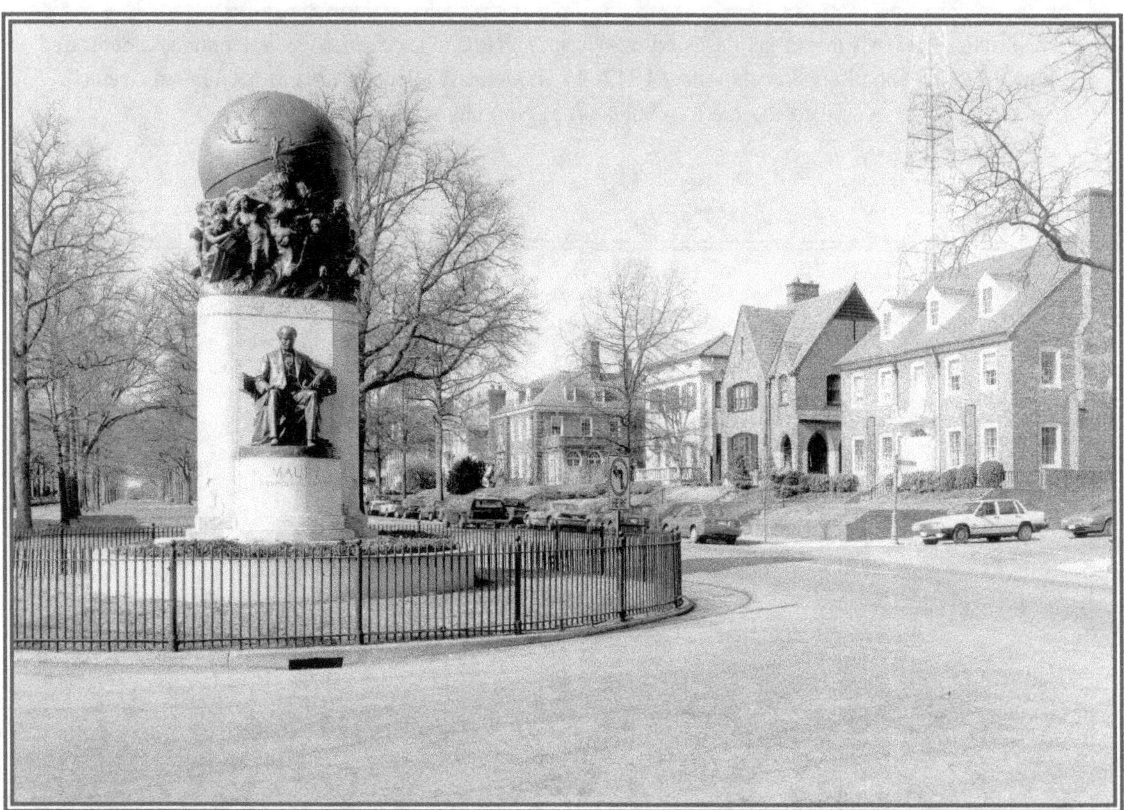

Fig. 6.7. Matthew Fontaine Maury monument, unveiled November 11, 1929, sculptor William F. Sievers. Houses. *Right to left,* 3100 Monument Avenue, Merrill E. Rabb house, 1926, W. Duncan Lee, architect; 3102 Monument Avenue, Irving and Elsie Greentree House, 1931, Carl Lindner, architect; 3104 Monument Avenue, Harold E. Calisch house, 1928, Davis Brothers, architects. Historic American Buildings Survey, Library of Congress.

## *Building on the Avenue*

While the Lee Monument and layout by Colonel Burgwyn was intended by Otway S. Allen to be the site of a prestigious neighborhood, nothing much happened between 1890 and 1901. The Allen family lots sold well to various speculators but no building occurred. The reasons are not far to seek. The great depression that gripped the United States in the 1890s hit Richmond hard—not until 1898 did the local economy recover to the levels of 1892. Similarly the city provided little in the way of urban amenities to people seeking to locate on the avenue. In spite of Burgwyn's (and Allen's) projection of lavishly planted central medians, the planting did not get under way until after 1900. In 1901 utilities were extended to the avenue and the first house was built. Henry James visited the Lee Monument in 1905 as part of his "pilgrim's return" and described the statue as isolated: "The place is the mere vague centre of two or three crossways, without form and void, with a circle half sketched by three or four groups of small, new, mean houses."[22]

James was too critical. In actuality the Lee Monument was laid out and defined, the roads were graded and graveled, curbs and sidewalks were installed, and at least twelve buildings were up with several more under construction.[23] By 1904 more than two hundred scarlet and sugar maple trees had been planted from what would be Stuart Circle along three blocks to the west.[24] In late 1905 the city of Richmond begin to lay out the remainder of the avenue westward from the Allen property to the Boulevard and in August 1906 the name formally became Monument Avenue.[25] Slightly earlier in 1904 the city permitted property owners to pave the sidewalks in front of their houses. Paving of the avenue with asphalt Belgian blocks did not commence until 1908 and it continued into 1910. These improvements occurred at the same time as the placement of the Stuart and Davis statues and the beginning of substantial home construction. Home construction, as both land records and photographs show, followed rather than led the westward progression of the monuments, which gave the avenue its distinctive character.

House construction began on the avenue in 1901. The deeds granting the property mandated "brick stone dwellings," set back twenty feet from the street, which changed to fifteen feet when sidewalks were introduced in 1904.[26] By 1905 fourteen houses had been built near the Lee Monument. By 1910 there were fifty-three houses on the avenue, with most clustered at the eastern end. In the next decade home building doubled to 109 houses between the Stuart and Jackson statues.

Monument Avenue from its beginning was a solid middle-upper-income neighborhood known for its prestigious residents and elegant houses. Among the earliest residents was Isaac Thalhimer, owner of a large city department store; O. H. Funsten, a leading realtor; Oliver J. Sands, president of the American National Bank; and D. C. Richardson, mayor of Richmond in 1908. Just before his death, Otway Allen commissioned a house (at 1631) in the block east of the Lee statue, but he did not live to see it completed. Several other members of the Allen family also built on the avenue over the years.

John P. Branch, who owned one of Monument Avenue's original tracts, never lived on the avenue, but a number of his children and other family members built extensively. The Branch money came from financial investments, especially their ownership of the Merchants National Bank, which was one of the largest firms in the South. John P.'s son, John K. Branch, was given a house site on the south side of Monument Avenue in 1903. John K. Branch and his wife, Beulah, did not build there until 1917, when they began construction of the largest house on the avenue after designs of John Russell Pope. The house, stylistically derivative of Compton Wynates in

Warwickshire, England, became one of Richmond's gems.[27] It stood in one of the most prominent locations on the avenue, a backdrop for the Davis statue. Intended as a showpiece for John Kerr Branch's extensive collection of furniture and tapestries, the house, while partaking of twisted chimney stacks of molded brick, diamond-shaped panes of windows, and other Tudor and early English Renaissance details, was in plan and in the balanced facades reflective of Beaux-Arts classical composition.

Stylistically the houses of Monument Avenue are varied. They range from the restless pyrotechnics of the earliest houses clustered between the Stuart and Lee monuments, which reflect the Richardsonian Romanesque and the Queen Anne, to a much calmer classicism that began to dominate after 1900. The early houses stand out with their towers and rounded bays. After 1900 the various classical idioms would dominate, but a few stylistic heretics did appear, such as the Jacobean house for Henry S. Wallerstein, and a couple of half-timbered designs. Other alternatives included the Mediterranean or the Italio-Spanish idiom, as with the house for J. Scott Parrish (president of a concrete company and a vice president of the Richmond Chamber of Commerce) designed by William Lawrence Bottomley in 1922. Although the light-colored stucco facades made the house stand out against the ubiquitous darker brick of much of the avenue, stylistically it was essentially classical. Bottomley also employed the Mediterranean idiom for the nine-story Stuart Court Apartments, 1924–26, located at the eastern end of the avenue at Stuart Circle. Another stylistic variation was the Italian Renaissance idiom as in the John Wilson house, 1911, at 2037 on the avenue. Wilson was a successful building contractor and may have used his own designers to create an Americanized—and indeed southernized—version of an Italian Renaissance palazzo in red brick and limestone trim.[28]

Although many styles are present, a common classical basis exists for most of the houses on Monument Avenue. The most prominent stylistic expression is a variation on the American Colonial, Georgian, and English revivals. Linked by their common bonds in that American Colonial is a derivative of English Georgian and also late-seventeenth- and early-eighteenth-century Queen Anne, these stylistic choices reflect an American Renaissance origin for the avenue. Additionally, there is a Virginia source for some of the stylistic choices, since the Commonwealth was the origin for a number of the red brick and white-trimmed colonial styles in use. Even more localized was the view that Southern Colonial meant columns and large porticos. Although in retrospect it is recognized that the large-columned portico is really a Federal and Greek Revival feature, still at the time it was widely believed to be genuinely Southern Colonial and specifically Virginian.[29]

This Colonial-Georgian revival had nationalistic and cosmopolitan connotations in that it was the style of the founders of the United States while at the same time having links to England and ultimately to the great classical heritage of Rome and Greece. The architecture on Monument Avenue, as with the monuments, was intended to demonstrate a connection to the great heritage of Western civilization. At the same time, the Colonial-English had particularized Virginia connections in that stylistic variants were generic to the state, and Virginians liked to claim their—real or imagined—English aristocratic connections. Here was an idiom both national and international, democratic and aristocratic, and capable of infinite variation.

Adding an air of architectural counterpoint to the residences was the ecclesiastical landscape. At the far eastern end, actually on Franklin Street and just beyond the avenue, stands St. James Episcopal Church, 1912, designed by Richmond architect William C. Noland. St. James's tall spire, inspired by Wren and Gibbs London churches and early American derivatives, provides a visual terminus to the avenue. At Stuart Circle, Charles Robinson designed the German Lutheran (now the First English) Evangelical Church in 1912, and Carl Lindner provided plans for St. John's United Church of Christ of 1932. Located in the middle of the next block is John Kevan Peebles's Grace Covenant Presbyterian Church, 1920–22. Peebles came from Norfolk and was one of the few turn-of-the-century Virginia architects to gain a reputation beyond the state.[30] These churches with their stumpy towers and finials break the three-story residential skyline and add a picturesque and medieval note to the avenue. Other churches were added to the avenue over the years, such as the very large and imposing Greco-Colonial First Baptist, located adjacent to the Boulevard. All of the churches on the avenue actually had been located closer in to the city core but were moved out as the population shifted to the west.[31]

## *The Modern Avenue*

The depression of the 1930s brought an end to virtually all building on Monument Avenue, and in the post–World War II years many of the original families sold their homes and departed to the suburbs. Some residences in the area closest to downtown were converted to rooming houses, apartments, or businesses. John Russell Pope's Branch house, for example, became an insurance office. Only a few postwar buildings were constructed on the avenue, the most prominent of which was the Lee Medical Building (1950–51) on Lee Circle. Still Monument Avenue remained an address of distinction and, beginning in the mid-1970s, a reverse trend was perceived as some houses were converted back to single-family dwellings and either renovated or restored. Assisting in this development was the designation in 1971 of Monument Avenue as a national, state, and local historical district. The Historic Monument Avenue and Fan District Association was created in 1976, and in 1998 Monument Avenue was listed as a National Historic Landmark. More problematical have been the monuments, because to many, and especially to African Americans, they symbolize an ignoble past. Consequently, there have been proposals to remove them or to construct monuments to the heroes of the civil rights movement. A statue honoring African American tennis player Arthur Ashe was dedicated in 1996 at the intersection of Roseneath (see chapter 14, "Contesting the Sacred: Preservation and Meaning on Richmond's Monument Avenue"). Small celebrations are still held on the birthdays of Lee and his accompanying cohorts, and every Easter a giant Easter egg hunt is held for the children of the neighborhood.

Created during the great wave of city rebuilding and civic art at the turn of the century, Monument Avenue remains one of the finest illustrations of the American Renaissance and the City Beautiful movement. With the revived economy that followed the depression of the 1890s, as well as the powerful influence of turn-of-the-century city beautification schemes in Washington, D.C., San Francisco, Denver, and other places, and with the many "White Cities" or expositions that were built across the country, Richmonders turned their attention to the avenue and installed more monuments and built houses.[32] Streets began to display harmonizing landscaping and architecture, a favorite feature of the emerging profession of city planning in the early twentieth century. Although Monument Avenue is part of the City Beautiful movement, it has a unique character that results from its completeness and overall level of thematic design, not to mention its mission as a memorial.

It may be a place of residences and churches, a street of movement and communication, but ultimately Monument Avenue is the site of memorials to the Confederacy. And it is back to these statues one must come, for their message cannot be ignored. The three equestrian statues of Lee, Stuart, and Jackson are all military memorials and give ample indication of a persistent strain on American culture—especially strong in southern culture—of a martial spirit. America proclaims its peace-loving nature, yet it fought on its soil one of the bloodiest wars of any nation. But the gore is gone from Monument Avenue. All that remains are ennobling portraits. Maury is essentially depicted as a man of peace, even though a few subtle symbols indicate his Confederate involvement. The Davis statue at the middle of the row is symbolically the center, protected by Lee, Stuart, and Jackson. Davis gestures toward the State House from which he ruled the Confederacy, and on the monument appears the inscription "Deo Vindice," or "God Be Our Vindicator." The meaning is clear—that right was on the side of the Confederacy; its battle for states' rights and to preserve slavery was a noble and just cause. Certainly there were noble individuals on both sides of the war, Union and Confederate, but there can be no question now of what was right and that the Lost Cause was a wrong cause. Henry James felt this when he viewed Lee's statue in 1905: "I looked back, before leaving it, at Lee's stranded, bereft image, which time and fortune have so cheated of half the significance, and so, I think, of half the dignity, of great memorials, I recognized something more than the melancholy of a lost cause. The whole infelicity speaks of a cause that could never have been gained."[33] If symbolically Monument Avenue recedes into a mixed past of both glory and deprivation of rights, still there is another and possibly a greater message.

As a grand plan, as a public space, as form, and as a unified streetscape, Monument Avenue is an important example of American city building. It represents a particularly American type of urban space, for it has evolved a certain unity in spite of the diversity of its parts. Seldom are great public urban spaces in American created as finite units; instead, they come into being over time. A good initial plan is essential, but on the scale on which Americans have built, few people can foresee the conclusion. The monuments added to the avenue over the years provide focal points, vertical thrusts against the march of the street and the buildings. On Monument Avenue the buildings are not identical units. Rather, they are closely spaced individual designs. Taken separately they represent a potpourri, an anarchy of styles and forms. They do not present a solid wall: some buildings project large windows and porches, others present facades nearly flush to the street. And there is variation in the size and height of the buildings, ranging from the tall medical center and apartment buildings at Stuart Circle to the different churches and many houses. But within this mixture of architecture, these counterpoints of rhythm, enough of a repetition occurs to provide order. These structures represent a concurrence of belief on the part of the architects and their patrons as to what makes appropriate architecture.

The greatest unity is provided by Monument Avenue itself. Spatially, it is long and linear; at times, as in the circles around the Stuart and Lee monuments, it pushes out, but ultimately it is a longitudinal space. It is the stretch of the street, its constant width, its paving, curbstones, and sidewalks that help provide unity.[34] The landscaping, the horizontal sweep of the green grass of the median, and the trees soften the conflicting architecture and provide a measured rhythm to the contrasting forms of buildings. The trees provide a necessary sequencing, a stepped pattern of space. And then there are the monuments: different and yet unified in their iconography, they are the focus. It is this interaction between the monuments, the buildings, the landscaping, and the street that makes Monument Avenue a unique American place.

## *Notes*

This essay is an abridged version of "Monument Avenue, Richmond," which appeared in *The Grand American Avenue, 1850–1920,* ed. Jan Cigliano and Sarah Bradford Landau (San Francisco: Pomegranate Artbooks; Washington, D.C.: American Architectural Foundation, 1994): 259–79. It is reprinted with permission of the Octagon, the museum of the American Architectural Foundation, Washington, D.C. A more lengthy treatment can be found in Sarah Shields Driggs, Richard Guy Wilson, and Robert P. Winthrop, *Richmond's Monument Avenue* (Chapel Hill: Univ. of North Carolina Press, 2001). For background and research I am greatly indebted to my former student Carden C. McGehee Jr. and his thesis, "The Planning, Sculpture, and Architecture of Monument Avenue, Richmond, Virginia" (master's thesis, Univ. of Virginia, 1980), and to the Historic American Buildings Survey and Kathy Edwards, Esme Howard, and Tony Prawl, *Monument Avenue, History and Architecture* (Washington, D.C.: U.S. Dept. of Interior, National Park Service Cultural Resources, HABS/HAER, 1992). During the post–World War II years, Monument Avenue was extended out into Henrico County for a total length of a little more than five miles; however, this area is of a different character and not integral to this article.

1. The term *New South* comes from Henry Grady, editor of the *Atlanta Constitution* in the 1880s. See Henry Grady, *The New South: Writings and Speeches of Henry Grady* (Savannah: Beehive Press, 1971). The classic study is C. Van Woodward, *Origins of the New South, 1877–1913* (Baton Rouge: Louisiana State Univ., 1951).

2. For Richmond, see Virginius Dabney, *Richmond: The Story of a City* (Garden City: Doubleday and Co., 1976), and Marie Tyler-McGraw, *At the Falls: Richmond, Virginia, and Its People* (Richmond: Valentine Museum, and Chapel Hill: University of North Carolina Press, 1994). On southern cities, see David R. Goldfield, *Cotton Fields and Skyscrapers, Southern City and Region, 1607–1980* (Baton Rouge: Louisiana State Univ. Press, 1982), and Blaine A. Brownell and David R. Goldfield, eds., *The City in Southern History* (Port Washington, N.Y.: Kennikat Press, 1977).

3. Howard N. Rabinowitz, "Southern Development, 1860–1900," in Brownell and Goldfield, *The City in Southern History,* 109.

4. Ginter Park, laid out in 1892, is to the north and is an exception to this observation.

5. *Richmond Dispatch,* May 25, 29–31, June 3, 1890, all cover the unveiling. Jay Killian Bowman Williams, *Changed Views and Unforeseen Prosperity: Richmond of 1890 Gets a Monument to Lee* (Richmond: Privately Printed, 1969) is an excellent study of the Lee Monument and the beginnings of Monument Avenue. Also of importance for chronology is "The Lee Monument at Richmond," *Southern Historical Society Papers* 17 (1890): 187–355. See also Driggs, Wilson, and Winthrop, *Richmond's Monument Avenue,* 37–55. The complicated story of the rival groups for the Lee monument and the issue of patronage and role of women with the different statues is treated in *Richmond's Monument Avenue.* Also see John M. Coski and Amy R. Feely, "A Monument to Southern Womanhood," in *A Woman's War,* ed. Edward D. C. Campbell Jr. and Kym S. Rice (Richmond: Museum of the Confederacy, and Charlottesville: Univ. Press of Virginia, 1996), 131–63.

6. "Statue and Sculptor," *Richmond Dispatch,* May 29, 1890. Additional accounts of debate for the site can be found in the *Richmond Dispatch,* June 19 and Oct. 12, 1886. See also Williams, *Changed Views,* chap. 3.

7. City of Richmond, *Common Council Journal, 1890–1894,* 262; and Williams, *Changed Views,* 41.

8. *Richmond Dispatch,* June 19, 1886.

9. "Equestrian Monuments, XLIV," *American Architect and Building News* 34 (Nov. 1891): 104–5. See also Ulrich Troubetzkoy, "The Lee Monument," *Virginia Cavalcade Magazine* 12 (spring 1962): 5–10. Homer

Saint-Gardens, ed., *The Reminiscences of Augustus Saint-Gaudens* (New York: Century Co., 1913), 2:47; see also 1:74–77.

10. Joseph T. Knox, "Le general Lee," *Virginia Cavalcade* 38 (autumn 1988): 76–85.

11. Richard Guy Wilson, Dianne Pilgrim, and Richard N. Murray, *The American Renaissance, 1876–1917* (Brooklyn: Brooklyn Museum, 1979).

12. Thomas L. Connelly, *The Marble Man* (New York: Alfred A. Knopf, 1977), covers the transformation of the Lee myth. Gaines M. Foster, *Ghosts of the Confederacy* (New York: Oxford Univ. Press, 1987) covers the various memorials and activities of the organizations.

13. For other opposing views on Monument Avenue's Confederate sculpture, see the essay by Brian Black and Bryn Varley in chapter 14 of this anthology. *Richmond Planet,* May 31, 1890, quoted in Williams, *Changed Views,* 60; and Dabney, *Richmond,* 242. See also Foster, *Ghosts,* 101–3.

14. *New York Times,* May 30, 1890; others quoted in Williams, *Changed Views,* 63.

15. Ulrich Troubetzkoy, "The Best Picture of General Stuart," *Virginia Cavalcade Magazine* 12 (winter 1962–63): 40–47.

16. John H. Moore, "The Jefferson Davis Monument," *Virginia Cavalcade Magazine* 10 (spring 1961): 29–34; Foster, *Ghosts,* 158–59.

17. *Richmond Times-Dispatch,* June 3–4, 1915.

18. Ibid., Oct. 11–12, 1919. Ulrich Troubetzkoy, "F. William Sievers, Sculptor," *Virginia Cavalcade Magazine* 12 (autumn 1962): 5–12.

19. *Richmond Times-Dispatch,* June 22–23, 1922; *Richmond News-Leader,* June 22–23, 1922.

20. Troubetzkoy, "F. William Sievers," 11; and *Richmond Dispatch,* Nov. 12, 1929.

21. *Richmond News-Leader,* Mar. 9, 1929.

22. Henry James, *The American Scene* (1907; New York: Horizon Press, 1967), 393. James originally published the Richmond section in *Fortnightly Review* 86 (1906).

23. Driggs, Wilson, Winthrop, *Richmond's Monument Avenue,* 100, 113, 247–54.

24. City Engineer, *Trees of the City* (Richmond: O. E. Flanhart Printing Co., 1904), 4. Maple trees are still used east of the Boulevard to Stuart Circle. From the Boulevard west to Roseneath pen oaks and willow oaks are used. West of Roseneath the landscaping is more varied, with various trees, and none near the end.

25. Richmond, Virginia, *Board of Alderman Journal 1901–1906,* entries for Aug. 14, 1906, and Oct. 11, 1906; and *Common Council Journal, 1902–1906,* entries for Jan. 2, 1906, and Aug. 16, 1906.

26. Williams, *Changed Views,* 47.

27. William B. O'Neal, "The Multiple Life of Space," *Arts in Virginia Magazine* 5, no. 3 (1965): 1–11, gives a basic history of the Branch house. According to Stephen Bedford, author of *John Russell Pope, Architect of Empire* (New York: Rizzoli, 1998), the design is probably the work of Pope's partner, Otto R. Eggers, with Pope as critic.

28. Wilson did some projects with William L. Carneal, and Carneal and Johnston probably designed it. However, the Wilson house also has some similarities to Noland and Henry Baskervill's YWCA in Richmond, at 6 North Fifth Street, of 1913. On Bottomley, see William B. O'Neal and Christopher Weeks, *The Work of William Lawrence Bottomley in Richmond* (Charlottesville: Univ. Press of Virginia, 1985), and Davyd Foard Hood, "William Lawrence Bottomley in Virginia: The 'Neo-Georgian' Houses in Richmond," (master's thesis, Univ. of Virginia, 1975).

29. For a fuller development of this topic, see my "Building on the Foundations: The Historical Present in Virginia Architecture, 1870–1990," in *The Making of Virginia Architecture,* ed. Charles Brownell, Calder Loth, William Rasmussen, and Richard Guy Wilson (Richmond: Virginia Museum of Fine Arts, 1992), 108–27.

30. Peeble's biography is frequently misstated; see Brownell et al., *The Making of Virginia Architecture*, 115–16, 382.

31. Ulrich Troubetzkoy, *Richmond City of Churches* (Richmond: Whittet and Shepperson, 1957), 18. The 130-room First Baptist was designed by Richmond architect H. L. Cain, with the University of Virginia professor (and later dean at Harvard) Joseph Hudnut as consulting architect in the late 1920s. In some cases, the land churches occupied on Monument Avenue came through gifts. For example, Whitmell S. Forbes, who built a giant house out beyond Roseneath, donated the land for the First Baptist Church.

32. For background on the City Beautiful movement, see Wilson, Pilgrim, and Murray, *The American Renaissance;* and William H. Wilson, *The City Beautiful Movement* (Baltimore: Johns Hopkins Univ. Press, 1989).

33. James, *The American Scene,* 394.

34. The paving of Monument Avenue in recent years has been a subject of controversy. After repeated protest against asphalt surfaces, some Belgian blocks remain between Stuart Circle and the Boulevard. See the essay by Brian Black and Bryn Varley, chapter 14 in this anthology, for further discussion of it. The remainder out to the end is a continuous asphalt surface.

# 7

# Personalizing the Political

## THE DAVIS FAMILY CIRCLE IN RICHMOND'S HOLLYWOOD CEMETERY

*M. Anna Fariello*

CONFEDERATE PRESIDENT JEFFERSON DAVIS, First Lady Varina Howell Davis, and their six children rest in a circular family plot at the southernmost corner of Richmond's Hollywood Cemetery. There, on a high bluff overlooking the James River, visitors may contemplate three larger-than-life sculptures (fig. 7.1), which artist George Julian Zolnay created between 1899 and 1911 to memorialize the former political leader and his two daughters. While the three memorials are similar in scale, they are strikingly different in design. Each eulogized an individual and appealed to a different audience; each is a symbol of the changing ideals and conflicts that marked life in the postwar South.[1]

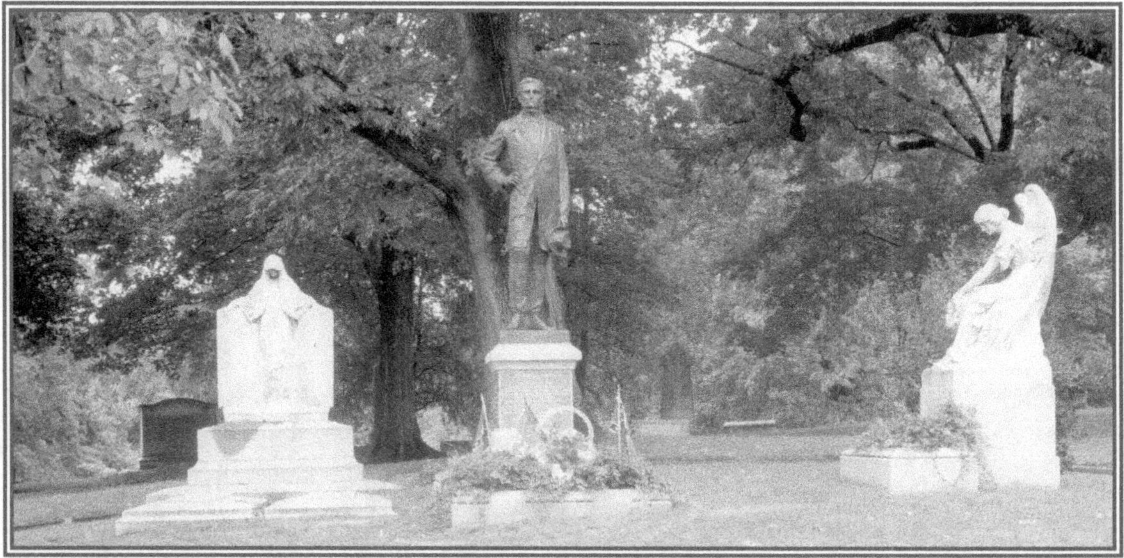

Fig. 7.1. Davis Family Circle, Hollywood Cemetery, Richmond, Virginia. The three figurative monuments, all designed by sculptor George Julian Zolnay, honor, *left to right,* Margaret Howell Davis Hayes (1911); Jefferson Davis (1899); and Varina Anne "Winnie" Davis (1899). Photograph by Sean McCormally.

In the center of the Davis family burial circle stands a realistic bronze figure of the former president. A portrait, in contrast to the allegorical figures marking the graves of his two daughters, it presents a rational, decisive, and dominating male presence. While Davis won a place in history as the first and only president of the Confederate States of America, his life—both political and personal—was marked by loss. Zolnay's dignified sculpture seems an effort to restore Davis's legacy as a gentleman and—given the circumstances of his defeat and capture—as a man. Confronting the viewer directly, the idealized likeness proclaims Davis's role as patriarch.

In contrast, the flanking memorials seem demure and deferential. The youthful innocence of Varina Anne "Winnie" Davis, beloved "Daughter of the Confederacy," is commemorated with a white marble winged figure that became one of Zolnay's most popular creations. Although its stylized and somewhat saccharine pose may seem to belie such a title, the image became known as the *Angel of Grief.*

The only twentieth-century statue in the plot marks the grave of Davis's eldest daughter, Margaret Howell Davis Hayes. In this later memorial Zolnay may have attempted a synthesis with regard to gender. A thoroughly androgynous figure stands with head bowed and arms outstretched within the open pages of a large book. Positioned at the outer edge of the family circle, the cloaked figure appears to be a detached observer, viewing the competition between chivalry and virtue— the traditions of southern masculinity and femininity—represented in the other two monuments.

The history of this sculptural triad intersects with the colorful personalities and personal stories of Davis, his daughters, and Zolnay, a Hungarian-born artist who completed numerous prestigious commissions in the United States from the 1890s until his death in 1949. The wide variation in the three works—from realism to sentimentality to a melancholy mystery—also is testimony to the persistence of specific gendered notions of life and death in late-nineteenth-century America. To appreciate these differences, one must examine the set of circumstances that led to the design of the three memorials: the Civil War that made Davis a tragic hero and daughter Winnie his angelic counterpart; the development of the rural cemetery, which gave public context to the monuments; and the aesthetic milieu in which the sculptures were created and in which they function today.

## *War and Death*

The Civil War was the most pervasive, and one could say collective, tragedy to befall nineteenth-century American life. The story of chivalrous planter-turned-soldier has been celebrated in popular culture, but the reality of the times was brutal and bitter. Many men who did not fall in battle died later of injuries and disease. Southern white women, by tradition restricted to the domestic sphere, usually served the Confederacy from a position safely within the accepted female realm. At the onset of the fighting, women organized sewing circles to produce uniforms and extra clothing for departing soldiers. Early on such activity was approached with a passion bordering on obsession, fueled as it was by a rising tide of patriotism for the cause. Later, when necessity demanded that women step outside the home, even "ladies" entered hospitals as attendants where women nursed the sick and held the hands of the dying.

Even before the war, it fell to women to care for the deceased, to wash, dress, and lay out the corpse, usually in the family parlor. Mourning and mourning rituals were part of daily life. For white Americans, life expectancy at birth did not exceed forty years at midcentury and death claimed infants and children in disproportionately high numbers.[2] While death from disease was common, accidental injury and the crude state of medical treatment often contributed to an early demise. Life was fragile for all, even for those buffered by privilege from economic deprivation. Thus throughout the nineteenth century conditions that could contribute to good health were foremost in the minds of informed citizens. Fresh air and sunshine were recognized as factors in warding off disease, while rest was considered important to recuperation. An interest in personal hygiene and environmental factors led to improved sanitation and contributed to a movement to bury the dead on the outskirts of cities rather than in cramped, deteriorating urban graveyards.

The first rural cemetery in America was Mount Auburn, established in Cambridge, Massachusetts, in 1831.[3] Although the initial impetus for a rural cemetery movement was practical—reflecting the growing national concern for better public sanitation and desire to minimize the spread of disease—practical concerns gave way to aesthetic interest as the popularity of rural cemeteries spread. Such cemeteries incorporated shrubs and flowers into a landscape dotted with ponds and bridge-covered streams to form inviting pastoral environments modeled after romantic English gardens. In recognition of their emphasis on botanical plantings, they also became known as garden cemeteries. Unlike traditional cemeteries where graves were laid out in a grid and

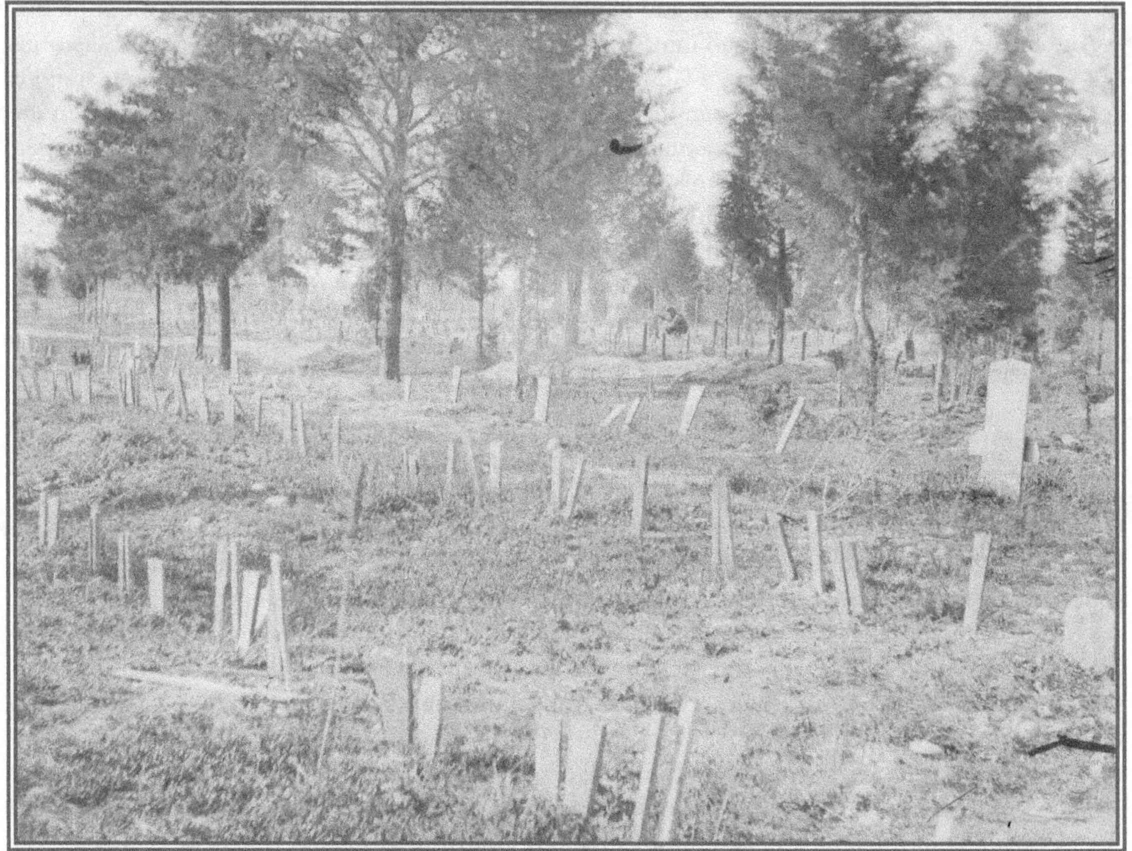

Fig. 7.2. Graves of Confederate soldiers in Hollywood Cemetery with temporary markers, often made of board, circa 1865. Prints and Photographs Division, Library of Congress.

surrounded by a fence or wall, these new cemeteries were designed with an inviting accessibility in mind. Often a short carriage ride from the city center, they incorporated meandering pathways and places to pause for remembrance or relaxation. Located away from the noise of the city, the rural cemetery took on an ambiance of nature, albeit controlled, and provided a public space for quiet contemplation. A poetic sketch by a Boston resident described Mount Auburn as a "place of beauty and death, of melancholy and delight." Rural cemeteries, which predated the establishment of centralized urban parks, became picturesque gathering places as well.[4]

By the mid-1800s the concept of the rural cemetery was gaining nationwide interest. Richmond, already a cultural center by the 1840s due, in part, to its position as an inland port, acquired its own rural cemetery in 1850. Located along the eastern perimeter of the city, a forty-five-acre wooded tract was carved from the Belvidere property, a former estate. With a view of the James River and Belle Isle, the new cemetery was heavily forested with an abundance of hollies, prompting the adoption of its original name, Holly-Wood.

Architect John Notman, who had recently completed Laurel Hill cemetery in Philadelphia, was commissioned to design and construct the new, rural burial ground in Richmond. He conscientiously utilized all features of the Hollywood site. In his report to the cemetery's financial backers, for example, Notman suggested that areas unsuitable for burials "be rendered highly ornamental to the main design by judicious planting[s] . . . of magnolias and other flowering shrubs of damp and watery natures."[5] Notman subdivided the entire wooded parcel by means of circuitous roads to provide access to the interior and bordered its perimeter with dense shrubbery to provide privacy. In this lovely, parklike setting there would be ample burial plots for Richmond's urban population. When the guns fired on Fort Sumter eleven years later, Hollywood Cemetery also would be ready for a wearisome service: receiving the bodies of Confederate fathers and sons, and eventually those of the Davis family.

## *The Davis Family*

On February 22, 1862—George Washington's birthday—Jefferson Davis took the oath of office in Richmond as the president of the Confederate States of America. The war of secession he led proved costly from the beginning, with 23,000 casualties at the battle at Antietam alone. A soldier recorded the carnage in a letter to home: "you could see the daggers [diggers] going and coming with the dead, dying and wounded, this was Tuesday after the battle on Sunday they did not git threw buriing the dead twel Saturday."[6]

By early 1864, a mood of disappointment was prevalent in the South. As the war progressed and led to increasing deprivation at home, the wearing of homespun by "ladies" accustomed to highly embellished finery was considered a "Confederate badge of honor." A lack of food and necessary supplies created a growing dissent among southern women of all stations. Richmond and other southern cities had been experiencing "bread riots" or "women riots" as popular support for the cause eroded. Women, brandishing hatchets, knives, and pistols, chanted "bread, bread, bread" as they took to the streets in search of food.[7]

The calamity that would plague Davis's Confederacy also entered his private life. A little more than two years after Davis's inauguration, his four-year-old son, Joseph, fell to his death April 30, 1864, from the portico of the Confederate White House. Private sorrow fused with public sentiment as Richmond children collected pennies to pay for young Joseph's grave marker in

Hollywood Cemetery.[8] The small stone, located on the perimeter of the Davis Circle reads, "Erected by the little boys & girls of the southern capital."

After the fall of Richmond and southern military surrender, Jefferson Davis was captured by Union troops and charged with treason. As if defeat and imprisonment were not enough humiliation, rumors surrounding the circumstances of his May 10, 1865, capture in Georgia—that he attempted to escape wearing a woman's cloak—would provide fodder for a barrage of scathing political cartoons and popular jokes.[9] Thus the year of sorrow that began with young Joseph's death marked a political as well as personal watershed for the Confederate president, for little more than twelve months later the cause also would be lost.

Varina Anne Davis was born in the summer of 1864 amid this stream of catastrophic events. In contrast to the tragic figure of her father, the youngest Davis offspring, known as "Winnie," would become a symbol of hope. Even as a child, Varina Anne's life had a political dimension, with external circumstances controlling her fate. In her first year, while her father was imprisoned, baby Winnie was placed under house arrest along with her mother. During her adolescence, she attended boarding school in Germany, which added to a feeling of estrangement from family and country. When seventeen-year-old Winnie Davis returned from Europe, she was fluent in German and French but spoke English with an accent.[10]

After serving two years in prison, Jefferson Davis reentered life as a private citizen, stripped of his political power, position, and, symbolically perhaps, his sense of manhood as well. Winnie accompanied her father on speaking engagements where, as a welcome guest at Confederate veteran functions, a measure of pride was returned to the aging statesman. In 1886 at a function in West Point, Georgia, Davis was too weak to speak and Winnie was called on to make remarks in his stead. It was there that she was first introduced as "the Daughter of the Confederacy . . . the war baby of our old chieftain." As her father's health deteriorated, Winnie Davis increasingly joined him at the podium. One witness described the enthusiasm with which she was frequently received, proclaiming that "as Winnie stepped forward, [she was] drowned in the noise of applause and cheering."[11]

The adoration and honorific title bestowed upon her by a devoted public would bring conflict, however, to her young life. She fell in love with Alfred Wilkinson, a Harvard-educated patent attorney who was not only a northerner but also the grandson of an abolitionist. After their engagement became known, Winnie received letters of disapproval from her public. She broke off the engagement, and neither she nor her beau ever married.[12] When Winnie took a respite from the political limelight to travel to Europe, her father's health declined. Before she could return, he died in New Orleans on December 6, 1889, at age eighty-one.

After a grand-scale funeral, Davis's body was laid in a vault in New Orleans' Metrairie Cemetery. This would not remain his final resting place, however; his body eventually would be returned to the Confederate capital. After several postponements, it was transported northward to Richmond in 1893 via a special funeral train, which made stops along the way to allow the public to pay respects. An official escort and an entourage of three hundred family members and distinguished guests accompanied the casket. In Virginia, ceremonies began with a formal escort to the state capitol, where Davis's body lay in state attended by an honor guard. The day was marked by solemn formality. Three thousand schoolchildren, each carrying flowers, marched two by two around the casket.[13]

Jefferson Davis's interment in Richmond was celebrated by formal pomp and circumstance; six white horses carried his body to its final resting place. The former statesman was laid in a simple

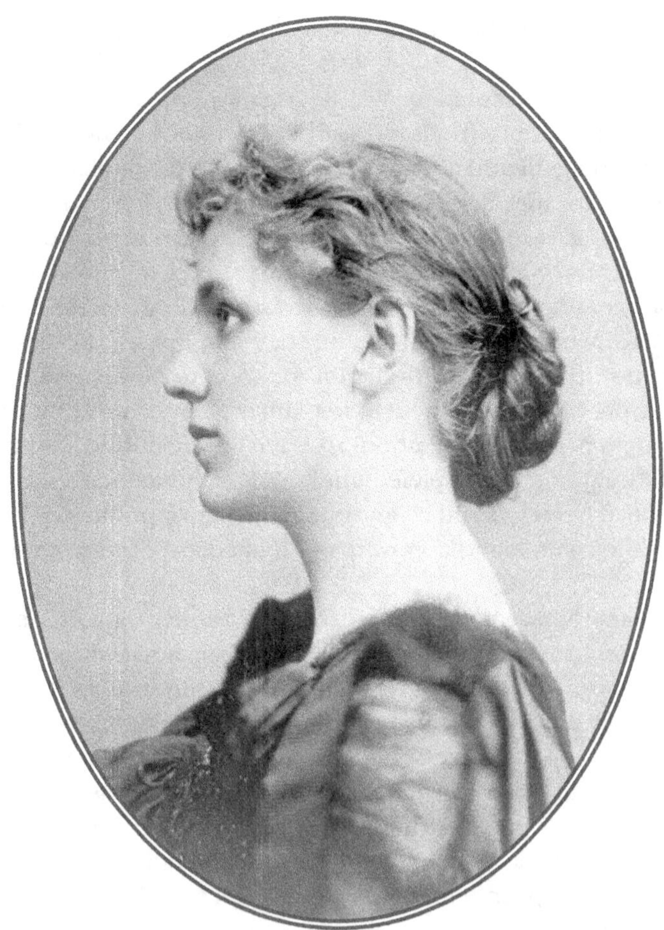

Fig. 7.3. Varina Anne "Winnie" Davis, circa 1890. Davis and Sanford photograph.
The Museum of the Confederacy, Richmond.

grave in Hollywood Cemetery on May 31, 1893, the city's Memorial Day. The events were enumerated in a *Programme of Ceremonies.* Although the program invitation was issued "at the request of The Jefferson Davis Monument Association," little or no progress was made to actualize a monument there for the Confederate president until much later.[14]

Winnie Davis (fig. 7.3) continued to face the impossible task of living up to the imagined standard of quintessential southern womanhood. After her father's death, she and her mother moved to New York City when Mrs. Davis was offered an annual salary for writing a weekly article for the *Sunday World.* Clearly, the two women were no longer able to maintain Beauvoir, the Biloxi, Mississippi, estate to which Jeff Davis had retired. They accepted the offer and moved North, where Winnie's health and spirit declined. Although her own writing met with some success, professional recognition was not enough to buttress the mounting disappointments in her personal life. Having by this time lost her father, four brothers to accident or illness, and her fiancé, Winnie Davis lamented, "I have very little joy in anything." She could not fulfill the role carved out for her by a sentimental and adoring public. As one newspaper had proclaimed, "all that will remain of

The Lost Cause is this young and beautiful woman." But on September 18, 1898, Varina Anne Davis died at age thirty-four.[15]

It appears that the idea of a memorial for Winnie began spontaneously. As reported in the *Richmond Dispatch,* her funeral drew "thousands of people [who] crowded the church, lined the streets to the cemetery, and gathered about the tomb."[16] A letter published in the newspaper on September 22, just four days after her death, is testimony to the immediate groundswell of support for a memorial, asking, "Are [you] in a position to accept my contribution of $5 towards erecting a monument to Miss Winnie Davis?" The editor's reply injected a cautionary note about not upstaging any forthcoming official tribute to the former Confederate president. "Yes, send it on. A monument to Miss Winnie Davis will certainly be built; but we presume that collections for it will be so timed as not to interfere with the effort, soon to be resumed, we believe, to raise funds to erect the long-promised monument to her father."[17] A cornerstone had been laid in 1896 for an elaborate Monument Avenue memorial to Davis in Richmond, but fund-raising for that project stalled and it would not be completed until 1907. Although Jefferson Davis's interment in Hollywood Cemetery had been marked by an ornate display of public celebration, public funds for a permanent gravesite commemoration were not immediately forthcoming in spite of the editor's optimism.

In a letter that appears to have been written shortly after her daughter's death in 1898, Mrs. Davis poured out her grief to a friend, writing on black-bordered mourning stationery, "[It] is almost more than I can bear." But Mrs. Davis tempered her emotion in discussing the proposed memorials. With politically motivated concern, she added, "I think it would be unfortunate if my Darling's tomb should overtop her fathers in the lot." Clearly she desired that her husband maintain his rightful and dominant place. The letter reveals that money was already being gathered for a monument to mark Winnie's grave. Mrs. Davis proposed to her friend "in confidence" that a "smaller monument" be made for her daughter and suggested that excess funding "be appropriated to a statue in front of the [Confederate] Museum," presumably a statue of the former president. She added that she and her daughter would incur "a heavy expense" for a "statue of Mr. Davis . . . to be erected as his grave."[18] Plans for Winnie's monument may have precipitated the commissioning of a cemetery memorial for her father almost ten years after his death. But his would be privately funded in contrast to the public outpouring that paid for Winnie's.

In the same letter, Mrs. Davis reported on the progress of commissioning the sculptures, writing, "My daughter [Margaret] and I are just arranging . . . for a statue of Mr. Davis" by a "noted sculptor . . . to give pleasure to our dear friends in Richmond." She proposed that Winnie's memorial be created by a "first-class artist here who knew her." Indeed, the "noted sculptor" and "first-class artist" recounted in Mrs. Davis's letter were one and the same. George Julian Zolnay eventually received both commissions.[19]

Zolnay (fig. 7.4) is as colorful a figure as one hopes to encounter in historical reading. Asked on one occasion to speak at a social function, the sculptor jumped up on a table and began to play his violin; at another, he was said to have served powdered donuts from the end of a sword.[20] Zolnay (1863–1949) attended the Royal Art Institute in Bucharest, Rumania, and soon after his graduation was offered the opportunity to travel to Chicago to work on the 1893 World's Columbian Exposition. In a memoir, Zolnay contrasted his first impression of New York City—"dull and wearisome [with] the deathly sameness of solid blocks of box-like brick buildings of the ugliest red"— with the challenge and inspiration "being prepared at the great Chicago exposition—the White

City—which opened the eyes of the country."[21] His work would always retain elements of the Beaux-Arts style that dominated the exposition.

After completing work in Chicago, Zolnay settled temporarily in the city he had earlier derided, where, in 1896, he met Mrs. Davis and her daughter, who assisted him in making important professional connections. In his memoir he credited them "more than anyone" as "instrumental in bringing about the turning point of my career. Through them I made my first connections in the South, which led to my work for the Nashville Centennial Exposition."[22] Zolnay's commission for the 1897 centennial included work on a replica of the Parthenon, where he completed the ninety-two sculpted metopes for the frieze, over five hundred feet of sculpted relief. Moreover, he would be invited back in the 1920s when the original work, in plaster and wood, was to be replaced with more permanent materials. Zolnay also would receive commissions for a portrait of local Confederate hero Sam Davis and a city monument for the unknown Confederate soldier. With the completion of public works for two expositions behind him, Zolnay established himself as a sculptor of some note in his adopted country.

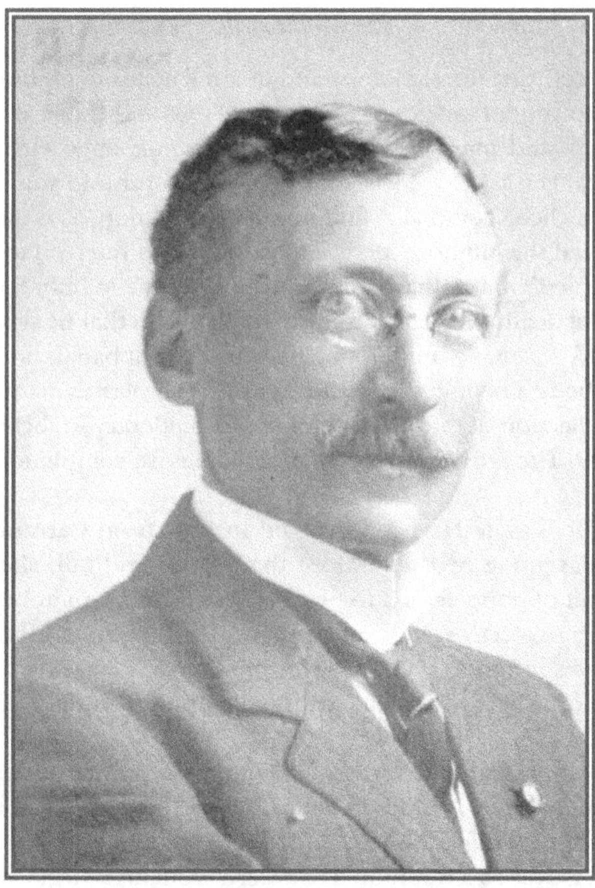

Fig. 7.4. Sculptor George Julian Zolnay, circa 1890. Zolnay papers, Archives of American Art, Smithsonian Institution.

Zolnay's lengthy *Memoir* (1929) sheds light on the commissioning of the three Davis memorials and illuminates the artist's aesthetic objectives. Following an account of his eight months in Nashville, Zolnay wrote of Winnie's death and the subsequent commissioning of her monument. Zolnay made it clear that it was the Daughters of the Confederacy, not Mrs. Davis, who requested a memorial for Winnie. "To honor her memory," he wrote, "the 'Daughters' commissioned me to erect a Memorial over her grave in Hollywood Cemetery of Richmond, Va. adjoining that of her father, Jefferson Davis, for which I was also making a monument."[23]

A June 1899 letter from Zolnay to Mrs. Davis outlines the financial arrangements for the Jefferson Davis monument. Mrs. Davis would be responsible for one-fifth of the cost; the rest would come from Margaret Howell, the surviving Davis daughter. Zolnay was thorough; he had borrowed Jefferson Davis's clothing and a photograph for use in refining the portrait, assuring Davis's widow that "I am still working on the statue, studying and revising details." The letter reveals that Winnie Davis's memorial was already complete. "Although I am still working on the statue [of the former Confederate president] . . . the angel is being cast meanwhile and will be sent abroad at once."[24] Before year's end, Zolnay had created two distinctive monuments.

## The Memorials

In the early nineteenth century, the skeletons and death's heads of eighteenth-century funerary markers had given way to gentler images of weeping willows and classical urns, weeping women, and genre figures of lambs and angels. By the end of the century angels in American art were considered clichéd by some: "The angel . . . has got to go," a lecturer told students at the Art Students League in 1888.[25] Yet the cliché could also find new interpretation, as it did in 1893 when Daniel Chester French completed the Milmore Memorial, a work also referred to as *The Angel of Death Staying the Hand of the Sculptor.* Zolnay knew and admired the Milmore Memorial, in which the angel is a gentle herald of death. He faced a similar challenge in that he wished to make "an angel in the nineteenth century . . . that would not be hackneyed; not banal; not to make a tombstone, but to translate and embody a people's love and a gift."[26] The plaster maquette of Zolnay's angel, which remains in the collection of the Museum of the Confederacy in Richmond, was sent to Florence, Italy, in June 1899. The artist soon followed to supervise completion of the full-scale monument (fig. 7.5).

Zolnay's memorial for Winnie Davis was carved in Italy from Carrara marble. The angel is seated atop a rectangular stone pedestal. More than seven feet tall, she reaches forward and downward with a garland of poppies as if to place them on the crypt at her feet. Her large wings form an arc resembling a protective shield at her back. Despite the sculpture's rather restrained and impassive pose, it was referred to in *Confederate Veteran* magazine within a month after its installation as an "Angel of Grief."[27] The name expressed public sentiment for the lost daughter of the cause.

The program accompanying the unveiling of Winnie's monument described it as resulting from a movement "inaugurated by . . . friends and admirers [from] both North and South." Winnie Davis was mourned by the "whole country," a country "touched by her blameless and heroic career."[28] But her "career" was as a traditional southern woman, a virgin symbol of the feminine. The popularity of the *Angel of Grief* is testimony to the power of public monuments to embody shared values. Perhaps Winnie's angel had the capacity to cleanse the war of reality, forgetting

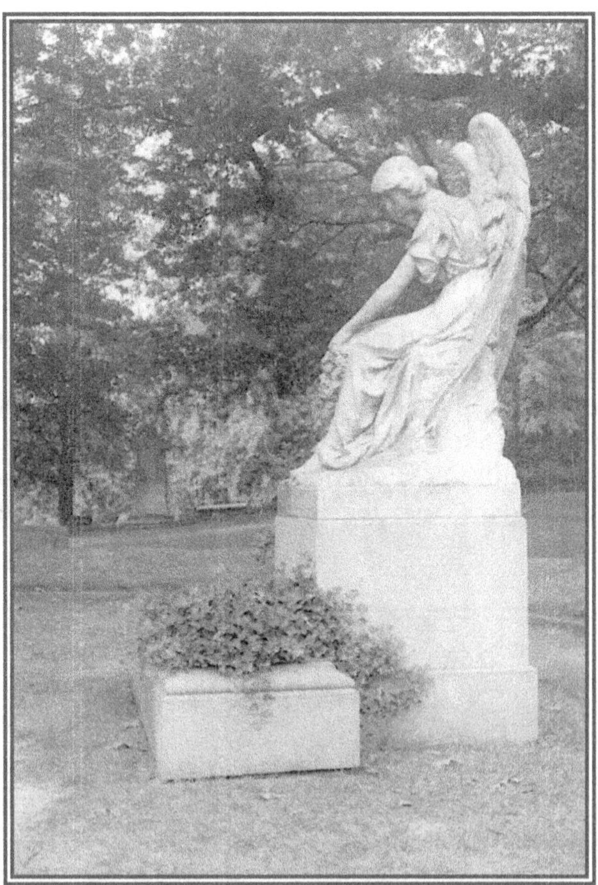

Fig. 7.5. Varina Anne "Winnie" Davis memorial, designed by George Julian Zolnay and dedicated November 9, 1899, Hollywood Cemetery, Richmond. Photograph by M. Anna Fariello.

cruelty and death. Winnie herself—her "blameless" innocence and youth—inspired hope, where her father's failure could at best command respect.

As if to shore up Jefferson Davis's reputation as a statesman, Zolnay depicted the Confederate president in a pose (see figs. 7.1 and 7.6) reminiscent of the well-known statue of George Washington by Jean-Antoine Houdon, modeled in 1788 for the Richmond capitol. In both portrait figures, the men are bare-headed and face squarely forward, one arm extended downward, the other upraised. Head held high, each wears contemporary dress, an expression of self-confidence, and an unflinching gaze of determination. It would have been appropriate for Zolnay to make such a visual comparison between George Washington and Jefferson Davis. After all, both men were "first presidents," and each attempted to establish sovereignty for their breakaway states. Zolnay expressed his philosophy on portraiture in his memoir, commenting that "a portrait, to be called great, must look more like the sitter than the sitter himself . . . . Not only is the sitter's appearance constantly affected by his physical condition and varying moods, but he registers according to the temperament of those who see him. Therefore, to be accepted by all as a good likeness, the artist must be able . . . to emphasize the sitter's fundamental traits, moral, mental and physical . . . [and] to coordinate his varying moods."[29]

Mrs. Davis may have had a premonition that Winnie's angel would be more memorable than the presidential portrait she had commissioned. Indeed, most subsequent writing on Zolnay mentions the *Angel of Grief* as one of his best-known works. Even before its installation, an interviewer visiting the sculptor in Florence asked "as a singular favor to be taken out to Zolnay's workshop to see the 'Angel' of which I had already heard so much through home papers." Zolnay asserted in his memoir, "[T]he work brought me so much publicity that suddenly I became known all over the country; in fact my notoriety at one time had reached such absurd proportions . . . .There is no doubt but what for about ten years I had more publicity than comes to most sculptors."[30]

The two Davis memorials were dedicated on the same day, November 9, 1899 (fig. 7.6). While a public outpouring of affection had enabled a rapid commemoration of the spirit of Winnie, the dedication came a full ten years after Jefferson Davis's death. Winnie's monument "was started by the Richmond chapter [of the UDC]," *Confederate Veteran* reported, "and without solicitation, contributions came pouring in from all over the South." The inscription on the base of her father's

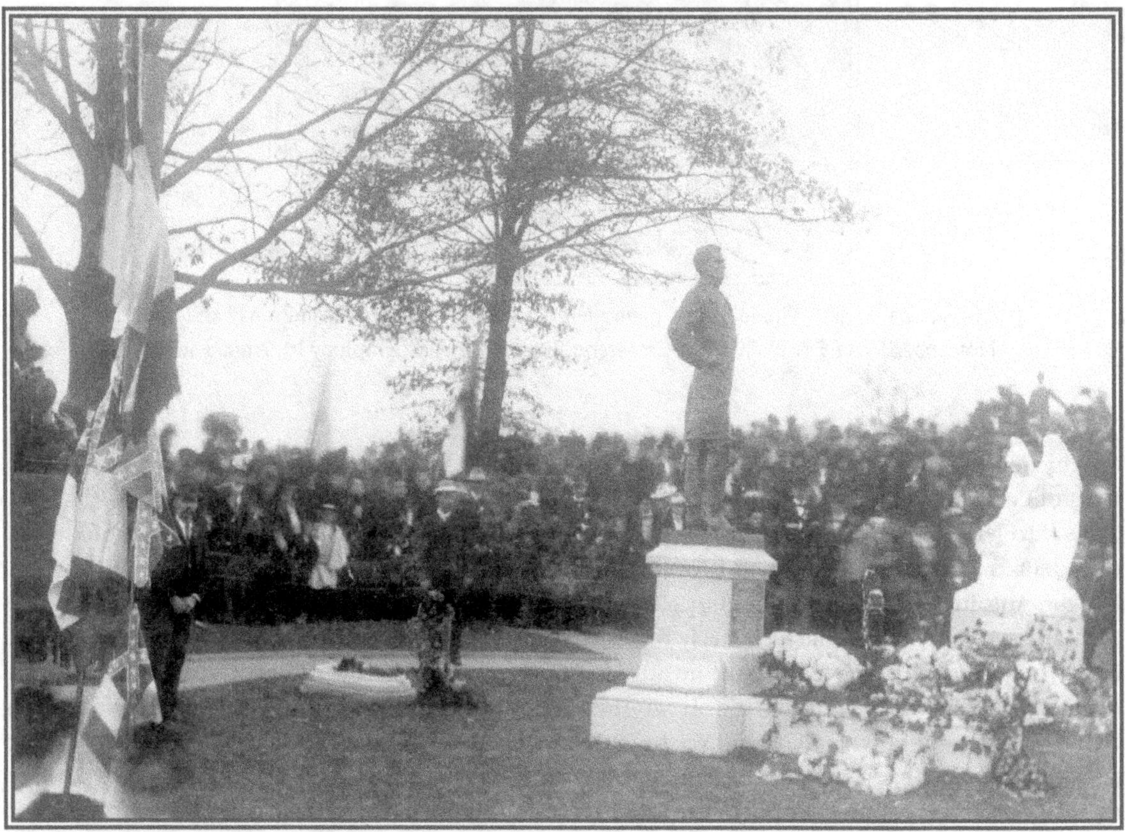

Fig. 7.6 Dedication on November 9, 1899, of memorials for Jefferson and Winnie Davis at Hollywood Cemetery, Richmond. Valentine Museum / Richmond History Center.

tomb—"erected by his wife Varina Howell Davis and his daughter Margaret Howell Davis Hayes"—reconfirms that, although he was a public figure, his cemetery memorial remained a private affair.[31]

A photograph showing the highly praised angel monument heaped with flowers illustrates the *Confederate Veteran* account of the dual dedications. Surprisingly, the author opined that "the bronze figure of President Davis is not pleasing. The sculptor explained . . . that he sought to combine the principles and conditions involved." In spite of such expressions of disappointment, Zolnay was dubbed the "Sculptor of the Confederacy" in numerous period writings and, in 1900, received an award from the king of Romania for his work. In *The New Age* a few years later, a writer suggested that the artist was awarded this royal citation on the strength of the *Angel of Grief* alone, a replica of which was acquired for the Royal Academy at Bucharest.[32] Had there been any real contest between the statues of the stoic statesman and the angel, Winnie's monument surely would have won.

The last sculpture created by Zolnay for the Davis Circle was the Hayes monument (fig. 7.7), completed in 1911, two years after the death of Margaret Howell Davis Hayes. Born in 1855,

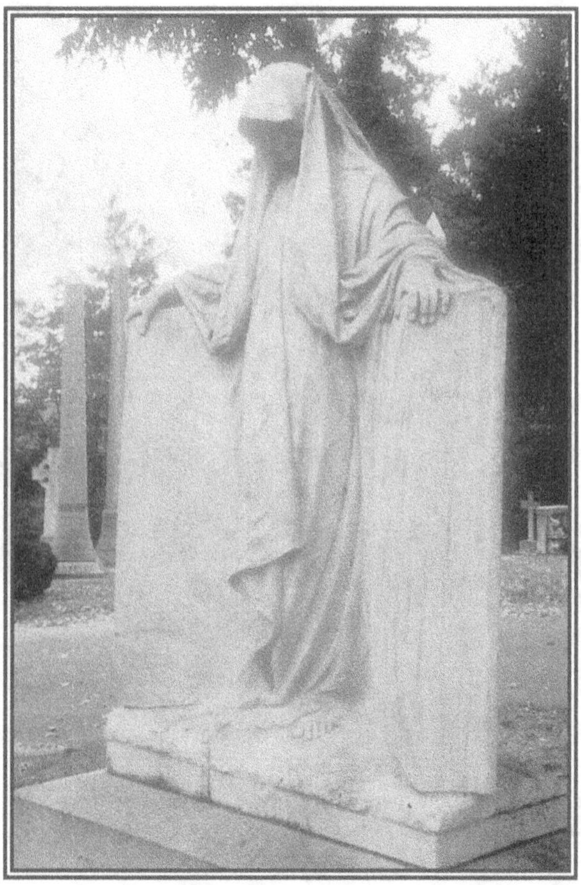

Fig. 7.7. Margaret Howell Davis Hayes Memorial, designed by George Julian Zolnay and completed 1911, Hollywood Cemetery, Richmond. Photograph by M. Anna Fariello.

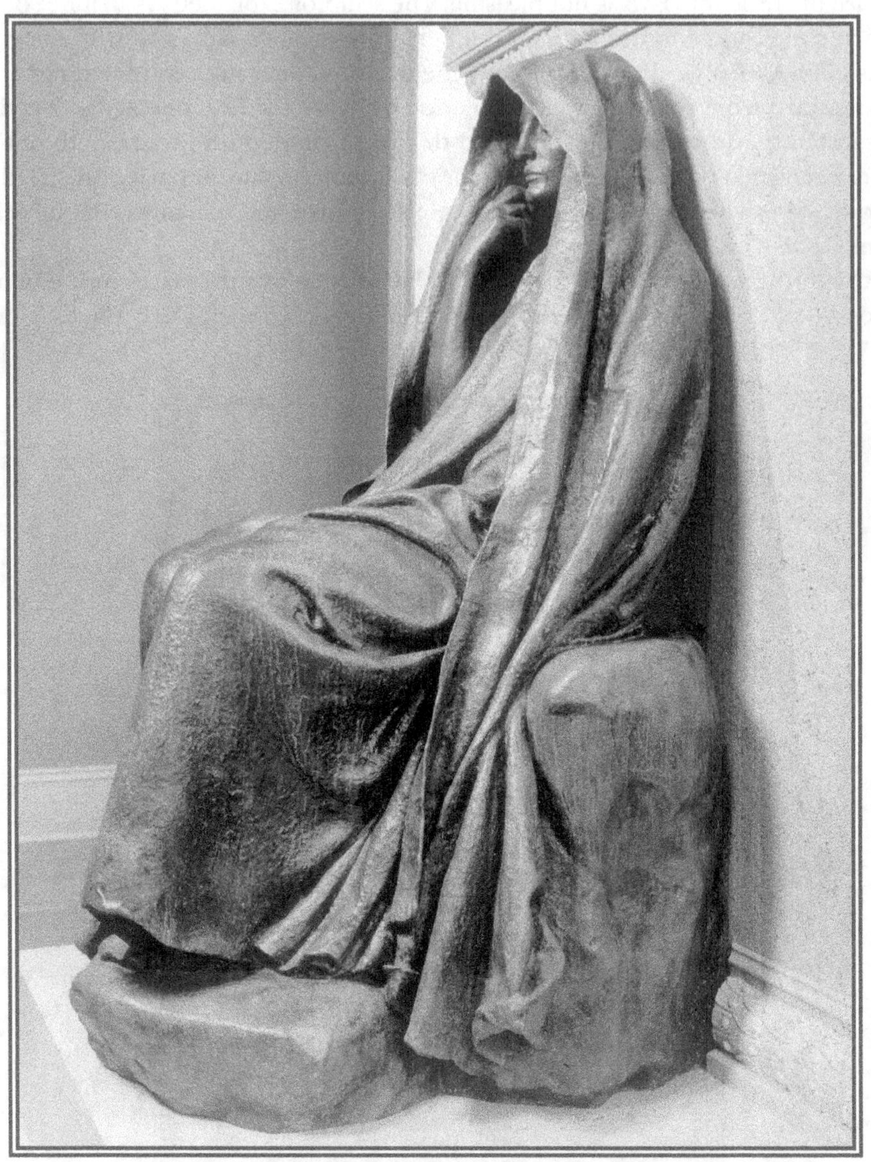

Fig. 7.8. Adams Memorial by Augustus Saint-Gaudens. Cast made from 1891 bronze figure in Rock Creek Cemetery, Washington, D.C. Smithsonian American Art Museum, Washington.

Margaret was the only one of the Davis children to marry and to outlive her parents. She was survived by four children and her husband, Joel Addison Hayes, who interred her ashes at Hollywood Cemetery and likely commissioned the monument. Zolnay later wrote that the Hayes Memorial was one of "various private commissions" he received after the turn of the century.[33]

The design of the monument may suggest Zolnay's deep admiration for the work of Augustus Saint-Gaudens, whom he called in his memoir "the foremost sculptor of the century," a man "we all looked up to . . . as a beloved friend and Master of the Craft." In 1891 Saint-Gaudens completed a bronze cemetery memorial commissioned by Henry Adams for the grave site of his wife, Marian Hooper Adams, who had committed suicide in 1885. Neither portrait nor virtuous allegory, the Adams Memorial (fig. 7.8) in Rock Creek Cemetery, Washington, D.C., was an enigmatic figure enfolded in mystery. Zolnay hailed the monument as a "mystically impressive . . . . great masterpiece of mortuary sculpture."[34]

In his memoir, Zolnay wrote about two particular funerary works by name: the Adams Memorial and French's 1893 Milmore Memorial, which also included a shrouded figure. Zolnay did not allude to the similarity they shared with his later Hayes Memorial. But all three works include figures swathed in an abundance of drapery with hooded faces in shadow. While the figure in the Adams memorial is more self-contained, the cloaked figures by Saint-Gaudens and Zolnay both are deliberately androgynous and partially concealed, adding to their ambiguity. With shadowed eyes, the two figures were interpreted by many as expressing a grief turned inward. The figure in the Hayes Memorial stands within a book imprinted with the simple Latin title *Pax*. With outstretched arms and hands gripping its edges, the figure appears to embrace the unwritten history of the future.

## Conclusion

George Julian Zolnay's final monument for the Davis Circle marked the threshold of a new century, hinting at hidden possibilities yet to come. Beyond its time was change. Hard-won female suffrage, unimagined weaponry, and the miracle of flight would greet the new century. Certainly, the Hayes Memorial is as ambiguous as the new age, leaving prescribed traditions of chivalry and virtue entombed in the past. In the Davis family circle, Zolnay was able to create a series of figures that also marked the passage of the times.

In her study *The Public Monument and Its Audience,* Marianne Doezema reminds readers that while scale and site are the tangible fundamentals of a public monument, it is the "capacity to mobilize ideas or values" that ultimately defines its success.[35] Clearly, Zolnay's conception of what made a suitable memorial changed over time—from a traditional nineteenth-century portrait statue and a sentimental allegorical angel to a later enigmatic figure embodying an ambiguity of meaning consistent with modern life. Zolnay's ability to negotiate changing cultural waters contributed to his success as a sculptor.

T. H. S. Escott, in the essay "Transformation of the Victorian Age," proposes that the turn of the century was a period of cultural demarcation.[36] When society redefines itself out of necessity, tradition becomes more pronounced. And so it was that ritualized mourning may have reached its zenith in the aftermath of the Civil War. Certainly the identity of the South's urbane citizenry evolved over the course of the nineteenth century from cultured to self-righteous to defiant and, eventually, to defeated.

In private ritual or public ceremony, it fell upon southern women to memorialize sons, lovers, fathers, and brothers. Soon after the end of the Civil War, Confederate Memorial Day activities were established to honor those martyred to the Lost Cause. A day was set aside to refurbish soldiers' graves and preserve their memory. Throughout history, such traditions and celebrations made for social cohesion, especially during times of crisis. While a large pyramid was dedicated in 1869 as an official remembrance of the Confederate dead, in reality the entire Hollywood Cemetery became a monument to the Lost Cause. Memorial sentiments were part and parcel of the age: "Let the soldiers' graves . . . be the southern Mecca to whose shrine her sorrowing women, like pilgrims, may annually bring their grateful hearts and floral offerings."[37] Perhaps the members of the Ladies' Memorial Society and United Daughters of the Confederacy buried more than their menfolk in Hollywood Cemetery. Laid to rest was a way of life and a faith in the ability of tradition to endure. The past lay buried within the Davis Circle as well. Marked above by sculptures heroic and sweet, the chivalry and virtue they represented seem distant in the twenty-first century.

## Notes

1. After 1855 a tendency to establish a "domestic circle" within burying grounds would distinguish a family from the broader community. Martha Pike and Janice Armstrong, eds., *A Time to Mourn* (New York: Museum at Stonybrook, 1980), 116. Interred within the Davis Circle are Jefferson Davis (1808–1889) and his wife, Varina Howell Davis (1826–1906); their sons, Samuel Emory (1852–54), who died of measles; Joseph (1859–1864), who suffered an accidental fall; William Howell (1861–1871); and Jefferson Davis Jr. (1857–78), who died of yellow fever; their daughters, Varina Anne "Winnie" Davis (1864–1898), who died after contracting malarial gastritis; and Margaret Howell Davis (1855–1909), who is interred with her husband, Joel Addison Hayes (1848–1919); and a few members of their extended family. Only the three graves discussed in this essay feature figurative sculptures; the rest are marked with small stones. Two plaques honor Mrs. Davis; one was placed by her daughter Margaret in 1907 and a second one by the United Daughters of the Confederacy in 1997.

2. Patricia Loughridge and Edward D. C. Campbell Jr., *Women in Mourning* (Richmond: Museum of the Confederacy, 1984), 7. See also Pat Jalland, *Death in the Victorian Family* (New York: Oxford Univ. Press, 1996), and *Historical Statistics of the United States: Colonial Times to 1970*, pt. 1 (Washington: U.S. Dept. of Commerce, Bureau of Census, 1975).

3. Subsequently, Laurel Hill was built in Philadelphia in 1836 and Green-Wood in Brooklyn in 1838. Holly-Wood would be established in Richmond in 1850.

4. See Ann Douglas, *The Feminization of American Culture* (New York: Knopf, 1977), 208–11, and Thomas Bender, "The 'Rural' Cemetery Movement: Urban Travail and the Appeal of Nature," in *Material Life in America, 1600–1860*, ed. Robert Blair St. George (Boston: Northeastern Univ. Press, 1988), 505–18.

5. Mary H. Mitchell, *Hollywood Cemetery: The History of a Southern Shrine* (Richmond: Virginia State Library, 1985), 15.

6. Davis had been inaugurated as president of the provisional Confederate government on February 18, 1861, in Montgomery, Alabama. He delivered what is known as his "second inaugural address" at the Virginia capitol in Richmond in 1862 "to usher into existence the Permanent Government of the Confederate States." The quotation is from a letter from Henry B. Wood to his wife, Sarah Jane, as cited in Loughridge and Campbell, *Women in Mourning*, 21.

7. Edward D. C. Campbell Jr. and Kym Rice, eds., *A Woman's War* (Richmond: Museum of Confederacy, 1996), 121, 9.

8. Mitchell, *Hollywood Cemetery*, 59.

9. See Nina Silber, "Intemperate Men, Spiteful Women and Jefferson Davis," in *Divided Houses: Gender and the Civil War*, ed. Catherine Clinton and Nina Silber (New York: Oxford Univ., 1992) for a discussion of concepts of virility and manliness in the South.

10. Museum of the Confederacy, exhibition script, *Lost Daughter of the Lost Cause* (Richmond: Museum of the Confederacy, 1998), unpaginated.

11. Tommie Phillips LaCavera, *Varina Anne "Winnie" Davis: The Daughter of the Confederacy* (Athens: Southern Trace Pub., 1994), 17, 27.

12. Ruth Ann Coski, "Winnie Davis, 'Lost' Daughter," *Museum of the Confederacy* newsletter (fall 1998): 4, and Museum of the Confederacy, *Lost Daughter of the Lost Cause* exhibition text.

13. Loughridge and Campbell, *Women in Mourning*, 7. The practice of reinterring the dead was common after the Civil War. Although a private business enterprise, once the war was under way, Hollywood Cemetery found itself with a moral responsibility for the burial of the Confederate dead as bodies arrived daily from the city's hospitals. By the end of the war 11,000 soldiers were buried there along with five Confederate generals. Eventually, 20,000 soldiers would be laid to rest in Hollywood. See *Hollywood Cemetery*, undated, unpaginated Richmond, Va., brochure, and Mitchell, *Hollywood Cemetery*, chaps. 5 and 6.

14. *Programme of Ceremonies*, Davis Family Collection (box 34), Museum of the Confederacy, Richmond.

15. LaCavera, *Varina Anne "Winnie" Davis*, 24. Winnie Davis died after contracting malarial gastritis. See note 1 for the deaths of her brothers. Quotation from Museum of the Confederacy, *Lost Daughter of the Lost Cause*.

16. LaCavera, *Varina Anne "Winnie" Davis*, 29.

17. Ibid., 62–63. LaCavera quotes from the *Richmond Dispatch*, Sept. 22, 1898.

18. Varina Howell Davis to Mrs. Daniel, circa 1898, Davis Family Collection, box 25, Museum of the Confederacy, Richmond.

19. Ibid.

20. Louise Davis, "Zolnay: Sculptor of the Confederacy," *Tennessean*, Aug. 28, 1988.

21. George Julian Zolnay, *A Memoir*, 59. This unpublished 1929 manuscript can be found in the Zolnay papers, Archives of American Art, Smithsonian Institution, Washington, D.C.

22. Ibid., 78.

23. Ibid., 82–83. While Zolnay did not specifically date events in his memoir, he did record his life sequentially, and the events he described appear consistent with my chronology.

24. George Julian Zolnay to Mrs. Davis, June 15, [1899], Jefferson Davis Papers, Univ. of Alabama, Birmingham. I am grateful to Ruth Ann Coski, librarian at the Museum of the Confederacy, for her assistance in locating these important letters.

25. Richard Murray, "Abbot Thayer's Stevenson Memorial," *American Art* 13, no. 2 (summer 1999): 7.

26. Mary Kelly Graves, "George Julian Zolnay, Sculptor," *New Age* (Jan. 1909): 19. Zolnay referred to the Milmore Memorial in his *Memoir*.

27. *Confederate Veteran* 7, no. 12 (Dec. 1899): 532–33. For a discussion of earlier uses of the term *Angel of Grief*, see Cynthia Mills, "The Adams Memorial and American Funerary Sculpture" (Ph.D. diss., Univ. of Maryland, 1996), 184–87.

28. Winnie Davis Monument Unveiling 1899, Davis Family Collection (box 33), Museum of the Confederacy, Richmond, and United Daughters of the Confederacy, "Proceedings at Annual Convention, Richmond, Va.," *Confederate Veteran* 7, no. 12 (Dec. 1899): 532–33.

29. Zolnay, *A Memoir*, 73.

30. Marguerite Hardy, "Reminiscences of Florence: An Interview with George Julian Zolnay," *Art Education,* ca. 1899, unpaginated; Davis Family Collection (box 33), Museum of the Confederacy, Richmond. Zolnay, *A Memoir,* 82.

31. United Daughters of the Confederacy, "Proceedings," 532–33. The inscription on Jefferson Davis's tomb states, "Defender of the Constitution . . . a Martyr to Principle. He lived and died the most consistent of American Soldiers and Statesmen . . . Erected by his wife Varina Howell Davis and his daughter Margaret Howell Davis Hayes." The inscription for Winnie Davis reads, "Erected by the United Daughters of the Confederacy. In the flower of her beauty . . . Brave and steadfast her loyal spirit was worthy of her peoples' glorious history."

32. United Daughters of the Confederacy, "Proceedings," 532–33. Zolnay, *A Memoir,* 84. Graves, "George Julian Zolnay, Sculptor," 23–24. On the replica, see Graves, 19.

33. Zolnay, *A Memoir,* 111.

34. Ibid., 72–74. Zolnay returned again to the motif of the shrouded figure in the mid-1920s when he created the David R. Francis Memorial for Bellefontaine Cemetery in St. Louis.

35. Marianne Doezema, *The Public Monument and Its Audience* (Cleveland: Cleveland Museum, 1977), 16.

36. T. H. S. Escott, "Transformation of the Victorian Age," in *The Invention of Tradition,* ed. Eric Hobsbawm and Terrance Ranger (Cambridge: Cambridge Univ. Press, 1983), 306. Escott proposes that in the nineteenth century cultural adaptation transferred downward from upper classes to lower, while in the twentieth century the direction reverses with the embrace of vernacular forms by the leisure classes. Twentieth-century jazz, ragtime, and tango provide a case in point; these filtered upward from the working class to take on the trappings of elite art forms. Whereas Memorial Day was celebrated formally by nineteenth-century upper and middle classes, today it marks the opening of public swimming pools and backyard barbecues.

37. The quotation is from a March 1866 open letter written by the secretary of the Columbus, Georgia, memorial association, as cited in Campbell and Rice, *A Woman's War,* 137. The concept of the Hollywood Cemetery as a shrine is underscored by the subtitle of Mary Mitchell's valuable text, *Hollywood Cemetery: The History of a Southern Shrine.* See also Ann Hunter McLean, "Unveiling the Lost Cause: A Study of Monuments to the Civil War Memory in Richmond, Virginia, and Vicinity" (Ph.D. diss., Univ. of Virginia, 1998).

# 8

# The Virtuous Soldier

CONSTRUCTING A USABLE CONFEDERATE PAST IN FRANKLIN, TENNESSEE

*David Currey*

DURING DEDICATION RITES for Battle Ground Academy in Franklin, Tennessee, in 1889, ex-Confederate general and former state governor William Bate proclaimed the school's brick edifice to be "an educational monument . . . in memory of that [Franklin] battle which occurred years agone." Twenty-five years earlier, he recalled, the soldiers of the Army of Tennessee had immortalized themselves on this very ground. Their valor deserved recognition. Yet the building of this all-male preparatory institution as a town memorial to their patriotism and heroism, Bate said, represented a new kind of commemoration. Most Confederate monuments built in the South in earlier decades had been placed in cemeteries, in remembrance of the South's dead soldiers and a dead cause. Bate argued that Battle Ground Academy was different because it combined the "practical with the sentimental." On this ground, consecrated by the blood of thousands of his compatriots, now stood a symbol of the South's modern rebirth—a place where Bate said "the history of the past and hope of the future unite . . . as kindred drops that mingle into one."[1]

Dramatic orations similar to the one Bate delivered were characteristic of the Confederate revival that swept the South during the 1880s and 1890s, accompanied by a boom in memorialization. In identifying the origins of this movement, scholars such as Gaines Foster rightly point out that industrialization and the integration of the South into a national economy produced tumultuous effects during the latter decades of the nineteenth century. The rise in tenancy, economic depression, political unrest, and black activism raised fears about the nature of a new corporate order many viewed as socially hostile and morally bankrupt. Confederate commemoration, Foster suggests, offered solace from the "tensions" of the period and transcended "the usual social and economic divisions of society." In his view, these rituals created a sense of social unity based on escape to a mythic past.[2]

The creation of a usable Confederate history did more, however, than provide comfort to communities caught in the midst of change. Instead, as this look at Franklin at the end of the nineteenth century will demonstrate, southerners used the process of commemoration to counteract and actively challenge what they saw as the decline and debauchery brought by the new industrial order. Key to this challenge was the construction of the pristine, virtuous Confederate common soldier as an icon of the South. The soldier's image, set in stone and bronze in hundreds of court-house towns, became the visual representation of the ideas Bate was attempting to convey with the BGA dedication. For him, the past was not solace but a model—a tool—used by southerners to mold the individual character of a new generation confronted with the South's, and the nation's, increasingly callous and calculating industrial expansion. A little more than a decade later, Franklin would muster enough will and resources to install its own soldier monument in its town square.

Creating a collective memory that emphasized southern character demanded an organized effort. The Lost Cause movement was no haphazard undertaking. As held true throughout the South, the work of the United Daughters of the Confederacy was critical to this enterprise in Franklin. From the organization's perspective, the advent of a new town culture was transforming the region's rural-based conception of work, family, and individual desire. The women worked to revitalize the social order formerly associated with the home. As a collective of well-placed wives and mothers who symbolized the essence of moral authority, they promoted the ideal of the

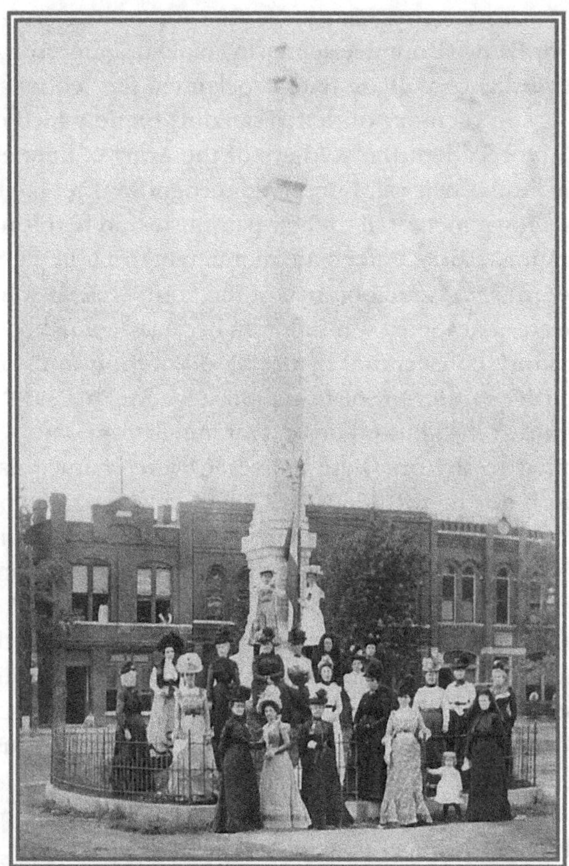

Fig. 8.1. Members of the local chapter of the United Daughters of the Confederacy in front
of soldier's monument, Franklin, Tennessee, 1905. Photograph used by permission of
Williamson County Archives, Franklin.

Confederate soldier as a standard for individual character: the devoted infantryman who had sacrificed everything to protect home, family, and society. In this way, the women could redevelop and recycle the southern domestic ideal left over from the antebellum period and use it to help a new generation of southerners see themselves as a people in, but morally above, the nation's new industrial order.[3]

## *Reconstructing the Conflict*

In Franklin, this active remaking of the Confederate past entailed reorganizing the town's memories of the war and the battle. When William Bate arrived in Franklin on October 5 by train from Nashville, twenty miles away, a local drum and flag corps escorted him from the depot to the ceremony grounds adjacent to the school, which was nearing completion. The site was familiar to the former Confederate major general. In the fall of 1864 he had served under John Bell Hood during the latter's ill-fated campaign into Middle Tennessee. For two weeks, from November 30, the day of the Franklin battle, to December 16, when the Battle of Nashville ended, Bate had witnessed the destruction of his division and with it the entire Army of Tennessee. Hood had entertained grandiose visions of recapturing the state's capital, a Union bastion if there ever was one, and then driving on into Kentucky and to the Ohio River. In reality, he met with disaster. The fighting at Franklin alone produced almost seven thousand Confederate casualties in five hours.[4]

For years following the war men such as Bate and Hood tried to explain to contemporaries their actions in the debacle. They hoped to preserve a sense of personal honor despite military loss. Hood, in particular, suffered close scrutiny for his actions. He had participated in some of the war's hallowed confrontations—Antietam, Gettysburg, and Chickamauga—but his personal memoir, published posthumously in 1880, was greeted with skepticism and hostility. His contemporaries protested that he never could admit blame for ordering the full frontal assault at Franklin across open ground against a fortified position. "They charge me with making Franklin a slaughter pen," Hood scolded his critics, "but, as I understand it, war means fight, and fight means kill."[5]

For their part, many of the Franklinites who were left to tend the thousands of Confederate casualties in 1864 did not bother to indulge in recriminations. Their initial response was to establish a cemetery for the Confederate dead. John McGavock, the wealthy owner of Carnton Plantation whose rooms had served as a field hospital in the battle's aftermath, partitioned two acres adjacent to the mansion for reburial of nearly fifteen hundred bodies disinterred in 1866 from shallow graves along the old Union breastworks. These men had been hastily buried after the battle, with many of the graves left unmarked. In an act that would be unthinkable thirty years later, local residents had stolen some of the makeshift markers for use as winter firewood. The new graves at Carnton would serve as a constant local reminder of the devastating Confederate defeat. Each May hundreds journeyed to the cemetery on Decoration Day to lay wreaths at the wooden headstones and pay their respects to the dead. The local newspaper, the *Franklin Review and Journal,* chided those who failed to participate.[6]

While annual grave site activities reinforced solidarity among southerners, they failed to produce a usable memory—focusing still on defeat of the South's cause. Franklin's morbidity was not alone. Until the mid-1880s, the majority of Confederate monuments were erected in cemeteries, and many were crowned with funerary urns. Each of these structures attested to the belief that, however noble, the cause had failed. As time passed, the names on the wooden grave markers at Carnton faded away. It seemed that the loss and destruction of the battle was about to be willingly forgotten.[7]

Instead, Franklin, along with the rest of the South, witnessed a dramatic change in how the Confederate past was remembered and commemorated beginning in the 1880s. Aided by a national spirit of reconciliation that lauded "the experience of battle" on both sides and a shifting cultural landscape shaped by industrialization, a hodgepodge of local bereavement exercises evolved into a regional celebration of the presumed southern values of self-sacrifice and honor. More important, Confederate commemoration began to feature a reconstructed memory of the war molded by the South's contemporary social and economic environment. Even some veterans who had fought at Franklin had a renewed outlook on the bloody confrontation.[8]

Sam Watkins was a veteran from Columbia, Tennessee, who had served with a local company called the Maury County Greys. Beginning in 1881, he penned a series of articles on the Army of Tennessee's exploits for his hometown newspaper, the *Columbia Herald.* Far from bitter about the war's outcome, Watkins sought public recognition for the "high private" who followed his orders and did his duty for his country. He told the story of a past "buried in oblivion," a past that lived only in the annals of his memory. His comrades on the battlefield, notably the foot soldier, were worthy of commemoration, he said. From "the proud and aristocratic stock of Cavaliers," they had surrendered their youth, and many their lives, for the southern cause.[9]

Watkins remembered the Franklin battle as the "blackest page in the history of the war." He and his comrades were not prepared that November afternoon for an assault on the Union line. Their regiments were strewn for twenty miles, from Spring Hill, eight miles south, to the outskirts of Franklin. But when the fighting began and "sheets of fire" ripped through their lines, he recalled, they continued to march "on down through the open field toward the rampart of blood and death." The forward line lit up all around them as the dead, Union and Confederate, filled the entrenchments. After midnight, when the battle finally ceased and the Union Army forces retreated toward Nashville, all that was left was a "grand holocaust of death."[10]

While Franklin was one of the worst defeats for the southern independence movement, Watkins hailed the soldiers' achievements. He hoped history would not remember these men who marched toward certain death as "an automation, a machine that works by the command of a good, bad, or indifferent engineer." At Franklin, he stressed, southern soldiers faced staggering odds. Yet these "noble and brave spirits" continued to fight, even though defeat appeared certain.[11]

Watkins's essays spoke particularly to those southerners who grew up with little or no memory of the struggle. The images he evoked of battle and of the unyielding participation of soldiers emphasized the South's devotion and character, not the actual political or economic aims of the Confederacy. Moreover, in this remaking of history, the North became a new kind of enemy. As Watkins described it, the Union won simply because of its overwhelming numbers. As one would expect from an army driven by industrial superiority, the northern troops were, in essence, characterless human machines that carried out their tasks according to their commanding engineers. Watkins's narrative suggests that contemporary southerners utilized the Confederate past not to recall themselves as supporters or descendants of slaveholders, or as believers in states' rights, but as men of spotless character confronting a modern world that often seemed chaotic and without integrity. For Watkins, the meaning of the war was taking on a new suit of clothes.[12]

The Columbia veteran's reworking of the glorious cause appealed to Franklin residents, who were experiencing the opportunities and dislocations of the New South. The Williamson County seat was fully involved in the economic and cultural transformations taking place during the 1880s and 1890s, as might be expected given its proximity to Nashville. The state capital had profited from the war more than any other southern city. Due in large part to Union occupation, local businessmen and transplants from other regions of the country took advantage of Nashville's expansive system of turnpikes and railroads that radiated out into the surrounding hinterland. By 1900 more than three thousand miles of track stretched between Ohio and the Gulf of Mexico, with Nashville serving as the hub. The city also was able to recruit northern capital to create a diverse manufacturing and financial base. Commercial enterprise extended beyond agricultural foodstuffs to embrace banking, lumber, publishing and printing, machine shops, and a workforce that included skilled mechanics and engineers who kept the distribution systems operating. At least until the turn of the century, when Atlanta and Memphis began to pose a challenge, Nashville dominated the South's commercial arena.[13]

Like people in other small southern towns, Franklinites both embraced and struggled with the regional process of development. The majority of Williamson County families survived, as they had in the past, on their abilities as farmers. Though most labored at home, some small farmers, both black and white, were forced by the poor economic conditions surrounding agriculture to hire on as extra hands on the large plantations still in operation. By 1889 local enterprise did offer Franklin's three thousand residents two gristmills and a broom factory, evidence of the area's industrial progress. In counties to the south, phosphate mines peppered once-prosperous farmlands. Increasingly, however, young people left the farm and ventured to town seeking employment. There men found work as clerks amid the crockery, tinware, iron stoves, and soap in several dry goods stores that lined the square. Women filled domestic jobs as seamstresses and cooks, and as teachers in the growing number of local schools.[14]

Those who remained on the farm saw their agricultural autonomy eroded by their participation in the region's expanding commercial economy. Cotton production in and around Franklin caught the eye of numerous small farmers. In concentrating on a single cash crop, their families were compelled to stake their livelihood on the consequences of the market. The editor of the local newspaper criticized the trend, saying, "'Cotton on the brain' is not a curable disease. All one can do is wait till those who have contracted it shall have died off, giving place to more sensible men and a more rational agriculture."[15]

The spread of the market economy was made more evident by Franklin's involvement with the railroad. By 1890, 90 percent of southerners lived in a county touched by rail. Towns fortunate to have a stop along the line quickly became centers of commerce, and train depots became the main staging grounds for community life. Twenty-five trains a day ran between Nashville and Birmingham, the Gulf corridor's other industrial leviathan, two hundred miles to the south. Though most locals traveled to the Tennessee capital to partake of its growing urban life, others, both professional and laymen, made the journey one way. "The most capable business men, lawyers, doctors, and preachers," noted a Vanderbilt University professor, "are practically all leaving the country for the town and city." Men from the rural hinterlands who had been too young to display their worth on the battlefield now made a name for themselves in the marketplace, ascending a new social hierarchy reliant on entrepreneurial enterprise. The building of Battle Ground Academy was an attempt by the people of Franklin to train young men for the experience.[16]

In early 1889 a group of local businessmen recruited Simeon Venerable Wall, the headmaster of the all-male academy in Culleoka, Tennessee, to establish an "entirely non-sectarian" school on battlefield land the group had purchased from a local family. The entire Culleoka student body and one teacher, William Mooney, accompanied Wall to Franklin. As a Confederate scout in Hood's army, Wall had participated in the Franklin engagement. His most notable claim to fame, however, had been escorting Jefferson Davis on his flight in May 1865 from Raleigh, North Carolina, to Irwinville, Georgia. As it turned out, Wall left Davis shortly before the Confederate president's capture—he claimed they parted near Dalton, Georgia—relieving the schoolmaster later of having to defend his lack of success in the affair. During the four-year war, Wall's family lost everything. He returned home to pursue a career in education.

His associate, William Mooney, was only two years old when the fighting began. The son of a Presbyterian minister in Huntsville, Alabama, Mooney was sent to the prestigious Webb School in Bell Buckle, Tennessee, and then to Southwestern Presbyterian University, where he earned a professional teaching degree. Mooney read and spoke Latin and Greek, and he combined his lifelong affinity for knowledge with the capability to coach football and baseball (fig. 8.2).[17]

According to the new directors, the academy could educate Franklin children and others "on a par with that of the best preparatory schools in New England." The curriculum would "subject boys to that discipline and training that may fit them to become learned, able, and Christian men." The school stressed its ability to cultivate self-control, truthfulness, and a sense of honor. Graduates, they noted, would possess the skills to attend such universities as Lehigh, Pennsylvania, and all the leading colleges of the South.[18]

The three-year college prep program at the academy exposed students to a broad range of subjects. Samuel Reynolds, a member of the class of 1909, joined BGA's Hamilton and Jefferson Debating Society and mixed in trips to Nashville's Vendome Theatre to see Shakespeare plays with his assignments in trigonometry, science, and French literature. He remembered that one of his favorite teachers, Mr. Hal, often lectured about such entrepreneurs as Andrew Carnegie, John D. Rockefeller, and Jay Gould.[19]

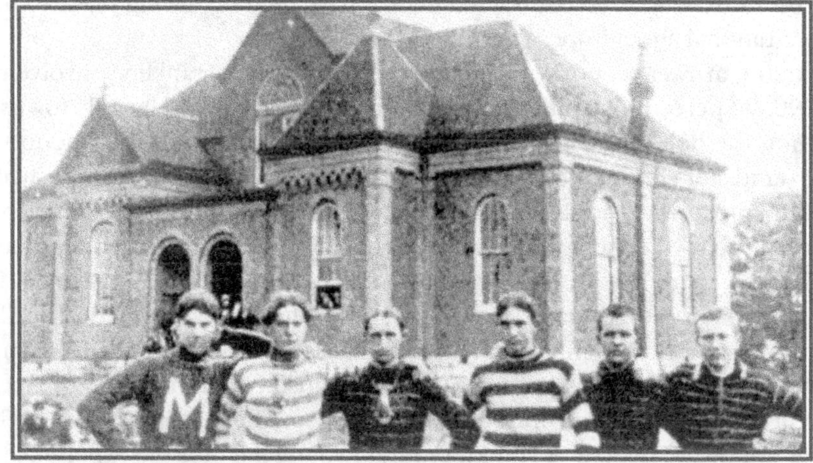

Fig. 8.2. Football team in front of original Battle Ground Academy Building, circa 1900. Williamson County Archives, Franklin.

Far more than any need to remember a war fading into history, it was Franklin's involvement in this enticing but threatening new order that prompted its people to begin celebrating the Confederate past. It was no accident that the revival process began in earnest not with cemeteries or even soldier monuments but with Battle Ground Academy. It was the world of the present and future—Mr. Hal and his lectures on Andrew Carnegie—that stirred the imagination of Williamson County. The Confederate past mattered indeed, but as a means to control Franklin's encounter with the real world of the 1880s and 1890s.

The academy's dedication was a community celebration. Almost three thousand onlookers pressed toward the speaker's platform to hear Bate pay tribute to the town's efforts. Since the end of the war the former governor had been a prolific speaker on the South's Confederate past, and in Franklin he chose to expound on the topic "patriotic." Bate hoped, as he had on other occasions, to link the values forged on the battlefield by Confederate soldiers, who, as he understood, were overpowered by the numbers and resources of his enemy, with the veterans who, "oppressed by unfriendly legislation" during Reconstruction, now made the best of citizens. The war had decided many things, among them the conflict between free and slave labor. But the people of Franklin had only to view the Battle Ground Academy and the rest of the changing landscape to see the "progressive prosperity" the Confederate soldier had been an "active agent in restoring." Bate asked his audience to "look around at church and school, at smiling field, at mill and factory, and ask whence this marvelous change? You will be told, it has not come from influences abroad, but from home people, among whom this same Confederate element has been a chief factor. It is a victory in peace." For Bate, the school was symbolic of that victory: a triumph that lay equally in the interests of the day and the actions of the past.[20]

In the course of an hour, Bate laid out the foundation of the new Confederate past. He described how, in his view, the framing of the Constitution had left sectional issues unresolved, and how the Confederacy was built on the principles of the founders. He continued, "The war was waged on principle. As evidenced by the veteran's earnestness in defeat, the sacrifices made by the Confederate soldier put to rest any question of motive. At no time was he doubtful of the legality and justice of his cause. There was never a time . . . that he did not feel he was fighting for his country."[21] The union of southern states is forever gone, Bate conceded, but "when we look into the casket of our interstate struggle for historic jewels, we will find none brighter or purer than those which adorn the Confederate side of this great drama." He challenged the academy's students to "turn the mirror of memory on this field" and preserve the "truth of history" concerning their heritage.[22]

### Building a Soldier Monument

Out of this interest in combining Confederate history with the area's progressive business community, local citizens soon turned to more symbolically direct methods to engineer a proper memory of the war. As early as 1887, several thousand former Confederates had gathered for a battlefield reunion. The parades and public speeches paid homage to their former comrades, both dead and alive. But more important, several citizens sought to build a monument memorializing the sacrifice and devotion of the Confederate soldier.[23]

In the months before the dedication of the Battle Ground Academy, a small group of Franklin women formed the Williamson County Monument Association. The WCMA's objective was to build a monument commemorating Franklin's fallen Confederate soldiers. In past years, the local Confederate veterans' group, the McEwen Bivouac, had achieved meager results in rallying support for this enterprise. Thus the WCMA inherited the project in the summer of 1889. Like other Ladies' Memorial Associations that sprang up in the South during the period, the group was composed almost exclusively of middle- and upper-class women whose families had been, and in most cases still were, part of the town's social and economic elite. The association offered these women the opportunity to expand their roles beyond the traditional domestic sphere while participating in an activity that kept "the memories of martyrdom alive."[24]

For the most part, veterans' groups identified the tasks involved in memorial work, such as fund-raising and monument building, as "particularly fitting to women." Male participation in these associations remained on the periphery, primarily in the role of sponsorship. In his speech at the academy, William Bate recognized the "noble women" of Franklin and their efforts to "teach our children and our children's children the history of our great struggle" through their monument work. He emphasized that the WCMA's activities should be an example to every county in the South.[25]

The WCMA held its inaugural meeting on Independence Day in 1889. The major result of the gathering was the establishment of an $8,000 fund-raising goal for construction of a monument to Franklin's Confederate dead. As a preamble to the monument campaign, the group decided to replace, with the help of the local United Confederate Veterans bivouac, the deteriorating wooden grave markers at Carnton. The cemetery held the dead from the eleven Confederate states and Kentucky. Each state legislature was asked to contribute $2 per man to fund new granite headstones, but only Louisiana, Mississippi, Missouri, and South Carolina responded to the appeal. The WCMA had to mount fund-raisers and solicit private donations to complete the project.[26]

By the fall of 1892 the women were far short of their $8,000 goal. Pledges gathered in the course of three years totaled less than $3,000. So in September the WCMA decided to abandon its efforts and cancel the remaining subscriptions. All but $300 was returned. Basing the project on preserving the graves of real Confederate soldiers apparently had not worked.[27]

In October 1895, however, the movement's fortunes changed with the emergence of a United Daughters of the Confederacy chapter in Franklin. Unlike locally oriented memorial associations, the UDC was a regional organization founded in Nashville in 1894, which personified the spirit of the nation's new corporate order.[28] It sought to do much more than commemorate the dead. Instead, the UDC's corporate mission was to mobilize a network of individual chapters (412 chapters by 1900) to mass-market a nostalgic mood, a mood made respectable because southern matrons cultivated it. The charters issued to each new chapter listed four primary objectives for memorializing the integrity of the Confederate soldier: the building of monuments, the research and writing of Confederate history, establishment of educational endowments for the sons and daughters of veterans, and the benevolent care of veterans. Emphasis was placed on the living, not graves and cemeteries.[29]

In the spring of 1895 the Nashville UDC encouraged members to establish new chapters in the Middle Tennessee area. Sallie Ewing Gaut, who lived with her husband in Nashville, organized an affiliate in her hometown of Franklin, for the most part composed of women formerly associated with the WCMA. Hattie McGavock Cowan, chapter president and daughter of John McGavock, the creator of the Carnton cemetery, headed a list of seventeen charter members. Others included Leighlia Perkins Cochran, whose husband had served in the war as a Confederate surgeon before

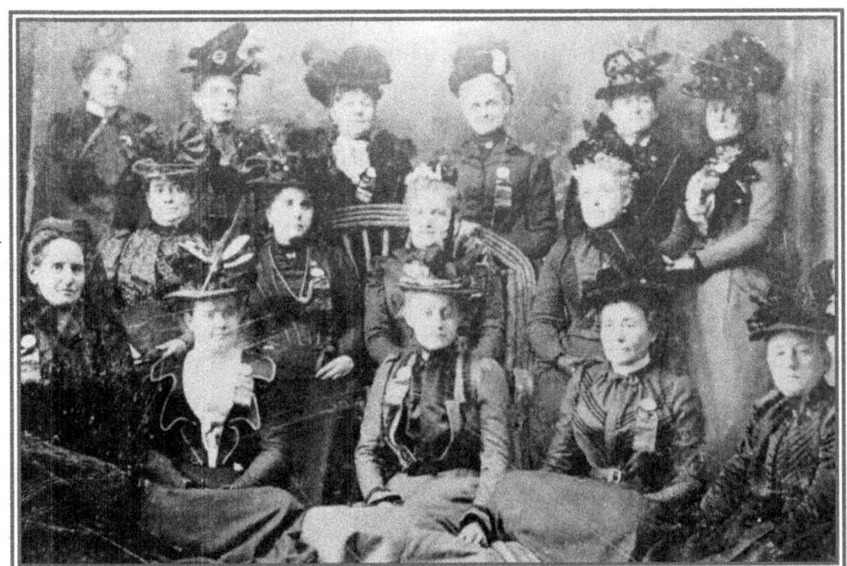

Fig. 8.3. Franklin Chapter of the United Daughters of the Confederacy, 1895.
Williamson County Archives, Franklin.

returning home to private practice; Martha Jones Gentry, the daughter of a Confederate surgeon, who now lived at Lynnhurst, one of Franklin's most prominent Victorian homes; Lulie Cochran Perkins, whose family had owned a plantation just outside of town before the war devastated their home; and Susie Gentry, one of the group's youngest members and already part of a national patriotic organization, the Daughters of the American Revolution.[30] The UDC chapter (fig. 8.3) rallied behind its motto, "The Truth Shall Shine in History," and geared up to resume Franklin's monument campaign. But before it moved into full swing, the women donated the funds left in their treasury—a little more than $400—to the proposed Battle Abbey in Richmond, a regionwide museum designed to hold Confederate memorabilia, regimental histories, and battle flags.[31]

When the women renewed Franklin's monument campaign, a debate ensued over where the memorial should be placed. Supporters of Carnton's Confederate Cemetery wanted the structure to be built near the graves of the "sacred dead," but the site was deemed "too far removed from the daily public contact." Others suggested the railroad depot, where those riding the train could view the monument against the backdrop of the battlefield. That idea quickly lost favor because, as one local saw it, "we don't build it for strangers; we build it for our children." Finally in 1899, when collections reached the UDC's goal, the town square was selected.[32]

By the end of the nineteenth century, the square had evolved into the center of public and commercial life in Franklin. Along with the railroad, a network of old and winding dirt roads channeled people and commodities into the town center from the surrounding countryside. Though most farmers visited infrequently, many people made the trip to peddle their goods to local merchants while picking up supplies for home. As commercial enterprise grew in places like Franklin, however, the larger businesses in town were less bound by ties to the area's small producers. They looked instead to brokers from larger cities to provide them with the majority of their wares.[33]

Within a dense configuration of new and old buildings, the most prominent local businesses were found on the square. A trip around its inner boundaries offered patrons a chance to see new items from distant places. Dry goods stores, with their showcase windows, helped create, as one historian puts it, a "public environment for desire." Shops displayed an assortment of merchandise, including things like gingham cloth, china, and name-brand soap. After the turn of the century, a stroll inside might even reveal a soda fountain serving Coca-Cola. Other businesses, such as the livery stable, the bank, saloons, stores, and the courthouse, also brought an array of shoppers and sightseers. The square offered all the features of the region's commercial progress.[34]

More often than not, the town square also presented an environment for vice and was singled out by social and religious reformers for its lack of virtue. As the new commercial economy became further entrenched in town, drunkenness, prostitution, and open profanity accompanied the throng of people, stirring temperance groups, moral and school reform organizations, and eventually anti–child labor advocates to respond.[35]

Franklin's decision to place the monument squarely within this maelstrom of social and economic activity attests to the town's interest and need to enlist the ideals of personal character and duty portrayed by the Confederate soldier. Complete with haversack, hat, and gun in hand, his image was thrust into the mainstream of southern town life in an attempt to revitalize and instill a sense of moral behavior in a world where character seemed to be all but abandoned for the interests of corporate commercialization and personal pleasure. The soldier's presence added a sense of Anglo-Saxon nobility not only to the aspiring sentiments of those harping the notion of a New South, but also to a reconciliatory nation on the cusp of imperial expansion.[36]

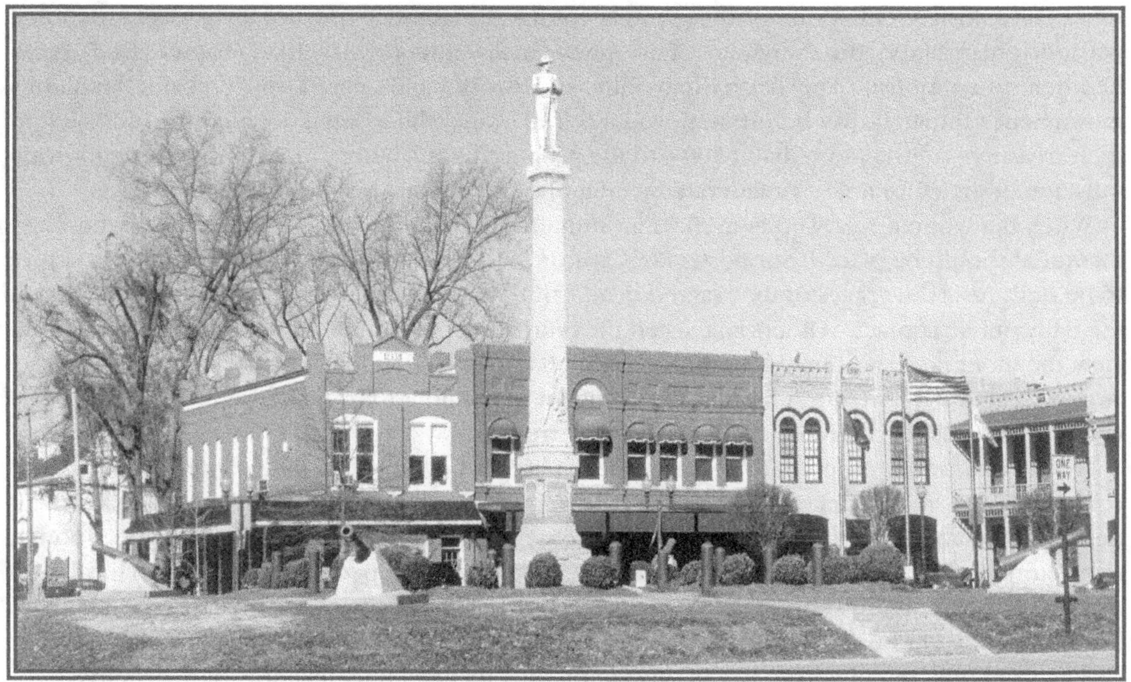

Fig. 8.4. Franklin Confederate Monument, 1999. Photograph by David Currey.

The Franklin monument was envisioned as a single shaft composed of Italian marble with a six-foot-tall marble soldier standing at parade rest on top (fig. 8.4). The base on which the shaft was supported was made of Vermont granite. The northern origin of the stone seemed to make little difference to locals in Franklin, but to some unreconstructed veterans in the South the use of Yankee granite was criminal. In 1888 when Gen. Jubal Early, a corps commander under Robert E. Lee, found that Maine granite rather than Virginia stone would be used for the pedestal of the monument to Lee in Richmond, he withdrew his $1,000 donation. The Franklin UDC was more reconciled.[37]

The final cost of the structure, including the property in the square, was $2,700. When the cornerstone was laid in September 1899, organizers placed a copy of the Franklin UDC charter inside the vault, along with a *Confederate Veteran* magazine and a list of those killed at Franklin in the war. Three weeks before the unveiling, as workmen were hoisting the statue to the top of the column, the pulley horses became tangled in the ropes and the soldier fell, breaking off a piece of his broad-brimmed hat. The UDC tried to no avail to fix the hat. It was decided that the piece would remain detached, and installation proceeded.

A cloudless blue sky and warm breeze welcomed an estimated ten thousand veterans, their families, and curious onlookers to the dedication day festivities on November 30, 1899. Even Tennessee Gov. Benton McMillan, who had greeted the First Tennessee Regiment in Nashville as they arrived home from the Philippines the previous day, was on hand. For at least a day, the town was awash in a sea of red and gray. Confederate flags and bunting "adorned the businesses along the square." A band struck up *Bonnie Blue Flag* and *Dixie* as members of the crowd, carrying portraits of Civil War heroes Robert E. Lee, Stonewall Jackson, and Jefferson Davis, sang along. Some veterans dressed in what remained of their old uniforms and joined in a parade from the railroad depot, up Main Street, to the center of town. J. H. Henderson, a local citizen, stood amidst the crowd and vowed that "future generations will point back with pride to the day . . . when all passions had subsided, all animosities had been buried, and all sections of our common country were at peace with each other as brothers."[38]

Local businesses got into the act as well. Buford Brothers, Franklin's largest dry goods store, sold souvenir plates produced in Vienna, Austria, and embellished with such battlefield landmarks as the Carter House, the Carter's cotton gin, the Carnton Confederate cemetery, and Battle Ground Academy, a symbol of the New South.[39]

Speeches about the Franklin battle filled the afternoon air. Gen. George Gordon described the first assault on the Union breastworks and his capture by Federal troops. At the height of his long-winded recitation, a "Rebel yell went out and pulses leaped." The war had returned to Franklin, but this time as a victory parade that celebrated the persistence of superior southern character in the form of the Confederate soldier. The soldier's image now stood in the center of Franklin's public life, a recognition of the value system that had opposed an overwhelming northern industrial machine during the war and now offered moral inspiration in the face of modernity's onrush. When the party finally broke up in late afternoon, veterans strolled up the street to the battlefield for less formal observations on their personal remembrances of the war. Organizers and participants alike perceived the ceremony as a way to "teach our children patriotism"—as one local put it—and exhibit for the citizens of Franklin, young and old, a distinct Confederate vision of the past. J. H. Henderson, a veteran of the battle, proclaimed that "while history for a season be colored by the conquerors, and thus shadow the truth, in time it will right itself, and the world will know as we know, that no age or country has ever produced the superior of our countrymen, in courage, fidelity, and nobleness of character."[40]

The need for a usable Confederate past during the 1890s led hundreds of small southern towns like Franklin to erect monuments to their fallen Confederate soldiers. Though some monuments continued to be built in cemeteries well into the twentieth century, the cause for which they stood no longer lingered in the cities of the dead. The Confederate past had been transformed into a response to industrialization's reordering of the region's social and economic institutions. In commodifying southern heritage, the UDC attempted to unify individuals and communities by extolling the patriotic values of the soldier who sacrificed his life for a cause greater than himself, protecting his home and family. The Franklin chapter would go on to promote Confederate textbooks in Williamson County schools, fund a women's dormitory at a Nashville teacher's college, and award academic scholarships for essays on Confederate history to high school students, girls and boys. In the end, however, the Confederate past the UDC celebrated was just that, a celebration, with little to do with the Confederacy.[41]

Over the course of the past century, the appearance of Franklin's cultural and physical landscape has been transformed by the region's further integration into a national, and now global, economy. Many of the sites associated with the memory of the Confederate soldier's sacrifice remain, however, as potent historical attractions. The monument continues to welcome those who converge on the square from one of four state highways. Small boxwoods and cannons have been added to the surrounding base to accentuate its commanding presence. Today Battle Ground Academy has added a new campus north of town that has increased the school's enrollment to well over six hundred. The school's hallways are filled with both boys and girls, and dozens of graduates matriculate each year to some of the country's most prestigious universities. The cemetery at Carnton also endures as a central component of annual memorial services and candlelight ceremonies. Though Franklin has changed over the years, these sites still convey the fundamental ideal important to their original and sustained relevance to the community: the value of personal character as a defining element of southern identity.

## *Notes*

1. William Bate, *Address at Battle Ground Academy* (BGA) dedication in Franklin, Tenn., Oct. 5, 1889. Copy in Tennessee State Library and Archives, Nashville, 3.

2. Gaines M. Foster, *Ghosts of the Confederacy* (New York: Oxford Univ. Press, 1987), 127–44; quotations on 127. See also Edward L. Ayers, *The Promise of the New South: Life after Reconstruction* (New York: Oxford Univ. Press, 1992); and C. Vann Woodward, *Origins of the New South, 1877–1913*, History of the South Series, vol. 9 (Baton Rouge: Louisiana State Univ. Press, 1987).

3. On the changing nature of family, see Steven Mintz and Susan Kellogg, *Domestic Revolutions: A Social History of American Family Life* (New York: Free Press, 1988), 43–65.

4. The most complete narrative of the Nashville and Franklin campaign can be found in Wiley Sword, *Embrace an Angry Wind: The Confederacy's Last Hurrah: Spring Hill, Franklin, and Nashville* (New York: Harper Collins, 1992).

5. John Bell Hood, *Advance and Retreat: Personal Experiences in the United States and Confederate States Armies* (New Orleans: G. T. Beauregard, 1880). An account of the day's proceedings can be found in "Battle Ground Academy," *Nashville Banner,* Oct. 7, 1889. Hood quotation is from Sword, *Embrace an Angry Wind,* 440.

6. The most detailed account of the cemetery's history can be found in a pamphlet published by the United Daughters of the Confederacy, *McGavock Confederate Cemetery; Franklin, Tennessee* (Franklin: privately printed, 1989). "Local Items," *Franklin Review and Journal,* May 20, 1875, 3.

7. Confederate Southern Memorial Association, *History of the Confederated Memorial Associations of the South* (New Orleans: Graham Press, 1904), 91–92.

8. Foster, *Ghosts of the Confederacy,* 6, 88–103.

9. Watkins's memoirs were first printed as a series of articles in the *Columbia Herald* in 1881–82. Quotations are from republication in book form: Sam Watkins, *Company Aytch; or a Side Show of the Big Show,* ed. M. Thomas Inge (New York: Plum, 1999), 5, 7, 213.

10. Ibid., 201–3.

11. Ibid., 8, 203.

12. Ibid., 7.

13. For the definitive study of Nashville's social and economic growth during and after the war, see Don H. Doyle, *New Men, New Cities, New South: Atlanta, Nashville, Charleston, Mobile, 1860–1910* (Chapel Hill: Univ. of North Carolina Press, 1990).

14. "Southern Scenes," *Franklin Review and Journal,* June 12, 1889, 2. Dept. of Commerce, Bureau of the Census, Williamson County manuscript census, 1880 (Washington D.C.: Government Printing Office, 1880), microfiche.

15. "Farm and Garden: Shall It Be 'All Cotton' This Year?" *Franklin Review and Journal,* Apr. 22, 1875, 4.

16. For a short overview of the railroad's impact on other towns, see Ayers, *Promise of the New South,* 9–13, 55–65; Vanderbilt professor's quotation, 63–64. On industrialization's impact on patterns of life, see Robert H. Wiebe, *The Search for Order, 1877–1920* (New York: Hill and Wang, 1967).

17. "Entirely non-sectarian" quotation is from "The Battle Ground Academy," *Franklin Review and Journal,* June 12, 1889, 3. Discussion of Wall and Mooney is from an unpublished manuscript by James French, "History of Battle Ground Academy," original at Battle Ground Academy, Franklin, Tenn. Wall claimed to have left Davis at Dalton, but the Davis escape route never neared Dalton, raising questions about Wall's account.

18. Battle Ground Academy, *The Mooney School: Battle Ground Academy, 1899–1900* (Nashville: Brandon Printing Co., 1899), 4–7.

19. Samuel Reynolds, "Recollections of Days at BGA," [1940?], typescript at Battle Ground Academy Library, Franklin, Tenn.

20. For an overview of the day's activities see *Nashville Banner,* Oct. 7, 1889. Bate, *Address at BGA,* 3, 9.

21. Bate, *Address at BGA,* 9.

22. Ibid., 7, 8, 15.

23. *Franklin Review-Appeal,* May 12, 1910.

24. "Unveiling of the Confederate Monument," *Franklin Review-Appeal,* Dec. 7, 1899.

25. Quotation and discussion is from Foster, *Ghosts of the Confederacy,* 38. See also Marjorie Spruill Wheeler, *New Women of the New South: The Leaders of the Woman Suffrage Movement in the Southern States* (New York: Oxford Univ. Press, 1993), 3–37. Bate quotes from *Address at BGA,* 15.

26. *Franklin Review-Appeal,* Dec. 7, 1899. UDC, *McGavock Confederate Cemetery,* 6.

27. Mary Pinkerton, "History of the Franklin Chapter: United Daughters of the Confederacy," *Franklin Review-Appeal,* Feb. 23, 1911.

28. "To Woman Goes the Credit," *Franklin Review-Appeal,* Nov. 30, 1899. Angie Parrott, "'Love Makes Memory Eternal': The United Daughters of the Confederacy in Richmond, Virginia, 1897–1920," in *The Edge*

*of the South: Life in Nineteenth Century Virginia,* Edward L. Ayers and John C. Willis, eds. (Charlottesville: Univ. Press of Virginia, 1991), 221. On the rise of the corporate order and "virtues" of organizational skills, see Alan Trachtenberg, *The Incorporation of America: Culture and Society in the Gilded Age* (New York: Hill and Wang, 1982), 70–100.

29. On the organizational policies and objectives of the UDC, see John Trotwood Moore, ed., *Tennessee: The Volunteer State, 1769–1923* (Nashville: S. J. Clarke, 1923), 793–94.

30. *Franklin Review-Appeal,* Feb. 23, 1911.

31. For motto see United Daughters of the Confederacy, Franklin Chapter Fourteen, *Yearbook 1994–1996* (Franklin: privately printed, 1994), 2. Foster, *Ghosts of the Confederacy,* 116–17.

32. *Franklin Review-Appeal,* Dec. 7, 1899.

33. The design of the town square has been described as a "magnet" in Edward T. Price, "The Central Courthouse Square in the American County Seat," in *Common Places: Readings in American Vernacular Architecture,* Dell Upton and John Michael Vlach, eds. (Athens and London: Univ. of Georgia Press, 1986), 124–45. Cynthia Tolbert looks at prewar development of Franklin in *Constructing Townscapes: Space and Society in Antebellum Tennessee* (Chapel Hill: Univ. of North Carolina Press, 1999).

34. Quotation from William Leach, *Land of Desire: Merchants, Power, and the Rise of a New American Culture* (New York: Pantheon, 1993), 40. In his work, Leach describes the rise of the growing consumer culture of the 1890s and how merchants played a vital role in creating the "cult of the new." For the importance of merchants bringing the outside world to southerners, see Ayers, *Promise of the New South,* 55–103.

35. For a glimpse of the rollicking town life and main streets, see Ted Ownby, *Subduing Satan: Religion, Recreation, and Manhood in the Rural South, 1865–1920* (Chapel Hill: Univ. of North Carolina Press, 1990), 38–55, 167–77. On southern women's reform movements and Progressivism, see William A. Link, *The Paradox of Southern Progressivism, 1880–1930* (Chapel Hill: Univ. of North Carolina Press, 1992).

36. Jackson Lears addresses the role of the "martial ideal" and the "wedding of virtue and commerce" in *No Place of Grace: Antimodernism and the Transformation of American Culture, 1880–1920* (Chicago: Univ. of Chicago Press, 1983), 97–102. Certainly the revival of the slaveholding cavalier is important to Lost Cause mythology, as Lears states, but the figure of the individual foot soldier, left out of the immediate postwar Lost Cause movement, is more representative of the response by late-nineteenth-century proponents such as the UDC to commercial society's lack of integrity.

37. "The Queen Bees," *Franklin Review-Appeal,* Dec. 7, 1899. Michael Kammen, *Mystic Chords of Memory* (New York: Alfred A. Knopf, 1991; reprint, New York: Vintage Books, 1993), 111.

38. *Franklin Review-Appeal,* Dec. 7, 1899.

39. Ibid., Nov. 30, 1899.

40. Ibid., Dec. 7, 1899.

41. On other UDC work see Patricia Faye Climer, "Protectors of the Past: The United Daughters of the Confederacy, Tennessee Division, and the Lost Cause" (master's thesis, Vanderbilt Univ., 1973).

# Part III

## CELEBRATION AND RESPONSES TO THE NORTH

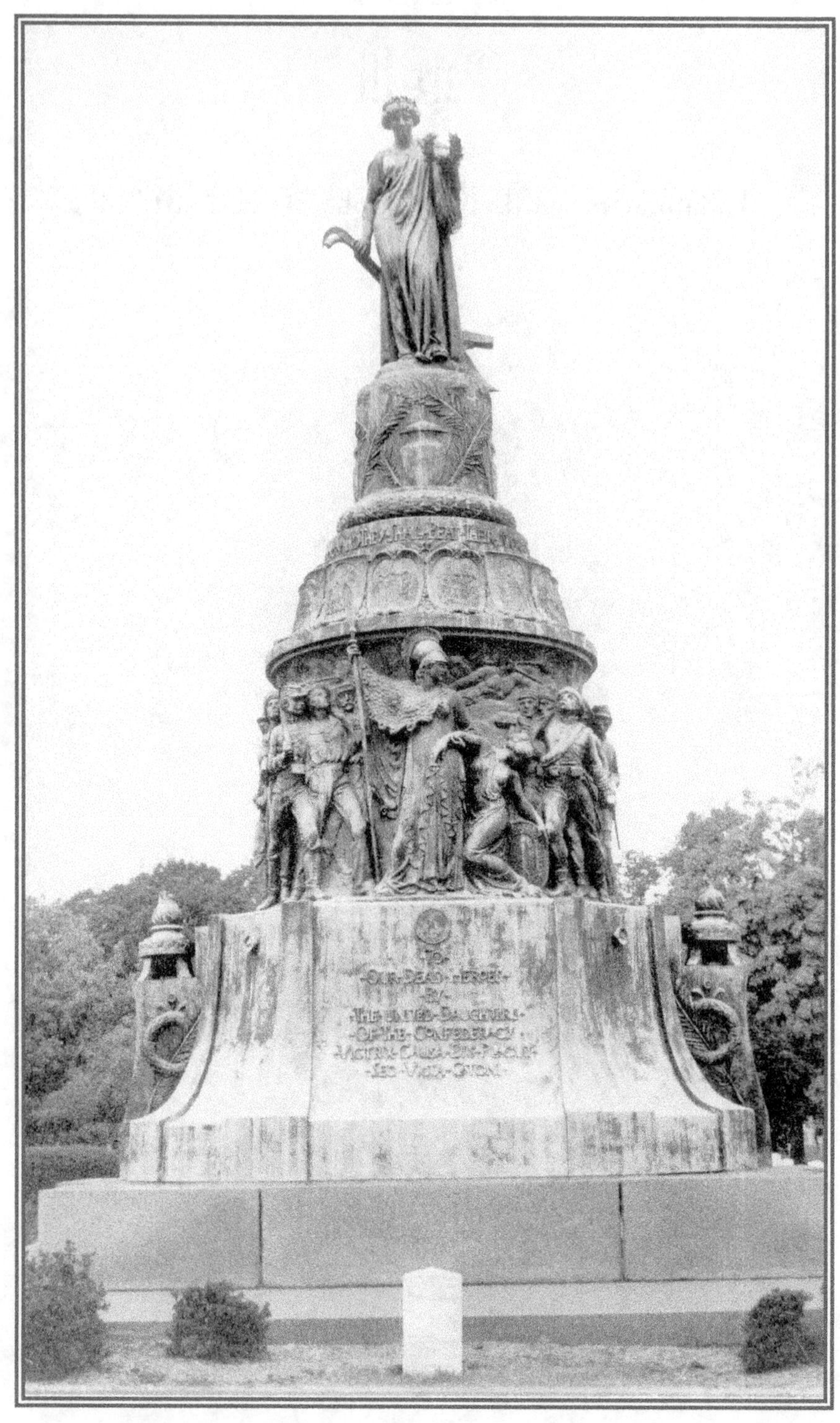

Fig. 9.1. Confederate Monument at Arlington National Cemetery, designed by sculptor Moses Ezekiel and dedicated June 4, 1914. Photograph by Sean McCormally.

# 9

# The Confederate Monument at Arlington

## A TOKEN OF RECONCILIATION

*Karen L. Cox*

A terrific thunderstorm broke over Arlington National Cemetery late yesterday while the President [Woodrow Wilson] was addressing a great crowd gathered for the unveiling of the monument erected there for the Confederate dead. Torrents of wind-driven rain drenched the blue and gray veterans and women and children before they could reach shelter, and then there was a wild dash for automobiles and trolley cars, participants and spectators alike forgetting the almost finished program.

Washington Post, *Friday, June 5, 1914*

LOST CAUSE DEVOTEES hailed the unveiling of the Confederate Monument in Arlington National Cemetery on June 4, 1914, as an extraordinary achievement for peace and reconciliation nearly a half century after the close of the Civil War. The Federal government had set the stage for this grand gesture by allowing the reburial of Confederate soldiers in the cemetery and by giving permission to the United Daughters of the Confederacy to build a tribute there. The impressive sculptural group that resulted, located just across the Potomac River from the White House, was conceived and constructed by the UDC as the influential organization's only "national" memorial, to be presented as a gift to the country. Military and political leaders from the North and South were invited to speak at its dedication, and the president of the United States joined them on the podium.[1] Yet upon closer examination, it is clear that the Arlington monument (fig. 9.1) had an even greater meaning than sectional peace for white southerners. For them, it also was about Confederate vindication. Vindication, after all, was the clearest path southerners could see to reconciliation and a truly reunited country.

Ever since the United Daughters of the Confederacy formed in 1894, the organization's underlying goal had been to vindicate the actions of its members' parents and grandparents, often referred to as the "generation of the sixties."[2] Confederate monuments served as one means of attaining this goal, and it is no coincidence that the Daughters placed them in the most publicly visible locations—on the grounds surrounding state capitols and county courthouses. By erecting images of their heroes on a political landscape, the Daughters insisted that the ideals of the Old South must be present in the creation of the New. Moreover, in a region that rejected women's right to full citizenship, monument-building was one way they could express their political beliefs. Monuments helped preserve Confederate culture for future generations and simultaneously allowed white women to show their support for a system of government that upheld the Confederate ideals of states' rights and white supremacy.[3]

The UDC had committed itself to build two other regional monuments before World War I— one to Jefferson Davis in Richmond, Virginia, and one to the soldiers buried at Shiloh, Tennessee. But the Arlington monument was unique among its projects, for it offers important evidence of how the national landscape was reconfigured to represent the white South's historical interpretation of the war.

### *Planting the Seed: McKinley's Words*

The movement to build the Arlington monument was initiated, in part, as a response to political rhetoric. Many southern whites pointed to a speech given by President William McKinley in Atlanta on December 21, 1898. There he made the statement that "in the spirit of fraternity we [the Federal government] should share with you in the care of graves of Confederate soldiers." Such words were salve for the wounded egos of white southerners, who had witnessed the Federal government's development of national cemeteries for Union casualties over the decades and heard former Confederates berated as "traitors" and "rebels." McKinley's comments also were timely, given the "romance of reunion" currently taking place between the North and South. Northerners and southerners had defeated a common enemy during the Spanish-American War, and in the 1890s white men from both regions were reveling in what historian Nina Silber has described as a "cult of Anglo-Saxonism." These shared experiences contributed to a new respect among northerners for Confederate veterans, an important step in reunification as well as vindication for southern men.[4]

Southerners took McKinley's words to heart and pushed to make sure that the Federal government followed through on his promise. On June 6, 1900, at the urging of southern veterans, Congress passed a law allowing the bodies of 267 Confederate soldiers buried on northern battlefields to be reinterred in a newly designated section of Arlington National Cemetery (fig. 9.2). Spokesmen for Lost Cause organizations regarded this as compelling evidence of a "fraternal love" between North and South.[5]

Talk of building a monument on these same grounds began almost immediately. Mrs. Magnus Thompson, president of the District of Columbia division of the UDC, called a meeting of Confederate organizations in the city on November 6, 1906. They discussed plans to build a monument in the area of Arlington Cemetery where the Confederate soldiers were buried; they also formed the Arlington Confederate Monument Association (ACMA). Hilary Herbert, a Confederate veteran and former secretary of the Navy under Grover Cleveland, headed the ACMA's executive committee. Florence Butler, the wife of U.S. Sen. Marion Butler of North Carolina, served on the executive committee, as did Thompson. Most committee members were representatives from local chapters of the UDC and the United Confederate Veterans (UCV). An all-male advisory board was

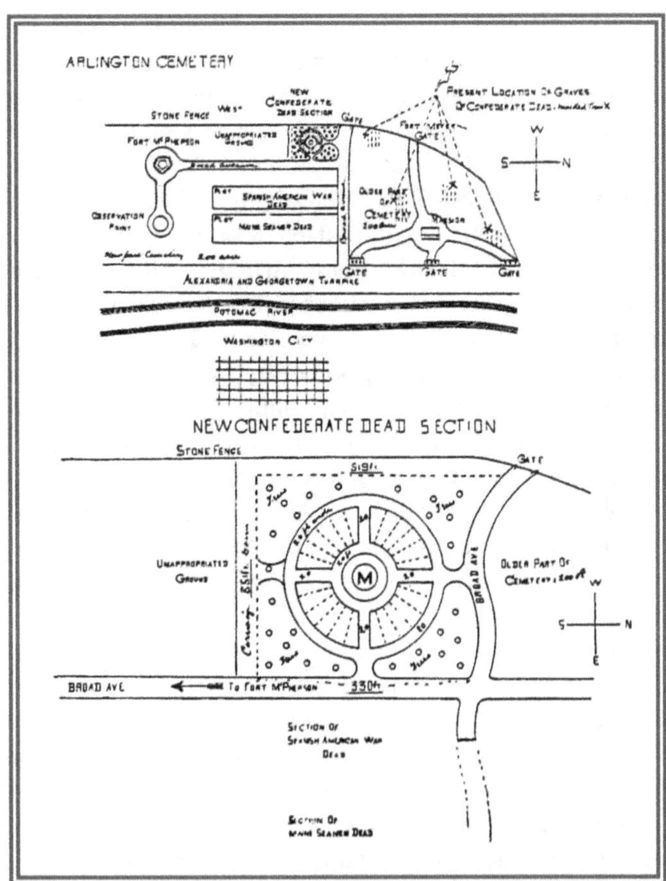

Fig. 9.2. Plan for location of Confederate graves and monument at Arlington National Cemetery, published in *The "Lost Cause,"* Louisville, Kentucky, 1907.

appointed, including among others Thomas Nelson Page, the U.S. ambassador to Italy who had gained fame for his dialect-driven plantation literature and novels critical of Reconstruction.[6]

The ACMA quickly gained permission from Secretary of War William Howard Taft to erect the monument and began its fund-raising campaign. Donations came in slowly, however, and within a year the group had raised little more than one thousand dollars. This was barely enough to erect the simplest monument, much less one worthy of placement on a national landscape and meant to convey the message that Confederate soldiers were heroic defenders of a just cause.[7]

The committee members soon realized that a citywide campaign could not generate the necessary funds. It was fortuitous, therefore, that on a visit to Washington in the summer of 1907, UDC President-General Lizzie George Henderson suggested that her organization take over the Arlington project. A national effort was required, and the UDC, a fund-raising powerhouse, was well known for its ability to complete its projects. For example, the Daughters had raised approximately fifty thousand dollars to erect the grand monument to Jefferson Davis in Richmond—a plan the UCV initiated but was unable to finish.[8]

At Henderson's urging, Colonel Herbert attended the Daughters' Norfolk Convention in 1907 and asked the Daughters to assume responsibility for completion of a monument of impressive scale and design. He suggested that delegates from UDC chapters in Washington could manage the project with the assistance of an advisory board of men. Convention delegates unanimously agreed to accept the work of the ACMA "without conditions."[9]

The Arlington project held great appeal for the Daughters. Building a Confederate monument near the nation's Capitol was symbolic in and of itself. Moreover, the monument would stand on land that surrounded Robert E. Lee's former home, Arlington House, which had been seized by Union forces. The timing, too, could not have been better. The Daughters had recently unveiled the Davis monument and were now free to devote their energy to a monument of national significance. The new project provided an opportunity to honor the "memory of the soldiers" buried at Arlington as well as to offer the nation a symbol of peace and reconciliation. Motivated by Herbert's charge that this monument be something extraordinary, the UDC employed its network of nearly 100,000 members in a fund-raising campaign destined for success.[10] The president-general acted as the ex-officio president of the ACMA, appointing a board of directors composed of one representative from each state division of the UDC. State directors were responsible for raising money to complete the Arlington monument, while a central committee in Washington oversaw local preparations.[11]

Progress was slow at first; the UDC raised less than twenty-five hundred dollars in the first year of its campaign. Committee chair Hilary Herbert was proud to note, however, that the donations included one from survivors of the Twenty-third New Jersey Regiment, proof of "brotherly love" between the veterans of both sections.[12] The following year, in 1909, the committee sent out more than three thousand letters and appeals, increasing the Arlington monument fund to thirteen thousand dollars by year's end. By this time several artists from around the country had written the ACMA asking what the organization expected to spend on the monument and offering to submit designs.[13]

The budget initially recommended for the monument was thirty-five thousand dollars, half the cost of the Davis Monument in Richmond, but a sizable amount nonetheless. Herbert advised the UDC to raise most of that amount before committing to "a plan, or an artist." This would ensure that the Daughters could "demand and secure a memorial that will be artistic, durable, appropriate, and worthy," he said. There also was concern that the monument reflect well upon Robert E. Lee, the "great leader at whose home it is to stand."[14]

## *Choosing a Design*

The committee on design first met at Herbert's home in northwest Washington in the summer of 1910 to consider what the completed monument should look like. It concluded that a depiction of Lee in the act of leading his forces would be most appropriate. While there had been many statues and monuments erected to Lee's memory, members said none had shown him "in action on the field of battle . . . with the love in which he was held by the private soldier under his command." The committee, made up of seven men and women, including UDC President-General Virginia Faulkner McSherry, also reasoned that a sculpture memorializing Lee and the "men behind the guns" was likely to "inspire a more active effort in the collection of funds."[15]

Raising money for monuments was becoming increasingly difficult. The number of Confederate veterans—the men who served as inspiration for building monuments—was rapidly dwindling. Younger southerners, who had no memory of the war, were less likely to support such projects. Thus emotional appeals from Lost Cause organizations had become less effective.

The Daughters employed numerous fund-raising strategies, including Confederate bazaars and ice cream socials. In 1910 the UDC hit upon the "scheme," as President-General McSherry put it, of selling "Confederate Christmas Seals." Noting the Red Cross's success in the sale of its stamps, McSherry believed the Daughters could raise thirty-five thousand dollars for the Arlington monument in eighteen months. With her approval, a UDC member from Florence, Alabama, created and copyrighted her design for Confederate Christmas Seals. The ACMA increased its budget for the monument to fifty thousand dollars in anticipation of the stamps' financial rewards.[16]

Confident that the Daughters would raise enough money for an impressive monument, the Arlington committee proceeded in its quest for an artist. In the spring of 1911 Thomas Nelson Page invited his friend, the sculptor Moses Ezekiel (1844–1917), to accompany him to Herbert's home. Ezekiel, who maintained his studio in Rome, was in the middle of a visit to the United States and unaware of the meeting's purpose. When members of the ACMA and the UDC invited him to create the Arlington monument, however, he accepted without hesitation. "I had been waiting for forty years," he recalled in his memoirs, "to have my love for the South recognized." He eagerly sketched the design he had in mind.[17]

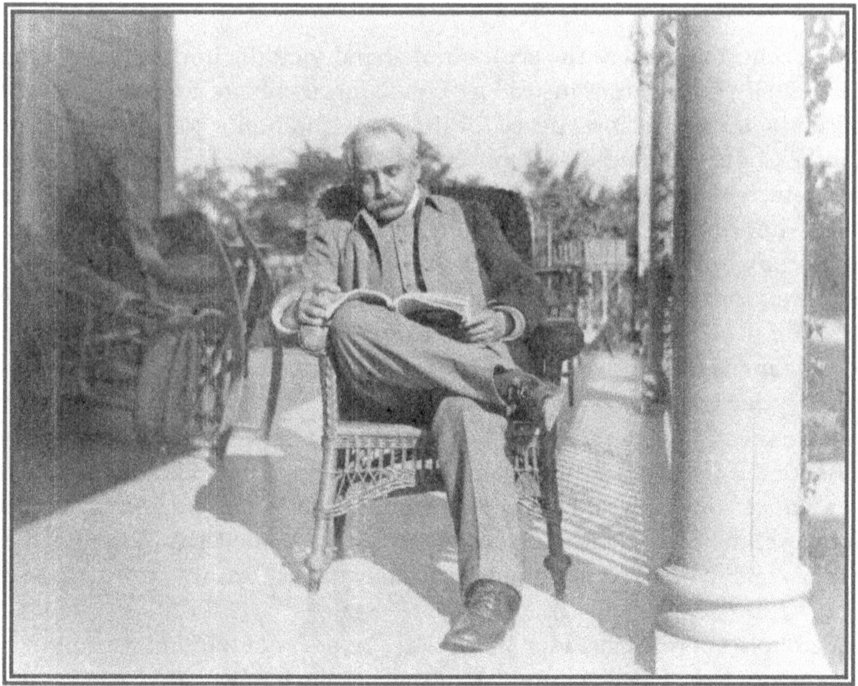

Fig. 9.3. Moses Ezekiel, circa 1910. Rader Marcus Center of the American Jewish Archives, Cincinnati campus, Hebrew Union College, Jewish Institute of Religion.

Ezekiel (fig. 9.3) the man, and Ezekiel the artist, proved to be an ideal choice. A native of Richmond, Ezekiel enrolled at the Virginia Military Institute (VMI) in Lexington, Virginia, in 1862, becoming its first Jewish cadet. He fought in the Battle of New Market in 1864 while a member of the VMI Cadet Battalion, and after graduation in 1866 he briefly studied human anatomy at the Medical College of Virginia. In May of 1869 Ezekiel went to Germany, where he studied at the Royal Academy of Art in Berlin. In 1873 he won the prestigious Michel-Beer Prix de Rome for a bas-relief entitled *Israel* and was awarded two years of study in Rome, all expenses paid. He made the Italian city his home and established his studio in the Baths of Diocletian, where he created numerous works that won him fame in Europe and the United States. By the time the UDC commissioned him to create the Arlington monument, he had earned a reputation for such works as *Religious Liberty* for the 1876 Centennial Exposition in Philadelphia, a statue of Christopher Columbus displayed at the 1893 Chicago World's Fair, and *Virginia Mourning Her Dead* at VMI, a moving allegorical figure dedicated in 1903 in honor of cadets killed at the Battle of New Market. A replica of Ezekiel's Stonewall Jackson statue for Charleston, West Virginia, also would be installed at VMI in 1912.[18]

Ezekiel felt strong emotional ties to the South and wrote to President-General McSherry that the Arlington commission was personally significant. "I am devoting myself to a subject that I have more at heart than any work I have ever done before," he told her. Referring to it as "our" monument, Ezekiel confessed, "I have given up every other commission in order to devote myself exclusively to this work, which occupies my thoughts all the time." He discouraged visitors from coming to his studio, in part to limit public discussions of the design before the work was completed.[19]

When the UDC chose Ezekiel as the sculptor, it abandoned the initial idea of a monument to Robert E. Lee and his army. Officials instead gave the artist complete control over the design. The agreed-upon central theme became "peace for the living and honor to the dead." Ezekiel sought to both honor the Confederate dead and convey peace through the heroic figure of a woman representing the South, with one hand extended and holding a wreath, the other hand "resting upon a plow-stock" as she "rests her faith in the future on labor." Directly below the bronze figure he planned four cinerary urns, one for each year of the war, and below them a frieze of shields bearing the coats of arms for each Confederate state plus Maryland, which was included because of the resources the state provided during the war. Ezekiel also wanted the monument to be flanked with tripods containing eternal flames.[20]

The theme of peace is less obvious in Ezekiel's ambitious plan for an eight-foot-high bronze frieze to complete the monument. He said the thirty-two life-size figures on the frieze illustrated "the enthusiasm of the South when the tocsin of war sounded" and exhibited "every phase of the heroism and sacrifices of the period."[21] Ezekiel's interpretation of the past was consistent with that held by many elite white southerners, especially those in the UDC. Certainly the Daughters did not labor for years to build a monument that unfavorably portrayed the actions of the South or its heroes.

The central grouping in relief includes Minerva, the goddess of war and wisdom, who "upholds the South [represented as a female figure] when she is sinking down and trying to sustain herself on the shield of the old Constitution, which she had set up at Richmond." The spirits of war appear behind Minerva, sounding their trumpets, calling southerners to aid their ailing mother. Those who answer the call to defend the South make up the remaining figures around the monument's base. These include soldiers marching furiously toward the front, a blacksmith who has forged his own sword preparing to leave his wife (fig. 9.4), and a young belle placing a sash around her lover's waist before he departs for war.[22]

Ezekiel accepted the commission for the monument although the UDC had only eighteen thousand dollars on hand for the project. He was confident that the group would raise the money to complete the contract price of thirty-five thousand dollars. For their part, the Daughters now pledged to raise fifty thousand dollars—substantially more than they offered in the original commission. They wanted a monument of national proportions and intended to use their status and influence to assure its successful completion.[23]

### *The Daughters Go to Washington*

To bring publicity to the Arlington monument, the Daughters decided to hold their 1912 annual convention in Washington. The UDC claimed that this was the first time the organization had held its meeting "outside" of the South—even though the organization had met in San Francisco, California, in 1905. The Washington convention did, however, represent a change in the Daughters' attitude toward the North. While the Spanish-American War was touted as the beginning of peaceful relations between the sections, participants in Confederate organizations were reluctant to embrace northerners wholeheartedly. This was especially true of UDC members, who still railed against what they perceived to be anti-Confederate sentiment in histories of the Civil War. Thus the meeting in Washington was a sign that many Daughters, though not all, believed the North had softened its stance that Confederate soldiers were traitors and rebels. The local press indicated this might be the case, as it predicted that the UDC's convention would "permanently mark the union between the North and the South."[24]

The nearly two thousand delegates who went to Washington for the November gathering received a welcome equal to the UDC's status as one of the South's most influential organizations. Members booked rooms and conducted their business in the posh new Willard Hotel and attended teas and receptions throughout the city, not the least of which was hosted by President and Mrs. William Howard Taft at the White House. The opening reception, held in the hotel ballroom, was one of the highlights of Washington's social season. As guests entered, they walked beneath an archway draped with "an electrically lighted Confederate flag." The *Washington Post* provided detailed descriptions of women's gowns, a sign of their elite status, referring to members of the UDC as "the flower of Southern Womanhood."[25]

While the Daughters were feted on several occasions during their convention, the highlight of their meeting was the laying of the cornerstone for the Arlington monument. Ritual generally accompanied monument unveilings, but the ceremony for this occasion offered new challenges. Florence Butler, in charge of the program, no doubt used her influence as a senator's wife to plan the day's events. She chose speakers to represent both North and South. Hilary Herbert spoke on behalf of the ACMA and, despite initial "murmurings of disapproval," James Tanner of the Grand Army of the Republic made remarks. Members of the UDC and the Daughters of the American Revolution (DAR) participated as well. Although he already had hosted the White House reception and given a welcoming speech at the convention, President Taft also delivered an address at the cemetery. The featured speaker of the day was William Jennings Bryan, nationally recognized orator and longtime leader in the Democratic Party.[26]

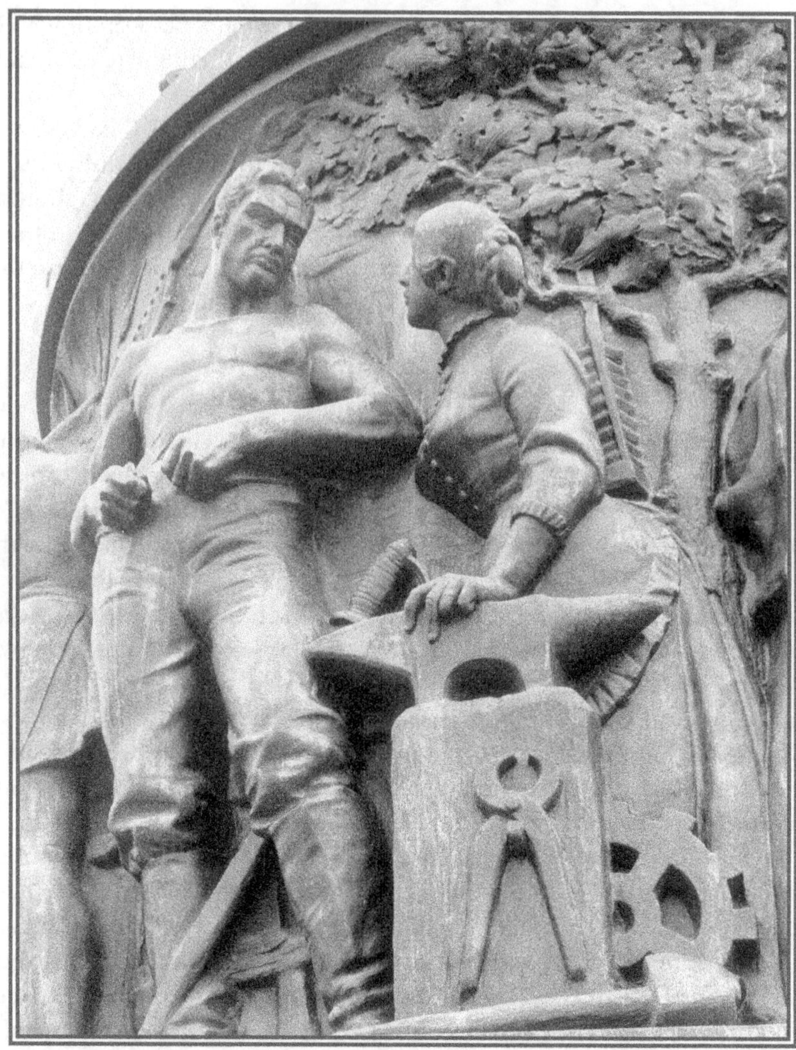

Fig. 9.4. Detail of frieze showing blacksmith and wife, Confederate Monument at Arlington National Cemetery. Photograph by Sean McCormally.

Bryan welcomed the day's ceremony as "evidence of a reunited nation." He carefully used his speech to place equal responsibility for the Civil War on North and South, declaring that both sections "shared the responsibility for slavery." Bryan acknowledged that the "wound of angry words . . . [had] not been so easily healed" and expressed hope that the Arlington monument would "breathe the spirit of national unity forever." He also praised the women of the UDC for building the monument, saying they "link us to the past" and "[point] us to the future."[27]

Bryan's comments about the Daughters described well the UDC's achievements since its founding in 1894. The organization had fought hard to ensure that the history, values, and culture of the Old South and the Confederacy would serve as the foundation for the New South—a term its members abhorred, but one that nevertheless described the changes in the region. The Daughters monitored school textbooks for their biases against the South, involved children in Confederate Memorial Day, gathered oral histories from both the men and women of the sixties, and erected hundreds of monuments across the South.[28]

For UDC members, there could be no future without honoring the past—no future without vindication for their parents and grandparents. Thus even as the phrase "reunited nation" inferred that people were looking forward, it necessarily had to be accompanied by an acknowledgment that the generation of the 1860s had participated in a noble cause. Though billed as a "peace monument," the Arlington sculpture's design honored the Lost Cause version of the past by presenting former Confederates as heroes.

## *Unveiling Vindication*

Nearly two years after the laying of the cornerstone, the monument was shipped in pieces to Washington for final assembly. Designed and modeled in Ezekiel's Roman studio, it had been cast in bronze by the Gladenbeck foundry in Berlin. Florence Butler of the local committee had the "disagreeable job," as she put it, of establishing the program for its planned June unveiling. "Of course there will be hundreds of requests to read poems, sing songs, and do other stunts which we cannot grant," she told UDC President-General Daisy Stevens. "Each speaker thinks he is the only person that the audience has come to hear." To ensure the program's success and bring honor to the occasion, she felt it important that there not be too many, or lengthy, speeches.[29]

The ritual for unveiling monuments had long been established, and the Arlington event followed a similar pattern. A platform was built for the ceremony and was festooned with flags of the United States and the Confederacy; well-known speakers were selected to present remarks. A child was chosen to pull the rope that would reveal the monument to those in attendance. This simple act was an important element of the unveiling ritual. While children always were involved in monument ceremonies, singing songs or forming a "living" Confederate flag on a nearby stand, the decision to have a child unveil the monument symbolically linked future generations to the past.[30]

The Arlington monument unveiling was a special occasion because it brought together citizens from North and South to admire and validate what white southerners heralded as a grand symbol of peace and sectional reconciliation. Gen. Washington Gardner, commander in chief of the Grand Army of the Republic, was a featured speaker, as was Gen. Bennett Young, the commander in chief of the UCV, along with Col. Robert E. Lee, grandson of the Confederate general. Veterans from Union and Confederate armies were present, as were leading members of the DAR and UDC. Moreover, Washingtonians were asked by the president of the city's chamber of commerce to decorate their homes and places of business in honor of the unveiling. Paul Herbert Micou, the eleven-year-old grandson of Hilary Herbert, was chosen to pull the cord that unveiled the monument.[31]

The ceremony on June 4, 1914, drew more than four thousand people who arrived in a "swarm of motors." They included many veterans who "had made weary pilgrimages from the far South and North to join once more in the fraternal spirit of the great Gettysburg reunion" held in 1913 to commemorate the fiftieth anniversary of the battle. Speaker after speaker commented on the spirit of fraternity that marked the occasion until the time finally arrived for the unveiling. At that moment, young Paul Micou walked over and jerked the cord, and the crowd's cheers at seeing the monument drowned out the sound of the band. Once the applause subsided, Mississippian Daisy

McLaurin Stevens approached the speaker's stand. Her role as leader of the South's most powerful women's organization was to present the monument as a "gift" to the United States.[32]

President-General Stevens, a well-known orator in Lost Cause circles, first paid homage to the Confederate soldiers buried at Arlington who rested "within the shadow of the home of [Robert E.] Lee and in the sight of the dome of the [United States] Capitol." She spoke of self-government but also included themes of reunification. The U.S. flag that day did not "wave above their [Confederate soldiers'] dust in cheering triumph," Stevens suggested, "but in loving protection." She also found it meaningful that "a president southern by birth and breeding and northern by choice of residence and training" was there to accept the Daughters' gift. She concluded by asserting her firm belief that the Arlington monument would long be important to all boys and girls; they would "look with reverence" at the striking bronze tableau and be thankful they were Americans.[33]

The theme of self-government was most appropriate, since Stevens presented the monument to Woodrow Wilson, a champion of self-determination on the world stage. In accepting the monument on behalf of the United States, he acknowledged the UDC's effort to present "a memorial of their dead" to the nation, yet he was quick to note that the government had also played a major role in its creation. The idea was inspired by President William McKinley, Congress authorized it, and another president, William Howard Taft, oversaw the laying of the cornerstone. The Virginia-born Wilson, therefore, saw his part in this chain of events as fitting and expressed pride in being able to participate in a ceremony that drew northerners and southerners together. His speech was cut short by a fierce thunderstorm that forced the large crowd to disperse in search of shelter. The full text of his address, however, made clear that Wilson saw the monument as a celebration of a united country. Reconciliation was the theme of the day for the unveiling of what sculptor Ezekiel described as a "peace monument."[34]

## A Textbook in Bronze

Most Confederate monuments are considered symbols of the Lost Cause; the Confederate monument at Arlington is no less than a pro-southern textbook illustrated in bronze. Herbert described Ezekiel's work as exactly that, "history in bronze." Noting that the "leading purpose of the UDC is to correct history," he suggested that Ezekiel had helped the organization to meet that goal. Actual textbooks offered children a version of the past that valued states' rights and white supremacy: benevolent masters, who subsequently became Confederate officers, ran southern plantations with the support of devoted mistresses. Slaves acted only as faithful servants. Confederate soldiers were always heroic figures, and during the period of the Confederacy, southern women made enormous sacrifices, not the least of which were the male members of their families.[35]

Similarly, the Arlington monument reads like a pro-southern text. The soldiers are not worn and defeated but walk determinedly toward the front lines of battle. Alongside these soldiers is a "faithful negro body servant following his young master, like Thomas Nelson Page's 'Marse Chan'" (fig. 9.5). The planter turned Confederate officer leaves his child in the trustworthy arms of the faithful black mammy (fig. 9.6). Herbert said this particular scene illustrated the "kindly relations that existed all over the South between the master and the slave." To him it told a story that could not be repeated often enough to "generations in which *Uncle Tom's Cabin* survives and is still manufacturing false ideas as to the South and slavery."[36]

Among the other scenes included in Ezekiel's sculpture, which he entitled *New South*, is the blacksmith forging his own sword (fig. 9.4) and a minister and his wife "bidding good-by to their

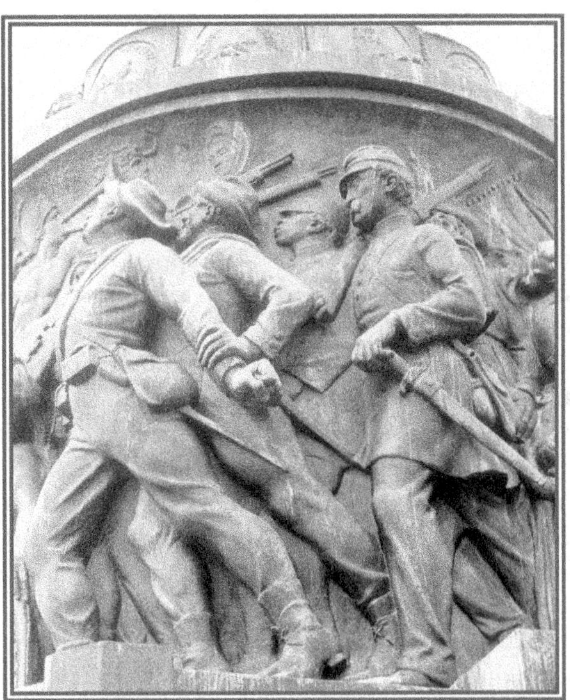

Fig. 9.5. Detail of frieze showing body servant and soldiers, Confederate Monument at Arlington National Cemetery. Photograph by Sean McCormally.

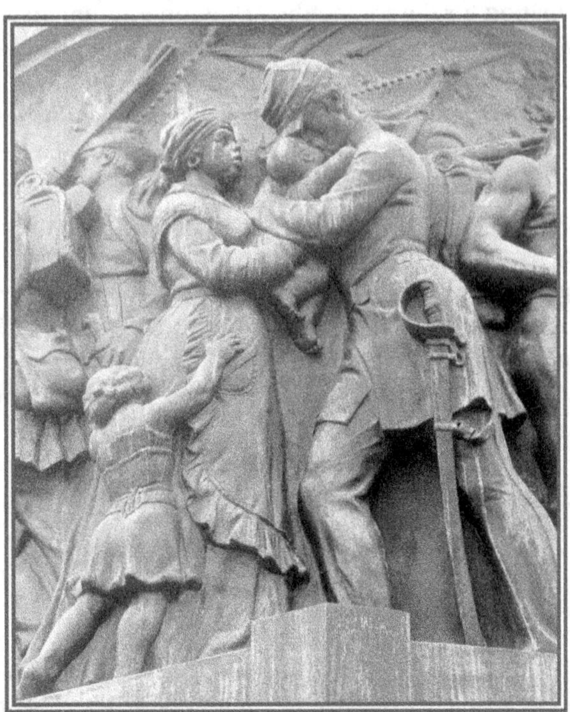

Fig. 9.6. Detail of frieze showing "black mammy," Confederate Monument at Arlington National Cemetery. Photograph by Sean McCormally.

schoolboy son." The latter provides a portrait of sacrifices made by both youth and families. Finally there is the new bride tying the sash around her soldier-husband, a symbol of young women's sacrifices—perhaps not unlike the women who were now members of the UDC, the organization that made the monument possible.[37]

The inscriptions are also significant because they provide the monument's literal meaning. Beneath the allegorical woman, whose "plow-stock" is topped with a curved blade, is an inscription from the prophet Isaiah: "And they shall beat their swords into plowshares, and their spears into pruning hooks." The message is plain: a region, dignified in defeat, is willing to put its swords to more productive use. Another inscription, this one on the rear of the monument, speaks to heroic sacrifice, a central theme of the Lost Cause: "Not for fame, not for place or for rank, not lured by ambition or goaded by necessity; but in simple obedience to duty as they understood it these men suffered all, sacrificed all, dared all—and died."[38]

Given that the monument offers an interpretation of events based on southern memory, and that the sculptor used the monument to emphasize that the South fought for "a constitutional right and not to uphold slavery," how can the Confederate monument at Arlington be viewed as a monument of either "peace" or "reconciliation"?

The two sections of the nation had made great strides toward reconciliation, especially after defeating a common enemy during the Spanish-American War. Reunions of the Blue and Gray brought Union and Confederate veterans together to swap stories and rekindle feelings of fraternity. Many men from both sections also shared similar assumptions about race and civilization. Allowing a monument to the Confederacy in Arlington National Cemetery, some southerners reasoned, was yet another example of the North's willingness to come together again.[39]

A more probable explanation for describing the Arlington monument as a monument of reconciliation is that *reconciliation* meant something different to white southerners. Members of the UDC and the UCV had long railed against the "biased" interpretations of northern historians, whom they believed cast a dark shadow over the Confederacy with their slurs of "traitor" and "rebel." The Daughters were loath to speak of reconciliation, in fact, as long as northerners treated southerners as second-class citizens. Had not the South, they asked, fought in defense of the Constitution? The Arlington monument helped assuage their feelings of resentment, since it symbolized the South's heroism and not its disloyalty. Moreover, its placement on a landscape of national significance suggested to them that the North finally had recognized the "truth" about the South. Marion Butler, the U.S. senator from North Carolina, explained it this way: "The whole spirit of the thing has been fostered by northerners, and they have helped the monument association in every way to bring its purpose to a grand success. It is a beautiful sentiment—the erasure of all party feeling and 'union forever' once more."[40]

It was a monument of reconciliation, but a reconciliation based on terms that the white South found to be acceptable. As a token gift to the nation, it acknowledged military defeat and nothing more.

## *Notes*

1. "Gray and Blue Join," *Washington Post,* June 5, 1914.

2. On the UDC, see Karen L. Cox, "Women, the Lost Cause, and the New South: The United Daughters of the Confederacy and the Transmission of Confederate Culture, 1894–1919" (Ph.D. diss., Univ. of Southern Mississippi, May 1997), and Cox, *Dixie's Daughters: The United Daughters of the Confederacy and the Preservation of Confederate Culture* (Gainesville: Univ. Press Florida, 2003).

3. This summary of monument building is informed in part by John J. Winberry, "'Lest We Forget': The Confederate Monument and the Southern Townscape," *Southeastern Geographer* (Nov. 1983): 107–21; and H. E. Gully, "Women and the Lost Cause: Preserving a Confederate Identity in the American Deep South," *Journal of Historical Geography* 19, no. 2 (Apr. 1993): 125–41.

4. On vindication and reunification see Gaines Foster, *Ghosts of the Confederacy* (New York: Oxford, 1987), 159; Nina Silber, *The Romance of Reunion: Northerners and the South, 1865–1900* (Chapel Hill: Univ. of North Carolina Press, 1993), 174–78; and Paul H. Buck, *The Road to Reunion, 1865–1900* (Boston: Little, Brown and Co., 1937). For more on the Federal burial program and Arlington Cemetery, see Catherine Zipf's essay about national cemeteries in chapter 2 of this anthology.

5. *Programme of the Ceremonies at the Unveiling of the Arlington Confederate Monument* (Arlington, Va., June 4, 1914), 15–16; "A Greeting from the New President General," *Minutes of the Thirteenth Annual Convention of the United Daughters of the Confederacy* (Nashville, Tenn.: UDC, 1907), 5. The annual *Minutes* will henceforth be cited as *UDC Minutes*.

6. *Programme*, 18. Thomas Nelson Page's novels about the South include *In Ole Virginia: Or, Marse Chan and Other Stories* (New York: Charles Scribner's Sons, 1882); *Two Little Confederates* (New York: Charles Scribner's Sons, 1888); and, with A. C. Gordon, *Befo' De War, Echoes in Negro Dialect* (New York: Charles Scribner's Sons, 1888). On Reconstruction, see Page's *Red Rock: A Chronicle of Reconstruction, Part I* (New York: Charles Scribner's Sons, 1903).

7. Report of the Arlington Confederate Monument Association, *UDC Minutes*, 1908, 275–76; and *Programme*, 17.

8. Report of the Arlington Confederate Monument Association, *UDC Minutes*, 1908, 276.

9. *UDC Minutes*, 1907, 5, 24. The phrase "without conditions" meant that the advisory board would have no formal control over the Arlington campaign.

10. Report of the Chairman of the Executive Committee, Arlington Confederate Monument Association, *UDC Minutes*, 1909, 279.

11. *UDC Minutes*, 1907, 59; 1908, 276.

12. Report of the Arlington Confederate Monument Association, *UDC Minutes*, 1908, 277. "Progress for the Arlington Monument," *Confederate Veteran* 16 (Apr. 1908). Henceforth, *Confederate Veteran* will be abbreviated *CV*.

13. Report of the Chairman of Executive Committee, Arlington Confederate Monument Association, *UDC Minutes*, 1909, 276–77.

14. Ibid., 278.

15. "Design for Arlington Monument," *CV* 18 (July 1910): 310.

16. Report of the Executive Committee, Arlington Confederate Monument Association, *UDC Minutes*, 1910, 291; "Confederate Christmas Seals," *CV* 18 (Nov. 1910): 500; "Construction of Arlington Monument," *CV* 19 (Apr. 1911): 147.

17. Joseph Gutmann and Stanley F. Chyet, eds., *Moses Jacob Ezekiel: Memoirs from the Baths of Diocletian* (Detroit: Wayne State Univ. Press, 1975), 439. See also Kathryn Allamong Jacob, *Testament to Union: Civil War Monuments in Washington, D.C.* (Baltimore: Johns Hopkins Univ. Press, 1999), 164–71.

18. *Programme*, 19–20; Albert Z. Conner, "Moses Jacob Ezekiel: From Confederate Cadet to World-Famous Artist," http://www.jewish-history.com/moses_ezekiel.html (1997), 1–6. Roberta K. Tarbell, "Moses Jacob Ezekiel's Sculpture and the Aesthetics in the Context of Nineteenth-Century Art and Philosophy," in *Ezekiel's Vision: Moses Jacob Ezekiel and the Classical Tradition* (Philadelphia: National Museum of American Jewish History, 1985), 19.

19. Letter quoted in "Construction of Arlington Monument," *CV* 19 (Apr. 1911): 147.

20. Gutmann and Chyet, *Moses Jacob Ezekiel*, 35, 441.

21. "The Monument at Arlington," *CV* 22 (July 1914): 296.

22. Ibid.

23. Report of Chairman of Executive Committee ACMA, *UDC Minutes*, 1911, 293.

24. Florence Butler to Mrs. Woodrow Wilson, Oct. 29, 1912, Florence F. Butler Papers, Southern Historical Collection (hereafter cited as SHC). Butler makes the comment about the convention being the first out of the South. She also sees this as an occasion to "demonstrate to the world that we are a united people." Quotation from "United Daughters of Confederacy Gather Here for Big Convention," *Washington Post*, Nov. 10, 1912.

25. "Host at Reception," *Washington Post*, Nov. 14, 1912; "Hosts to the UDC: Mr. and Mrs. Taft Will Receive Delegates Nov. 14," *Washington Post*, Nov. 4, 1912.

26. "Laying Cornerstone for UCV Shaft in Arlington," *Washington Post*, Nov. 13, 1912. See also "History of the Monument," in *Programme*, 17. The Daughters originally invited Woodrow Wilson, then governor of New Jersey, to speak. See Florence Butler to Mrs. Woodrow Wilson, Oct. 29, 1912, Florence F. Butler Papers, SHC.

27. "Laying Cornerstone for UCV Shaft in Arlington," *Washington Post*, Nov. 12, 1912.

28. Cox, "Women, the Lost Cause, and the New South."

29. An inscription says the casting is by "Atkien-Gesellschaft Gladenbeck/Brunze Foundery/Berlin-Friedrichshagen." Quotations are from Florence Butler to Daisy Stevens, Jan. 22, 1914, Florence F. Butler Papers, SHC.

30. Regarding children's involvement in unveiling ceremonies, see Cox, "Women, the Lost Cause, and the New South," 100–103.

31. "Arrive for Unveiling," *Washington Post*, June 4, 1914; "Child to Bare Memorial," *Washington Post*, June 3, 1914.

32. Report of the President-General, *UDC Minutes*, 1914, 102–3; "The Monument at Arlington," *CV* 22 (July 1914): 292–96; "Gray and Blue Join," *Washington Post*, June 5, 1914.

33. Address of Daisy Stevens, "The Arlington Monument," *CV* 22 (Aug. 1914): 346–47; "The Monument at Arlington," *CV* 22 (July 1914): 292–96; *Washington Post*, June 5, 1914.

34. "The Monument at Arlington," *CV* 22 (July 1914): 292–96; "Turn Your Faces to the Future . . ." *Washington Post*, July 5, 1914.

35. Herbert's quotations from Hilary Herbert, *History of the Arlington Confederate Monument at Arlington, Virginia* (United Daughters of the Confederacy, 1914), 77. The campaign to eradicate bias in southern textbooks has been covered extensively by historian Fred Bailey. See, for example, "The Textbooks of the 'Lost Cause': Censorship and the Creation of Southern State Histories," *Georgia Historical Quarterly* 75 (summer 1991): 507–33.

36. Herbert, *History of the Arlington Confederate Monument*, 77.

37. Ibid.

38. "The Monument at Arlington," *CV* 22 (July 1914): 296; This inscription was written by Rev. Randolph McKim, a Confederate veteran who was pastor of the Epiphany Church in Washington, D.C. Ezekiel is buried at the foot of the monument.

39. On sectional reconciliation, see Silber, *The Romance of Reunion*, 178–85; Paul Buck, *The Road to Reunion*; and Gaines Foster, *Ghosts of the Confederacy*, 152–56.

40. "Unite Again in Reception," *Washington Post*, June 5, 1914.

# 10

# Planning a Temple to the Lost Cause

## The Confederate "Battle Abbey"

*William M. S. Rasmussen*

THE IDEA for a grand "Temple to the Lost Cause" that would venerate southern history was conceived in 1894 at a time when the Union army and its cause were being honored by the Grant Monument (popularly known as Grant's Tomb). Plagued by delays, the Confederate Memorial Institute eventually was built in Richmond, Virginia, in 1912–13 in defiance of the congressional vote to remember Abraham Lincoln, the former northern commander in chief, with a national memorial. The story of the institute reveals much about the South and Virginia at the turn of the century, and it is an important example of an American architectural competition with a national audience. The 1910 competition to design the memorial building (often called the South's Battle Abbey) attracted far-reaching attention, prompting letters of inquiry from some 350 architects across the nation and entries from sixty-eight firms. But the project's history is marked as much by missed opportunities as by lofty objectives. The strong winning design ultimately had to be amended to meet budget constraints.

## *Origins of the Memorial*

The project was the brainchild of Charles Broadway Rouss, a former Confederate private who had amassed a fortune in the dry goods business in postwar New York City and who was a witness to the building there of the Grant Monument. In 1885 the Grant Monument Association had announced plans to erect a spectacular tomb and memorial in Riverside Park for "the grandest character of the century," the Union general and eighteenth president who already was memorialized in nearly two dozen adulatory biographies. Rouss watched as the sum of $600,000 was raised for the project by popular subscription and as ground was broken in 1891. Three years later—and three years before the monument was completed—this former Virginian sent a letter to various camps of Confederate veterans, calling for a Confederate Memorial Association (CMA) that would honor Grant's former opponents. It would collect and preserve Confederate records and relics, particularly portraits. Six months later, Rouss pledged $100,000 toward construction of the building in which these objects would be housed. According to his scheme, that amount was to be matched by an equal sum, so that this "national memorial hall" could be constructed on an appropriately grand scale.[1]

If Rouss was prompted to action by the movement that built the memorial to Ulysses S. Grant, he also may have been motivated by the issue of redemption. Southern traditionalists leveled part of their criticism for the ills of contemporary society on the northern robber barons who were driven by greed and on those in the New South who would match them. But they found especially shameful those who "sold their birthrights for a mess of pottage and deserted the old Southern ideals" to become "millionaires" in the North. To the thinking of traditionalists, atonement was in order for Rouss, as it was for Thomas Fortune Ryan, another Virginian who had become affluent in New York City. Ryan was the patron who fifteen years later would fund a cycle of mural paintings for the Confederate memorial. It is at the least ironic that these two products of a perceived moral crisis in the postwar South would fund the premiere Confederate museum. A purpose of that institute, through its celebration of antebellum behavior and its presentation of inspirational role models, would be the rectification of the very disorder in American society that bred the likes of Rouss and Ryan.[2]

The South was a world turned upside down by a humiliating defeat. In the 1890s, a quarter century after Appomattox, the wounds had not healed for many southern veterans, and they even appeared with time to be reopening. If it seemed at first that a Confederate memorial could be established relatively easily and quickly, the reality proved to be different. Not a single brick for the building would be laid within Rouss's lifetime.

The veterans, already immersed in their cult of the Lost Cause, could readily endorse the idea Rouss proposed, because a memorial would give permanence to their efforts to right the present by preserving the Confederate past. For the previous several years, during a difficult period of social transition, they had organized meetings and parades and had erected statues, all in an effort to give high visibility to the Confederate past. They found that the presence of that past served to reaffirm southern white dignity and to reinforce the structure and values of antebellum southern society.

But Rouss had presented a goal that proved elusive for the veterans. They may have once come together as Confederates, but now the vast geography of the South and social standing divided them. They felt allegiance first to their own states, and many members of the veterans' groups were conscious that their middle-class origins separated them from the Old South aristocracy that had directed the Confederacy. It was a relatively easy matter to plan parades and meetings, and even to erect some statues. It was another to conceive a large complex of undefined plan, size, and shape and to choose a single location for it. How could they agree on what the proposed memorial should be, which veterans it should honor, and where it should be located? How could they accept money from northern industrialists, their only substantive source of funding? And if they would not take northern money, should the scant southern funds available be directed to a national Confederate memorial? It would be fifteen years before all of these questions were answered.[3]

Toward the end of the long period of indecision that preceded the competition of 1910, there also would be a regional element in the equation. Once the site for the Confederate memorial was decided, the entire scheme would have to be reconsidered by the veterans resident in that state. The memorial would become less a southern one and more a Virginia one. The Virginians had a slightly different agenda than their counterparts in the Deep South, one dictated by an aristocratic bias that influenced their will to preserve the colonial past along with the Confederate heritage. White Virginians would influence how the project would be brought to fruition and, as virtually the only audience, would govern how it would be received. Their monument, the one that was built, was notably different from the "national" shrine that Rouss had proposed and would have placed in Washington, D.C., the nation's capital.

Soon after Rouss announced his pledge, various opinions were offered as to what the building should be. A committee of the United Confederate Veterans (UCV) wanted it "large," with a "spacious hall for confederate gatherings" at its core. Nearly 100,000 of the faithful made pilgrimages to the annual UCV reunions. The committee called as well for multiple galleries—these could surround the core—to house "a great library" and Confederate objects of all sorts—"portraits, paintings, [and] photographs . . . of Confederate people, places, and things." In theory at least, the Confederate states would "vie among themselves to be foremost in sending these sacred and invaluable momentos." "Medallions and statuary" would "adorn the grounds and buildings." At the annual reunion of 1896 (when the Confederate Memorial Association was incorporated for

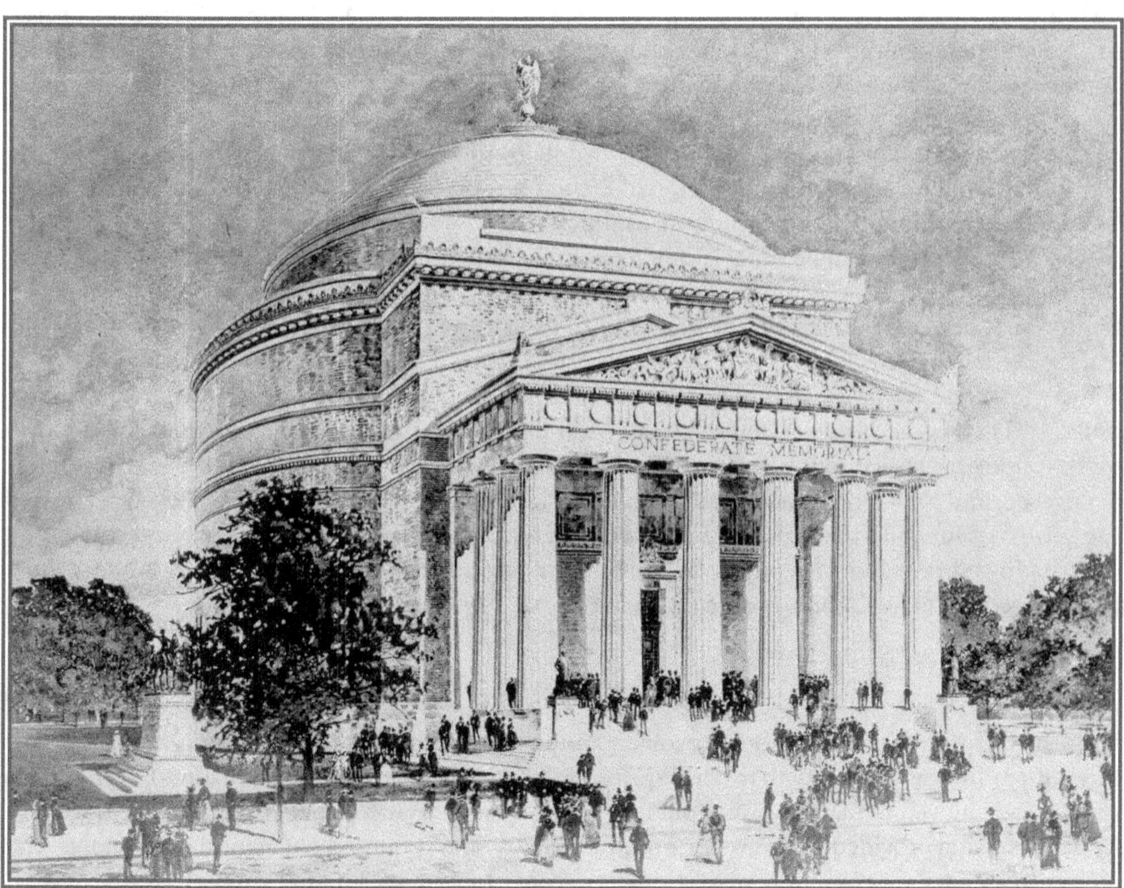


Fig. 10.1. Detail of Stanford White drawing for Confederate Memorial Institute, Richmond, 1900. Photograph of lost drawing courtesy of Avery Library, Columbia University.

the purpose of building the Confederate Memorial Institute), these same ideas were repeated by Col. A. G. Dickinson, authorized by Rouss to speak to the veterans on his behalf. In further prescribing departments of history, "art and sculpture," and "industrial and agricultural resources" for the institute, Rouss and Dickinson envisioned exhibits that would preserve, at least in a gallery setting, the culture and economy of the Old South.[4]

As it turned out, the plethora of art objects that would have necessitated the multiple galleries never were forthcoming from the various Confederate states. But the early proposals that describe a large meeting hall, satellite galleries, and a program of sculptural decoration were remembered in the first design for the memorial (fig. 10.1) and in all five of the winning entries fifteen years later. And Dickinson's description of the South as the "Athens of America," along with Rouss's use of the phrase "Temple to the Lost Cause" to describe the proposed institute, sketched a vision of it as the type of classical structure that would be depicted in all five winning entries.[5]

One man, J. Taylor Ellyson, served as a sort of institutional guardian of these early ideas, which he clipped from newspaper accounts and then brought to fruition after the originators of the project had died. In 1910 Ellyson was not only the president of the CMA and one of the three jurors of the competition; he was also presumably instrumental in determining the configuration of that jury. A former Confederate private and then mayor of the city of Richmond, Ellyson was three times lieutenant governor of Virginia and for twenty-five years served as chairman of the Democratic State Committee. He also advised the Association for the Preservation of Virginia Antiquities, which his wife headed. As a guardian of both the Confederate and colonial pasts, Ellyson embodied the peculiar duality that distinguished Virginia in this period and that would impact on the institute when the question of its location in Richmond was settled. That decision was made at the 1898 annual reunion, held in Covington, Kentucky.[6]

Though the former capital of the Confederacy, Richmond was not an ideal site for the institute. Not only did the state present the distraction of a rich colonial legacy, but the Confederate celebration had been a popular crusade centered in the Deep South, not in Virginia, arguably America's most aristocratic society. In 1889 the social crisis in Virginia that had fueled Confederate activity lessened when the liberal party of change, the Readjusters, was soundly defeated at the polls. And two decades earlier, the state had been the battleground of a failed revitalization movement to look backward to the Confederacy.[7] Proponents for the cities of Nashville and Memphis, Tennessee, and New Orleans, Louisiana, protested the selection of Richmond and even requested the return of funds. Their reaction is evidence of a lessening interest in the project, which was overshadowed the same year, 1898, by the Spanish-American War. There southern military units participated with equal status beside northern ones.


## *The Underwood Debacle, 1898–1906*

With the location for the memorial resolved and in the aftermath of the dedication of the Grant Monument in New York City that same spring of 1898 (before an audience of a million people), the veterans moved to match Rouss's pledge. They replaced an ineffective fund-raiser with John C. Underwood and provided incentive for prompt success—the promised payment to this veteran and former lieutenant governor of Kentucky of 25 percent of whatever sum he could raise. Underwood demonstrated remarkable initiative that reaped pledges just as quickly as it angered UCV leaders, who eventually deposed and discredited him.

Rouss had suggested that Confederate veterans fund the institute, but Underwood recognized that the desired sum could never be collected in the impoverished South. He traveled to New York City to find most of his patrons. Underwood produced a list of subscribers to the memorial that runs for pages and includes such recognizable northern names as J. Pierpont Morgan, Henry Flagler, and the Carnegie Steel Company. Morgan had been the treasurer for the Grant Memorial Association.[8]

If by itself this promise of northern support did not outrage Confederate veterans, Underwood's other steps did. On his own authority, he solicited architectural drawings for the memorial and plaster models of statues to adorn that building, and he commissioned fifteen to twenty portraits of Confederate leaders to hang inside it. He presented some of these paintings at the annual meeting of 1899 in Charleston, South Carolina, and additional portraits, along with architectural plans and models of sculpture, in 1900 in Louisville, Kentucky. The audiences applauded his presentations. The architectural scheme (fig. 10.1) was even approved by the trustees of the association. But the portrait issue set off a powder keg.[9] What caused the furor was the difficult question of who should be depicted in memorial portraits. Some veterans would not allow a collection agent to make this decision for them. Underwood was dismissed. He successfully sued the association, only to see his award overturned by an appeals court in 1906. In the process, the Confederate memorial was delayed for eight years.[10]

With Underwood's removal, the institute never would be adequately funded and the strongest design ever made for the building was discarded. Underwood may or may not have approached portraitists of great merit (no record has emerged), but he had turned to sculptors of national reputation, Charles Niehaus and John Massey Rhind, and to a leading architect, Stanford White.[11]

Only four years earlier, in 1896, White had been called to the University of Virginia to rebuild the centerpiece of the lawn there, Thomas Jefferson's library building, which had burned. For the Confederate memorial in nearby Richmond, White would simply duplicate Jefferson's pantheon or rotunda, replacing its ornate Corinthian order, appropriate for a university, with the more solemn Doric order. According to a contemporary account in a Richmond newspaper, White's design (fig. 10.1) evoked qualities that one could associate with the Confederacy—"dignity," "monumentality," and "seriousness of purpose." The "immensity" of the building would make the experience of viewing it "overwhelming," because White proposed to nearly double the size of the University of Virginia Rotunda (seventy-two feet wide) to approach the size of the Pantheon in Rome. The structure was to be "roofed by a dome 130 feet in diameter covering the entire building and [one of] the largest in the world." Statues of Jefferson Davis, Robert E. Lee, J. E. B. Stuart, and Nathan Bedford Forrest would stand before the portico and on the grounds.[12]

The imposing facade was matched within. White encircled the central rotunda with galleries set off by a grand Ionic colonnade, eighty-six feet in diameter and lined with statues of Confederate heroes. Portraits were to be hung on the second floor, along the barrel supporting the dome and visible from below on entering the room. Off the entrance vestibule would be a library with a thirty-foot ceiling. As recognized at the time, "the entire scheme and purpose of the building [would be] unfolded at a single glance." It seemed that this design, "based on simplicity," could "not fail of . . . impressiveness."

Admittedly the structure would have been expensive: one contractor estimated that the cost could be kept to $300,000. But Underwood thought the sum was attainable. Nothing further came of this design, however, for a decade later White was dead and the firm of McKim, Mead and White would not choose to enter the national competition.[13]

## *The Project Revived and Delayed*

With the rejection of Underwood's effective policy and White's impressive design, the memorial project was faltering. To make matters worse, Charles Rouss and George Moorman, one of the UCV's principal leaders, both died in 1902, the same year Underwood was dismissed. Moreover, the state of Virginia at this juncture adopted a new constitution to disfranchise much of the new electorate that had threatened traditionalists since the days of Reconstruction. This legislation of 1902 allowed Anglo-Saxon Virginians to feel less threatened and less dependent on Confederate celebrations.

But with or without social unrest, the Memorial Institute was wanted by Virginia's white majority. Curiously perhaps, a number of Virginians were now more ardently Confederate than before, and the institute would be a jewel in Richmond's crown. In 1903 the Richmond City Council—encouraged by Peter Rouss's vow to honor his father's pledge to build the memorial—voted the large sum of $50,000, half the match of the Rouss pledge, to help fund construction. Five years after the decision to locate in Richmond, council members must have feared that the proposal might not become a reality without their action.[14]

The City Council gift was sizable, but fund-raising was impeded during the next three years as the Underwood controversy dragged on in the courts. Even after the resolution of that case in 1906, new funds were not forthcoming. It is ironic, however, that funding was the primary issue that kept the project from moving forward until 1909, because the sum of the Rouss and City Council gifts, $150,000, would constitute the entire final budget for the memorial.[15]

On the Virginia front there was an additional reason for the long delay. The keepers of the past there were distracted in these years with other equally compelling activities that would culminate in 1907. One event centered around Jamestown, for the year 1907 was the three hundredth anniversary of the founding there of a settlement that seemed to prove the state's importance. Virginians would not miss the opportunity to make the site a pilgrimage place. This was also a time of Confederate celebration in Richmond on the eve of the hundredth anniversary in 1908 of the birth of Jefferson Davis. For decades the former president of the Confederacy had been the target of northern abuse, and southerners would now vindicate his memory. In 1907 statues of both Davis and Confederate Gen. J. E. B. Stuart were unveiled with fanfare on the city's grandest esplanade, Monument Avenue.[16]

Only in 1909 would interest in the Confederate Memorial Institute be revived. Ironically the impetus would come from the North and be sufficiently strong to push aside the issue of inadequate funding. The hundredth anniversary of Abraham Lincoln's birth was at hand, and white Virginians were in no mood to lose another Appomattox—this time the battle between the North and the South that was being replayed in the history books. As with Grant, Lincoln was first deified by the northern press and then honored with a monument. The adoration that anticipated the 1909 centennial of his birth led eventually to a congressional commission (1911) and then an act (1913) that authorized $2 million to build a national memorial in Washington, D.C., to the president who had preserved the union.[17] This adulation incited Confederate veterans to action.

The intensity of anti-Lincoln sentiment in the South is easily measured by an address delivered in Richmond in the centennial year by a member of the CMA's executive committee who was Ellyson's principal assistant through the competition of 1910 and the building of the institute. Judge George L. Christian proclaimed that the commander in chief was "one of the greatest tyrants of any age," saying it was Lincoln who had sanctioned the Union army's uncivil treatment of noncombatants during the war. Christian worried particularly about the children of the South: "If we remain silent," he argued, "will they not rather interpret our silence as a confession of guilt, and that we deemed our cause an unholy one?" This "duty" to "our children and our children's children," as well as to "the memories of our dead comrades [and] to ourselves" prompted the veterans to revive the project at the precise moment of Lincoln's deification in the North. Only the institute could answer the newest slander of the northern press.[18]

Thus in 1909, the anniversary year of Lincoln's birth, the association solicited "several tentative drawings" from the New York firm of Snelling and Porter, to be presented at the annual UCV meeting in Memphis. There the executive committee of the CMA directed Ellyson and Christian "to secure plans and specifications for the building, and to offer as a reward for the best plan, or plans, a sum" not to exceed $1,000. Whatever designs the Richmonders solicited they would pass back to the full executive committee for a final selection.[19]

The committee essentially ordered a limited competition, a format that had yielded strong results in post–Civil War America. But the panel failed to structure its contest in terms of defining it and setting dates for the receipt of entries. Also no one on the committee knew what architects to approach. The chance of success was slim. Here began a series of awkward entanglements for the association that after twelve months would yield no acceptable scheme but instead virtually force an open competition.

Ellyson continued to correspond with minor architects like Snelling and Porter, and young Rossel Edward Mitchell of Norfolk, but he did have the vision to pursue Ralph Adams Cram as well. The established Boston architect recently had been chosen to design the new Richmond College (now the University of Richmond), where Ellyson served as chairman of the committee for new buildings, but Ellyson could not extract a plan for the institute from Cram. He also failed to control a group of unsolicited architects who in 1909–10 sought the Confederate commission.[20] By the time of the UCV's 1910 reunion in Mobile, Alabama, Ellyson and Christian had little to show. At least they had no design that the executive committee cared to endorse. Almost as a last resort, the idea of an open competition was put forward.[21]

Several days before the reunion and in anticipation of it, the specific Richmond site for the institute was determined. For the past fifteen years members of the Confederate Memorial Literary Society, a local women's association that had rescued the former White House of the Confederacy from demolition, had put forward that site as appropriate for the institute, which they even imagined that they would themselves administer. Beginning in 1890 the ladies had transformed Jefferson Davis's wartime residence, which today is adjacent to and a branch of the Museum of the Confederacy, into what they perceived as the paramount Confederate museum, one that already performed many of the functions proposed for Rouss's institute.[22] But the White House site, located in an old part of the city near Thomas Jefferson's capitol, was too steeply sloped to accommodate very well the large civic building envisioned by the CMA. The Lee Camp of Confederate Veterans, the audience for Judge Christian's anti-Lincoln address a year earlier, voted in the spring of 1910 to donate a portion of its flat, spacious park to the association. This land was also sanctified because it is within sight of Richmond's Monument Avenue, a street by then well established as the premier Confederate corridor in the nation. The institute would be placed near this street, which came to symbolize New South progress, Old South gentility, and the reestablishment of the old order of white supremacy.[23]

## *The Competition of 1910*

The staging of a large competition was by no means a radical course for the Confederate veterans to follow. After all, contests with this format were announced almost daily in Victorian England and, by the 1890s, the formal competition was a frequent solution to the dilemma faced by sponsors of large public and semipublic edifices. But the open competition was always a risk; its history was marked with the scandal of unfair administration, receipt of entries over budget, and complaints from the entrants. And competitions open to all architects generally failed to attract established firms.[24]

Following the common practice in this era of engaging professional advice, Ellyson immediately enlisted as an advisor and juror the Richmond architect William C. Noland, who guided the competition process so well that in the end it won more acclaim than criticism.[25] Through the summer of 1910 the competition was announced in major architectural magazines and selected newspapers. Prominent among the candidates who responded were John Russell Pope and the firm of Shepley, Rutan and Coolidge. Neither, however, actually entered the competition.[26]

Noland and Ellyson conceived a competition format that consisted of two judgings, the first of which would establish ability. By October 15, 1910, candidates were to submit three blueprints and one photograph for each of two major buildings they had designed and erected. Qualifiers next faced a second deadline of December 22 for submission of designs. As intended, this format reduced the number of competitors—from the unwieldy quantity of 350 who inquired to the 97 who responded to the first deadline. The 88 architects who were approved by Noland and Ellyson, mostly New York and Philadelphia figures, made up a large enough field of candidates but contained too few names of prominence.[27]

"Instructions to [the eighty-eight] Competitors" were provided in a seven-page printed booklet. It listed a budget of $150,000. The winner would become architect of the building; as such he would receive 6 percent of the contract cost, or $9,000, a large prize for a competition. The runner-up would win $400, while three third-place entrants would each collect $200. These prizes helped to entice sixty-eight of the eighty-eight qualifiers to submit actual designs for the institute.[28] Although the booklet promised a "Program of Requirements" that would discuss the general purposes of the building, this apparently was never prepared. In its absence, a flood of mostly practical questions was received by the association. These were printed, along with the answers, and mailed to all competitors in November.[29]

In December a second professional juror, James Knox Taylor, was added to assist Noland and Ellyson with what would be a difficult process. As supervising architect of the U.S. Treasury from 1898 to 1912, Taylor was accustomed to examining and passing judgment on plans.[30] By January 24, 1911, the jurying was over, the executive committee had given its approval, and the winners of the competition were announced. The process had taken less than a month. No records document how the jurors made their decisions. The submitted drawings were returned to the applicants and nearly all are now lost. Probably most were classical in style.

A group of entries were rotunda buildings. Perhaps the most inspired of these was the grand baroque structure by Rossel Edward Mitchell, the young Norfolk architect so much encouraged by Ellyson and Christian (fig. 10.2). This domed building, embellished with sculpture, is reminiscent of such great derivatives of St. Peter's Cathedral as the seventeenth-century Church of the Invalides in Paris by Jules Hardouin-Mansart. Verticality is stressed both outside and within. On the interior, the sheer height of the dome is enhanced by the use of illusionistic devices of lighting and perspective. An inner shell to the dome opens to a lit vista of even greater distance. The shell would be painted not with a traditional depiction of otherworldly glory but would offer instead an apotheosis of the Confederate soldier at war. The Roman Pantheon was the prototype for two other rotunda designs also rejected by the jurors. The architects were Walker and Hazzard and Wendell P. Blagden, of New York City, and Rankin, Kellogg and Crane, of Philadelphia. The strength of each design is its fidelity to so commanding a model; the weakness is the invented element added to both—a one-story surround to provide gallery space.[31]

Many, if not most, of the competition designs presented rectangular temples of one type or another. This kind of building answered both the inspirational and physical needs of the Confederate commission. The temple-form structure carries sacred associations and dignity, and it allows, better than do rotunda types, a workable plan of galleries surrounding a large central hall.

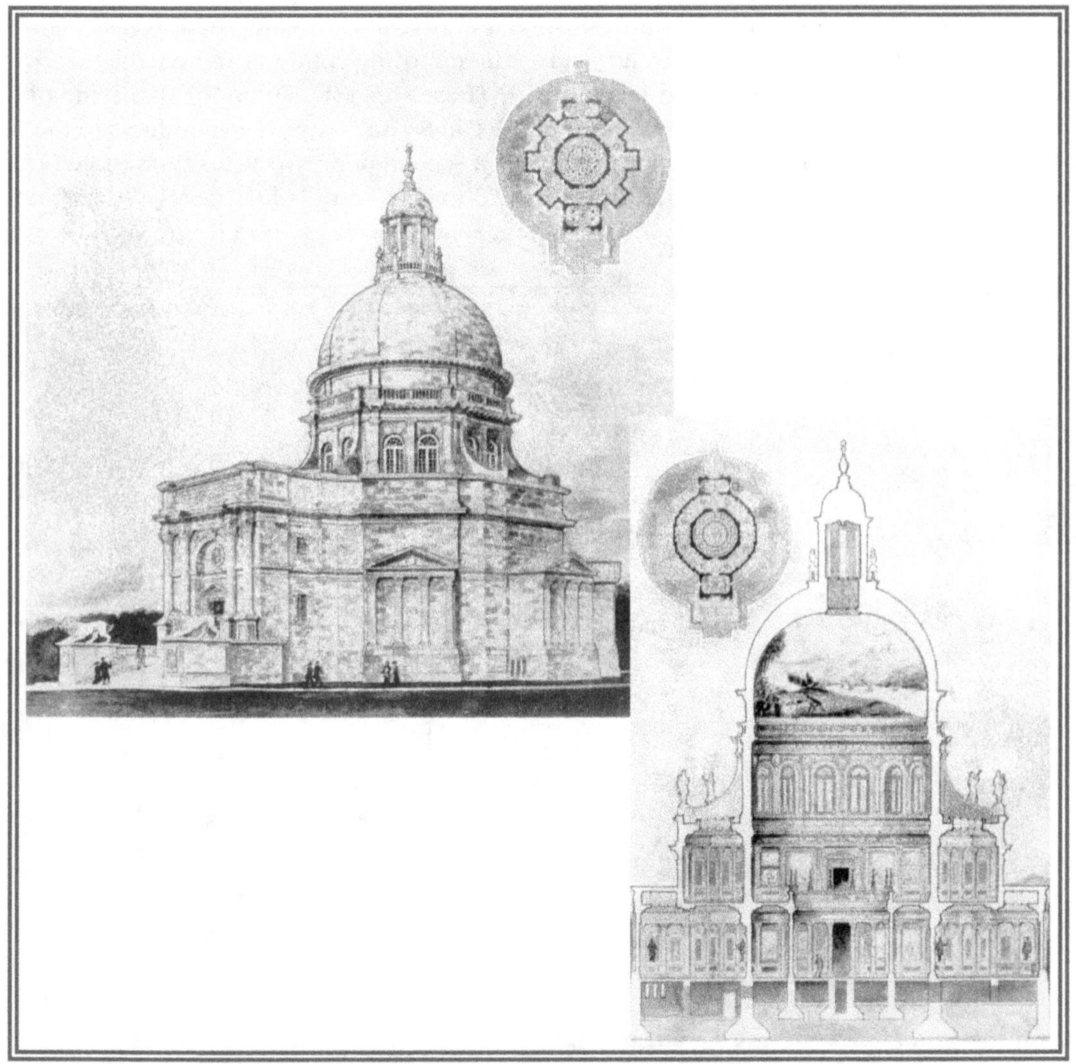

Fig. 10.2. Rossel Edward Mitchell competition drawing for Confederate Memorial Institute, 1910, published in *American Architect*, March 15, 1911.

If anything, the jury was consistent in that it awarded all five of its prizes to remarkably similar designs. In each, a six-columned giant portico dominates the elevation and gives an indication of the large scale of a central hall behind it. That core space is surrounded by smaller galleries that find expression on the exterior in the wings that flank the portico. Unlike the rotunda-style schemes, the lateral additions in the prize-winning temple-form entries do little to diminish the solemnity of the building. Each facade is loaded with sculptural embellishment. Answering what they perceived to be the requirements of the commission—a need for a sufficient number of galleries to honor the many Confederate states, the appropriateness of stone construction enriched with sculptural reliefs, and a capped budget—five firms (and probably more) independently developed elevations and plans, and even square footages, that are more alike than different.[32]

It is easy to see why the third-place entry by the New York City firm of Wilder and White attracted the eyes of the jurors (fig. 10.3). This Doric temple is a striking exercise in the adaptation of Greek classical proportions to generous, though nontraditional, square footages, a familiar characteristic of Greek Revival style architecture. The imposing columns and entablature are as massive as the sculptural decoration is abundant. These suggest a splendor that sympathetic viewers would have associated with memories of the Old South. There is a soundness to the proportioning and a virtuoso control of profuse detail.[33] A second design to win a third-place prize is a variation on the same Doric theme. If the portico in this entry is less massive than that by Wilder and White, it is more graceful. The pediment is just as solidly packed with sculpture, and

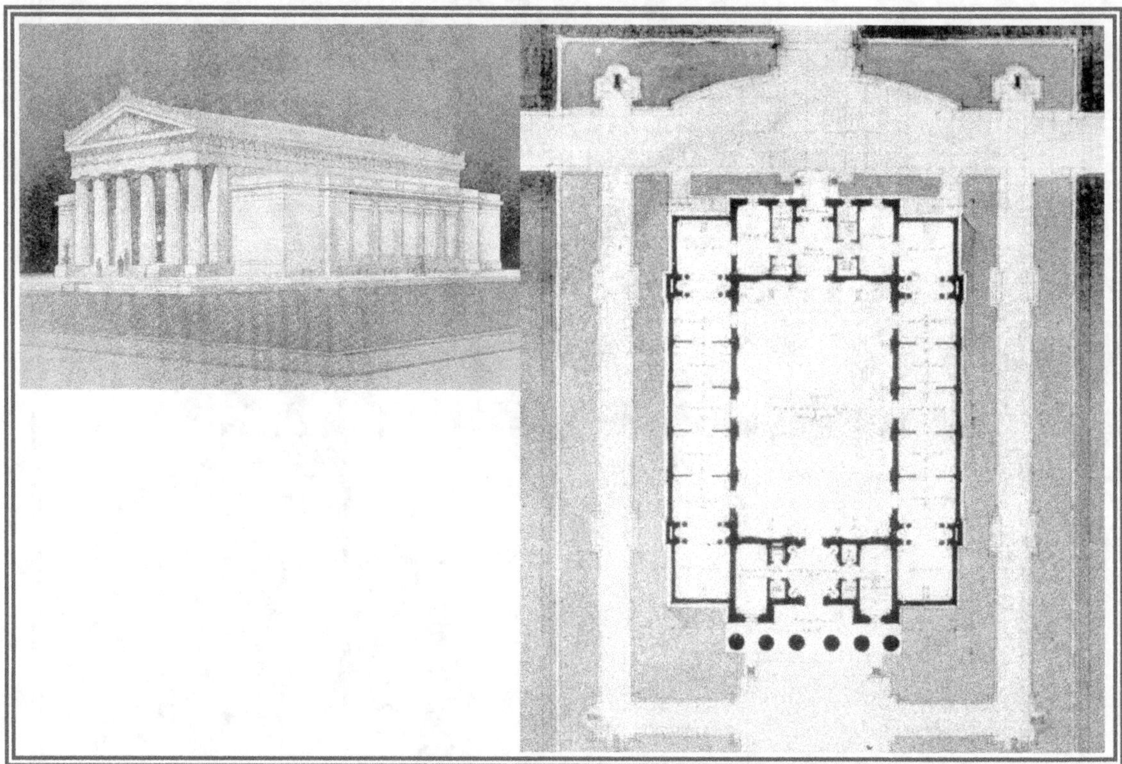

Fig. 10.3. Wilder and White competition drawing for the Confederate Memorial Institute competition, 1910, which won third place. Published in *American Architect,* March 15, 1911, and the Year Book of the Philadelphia Chapter American Institute of Architects and the T Square Club, 1911.

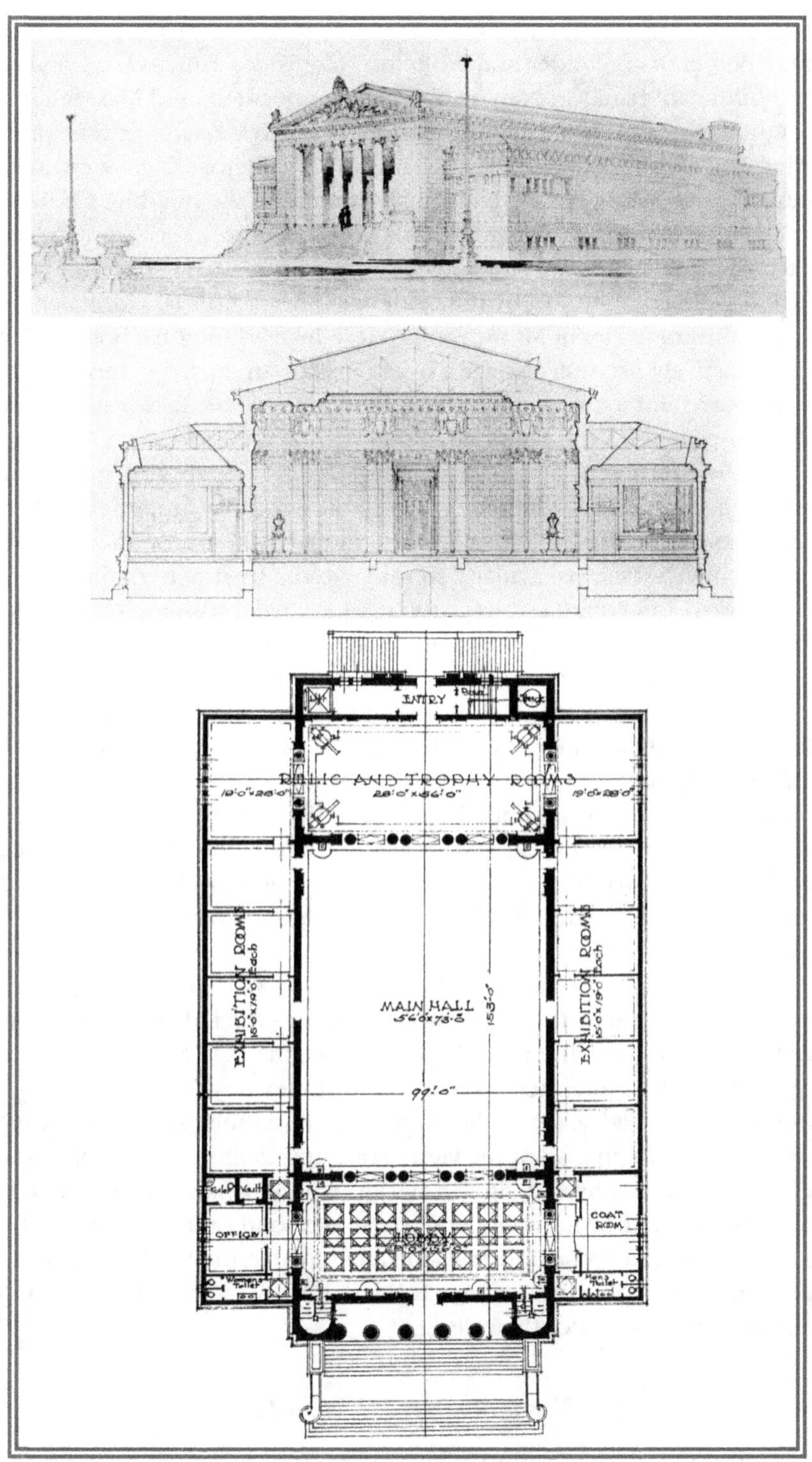

Fig. 10.4. Hewitt and Brown competition drawing for the Confederate Memorial Institute, 1910, which won second place. Published in *American Architect,* March 15, 1911.

again the elevation is an appropriate expression of a sensible floor plan. The architects, Dennison and Hirons, were neighbors of Wilder and White on New York's Fifth Avenue and had established a reputation as builders of banks in New York State, Connecticut, and Massachusetts.[34] The final design to win a third-place prize is yet another creative revival exercise, this time in the Roman Corinthian order. The architects, Averill and Adams of Washington, D.C., were able to combine a sense of the monumental with a notably graceful treatment of the building's portico.[35]

It must have been the two professional jurors who awarded the second-place prize to a design of a classicist temple that stands apart for its modernity (fig. 10.4). The architects, Hewitt and Brown, qualified for the competition by the evidence of a traditional Gothic church, St. Mark's, that they built in their home city of Minneapolis. Here instead they are bold and inventive, even whimsical. They effectively use wall surfaces, necessary for an enclosed modern temple, as a foil for both relief sculpture and for screens of columns that pierce the facades. To tie the parts to the whole, both the sculpture and the columns of the portico are revived on the wings—in panels, squat pilasters, and modern windows. These decorative areas start and stop unpredictably and invigorate the design. A "classical" chimney for the boiler room is at the rear, a further reminder that the requirements of modern buildings demand modern solutions. The cross-section drawing suggests that the architects were particularly sensitive to the treatment of the satellite galleries.[36]

The first-place award and commission for the institute went to Bissell and Sinkler, a Philadelphia firm as little known as the other prize winners (fig. 10.5). Elliston Perot Bissell and John Penn Brock Sinkler had established a partnership in 1906. For the five years preceding the Confederate competition, their body of work fills a short list of mostly residential commissions. Their later careers are exceptional only for their shared interest in restoration work and Sinkler's service as city architect of Philadelphia.[37]

Bissell and Sinkler presented essentially the same floor plan, square footage, and type of expanded temple building as did the other four award winners. But better than their competitors, they understood that the romantic classicist architect can incorporate both lavish detailing and a sense of monumentality into the design of a modern building. That combination was appropriate for the Confederate commission.

The architects offered what was arguably the most successful sculptural program, in that the details of the polychrome reliefs, the full entablatures, and the balustraded roof line suggest by their opulence both the cultural and material abundance that had been stripped from the South by defeat. The memorial was intended to preserve that memory. The Bissell and Sinkler design provided as well a pronounced sense of the monumental, on the exterior and within. The building seems larger than it is. In an instant the viewer recognizes this as a "temple to the Lost Cause" and is told that the cause was heroic. Such a design would satisfy the veterans, so that Ellyson could approve it. Noland and Taylor could endorse it as a solid exercise in romantic classicism.[38]

Bissell and Sinkler had given visual form to the analogy that the South was the Athens of America. Unfortunately, due to cost considerations, this lavish classical scheme would not be built. The architects would be directed to alter their design.

## *Aftermath of the Competition*

Significantly, one objection to the results of the competition came from the one person who mattered, patron Peter Rouss. His agent, Louis D'Auby, wrote immediately to Ellyson that the illustration of the selected design "would give the impression that the building was constructed to be set into a narrow city lot, and if this be the case we are somewhat disappointed in the general

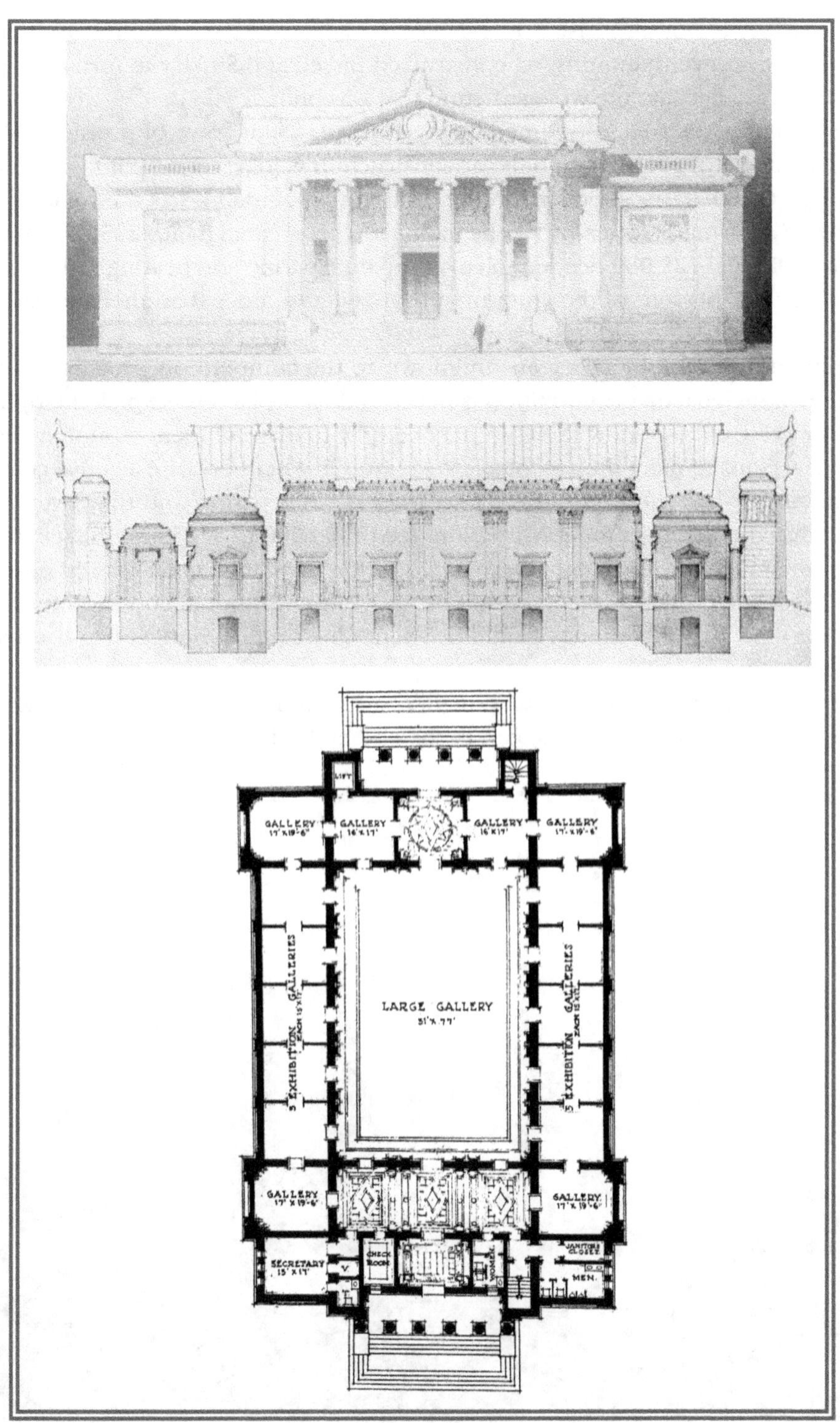

Fig. 10.5. Bissell and Sinkler competition drawing for the Confederate Memorial Institute, 1910, which won first place and was built in an altered form. Published in *American Architect,* March 15, 1911, and the Year Book of the Philadelphia Chapter American Institute of Architects and the T Square Club, 1911.

results." Ellyson would not displease Rouss. No doubt it was the association's president, at some point during the next twelve months, who instructed Bissell and Sinkler to turn their plan ninety degrees on its axis to become the wide structure that was built.[39]

At the very point when success seemed finally at hand, a new wave of problems shocked the association. In August of 1911, when bids for construction were received, all fifteen far exceeded the sum of $150,000 that was stipulated in the competition guidelines as the ceiling for the project. The lowest bid, from Metzger and Wells of Philadelphia, came in at $225,000. Added to that would be an additional $25,000 needed to cover separate wiring and heating estimates. The total of $250,000 was 167 percent of the amount authorized and more than the association's entire resources.[40]

Over-budget designs are by no means unknown to the competition process. Besides, some would argue that the goal of a competition is not to choose a plan but to pick the right designer. The architects were selected; now the CMA needed only to instruct them to modify their scheme and submit new plans to meet the acceptable cost level. But neither the executive committee nor the young architects had the experience to weather the new storm and they overreacted. The committee reduced the budget for construction from $150,000 to $125,000. Bissell and Sinkler's altered design was submitted in December 1911. The low bid for it, again offered by Metzger and Wells, was $90,625, to which $10,000 would be added for additional contracts for heating and electricity. This time, too little money would be spent. The original budget had been diminished by a third.[41]

The new building (fig. 10.6) would be a smaller, stripped-down version of the original, turned on its axis as suggested by Peter Rouss, and in the end built of Indiana limestone rather than the

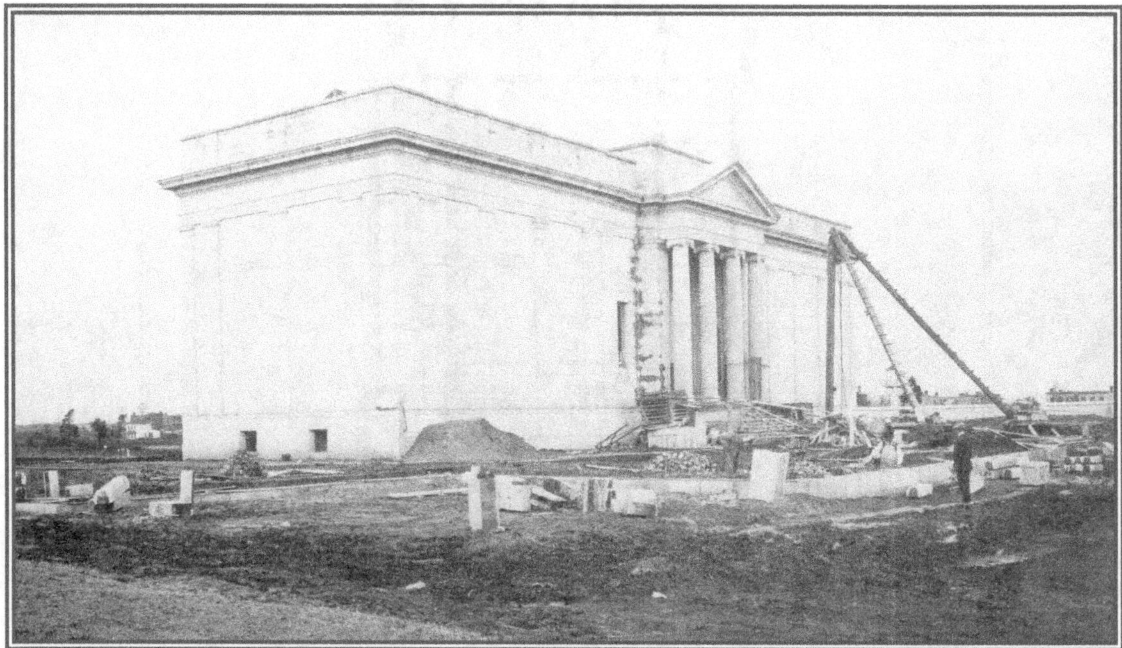

Fig. 10.6. The Confederate Memorial Institute, Richmond, January 8, 1913. Bissell and Sinkler, architects. Photograph courtesy of Virginia Historical Society.

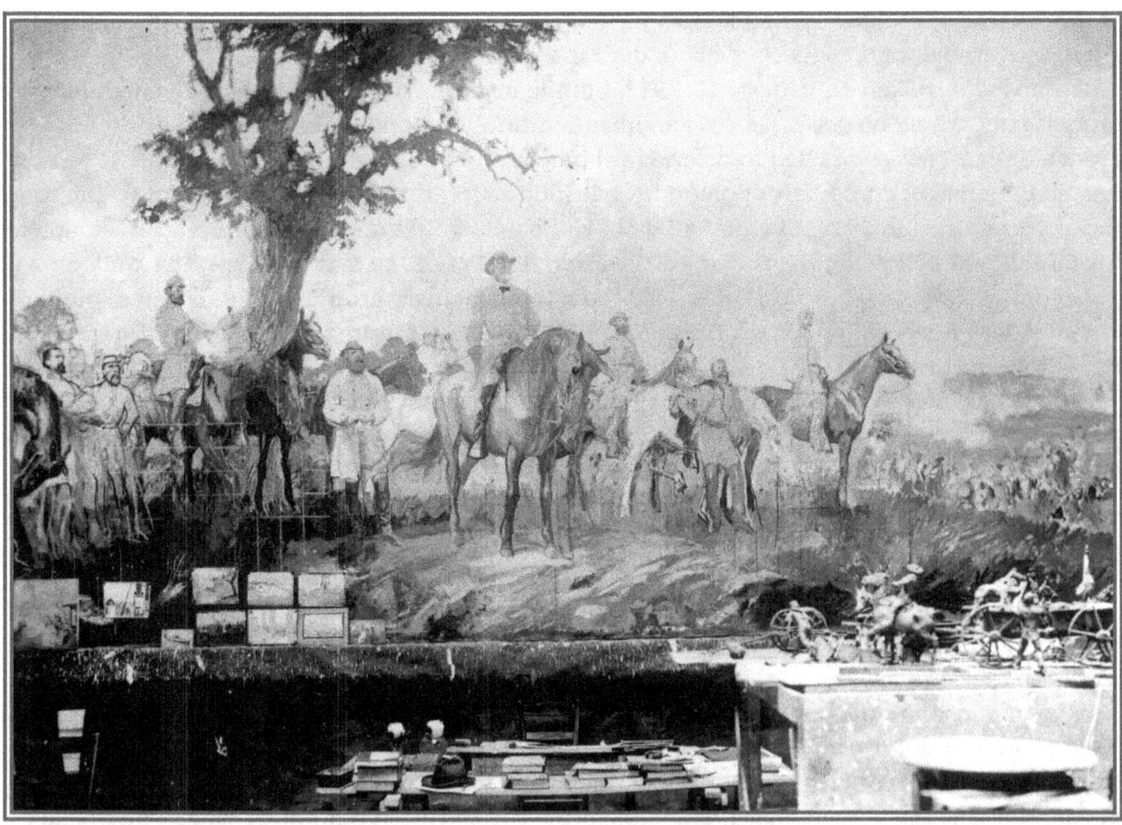

Fig. 10.7. *Summer* panel from *The Four Seasons of the Confederacy* mural by Charles Hoffbauer, as it neared completion about 1920. Photograph courtesy of the Virginia Historical Society.

expensive Georgia marble that had helped to push the first estimates beyond anticipation. The second Bissell and Sinkler design—the one that was constructed and survives today—is a building with a stark and bare facade. Its small portico has four columns instead of six, and strangely blank panels still await the relief sculpture that never would be carved. What would have been a vast interior space was cut in half: in the new design there would be no large gallery encircled by smaller ones—only an entrance flanked by a memorial hall and a library.[42] Bissell and Sinkler, however, did maintain in their second scheme segments of the architectural detail they had initially proposed, and they did keep the imposing scale of the old building—including its height (forty-four feet). If it no longer was a deep structure, at least it now was wide (150 feet). And the workmanship for the building was sound.[43]

The executive committee could accept the reduced square footage of the second design because a long-standing crisis had never been resolved. Not one of the Confederate veterans groups—including even the Lee Camp that was resident adjacent to the site for the institute—had come forward to provide the anticipated gifts of paintings and sculptures that would have filled the galleries of the original design. Ellyson was compelled to find an additional benefactor who would commission a muralist to create new art for the "memorial hall." The patron was Thomas Fortune Ryan, who as a financier of municipal railways and lighting systems had amassed in New

York City one of the great personal fortunes of the era. The painter was a Frenchman, Charles Hoffbauer, winner of the Prix National of the Paris Salon in 1906.

Ground was broken on January 22, 1912, but the institute, which was to have opened thirteen months later, would be delayed for yet another decade. At the outbreak of the First World War, the French muralist felt compelled to defend his homeland. The aging veterans, desperate to see the finished memorial, could only applaud his patriotic action that repeated their own. By the time the artist returned in 1919, Ellyson had died. Hoffbauer would take two more years to complete his mural cycle following the theme of *The Four Seasons of the Confederacy.* The well-known panel entitled *Summer* (fig. 10.7) is conceived as an imaginary grouping of illustrious southern commanders surrounding Robert E. Lee. The murals depict Virginia campaigns of the Civil War but ignore the conflict in the West, for the institute had become largely a Virginia memorial.[44]

While Hoffbauer worked, a wing was added to the rear of the building by the Richmond firm of Baskervill and Lambert. As early as 1912 the executive committee had recognized the surplus in its bank account, but it acted only when the Lee Camp of veterans in 1919 pledged to place its portrait collection in the institute if its meetings could be held there. By 1921, when that rear wing was completed and the institute finally opened, there were few surviving veterans, at Lee Camp or anywhere else in the nation.[45]

The opening of the building marked the end of the last Confederate campaign. Its story, one of advances and retreats, is a record of the will of the survivors of the Confederacy to perpetuate old southern ideals and values in the face of modern forces of change. As to the architecture of the project, the institute ultimately was less inspired and less ambitious than the structure that had been proposed in 1900; Stanford White's pantheon would have been a striking national monument, one with remarkable dignity and monumentality, as its advocates had noted. The Bissell and Sinkler building also did not match in grandeur the two northern buildings that had provoked its creation and its resurrection, because the Grant Monument and the Lincoln Memorial had budgets five and sixteen to twenty times as large. But the competition of 1910 was fairly and competently staged, it yielded a strong design, and the final product is impressive if not lavish. The Confederate veterans were described in a southern novel of 1909 as "dead men . . . moving among the living as ghosts." Their persistent memories and intense emotions made the memorializing of their cause an arduous and protracted exercise.[46]

## Notes

This essay is an abridged version of "Planning a 'Temple to the Lost Cause': The Confederate Memorial Institute and the Design Competition of 1910," *ARRIS* 8 (1997): 6–23. My thanks to Richard Guy Wilson for reading an early draft of this paper and offering helpful advice and ideas.

1. David M. Kahn, "The Grant Monument," *Journal of the Society of Architectural Historians* 41 (1982): 212–31; Confederate Memorial Assoc., *The South's Battle Abbey* (Atlanta: Respress Co., 1896?), 2–4. The Confederate Memorial Institute (CMI) has largely been overlooked by architectural historians, though it is cited in Charles E. Brownell, Calder Loth, William M. S. Rasmussen, and Richard Guy Wilson, *The Making of Virginia Architecture* (Richmond: Virginia Museum of Fine Arts, 1992), 117.

2. Gaines M. Foster, *Ghosts of the Confederacy* (New York: Oxford Univ. Press, 1987), 114; James M. Lindgren, *Preserving the Old Dominion: Historic Preservation and Virginia Traditionalism* (Charlottesville:

Univ. Press of Virginia, 1993), 187. The quotation about "pottage" is from Lyon Tyler, a president of the College of William and Mary.

3. The veterans debated Rouss's proposal through UCV meetings, committees, and the magazine *Confederate Veteran*.

4. Confederate Memorial Assoc., *South's Battle Abbey*, 16. "The Battle-Abbey Scheme, Mr. C. B. Rouss Submits an Additional Proposition on the Subject," *Times-Richmond*, June 1, 1896, in "Confederate Memorial Institute, A Scrap Book," n.p. (arranged chronologically), compiled and edited by Mrs. J. Taylor Ellyson, 1925, Confederate Memorial Association Records, Virginia Historical Society, Richmond. Dickinson even discussed having burials there, "in imitation of Westminster Abbey."

5. "The Battle-Abbey Scheme," n.p. At this early date, Sen. John W. Daniel of Virginia called the proposed memorial the "Battle Abbey of the South." That term for the building survives today and makes clear the sanctity that many southerners attached to the Lost Cause. Confederate Memorial Assoc., *South's Battle Abbey*, 5. But there is no evidence that this "abbey" ever was to have been in a medievalist style.

6. It was Ellyson's newspaper clippings that were arranged by his widow in "Confederate Memorial Institute, A Scrap Book."

7. The revitalization movement had been led by former Confederate Gen. Jubal Early, who in defiance of Robert E. Lee's pleas to forgive and forget, preached militant sectionalism and became obsessed with Confederate culture and the issues of the war. Foster, *Ghosts of the Confederacy*, 47–62.

8. Even though he called for a "national" shrine, Rouss argued provincially that the "easy task [of] secur[ing] the [matching] money for the proposed work from a few rich men" in the North was not desirable. Instead, "every confederate veteran" should contribute something, giving "proof of the existence of that sentiment which every confederate veteran cherishes in his heart" (Confederate Memorial Assoc., *South's Battle Abbey*, 3). This idea was unsound, because even outside the impoverished South public subscriptions at this time often fell far short of their goal. The Grant Memorial Association had failed to raise the million dollars it initially projected. For a discussion of public subscriptions for Civil War monuments, see Kirk Savage, "Race, Memory, and Identity: The National Monuments of the Union and the Confederacy" (Ph.D. diss., Univ. of California at Berkeley, 1990), 119–41. When confronted with Underwood's success at accumulating pledges and checks for more than $123,000, Rouss reversed his position.

9. *United States Circuit Court of Appeals for the Second Circuit, The Confederate Memorial Association vs. John N. Shaugnessy, Transcript of Record, Error to the Circuit Court of the United States for the Eastern District of New York* (Printed under the Direction of the Clerk, n.d.), 31, 185, 171–75, 192. Many of the architects and artists Underwood chose were northerners. Underwood paid for the portraits himself and intended to donate them to the association.

10. The most vocal opponent of Underwood's action was S. A. Cunningham, the stubborn sectionalist editor of the magazine *Confederate Veteran,* which served as the voice of the UCV and the Confederate celebration. Cunningham called Underwood's Charleston report "nauseating," "insolent," and "an outrage," asking, who was Underwood "to be the judge as to whose pictures should go in it [the memorial building]?" *Confederate Veteran* 7 (June 1899): 257, 349–50.

11. Underwood also had solicited a second design from a now-unknown architect. According to a newspaper account of the 1900 reunion in Louisville, two designs would be submitted for consideration, but White's was much preferred and probably would be accepted. "Great Confederate Battle Abbey Which Is to Be Erected in This City," *Times-Richmond*, June 3, 1900.

12. The reworked White drawing is published in "Great Confederate Battle Abbey." Scholars with no access to this newspaper account have misdated the drawing to 1910. The article makes no mention of White's

name, either because he was a northern architect or because Underwood had not revealed his identity to the paper. Flanking the grand steps to the portico were to be statues of Davis and Lee. Equestrian statues of Generals Stuart and Forrest were projected for the grounds, as suggested in White's presentation drawing. Forrest, a Tennessee hero, would be forgotten by the Virginians who after 1912 would decorate the institute. Underwood displayed to the veterans two plaster models for the proposed statue of Lee, one by Niehaus and one by Rhind, as well as a plaster model of a proposed statue of Davis by Niehaus.

13. Quotation on the scheme unfolding "at a single glance" is from "Great Confederate Battle Abbey," *Times-Richmond,* June 3, 1900. Charles McKim may never have desired any association with the CMI, for he was from an abolitionist family and in the years around 1910 was involved instead with the Lincoln Memorial and the civic beautification project for Washington, D.C. Savage, "National Monuments," 202–3.

14. Richmond newspaper publisher Joseph Bryan wrote in 1900, "I am a hotter Confederate now than I have been in fifteen years . . . . It is a case of streams wearing their channel deeper." Lindgren, *Preserving the Old Dominion,* 173–74. For the council funding, see "Money for the Abbey," *Richmond Times-Dispatch,* May 13, 1903, in "Scrap Book," n.p.

15. In 1906 when the New York firm of Carpentier, Blair and Gould submitted to the association an unsolicited but handsome design (Special Collections, Univ. of Washington Library) projecting a classical domed building that is essentially an opera house, no serious consideration was given to the proposal.

16. Lindgren, *Preserving the Old Dominion,* 128, 123, 97; Foster, *Ghosts of the Confederacy,* 158–59.

17. For earlier efforts to build a Lincoln memorial, see Savage, "National Monuments," 48–65, 94–101, 141, 201–15.

18. This postwar southern view of Lincoln has been largely forgotten. Christian argued that to say Lincoln was "the greatest, wisest and godliest man that has appeared on the earth since Christ" was a "positive fraud on the public" and an "outrage on the truth of history." George L. Christian, *Abraham Lincoln. An Address Delivered before R. E. Lee Camp, No. 1, Confederate Veterans, at Richmond, Va., on October 29th, 1909* (Richmond: n.p., 1909), 38, 4, 7, 12, 20–25, 40.

19. Robert White to Ellyson, Mar. 24, 1909; Ellyson to White, Apr. 14, 1909; Board of Trustees Minute Book, May 22, 1909, CMA Records. (The Snelling and Porter drawings are lost.)

20. Mitchell to Ellyson, Feb. 17 and May 27, 1910, CMA Records; Cram to Ellyson, Apr. 9, Oct. 3, and Oct. 14, 1910, CMA Records.

21. The executive committee had hoped to endorse a design at its meeting. Members even talked of laying the cornerstone a month later, on June 3. See Robert White to Ellyson, Apr. 4, 1910, CMA Records. It is not known who on the committee suggested that a competition be held or when the final decision on it was approved. But the idea had been talked about in the committee for at least half a year. As early as January, J. Stewart Barney had tried to dissuade Ellyson from considering it. See Barney's letter of Jan. 5, 1910, CMA Records.

22. See John M. Coski and Amy R. Feely, "A Monument to Southern Womanhood: The Founding Generation of the Confederate Museum," in *A Woman's War,* ed. Edward D. C. Campbell Jr. and Kym S. Rice (Richmond: Museum of the Confederacy, 1996), 131–63.

23. For more on Monument Avenue, see essays by Richard Guy Wilson, Brian Black, and Bryn Varley in this anthology. The CMI site fronts a major cross-axis, the Boulevard, two short blocks from Monument Avenue. The juncture of the two streets had been considered earlier; in 1909 Snelling devised a circular building for that site with an ambulatory and upstairs gallery. The equestrian statue of Stonewall Jackson was placed there instead in 1919. Letters of Apr. 28 and June 17, 1909, and May 27, 1910, to Ellyson, CMA Records.

24. Hélène Lipstadt, ed., *The Experimental Tradition, Essays on Competitions in Architecture* (New York: Princeton Architectural Press, 1989). The two-stage format, whereby the winners of an open competition

would compete with a select group invited to participate in a second round, could not be used because no short list of invited architects could be devised to satisfy both the New York sponsor and the Confederate veterans. An open competition seemed somehow different than inviting a Yankee architect. Once enrolled in the Confederate competition, the northerner would be free from sectionalist bias because the jurying process was "blind," as stipulated since 1870 in the American Institute of Architects' code of regulations. Lipstadt, *Experimental Tradition,* 61.

25. On advisors, see Lipstadt, *Experimental Tradition,* 65. Noland, trained in the office of Cope and Stewardson in Philadelphia, became the "dean" of his profession in Virginia—the first president of the Richmond Architects' Association (1911), a founder of the Virginia chapter of the American Institute of Architects (1914), and the first to be certified by the state as an architect (1921).

26. Announcements of the competition were placed in *The American Architect, The Architect's Review,* and the *Brickbuilder.* See E. R. Will, Pope's office manager, to Ellyson, Sept. 1 and Oct. 27, 1910, CMA Records.

27. The number of competition qualifiers, eighty-eight, matched the number of entries submitted to the muchpublicized New York Public Library competition of 1897. Lipstadt, *Experimental Tradition,* 66–72. The architects represented many states of the union, but almost half (close to thirty) were from New York. The fourteen entries from Philadelphia nearly equaled the total from the entire South. Only seven resident Virginians applied.

28. The Grant competition had paid a lesser premium and offered the winner no guarantee of employment as project architect. As a result, only twenty-three Americans and a total of sixty-five architects entered that contest. Kahn, "Grant Monument," 219.

29. Questions included the following: What style of architecture is wanted, Gothic or Classical? The answer: This is "left to the option of the competitor. The question of style of architecture has never been discussed by the Executive Committee."

30. Taylor was selected by AIA President Irving Pond and was to be paid $100 or $150 for his service. Pond to Noland, Feb. 4, 1911, CMA Records. On Nov. 16, at too late a date, Henry Bacon requested information about the competition, only to be denied entry. Bacon to Ellyson, Nov. 16, 1910, CMA Records.

31. Mitchell to George Christian, May 27, 1910, CMA Records. Mitchell further explained that the great height of the dome "would give a monumental grandeur to the interior," and "the two surrounding galleries would make magnificent settings for paintings, busts, relics etc., of the different states." The Walker and Hazzard and Wendell P. Blagden design is illustrated in *American Architect,* March 15, 1911. The Rankin, Kellogg and Crane design is illustrated in the *Year Book* of the Philadelphia AIA and T Square Club, 1911.

32. The dimensions for the monumental halls proposed by Bissell and Sinkler, Hewitt and Brown, Wilder and White, and Averill and Adams are 31 x 77, 56 x 73, 50 x 80, and 58 x 69 feet. The four firms, listed in the same order, proposed sixteen, thirteen, fourteen, and fifteen galleries. Dimensions in the photo of the Dennison and Hirons plan, which had thirteen galleries, are not legible.

33. Walter Robb Wilder and Harry Keith White qualified for the competition by the evidence of minor commercial work, none of national distinction. Wilder and White to Ellyson, Oct. 12, 1910, CMA Records.

34. The design is illustrated in *American Architect,* May 10, 1911. Dennison and Hirons to Ellyson, Oct. 11, 1910, CMA Records.

35. The design is illustrated in *American Architect,* May 10, 1911. In establishing their eligibility, Frank L. Averill, a structural engineer, and architect Percy C. Adams claimed experience in Washington with government buildings. Averill and Adams to Ellyson, Oct. 12, 1910, CMA Records.

36. Hewitt and Brown to Ellyson, Oct. 12, 1910, CMA Records.

37. Bissell and Sinkler were Philadelphia natives and graduates of the University of Pennsylvania's school of architecture. Elliston Bissell then interned with the medievalist firm of Cope and Stewardson. John Sinkler

trained in a classicist style at the École des Beaux-Arts in Paris. Sandra L. Tatman and Roger W. Moss, *Biographical Dictionary of Philadelphia Architects: 1700–1930* (Boston: G. K. Hall, 1985), 72–74, 727–29.

38. Eight months earlier, Judge Christian had criticized one of Grenville Snelling's designs for offering a building that was "not . . . sufficiently imposing." Snelling to Ellyson, May 27, 1910, CMA Records.

39. Louis D'Auby to Ellyson, Jan. 26 and Feb. 10, 1911, CMA Records.

40. Executive committee meeting, Aug. 7, 1911, CMA Records; George Christian, "letter to the editor," *Richmond Times-Dispatch*, Nov. 2, 1911, in "Scrap Book," n.p.

41. Meetings of Aug. 18 and Dec. 18, 1911, of the executive committee, CMA Records. The second set of bids is curiously absent from the records of the association.

42. The specifications of Dec. 1, 1911, still called for "clear white Georgia marble," which was dropped when bids were received later that month. Bissell and Sinkler, *Specifications for the General Construction of the Confederate Memorial Institute* (Philadelphia, 1911). At the 1914 reunion, Ellyson hoped that "at no distant day [the large facade blocks] will be transformed by the art of the sculptor into . . . suitable memorials of some of the great events of that time which the whole building is designed to commemorate." "Confederate Memorial Institute Report Read at Great Reunion," *Richmond News Leader,* May 7, 1914, in "Scrap Book," n.p.

43. "Confederate Memorial Institute Report Read," in "Scrap Book," n.p. The firm published a sixty-six-page book that contains some 387 stringent regulations: details would be "first-class in every respect" or rejected. Bissell and Sinkler, *Specifications,* par. 139. While the changes were dramatic, alterations are to be expected with a competition project. For example, the Grant Monument was not constructed as designed, because even its large budget was insufficient. Kahn, "Grant Monument," 230–31.

44. William M. S. Rasmussen, "Making the Confederate Murals, Studies by Charles Hoffbauer," *Virginia Magazine of History and Biography* 101 (1993): 433–56.

45. George L. Christian, *Sketch of the Origin and Erection of the Confederate Memorial Institute at Richmond, Virginia* (Richmond: n.p., 1921), 19; "Memorial Institute Here to Be Greatest Confederate Building," *Richmond News Leader,* May 9, 1912, in "Scrap Book," n.p. Still missing on the exterior was the surrounding environment of "beautiful lawns and gardens, with trees and shrubbery, with emblematic fountains, . . . and statues" that Charles Rouss and Colonel Dickinson had envisioned. "The Battle-Abbey Scheme," in "Scrap Book," n.p. The statues were no longer essential since sculptures of Lee, Davis, and Stuart stood nearby on Monument Avenue.

46. Walter Hines Page, *The Southerner, or the Autobiography of Nicholas Worth* (New York: Doubleday, Page and Co., 1909); cited in Richard M. Weaver, *The Southern Tradition at Bay, a History of Postbellum Thought* (New Rochelle, N.Y.: Arlington House, 1968), 372. In 1946, when practically no Confederate veterans survived, the Confederate Memorial Institute was absorbed by the Virginia Historical Society. It serves today as the core of the society's headquarters complex. The three Bissell and Sinkler rooms remain largely as they were built.

# 11

# Gratitude and Gender Wars

MONUMENTS TO THE WOMEN OF THE SIXTIES

*Cynthia Mills*

AFTER A LONG FUND-RAISING STRUGGLE, aging veterans of the Civil War erected seven state monuments to the Women of the Confederacy between 1912 and 1926. The old soldiers had launched a major, regionwide campaign at the turn of the century to build these monuments, defining their drive as an exclusively male venture. They said its aim was to create a united, enduring expression of the men's gratitude to southern wives, mothers, sisters, and daughters for their valor, self-sacrifice, and strength of character in the war years.

The veterans never were able to reach agreement, however, on the exact note they wished to strike with their tributes to the "Women of the Sixties," and they failed to meet their early goal of placing casts of the same sculptural group on the Capitol grounds of each seceding state. Instead a peculiar assortment of public sculptures emerged over the decades. Five Confederate states failed to build women's memorials. The others—Arkansas, Florida, Mississippi, North Carolina, South Carolina, and Tennessee, as well one border state, Maryland—raised monuments of widely varying designs.

Why was this unusual assortment of monuments, putting woman's achievement on a pedestal, born in the South at this time? A close look at the surviving sculptures and the extended feud over their creation reveals more complex motivations than mere gratitude. It suggests that a lingering contest between northern and southern definitions of manliness was being played out in an era when urban beautification efforts produced a wealth of new public sculpture in the United States and abroad. A gender competition with the women of the South, who had successfully commissioned a multitude of monuments to the Confederate soldier, also was implicit. Many women rejected the veterans' campaign as irrelevant to their new roles in society. This essay will trace the origins of this sculptural group and then examine each of the completed state monuments. The bronzes portraying elite white women ultimately expose the decay of myths about antebellum gender relations and the awkward way in which a damaged value system collapses.

Ladies' Memorial Associations had often been the first to erect Civil War memorials, as several of the essays in this volume demonstrate. After its formation in the 1890s, the United Daughters of the Confederacy led many successful monument drives glorifying southern soldiers and political leaders. Dedications of Confederate monuments of all kinds soared between 1905 and 1912, in part because of improved financial conditions in the South and a sense that the clock was running out for the aging war generation. Shafts topped by a single figure of a Confederate soldier dotted courthouse lawns, public squares, and cemeteries across the South. These, along with battlefield memorials and monuments to such Lost Cause heroes as Generals Robert E. Lee and Stonewall Jackson, helped rebuild a regional identity.

It was in this period that the veterans finally acted upon a long-discussed idea of building a major men's memorial to the war women.[1] The public drive to honor the special qualities of southern women had gained strength in the 1890s after the formation of the United Confederate Veterans, a regionwide group that organized annual reunions. The veterans group worked to institutionalize "correct" memories about the war in a variety of ways, including a major textbook campaign. In their drive to build a monument to southern women, the former soldiers advanced the argument that family was at the heart of the war effort. They sought to combat what they perceived as "false" history about southern gender relations as well as "false" northern arguments that the war was fought over the issue of slavery.

The veterans retained memories of northern wounds to southern whites' masculine pride—wounds that were expressed in verbal and pictorial form as well as in physical conflict. Scholar Nina Silber has described how after the war and President Abraham Lincoln's assassination,

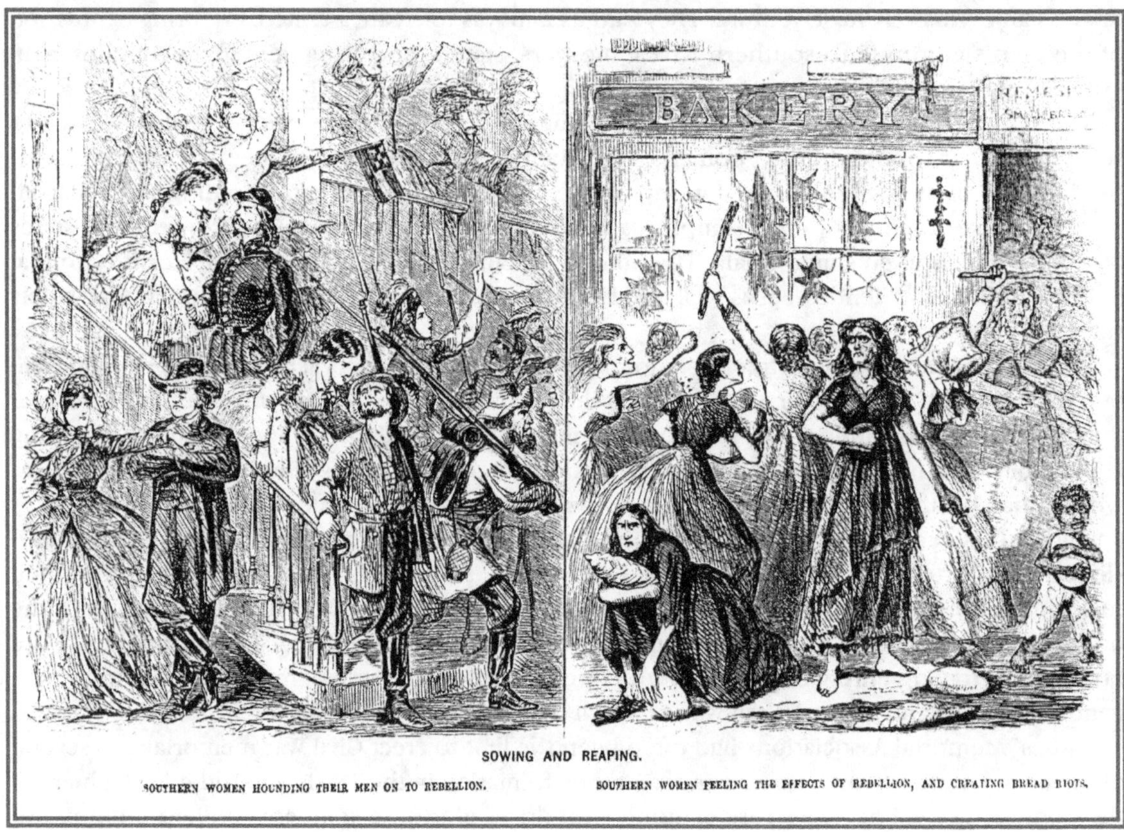


Fig. 11.1. "Sowing and Reaping." Wood engraving from *Leslie's Illustrated Weekly News,* May 23, 1863.

northern men "attacked the manhood of southern leaders, chiding the 'chivalry' for their dissipative, idle, and intemperate ways and suggesting that Southern masculinity lacked that quality of restraint which was one hallmark of Northern manliness." Prominent speakers and journalists in the North "frequently savaged Southern ladies for what was seen as their excessive support of the Confederacy." This abusive language saw the southern elite as embodying "corruptions of proper gender codes," including "emasculated Southern men" and "spiteful and unruly Southern women."[2] A wood engraving entitled *Sowing and Reaping* in *Frank Leslie's Illustrated News* (fig. 11.1) is a pictorial example of the vituperative northern imagery of southern women. The first panel shows southern belles, dressed in fine clothes, imperiously ordering their men off to war. The second shows the women, gaunt and in homespun dresses adopted during the war, wielding clubs and guns during wartime bread riots. All of these statements and pictures suggested the southern woman was shrewish and strident, marked by bellicose characteristics, while southern males were soft and undisciplined—not only in war but at home, where they could not control their women.

The attack on the masculinity of the southern male reached a high pitch with the northern ridicule that followed the 1865 arrest in Georgia of Confederate President Jefferson Davis, who, according to legend, put on some of his wife's garments—most likely a cloak or shawl—to disguise himself from pursuing Union soldiers. He was mercilessly lambasted as the petticoat president in the northern press, and with him all of southern manhood and the whole cult of southern womanhood that supported it.[3]

Significantly, it was Davis who led the drive to elevate the southern woman after the war by dedicating his 1881 book, *The Rise and Fall of the Confederate Government,* to "The Women of the Confederacy,"

> Whose pious ministrations to our wounded soldiers
> Soothed the last hours of those
>> Who died far from the objects of their tenderest love;
>> Whose domestic labors
>> Contributed much to supply the wants of our defenders in the field;
>> Whose zealous faith in our cause
>> Shone a guiding star undimmed by the darkest clouds of war;
> Whose fortitude
> Sustained them under all the privations to which they were subjected;
>> Whose annual tribute
>> Expresses their enduring grief, love, and reverence
>> For our sacred dead.[4]

Supporters of the campaign for women's memorials quoted Davis's dedication frequently, and it appeared on at least two of the completed monuments. The statement served as a building block in the postwar construction of the Lost Cause narrative, and it helped define the monument building movement that blossomed at the turn of the century.

Partly in response to the northern assault on southern gender relations, southern veterans made their women part of all public remembrances of the war and repeatedly expressed public gratitude for their qualities of beauty, morality, and loyalty. At veterans' reunions, women played a major role as maids of honor, and "representative" young women of the South rode in the parades alongside the aging former soldiers. Davis's daughter Varina, known as "Winnie," was the subject of many tributes, even in death. Elderly women were given honored places on platforms, and lists of the dwindling number of surviving "Confederate mothers" were published in the veterans' magazine. The desire to counter the "wrong" image of Confederate women—and men— clearly was an important factor in the grassroots monument movement.

## *Monumental Choices*

Once the decision had been made to honor women, the first question to be addressed was whether to build a physical monument, like an obelisk or a bronze figurative group, or whether the tribute should take some other form. Early discussions of the project in the *Confederate Veteran,* the chief publication of the veterans' group, repeatedly mentioned that women opposed a monument of bronze and stone. The magazine always ascribed this opposition to modesty, but comments from some women suggested that they preferred a memorial in another, more constructive form, such as scholarships to help educate the new generation of women.[5]

In 1906, for instance, Martha S. Gielow, president of the Southern Industrial Educational Association, wrote that there was an "almost universal objection to a 'shaft' by the women of the South." She suggested the proposed memorial take the form of an industrial college instead. Sada Foute Richmond of Memphis urged endowment of a "Southern Mothers' Scholarship" in each southern state instead of "a heap of stones, in repetition of aboriginal ideas." She wrote in the *Confederate Veteran* in 1907, "That a monument should be built to the mothers and grandmothers of the Confederacy is unquestioned . . . but let it not be a monument of insensate stone or pulseless clay, but one that will be a continual blessing to all Southern womanhood."[6]

Sallie S. Hunt of the Stonewall Jackson Institute in Abingdon, Virginia, suggested a "Dixie Home" for poor but ambitious southern girls. In Tennessee, the United Daughters of the Confederacy (UDC) asked the state to apply money to the payment of veterans' pensions rather than appropriate $6,000, as a state senator proposed, toward a women's monument. In Alabama, UDC member Mabel Wrenn introduced a resolution, saying "it is better to found scholarships than to erect monuments."[7]

The veterans ultimately spurned these suggestions. C. Irvine Walker of Charleston, South Carolina, the United Confederate Veterans (UCV) general who led a joint committee formed by the UCV and the Sons of Confederate Veterans, defended the final choice of a traditional bronze figurative monument or series of monuments in a proposal he first drafted in November 1905. The veterans could not raise the large amount of money needed "to endow some school, hospital or other work which would produce some practical good to humanity" in perpetuity, he said. "Monuments, however, if substantially built, would after erection require no further outlay of money."[8]

The men may have wished to show that they could compete with women's groups, which had so successfully raised money for public sculptures. "Every man in the South knows that the monuments erected everywhere to the Confederate soldier have been planned and the money raised for them by women," Bridges Smith, the mayor of Macon, Georgia, noted for example.[9] They may have suspected that the women had an unspoken objective—avoiding rivalry with their own ongoing monumental efforts. Awareness of women's changing role was another factor. By the turn of the century, increasing numbers of upper-class women in the South were engaged in activities outside the home. More women of all classes were working for wages in an economy far removed from the plantation culture that some veterans remembered with nostalgia. White women found

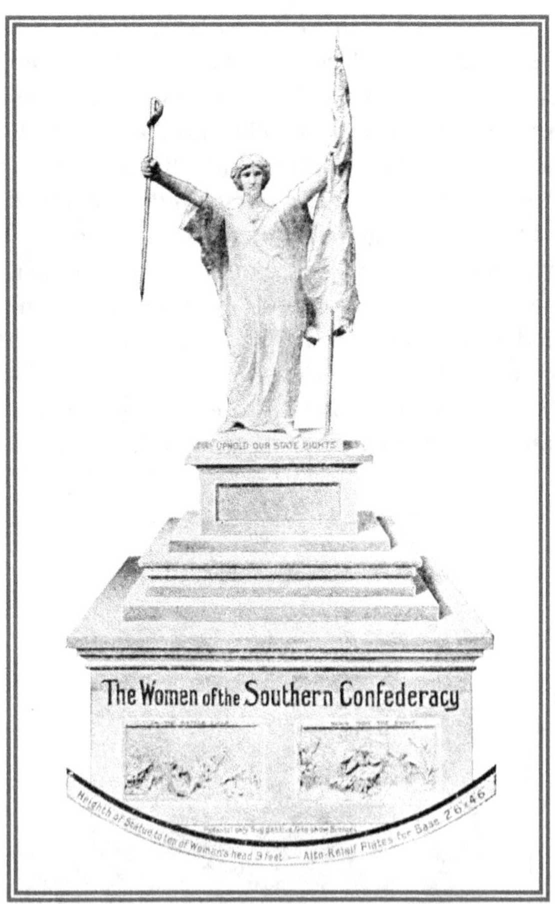


Fig. 11.2. Proposal by sculptor Louis Amateis for a regionwide monument to Confederate women, presented to 1909 reunion of Confederate veterans in Memphis, Tennessee. Photograph from April 1909 *Confederate Veteran.*

positions as teachers, governesses, nurses, millworkers, stenographers, and saleswomen, and a small number became doctors and lawyers. In tandem with these new duties and opportunities, some southern women, including some members of the UDC, were joining the suffrage movement just as the veterans' campaign for monuments to the women of the sixties was gaining steam. A monument would provide a countermodel for future generations.[10]

At first, the veterans considered building one grand monument, perhaps in Richmond, the Confederate capital. However, to avoid regional feuding and encourage fund-raising, Walker eventually proposed having a monument to the southern woman in each seceding state. He suggested that the veterans settle on one design for a bronze sculpture, with the artist to be paid a large fee—perhaps $25,000—for the design from a common fund. Then casts of this same design could be furnished at cost to each state for erection on state capitol grounds.[11]

Walker's solution became the accepted one, but finding a design that all the state delegations would accept ultimately proved impossible. In 1909 the regional monument committee finally endorsed a design by the Italian-born sculptor Louis Amateis after years of fund-raising and an unsuccessful 1907 competition in which all seventy-five suggestions were rejected. Amateis's plaster model (fig. 11.2) showed a woman in classicizing dress standing assertively with arms aloft—one hand gripping a sword by its blade and the other holding a loosely furled Confederate flag. The base below her feet is inscribed: "Uphold Our State Rights." Two bas-reliefs on the pedestal depict the Confederate woman at home and as a nurse on the battlefield.[12]

Critics promptly insisted that this design completely missed the point. H. M. Hamill of Nashville, Tennessee, for example, took umbrage at the "defiant pose" of the nine-foot-tall "brawny Southern amazon," with "not a line of womanly grace or modesty or tenderness, not a hint of the dear home keeper . . . of the Southland, not a reminder of the . . . patient, self-sacrificing, unwearied helper and comforter of the boys in gray." The *Confederate Veteran* editorialized that the model was "most objectionable," despite General Walker's proposal that the sword could be placed in its scabbard "to prevent its cutting the woman's hand." At the annual reunion of Confederate veterans

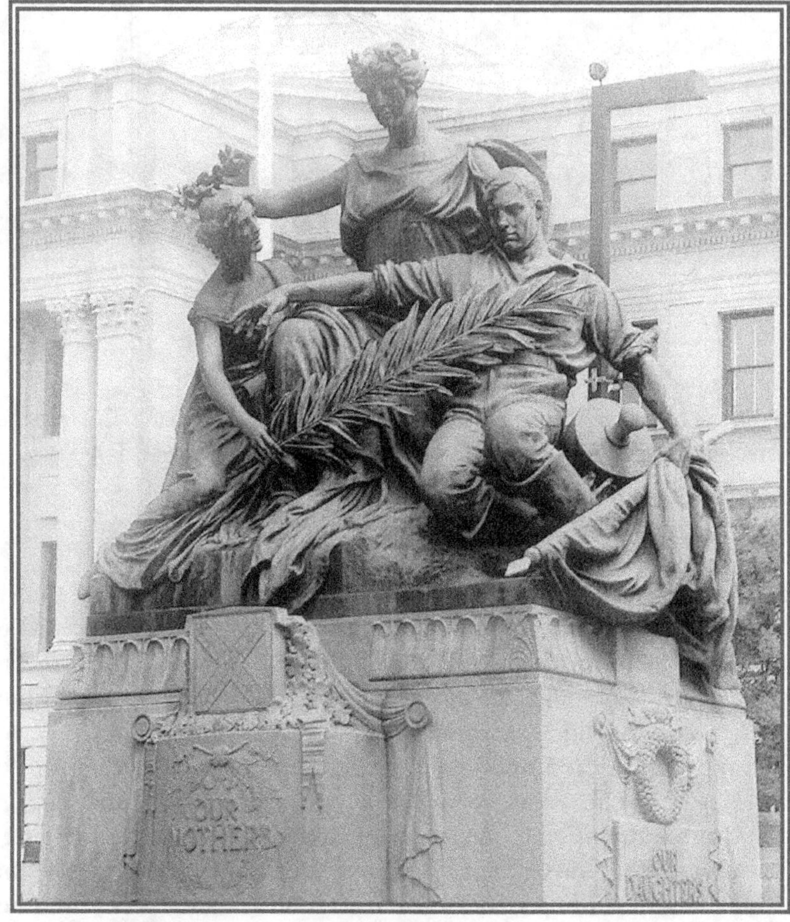


Fig. 11.3. Mississippi monument to Confederate women, Jackson, sculpted by Belle Kinney and cast in 1917. A monument of the same design also was dedicated in Nashville, Tennessee, October 10, 1926. Photograph by Chris Todd.

in Memphis in June 1909, Walker showed lantern slides of the model. But speaker after speaker rose to complain that this militant allegorical figure—armed and holding a flag—did not reflect the qualities of sentiment, grace, and self-abnegation in the women that they wished to honor. An enlarged monument committee was formed to search for a less assertive design.[13]

The panel met in December and, despite a schism with delegates from the Sons of Confederate Veterans, chose another allegorical design, this time not by a foreign-born sculptor but by a home-grown Tennessean, twenty-three-year-old Belle Kinney, a veteran's daughter who grew up in Nashville. A serene figure of Fame supports a dying Confederate soldier with her left arm while placing a wreath on the head of a southern woman with her right hand. The kneeling woman, seemingly unaware that she is being honored, is about to place a palm of glory on the recumbent soldier, an emblem of her belief that he is triumphant even in death. General Walker said Kinney's creation of this circle of honor embodied "the idea of woman's loyalty to the Confederacy and how unconsciously she is being rewarded for what she did." The suggestion was that this paralleled the modesty of women who were resisting the monument campaign.[14]

The commission was labeled in the press "the largest contract for sculpture ever awarded to a woman." Kinney, who had trained and taught at the Art Institute of Chicago with the encouragement of noted midwestern sculptor Lorado Taft, later moved her studio to New York, where she prepared the full-scale, nine-foot plaster model from which the casts were to be made by Tiffany Studios.[15] But as state veterans groups and legislative committees, which each raised their own funds, met later to consider the issue, any consensus for Kinney's design dissolved. Only Mississippi (fig. 11.3) and Kinney's home state of Tennessee would erect slightly modified casts of her monument. The other states that completed women's monuments, acting perhaps out of local pride, each went their own way—choosing designs by male sculptors.

## *State Dedications*

South Carolina, the state where the Civil War began, actually was the first to erect a monument to Confederate women (fig. 11.4). Frustrated by the failure of organized veterans to settle on a regional design, backers pushed a $7,500 appropriation for a monument through the state legislature by February 1909. The money was to be matched with contributions from "male inhabitants" of the state through an extensive newspaper fund-raising campaign.[16] In May, the state commissioned academic sculptor F. Wellington Ruckstuhl to make its monument, acting before the regionwide veterans committee had even chosen Kinney's design. Ruckstuhl, who was born in Alsace, raised in St. Louis, trained in Paris, and worked in New York, had created Baltimore's *Spirit of the Confederacy* monument in 1903 and would take on many other southern commissions. His ideas were idealizing and often grandiose.[17]

Ruckstuhl wrote that he had developed an elaborate conception for a southern women's monument some years earlier, when it seemed one large, much more expensive regional memorial might be commissioned at Richmond: "I imagined a Greek, semi-circled marble colonnade, between the columns of which there should be a dozen portrait busts of famous women of the Confederacy, while, on the face of the colonnade were to be about a score of small bronze bas-reliefs to illustrate the various characteristic activities of the war-women—from inspiring a whole people to fight for their homes, to burying their dead. . . . In the center of this decorative semi-circle was to be a large group—symbolizing the South and her children glorifying the women."[18]

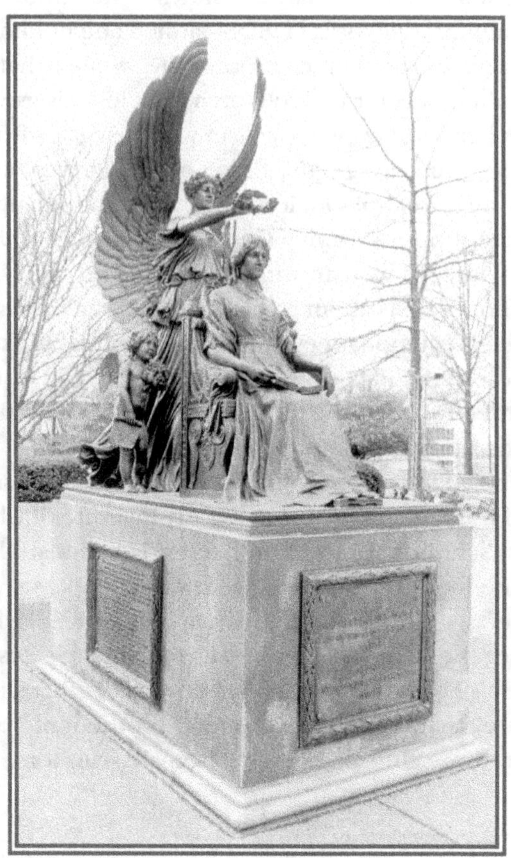

Fig. 11.4. South Carolina monument to Confederate women, Columbia, sculpted by
F. Wellington Ruckstuhl and unveiled April 11, 1912. Photograph by Mark Taylor.

Since South Carolina hoped to erect a monument for just $15,000 on the south plaza of the
statehouse (in the end $21,000 was raised), Ruckstuhl only completed the central group he had
envisioned: A dignified woman who the sculptor described as "40 years of age but still handsome,"
holds a Bible in her lap to denote her faith and a "Louis XIV fan" to denote the elegant plantation
culture in which she had lived. She looks outward over history "in lofty contemplation of her war-
work" and of her region's past and future. She is dressed in the simple gown that Ruckstuhl said
"was generally worn at the end of the war" and a chiffon scarf, but she sits in a thronelike chair of
state. A winged Genius of State stands behind, about to crown her. At the woman's left is a winged
boy, who rushes forward to place an armful of flowers on her lap. At her right a winged girl advances
more timidly, holding in one hand a bouquet and in the other a scroll bearing the words "Enacted
by the General Assembly of South Carolina" and the state seal.[19]

Ruckstuhl, a frequent traveler to France, cited the 1883 Monument to the Republic in Paris by
Charles and Leopold Morice in discussing his original conception for a grand regional monument.
But he appears to have been more influenced in the final result by Jules Dalou's competing
*Triumph of the Republic,* unveiled in 1899 in Paris. Dalou's monument revived the idea of the

triumphal procession, with realistic figures that stand for the People, the Republic, Labor, and Prosperity joining in an energetic forward movement. In Ruckstuhl's South Carolina adaptation, the southern woman becomes the main figure. The Columbia sculpture lacks the unity and power, however, of either French model. The winged genius and children stride forward in a joyful harmony of movement, but the enthroned woman is static and hermetic. She is an allegory from another, seemingly more lifeless realm—a figure from the past that is not, like Dalou's vibrant Republic, heading into the future.

Ruckstuhl said he made a "composite" head for the southern woman, who he described as thinking of things beyond the material world. The southern woman is being honored for virtues not ordinarily placed on public display—modesty, her thoughts for others over herself, her stoicism, control, and passivity. Here "woman" is carrier of family faith and values, staying inside a prescribed sphere of gender activities. Her traits are opposites of the aggressive, "spiteful" women critiqued in northern assaults.[20]

The unveiling ceremony at noon on April 11, 1912, drew a crowd estimated at nearly ten thousand to the south plaza of the South Carolina statehouse, where the monument was undraped after a series of speeches and a twenty-one-gun salute. General Walker spoke first, urging the younger generation in the assemblage to let "all the false teachings, the perverted histories you have had to study from, fall upon barren ground in your minds" and to remember their parents' sacrifices and achievements when others tried to impugn their southern heritage.[21] Protestations that the war was fought for family and home would be repeated at dedications of all the sculptures to women.

In the keynote address, Joseph W. Barnwell of Charleston delivered an appeal to the current generation of women to know their place in southern gender relations: "Women of Carolina! Among the vast changes of the last 60 years none has been greater than in the position of your sex. . . . but do not forget that in competing with men you must not surrender the influence of your sex. Shall sentiment depart? Shall grace be banished and beauty be neglected or despised? So did not think the women of the war. . . . Do not forget that after all you are not, and cannot be, men, and that love and admiration are as well worth winning as an acknowledgment of superiority or cold respect."[22]

Despite South Carolina's success in erecting a monument to the state's Confederate women, the *Confederate Veteran* "deeply regretted" that the state had not used Kinney's design. "It was planned that while each state should erect its own monument, yet by the similarity of the bronze group that all the women of the South would be honored as well as those of each state," the magazine complained. It suggested, in vain, that South Carolina build a second monument, this time of the Kinney design, "to be in line with the other Southern states."[23] This did not happen, however, and more disappointments were in store for those seeking regionwide unity.

Gen. Charles Coffin of Barnesville, Arkansas, who was a persistent advocate for Kinney's design, said problems arose soon after the United Confederate Veterans committee entered into a contract with Kinney in 1910 to make multiple reproductions of her design. "Men who could not design a plow stock suddenly became 'art critics' and began to decry the Kinney design," he observed. Women also were among the leading critics. Margaret Drane Tichenor, a UDC activist in New Orleans, waged a vigorous letter-writing campaign mobilizing opinion across the South against the McKinney design on grounds that it would "stamp a false conception of our Mothers on the youth of the South" by overemphasizing themes of defeat and loss. "It was a period that called for immediate action, not for timid shrinking and fearfulness of spirit," she wrote. "Our mothers met the call of the hour courageously, undauntedly, and when Appomattox came, faced defeat as proudly as once they exulted in success . . . but the design has singled out one feature, Appomattox alone." Tichenor said she had little feeling for "the willowy, sentimental, frivolous girl with a palm branch in hand" depicted by Kinney. The UDC refrained from endorsing the design, and these arguments may have helped to persuade other groups to withdraw their support.[24]

The Arkansas veterans committee, for example, aided by a $10,000 appropriation from the state legislature, initially considered purchasing a cast from Kinney. But the state committee, first formed in 1906 to cooperate with the regionwide Confederate committee, divided three to three on approving her design once the funds had been raised. A seventh member, added to break the tie, voted down Kinney's model. The panel eventually selected a very different design by Swiss-born artist J. Otto Schweizer from twenty-eight entries in a competition. Schweizer worked in Philadelphia, where he made historical monuments of all types, mostly in the North.[25]

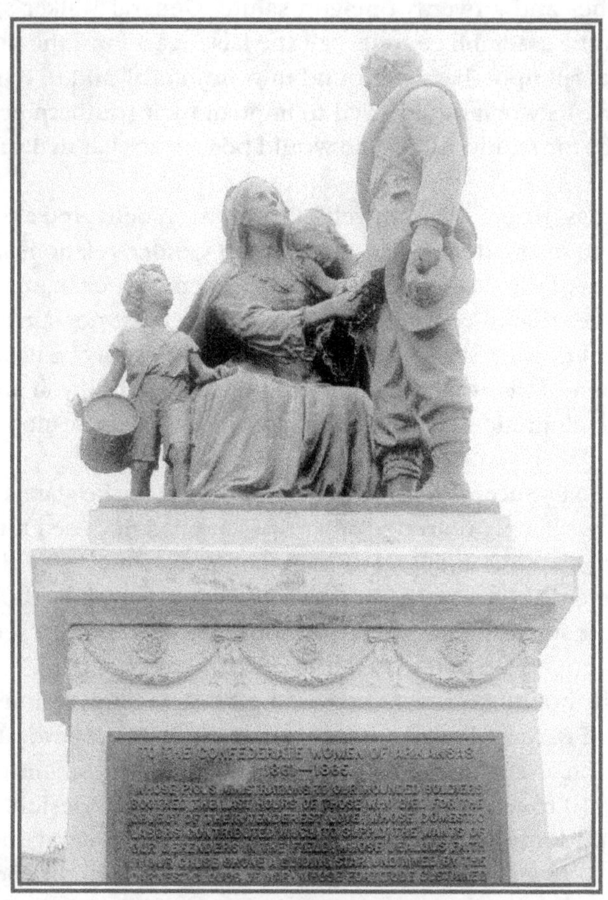

Fig. 11.5. Monument to the Confederate Women of Arkansas, Little Rock, sculpted by
J. Otto Schweizer and unveiled May 1, 1913. Photograph by Karen Segrave.

Thousands attended the unveiling May 1, 1913, at the new capitol grounds of his Monument to the Confederate Women of Arkansas (fig. 11.5), which consists of four life-size figures on a fifteen-foot granite base that quotes Jefferson Davis's tribute. In a realistic narrative style, it represents a seated woman bidding farewell to her young son who is heading off to war. A younger daughter rests her head on her mother's shoulder, while a boy—perhaps four or five years old—beats a toy drum at her side, too young to realize anything but the glamour of war. Contemporary descriptions presume that the mother already has sacrificed her husband to the conflict.

The Arkansas monument, lacking the allegorical elements of Kinney's design or the South Carolina monument, may have been seen by the veterans as having a truer regional flavor, portraying the southern woman as a unique resource that helped define a superior culture. It shows her as mother and wife, bearing up with dignity as her children enact their gender roles. The little girl has no function in war but to wait at home and grieve. The small boy is more active, preparing to become the new patriarch. The woman suffers in silence as she sends her older son off to possible death. The family is tightly clustered in the absence of the father, its status-giver and protector. Home is the woman's realm, damaged though it may be by war.

The double-edged theme of the glory and tragedy of war, with woman surviving to provide the cultural memory for both, is repeated in the next state memorial to be dedicated—in Raleigh. This monument to southern women was built with a $10,000 contribution from one old veteran, Col. Ashley Horne. Horne had volunteered for the war at age twenty and served most of his time under General Lee in the Army of Northern Virginia around Richmond. He was one of a small unit assigned to deliver the news of Lee's surrender at Appomattox to Sherman's army at Durham and Johnston's at Greensboro. He returned home to laboriously rebuild his family's plantation, eventually becoming one of the state's most prominent businessmen. After the war, he lived with his mother, who had lost three of her six sons in the conflict. He married twice and had one daughter.[26] At age seventy, Horne wrote Secretary of State J. Bryan Grimes: "I have been thinking for a long time that the State would never build a Woman's Confederate Monument, and I, being a soldier of Lee's Army for four years and seeing the work that the women of my State did in carrying food and clothing . . . I have decided to build this monument myself."[27]

The state accepted the offer and dedicated a site in the capitol square. It was initially speculated that Horne might erect a cast of Kinney's design. But a committee of four prominent North Carolina men and one woman, which he appointed, chose instead a conception by Richmond-born sculptor Augustus Lukeman. Lukeman, who was Paris-trained and had his studio in New York, created soldiers' memorials for both North and South. He also was commissioned to complete the Stone Mountain Confederate Memorial in Georgia, begun by Gutzon Borglum. His women's monument (fig. 11.6) was unveiled by Horne's grandson on June 10, 1914, six months after the old soldier's death.[28]

Its central figure is a Confederate woman, touched by grief and age, who holds a large book in her lap. According to one contemporary account, she "has been reading to her grandson the heroic story of that tragic four years" of war. The young boy, holding his dead father's sword, half leans against the knees of the seated woman. The eyes of both are fixed with distant gazes—the boy perhaps thinking of the glory of war and the woman of the losses.

The monument is full of ambiguities and conflicts. Is the boy about to take the sword from its scabbard, or has he just placed it there after testing its blade? While the boy is dressed in postwar city clothing—double-breasted jacket, tie, knee-length pants, and leather shoes—the grandmother

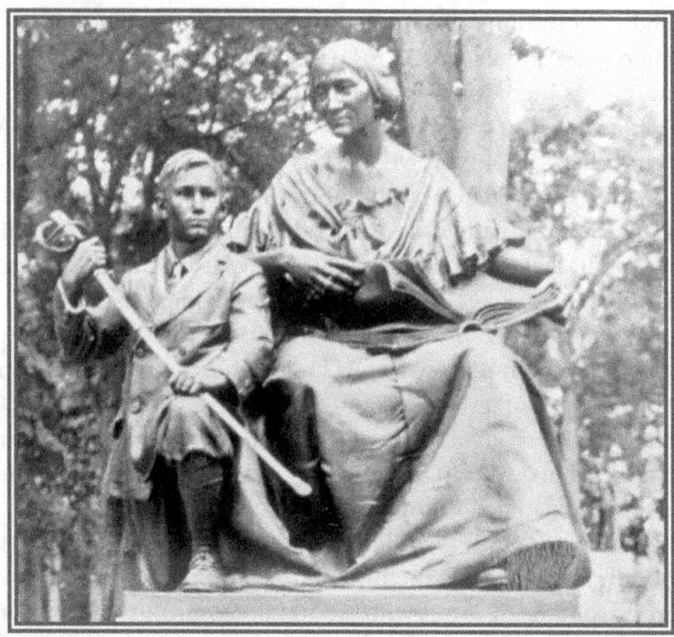

Fig. 11.6. North Carolina monument to Confederate women, Raleigh, sculpted by Augustus Lukeman and dedicated June 10, 1914. Photograph by Keith Sinzinger.

wears an older-style dress and shawl. The woman again appears to be from a past time. At the dedication ceremony, spectators commented on the plainness of her aging face and the jarringly low cut of her dress, perhaps more appropriate for the younger woman she once was.[29] The two ages of woman—prewar and postwar—seem to be contained in one figure. The pages of the book the woman holds are blank.

The disjunctions continue on two bas-reliefs on the monument's base. One of the bronze reliefs shows a southern woman in allegorical dress who raises one arm, sending soldiers on foot and horseback off to war. It is the only hint of Amateis's original, more militant design to appear on any monument. A second relief shows one southern woman tenderly kissing a survivor who returns from war and another receiving the corpse of a casualty. Architect Henry Bacon placed benches on either side of Horne's monument to the Women of the Confederacy so that pedestrians could pause and ponder its significance. The monument still stands at its original location, near the intersection of Morgan and Salisbury Streets, with the state capitol behind it.

The theme of the mother instructing her children in the "true history" of the South was carried on in Florida's choice of a costlier, more elaborate monument (fig. 11.7), which was dedicated October 26, 1915, in the Confederate Park in Jacksonville. The bronze central group, modeled by sculptor Allen George Newman of New York, features a seated woman "in the costume of the '60s" holding an open book on her lap. She is teaching the facts of war to a small boy on her right and a girl on her left. The figures, five feet seven inches high, were placed on a pedestal inside an open granite-columned structure. A thirteen-foot allegorical woman stands atop the stone structure, wearing classicizing drapery and holding the fallen banner of the Confederacy.[30]

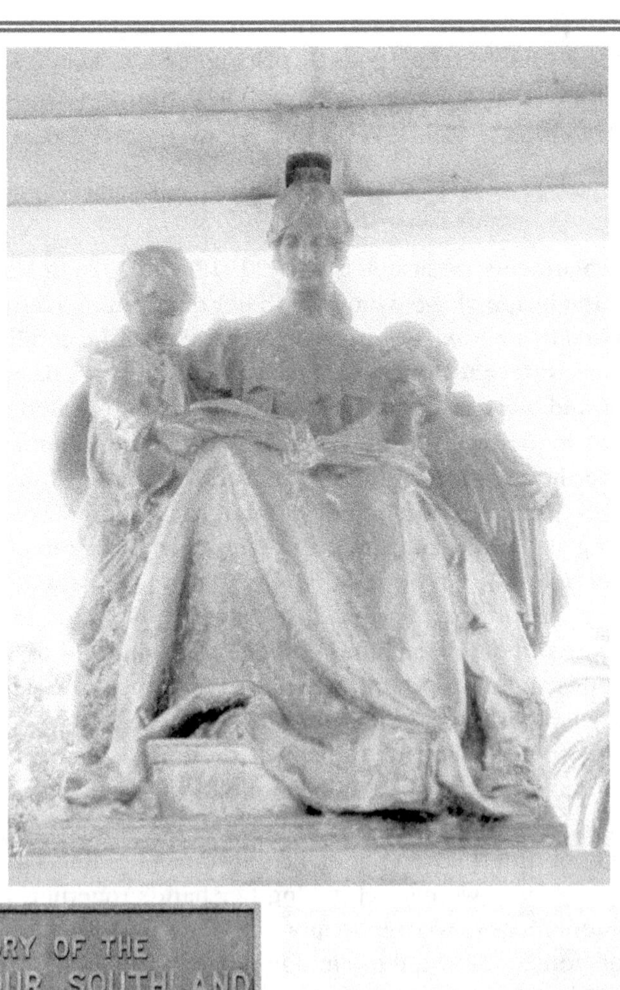

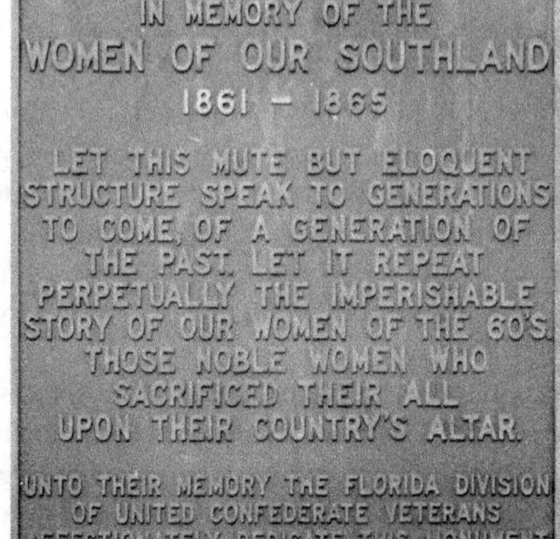


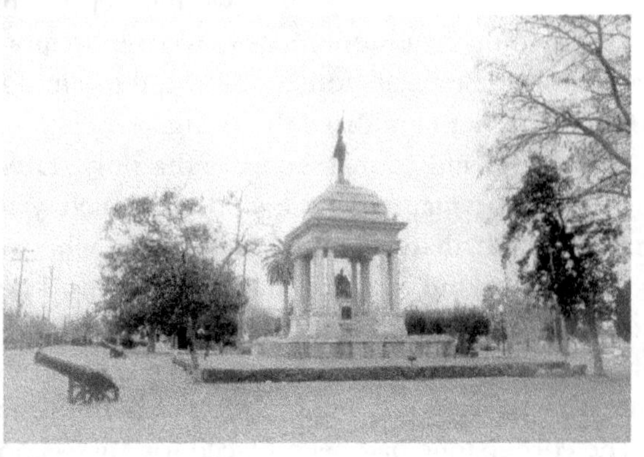

Fig. 11.7. Florida monument to Confederate women, Jacksonville, sculpted by Allen G. Newman and dedicated October 26, 1915. Photographs by Oscar Sosa.

Newman wrote that placing the central group in this architectural setting was meant to enshrine it, as the Greeks honored their gods by placing them in temples. "The group represents the woman of the South instructing future generations as well as showing her as the most privileged guardian of the home ties," he said.[31]

## Universal Themes

The final three state monuments, dedicated in 1917, 1918, and 1926 in Mississippi, Maryland, and Tennessee, cast aside the image of the woman with her children in a fatherless household. With Western Europe engulfed in a new war even more horrible than the conflict in the United States a half century earlier, Mississippi and Tennessee held to Belle Kinney's design of a woman reaching out to a dying soldier, and Maryland, a border state with strong Confederate sympathies during the Civil War, adopted a modernized version of that theme. The monuments seem less regionally distinctive and time specific and more attuned to universal themes of suffering and reconciliation.

Maryland supporters commissioned Baltimore sculptor Joseph Maxwell Miller to make their state's bronze group (fig. 0.4), unveiled Nov. 2, 1918, at the intersection of Charles Street and University Parkway. The *Baltimore Sun* reported on page 10 that there was little interest in the monument unveiling in comparison with earlier Lost Cause dedications in the South, which had attracted thousands. "A crowd of several hundred persons, composed of former supporters of the Confederacy, their friends and descendants, assembled to witness the unveiling," it said, and the Daughters of the Confederacy sent "a large delegation."[32]

Judge James Trippe of the Appeal Tax Court was the principal speaker, and he brought the monument movement into modern times, hailing not only the women of the Lost Cause fifty years earlier but also those helping in the new war in Europe. The monument no longer seeks to set history straight with a book and children but depicts a woman holding a dying soldier in her arms. Behind them stands a younger woman, clutching her hands together, perhaps looking to the future. It could be a monument to women in any war. The inscription, on a red granite pedestal, reads "To the Brave at Home. / They fed the hungry, / They clothed the needy, / They nursed the wounded, / They comforted the dying."

Mississippi and Tennessee were the only states to erect Belle Kinney's design as a memorial. The casts were made at Tiffany Studios in New York in 1917. The story was told, apparently by Kinney herself, that five of the young men who worked on the casting were World War I draftees or volunteers, and some of them had received permission to delay their departure to finish the project. All five "put on their hats the moment the bronze was finished and started for the training camps."[33] Kinney also told an interviewer that one of the plaster models for the monument was lent to a New York recruiting station to help inspire volunteers.

The cornerstone had been placed for Mississippi's monument on June 3, 1912, the anniversary of Jefferson Davis's birthday. Davis's words honoring southern women are carved on the front of the elaborate pedestal, but for a variety of reasons Mississippians had to wait another five years before the bronze sculptural group was finally in its place on top.[34] Tennessee's monument took even longer to erect. The Tennessee legislature had by 1911 approved $6,000 for a memorial on the Capitol grounds in Nashville, and veterans began a drive to raise $8,500 more. A state monument committee chose Kinney's design in 1916 after a competition in which nineteen other sculptors took part. The monument, placed in the sunken garden of the Tennessee War Memorial, was not dedicated until October 10, 1926, in a world far removed from the heat of the conflict that sparked the campaign to build the monuments. World War I veterans who were descendants of Confederate soldiers served as ushers.[35] J. I. Highsaw of Memphis, commander of the state Sons of Confederate Veterans, told the audience of the passing generation's long memory, "The news of the dedication of this monument to the women of the Confederacy will bring joy and pleasure to every living veteran in that thin line of gray. It was their fondest hope and dream."[36]

Historian Neil Harris has noted that a monument commemorates both the subject that it honors and the generation that remembered it in sculpture. The choice of form and style, the size and durability of material, all reflect the taste, recollections, and judgment of those who commissioned the monument. In the end, "a beautifully circular" gesture remains, he said.[37] This circle can be a closed one when a monument's message does not ring true to future generations and is remote from their aspirations. The monuments to the Women of the Confederacy take on new interest to us, however, when we view them as pieces in a complex discourse about nineteenth- and early-twentieth-century gender relations and the veterans' yearnings for "better times" of the past.

The southern lady of these monuments is a well-to-do white woman who is the self-denying queen of a harmonious domestic realm, an asexual saint who upholds high moral standards, the "nurturing professor" of the next generation, and a loyal and submissive wife who does not wish to step outside her allotted sphere. In his keynote speech at the dedication of the Raleigh monument, Daniel Harvey Hill spelled out these virtues that veterans believed they were enshrining, declaring, "The woman of the Confederacy was a womanly woman. She craved no queenhood except the sovereignty of her own home. She desired no subjects save those of her own household. . . . Accustomed to manage large households of children and of slaves, she early acquired dignity, earnestness, and the self-control which enables its possessor to control others. She never thought of doubting that her sphere of action was the home, and she centered her efforts on making that home a place of refinement and comfort."[38]

But the monuments' message hailing the "old" ways was at cross-purposes with younger women's vision of their role in society and older women's recollections of antebellum life and the harsh realities of the war. For instance, the monuments make no reference to the slaves who supported the southern plantation economy and who worked closely with the veterans' wives and mothers; they also ignore women from other classes and many of the ugly truths of war. Recent scholarship has exposed a vast gap between the truth of antebellum life and the monuments' nostalgic iconography of family harmony and loss.

These peculiar sculptural groups, promoted as men's expression of gratitude to the women of the South, instead were carriers of another agenda. By appropriating the image of the patrician Confederate white woman, the veterans sought to validate their own definitions of masculinity and family relations, which had been maligned in the North-South war and were withering in the postwar world. In the end, the monuments were tributes to a lost past that could no longer be a model for southern women—or southern men.

## Notes

This essay is reprinted in slightly abridged form from the *Southeastern College Art Conference Review* 13, no. 3 (1998): 229–40. My thanks to Josephine Withers and Pamela Simpson for their assistance during its evolution.

1. Probably the first recorded public call for a monument to Women of the Confederacy was made in 1866 by veteran E. P. Morrisett at a camp meeting in Montgomery, Alabama. He proposed a "lofty Corinthian monument whose . . . graceful shaft shall . . . commemorate in our native language the names and glorious

deeds of the women of our own dear Southern land." "Monument to the Women of the Confederacy," *Confederate Veteran* 11, no. 10 (Sept. 1903): 415. A number of local monuments were built, with some of the earliest examples in Fort Mill, South Carolina, in 1895; Rome, Georgia, 1910; and Macon, Georgia, 1911. *Confederate Veteran* (1893–1932), the official organ of the United Confederate Veterans, will be cited hereafter as *CV.*

2. Nina Silber, "Intemperate Men, Spiteful Women and Jefferson Davis," *American Quarterly* 41, no. 4 (Dec. 1989): 614–15, 622–23. Also see Drew Gilpin Faust, *Mothers of Invention* (Chapel Hill: Univ. of North Carolina Press, 1996), 207–12.

3. For satirical images of a feminized Davis, see "The Belle of Richmond," chap. 8 in *The Confederate Image: Prints of the Lost Cause,* ed. Mark E. Neely, Harold Holzer, and Gabor S. Boritt (Chapel Hill: Univ. of North Carolina Press, 1987), 79–96.

4. Jefferson Davis, *The Rise and Fall of the Confederate Government,* vol. 1 (New York, 1881), frontispiece.

5. In 1905, for instance, "The general association of the U.C.V.s, in convention assembled in Nashville, Tennessee, confessed their failure to raise funds for the building of a monument to the memory of the 'Women of the Confederacy.' . . . It is not indifference to the cause, but lack of information as to where and what to build. . . . The fact that 'the women don't want it' is still another reason why the monument is not built." From "Southern Women Deserve a Monument," *CV* 13, no. 4 (Apr. 1905): 18.

6. "Such a monument [the industrial college] would be the noblest memorial they [veterans groups] could erect," Gielow wrote. "If they desired, there could be a lofty dome crowned with a figure of a Southern woman, with a tablet dedicating it to the Women of the Confederacy." Martha S. Gielow, "Woman's Monument—Plan Suggested," *CV* 14, no. 4 (Apr. 1906): 159. Sada Foute Richmond, "The Southern Mothers' Scholarship," *CV* 15, no. 8 (Aug. 1907): 351.

7. "Tennessee Gives to Woman's Monument," *CV* 17, no. 8 (Aug. 1909): 391. "Scholarships or Monuments," *CV* 23, no. 3 (1915): 131.

8. "Confederation News," *CV* 13, no. 11 (Nov. 1905): 493.

9. Bridges Smith, "Woman's Monument Movement in Macon," *CV* 13, no. 6 (June 1905): 272.

10. There is now a growing body of published work on the status of southern women in the postwar period. A pioneering work was Anne Scott Firor's *The Southern Lady* (Chicago: Univ. of Chicago Press, 1970), followed by, among others, George C. Rable, *Civil Wars: Women and the Crisis of Southern Nationalism* (Chicago: Univ. of Chicago Press, 1989); Faust, *Mothers of Invention;* and Edward D. C. Campbell Jr. and Kym S. Rice, *A Woman's War* (Richmond: Museum of the Confederacy, 1996). See also Nina Silber, *The Romance of Reunion* (Chapel Hill: Univ. of North Carolina Press, 1993) and Anastatia Sims, *The Power of Femininity in the New South* (Columbia: Univ. of South Carolina Press, 1997).

11. Under this plan, each state could determine the size and design of its pedestal, or even the size of the bronze cast. "Confederation News," *CV* 13, no. 11 (Nov. 1905): 493.

12. Amateis (1855–1913) came to the United States in 1884 from his native Turin and settled in the Washington, D.C., area, where a number of his sculptural works remain. His son, Edmond, also was a sculptor. See Glenn B. Optiz, ed., *Dictionary of American Sculptors* (Poughkeepsie, N.Y.: Apollo, 1984), 9, and James M. Goode, *The Outdoor Sculpture of Washington* (Washington D.C.: Smithsonian Institution Press, 1974), 349, 510–11, and 544 in hardcover appendix.

13. H. M. Hamill, "Confederate Woman's Monument," *CV* 17, no. 4 (Apr. 1909): 150. For another view, see Wallace Streater, "Favors Design for Woman's Monument," *CV* 17, no. 6 (June 1909): 285. For accounts of the 1909 meeting at which the Amateis design was rejected, see coverage in the *Atlanta Journal,* June 9, 1909;

"Monument Design Is Disapproved," *Memphis Commercial Appeal,* June 9, 1909; and "Not a Woman Militant," *New York Times,* June 10, 1909.

14. "Concerning Southern Woman's Monument," *CV* 17, no. 8 (Aug. 1909): 371.

15. For information on Kinney (1890–1959) and the monument commission, see "Miss Belle Kinney Designs Confederate Women Memorial," *Atlanta Journal,* Dec. 30, 1909; "A Monument to the Confederacy," *Harper's Weekly,* Mar. 12, 1910; "Memorial to Women of Confederacy; Unique Design by Southern Sculptor," *Brooklyn Daily Eagle,* July 31, 1910, Sunday section; "Belle Kinney" entry, *Who's Who in Tennessee,* 1911; "Women Sculptors Nobly Upholding the Art in America," *New York Sun,* Oct. 28, 1917, Sunday section; "Belle Kinney, Sculptor, Dies," *New York Times,* Aug. 28, 1959; and Elise L. Smith, "Belle Kinney and the Confederate Women's Monument," *Southern Quarterly* 32, no. 4 (summer 1994): 7–31.

16. The exclusively male nature of the project was reinforced by the public call for proposed inscriptions for the monument, which stated, "The men are requested to send in their suggestions, as modesty would prevent women doing full justice to the subject." "Inscriptions for Woman's Monument," *CV* 17, no. 10 (Oct. 1909): 514.

17. For background on Ruckstuhl (who later Americanized the spelling of his name), see Cynthia Mills, "Frederic Wellington Ruckstull: In Defense of the Ideal" (master's thesis, Univ. of Maryland, 1988) and "Autobiographical Notice," in F. Wellington Ruckstull, *Great Works of Art and What Makes Them Great* (New York: G. P. Putnam's Sons, 1925), 517–42.

18. F. Wellington Ruckstuhl, "Sculptor Interprets the Memorial," *Columbia State,* Apr. 12, 1912, special memorial section.

19. Ibid.

20. There had been earlier suggestions about creating a monument design of a woman with a Bible. J. Dupree of Ivanhoe, Texas, had suggested in 1909, for example, that the Women's Memorial Committee commission "a plain picture of a Christian Southern woman with Bible in hand and her eyes lifted toward heaven." He thought the women's monument should take a cue from a widely distributed print, *The Burial of Latane,* after the 1864 painting by William D. Washington depicting women, with the aid of slaves, acting as ministers during the war. "Southern Woman's Monument," *CV* 17, no. 7 (July 1909): 362. For *The Burial of Latane* prints, see Neely, *The Confederate Image,* ix–xiv.

21. For accounts of the dedication, see "First State Memorial to Southern Women," *Monumental News* 24, no. 5 (May 1912): 388, and extensive coverage in the *Columbia State,* Apr. 12, 1912.

22. "Addresses at Monument Unveiling Yesterday," *Columbia State,* Apr. 12, 1912.

23. "Uniformity of Design Desirable," *CV* 20, no. 1 (Jan. 1912): 3.

24. "Monument to Women of Arkansas," *CV* 21, no. 6 (June 1913): 285. A 1910–11 scrapbook kept by Margaret Drane Tichenor and now held by the Museum of the Confederacy, Richmond, contains hundreds of letters to and from UDC/UCV groups and leaders mobilizing opinion against the Kinney design. Tichenor quotations here are from Elise Smith, "Belle Kinney and the Confederate Women's Monuments," 19, and Foster, *Ghosts of the Confederacy,* 177–78.

25. For information on the commission and dedication of the monument, see "Arkansas Monument to Confederate Women," *CV* 20, no. 8 (Aug. 1912): 367; "Monument to the Women of Arkansas," *CV* 21, no. 6 (June 1913): 285; and "Handsome Tribute to Wartime Women," *Little Rock Arkansas Democrat,* May 2, 1913. Also see Arkansas Historic Preservation Program, "Something So Dim It Must Be Holy!: Civil War Commemorative Sculpture in Arkansas, 1886–1934," a filing with the National Register of Historic Places, 1996.

26. For biographies of Horne (1841–1913), see "Horne, Ashley," *National Cyclopaedia of American Biography,* 15:62; "Col. Ashley Horne True Son of State," *Carolina and the Southern Cross* 2, no. 3 (June 1914): 1–3; *Raleigh News and Observer,* June 11, 1914; and "North Carolina Woman's Monument: Letter from Hon. Ashley Horne," *CV* 20, no. 9 (Sept. 1912): 412.

27. R. D. W. Connor, *Addresses at the Unveiling of the Memorial to the North Carolina Woman of the Confederacy* (Raleigh, 1914), 5–6.

28. "Monument to North Carolina Women," *CV* 22, no. 8 (Aug. 1914): 340. "Augustus Lukeman," Opitz, *Dictionary of American Sculpture;* New York Public Library artist's file on Lukeman.

29. *Raleigh News and Observer,* June 11, 1914.

30. "The Woman's Monument in Florida," *CV* 23, no. 4 (Apr. 1915): 1. "Monument to the Women of the Confederacy Now Ready to Be Unveiled in Confederate Park," *Jacksonville Florida Times-Union,* Apr. 2, 1915. The Florida monument was funded by a $12,000 appropriation made by the state legislature in 1913 and at least $10,000 more from a private subscription drive begun in 1910, most of that coming from Confederate veteran camps.

31. *CV* 23, no. 4 (Apr. 1915): 1.

32. In this case, the Daughters of the Confederacy helped lobby for funds. In 1914, the Maryland legislature appropriated $12,000 for the monument. A private subscription drive supplemented that money. "Proposed Monuments," *Granite Marble and Bronze* 24, no. 3 (Mar. 1914): 54. "Monument Unveiled," *Baltimore Sun,* Nov. 3, 1918.

33. "Women Sculptors Nobly Upholding the Art in America," *New York Sun,* Oct. 28, 1917, Sunday section.

34. "Woman's Monument at Jackson, Miss.," *CV* 24, no. 7 (July 1912): 324–26.

35. J. Hickman, "Women of the South to Be Honored," *CV* 19, no. 4 (Apr. 1911): 160. "Monument for Confederate Women," *Granite, Marble and Bronze* 26, no. 5 (May 1916): 44.

36. "Monument Is Unveiled," *Nashville Banner,* Oct. 11, 1926. The sunken garden in which the Tennessee women's monument once sat has since been converted into the Tennessee Vietnam Veterans Plaza. Kinney's sculptural group now overlooks the tribute to a later war. See Suzanne Woolley Smith, "The Tennessee Monument to the Confederacy," *Border States: Journal of the Kentucky-Tennessee American Studies Association* 11 (1997).

37. Neil Harris, *The Artist in American Society* (New York: Simon and Schuster, 1970), 197.

38. *Raleigh News and Observer,* June 11, 1914.

# Part IV

## Changing Times, Reshaping History

# 12

# Commemorating the Color Line

The National Mammy Monument Controversy of the 1920s

*Micki McElya*

IN FEBRUARY 1923 Neval H. Thomas, a board member of the National Association for the Advancement of Colored People (NAACP), sent an open letter to the U.S. Senate, the United Daughters of the Confederacy, and two mainstream newspapers, the *New York World* and the *Washington Evening Star*. In this letter, which was reprinted in a number of black newspapers, Thomas decried a bill before the Senate to allot land in the nation's capital for a monument to the "faithful colored mammies of the South." Urging the senators to deny the land grant, he argued, "Democracy is the monument that the noble 'black mammy' wants erected to her, and not this marble shaft which can only be a symbol of servitude to teach white and black alike that the menial callings are the Negro's place in the scheme of things."[1]

Thomas's letter and other early challenges to the UDC's proposal failed initially, as the Senate on February 28, 1923, approved Bill S4119 to grant the southern women a place in Washington, D.C., for their memorial. But a flood of protests followed, and the bill never reached the floor of the House of Representatives for a vote. While struggles continue to this day to realize the democracy Thomas sought, the national mammy monument drive came to its end in 1924 when it was left to languish in a House committee.

This brief episode in the history of the production of public memory has much to tell us about the formation of racial identities and categories, efforts to expand the parameters of American citizenship, and southern regionalism in the early twentieth century—the "scheme of things" in Thomas's words. From the Daughters who conceived of the monument to the various African American organizations and journalists who opposed it, those enmeshed in the controversy used the image of the mammy to articulate contrasting visions of what this scheme of things ought to be and where they should fall within it. The complex debate that ensued may be best understood by first considering the motivations of the United Daughters of the Confederacy, whose members shared a particular vision of segregation and racial fantasy embodied in the figure of the mammy. Any analysis of the battle over the monument also must explore the Daughters' choice of a medium—public sculpture—to promote their views.

Confronted with growing black radicalism after World War I and the continuing exodus of African Americans from the South, the monument's supporters nationwide longed for a black mammy. They wanted to render in stone and bronze a permanent marker of appropriate, safe, and appealing blackness. Significantly, the figure they chose for veneration held particular gender, class, sexual, and regional connotations. In popular representation, the mammy had been the most loyal, because she was content with her servitude and sanctioned white supremacy. For monument advocates, she embodied the best potential for interracial relations. Their support of the campaign and its initial success did not just indicate whites' belief in their own racial superiority but also affirmed whites' wish for African Americans to believe in that superiority too. In their view, mammy did not just serve, but was happy to do so, and held genuine affection—even unconditional maternal love—for her white masters and charges.

The desire to fix for all time the contours of such a devoted servant suggests the fear of another kind of blackness—presumed to be unruly, dangerous, and destabilizing—that was visible in America in the postwar period. In his compelling study of race and monuments in the nineteenth century, art historian Kirk Savage describes twin catalysts of commemorative movements: the hope of molding a particular historical narrative into concrete form and the participants' wish to claim a broad consensus for their view. Noting that public sculpture drives have often been controversial, Savage argues, "to commemorate is to seek historical closure" and to secure the past "against the vicissitudes of the present."[2] Indeed, the United Daughters of the Confederacy and their supporters sought to locate black people and national race relations within a history of their own invention. Yet their monument drive was more than an attempt to herald a cause long lost and to portray slavery as a benign institution. The campaign reveals much more—the articulation of a new cause for an uncertain future.[3]

## Women's "Visible" Work

Founded in 1894, the United Daughters of the Confederacy initially acted as an umbrella organization for local Ladies' Memorial Associations and other Confederate women's groups. By the early 1900s, it was an exceedingly popular organization among white, bourgeois, and elite southern women. Its membership steadily increased in the early twentieth century, growing from about 17,000 members in 1900 to 68,000 by 1920.[4] White women established chapters throughout the South and in areas as far flung as New York City; Helena, Montana; and Paris, France.

While commemorative activities and public spectacles of mourning for the Confederate dead remained central to the UDC in the early twentieth century, the group pursued a broader social and political agenda than the earlier Ladies' Memorial Associations. Of primary importance was the "preservation" of a glorious memory of the Confederacy as well as women's roles as keepers and disseminators of this "truth." Rather than simply maintaining an extant collective understanding of the historical past, however, the Daughters worked persistently to reinvent the Old South and Confederate traditions. Like other turn-of-the-century women's groups, UDC members saw themselves as particularly suited to reform and patriotic education. To this end, they not only raised monuments and orchestrated Confederate Memorial Day events throughout the South but also campaigned to remove from southern schools certain textbooks deemed hostile to the Confederacy, founded and staffed memorial homes to care for aged Confederate men and women, organized a children's auxiliary called the Children of the Confederacy, and sponsored historical research.[5]

Public memorialization remained a crucial means for the dissemination of this history and Confederate pride. Writing of the UDC's extensive commemorative activities in an organizational history published in the early 1930s, Rassie Hoskins White asserted the special importance of public monuments in the group's social and political agenda. The Daughters devoted so much time, labor, and money to statues, White explained, because "they knew monuments would speak more quickly, impressively, and lastingly to the eye than the written or printed word—attract more attention." She wrote, "The [UDC] chapters, State Divisions, and the general organization have done remarkable work in other lines, unseen work, but it is this *visible* work—great monuments and memorials—that has brought the organization publicity and acclaim for these thirty-five years of work, for they have spoken and will speak to a world indifferent to that vast amount of work which is invisible."[6] While the monuments commemorated martial honor and a patriarchal system, she argued that they also denoted the power and prowess of the women whose fund-raising, political savvy, and time had enabled their existence. White's insistent emphasis on making "visible" the Daughters' "work" points to this contradiction in UDC members' struggles to define public authority for white women by celebrating Old South hierarchies.

In their articulations of Confederate pride, whether through monuments to fallen military heroes or "proper" history texts, the Daughters created southern identities based in shared assumptions about the qualities of the region, white supremacy, and elite privilege. Of the UDC's membership, historian Anastasia Sims has noted: "Their loyalty to white supremacy was implicit; they also sharply delineated class distinctions among whites. Eligibility was based on ancestry, on an applicant's ability to document a satisfactory answer to that quintessentially southern question, Who are your people?"[7] The UDC carefully policed the boundary of its membership by defining who could *not* be a part of its honorable South—African Americans and the poor of any race.

If African American contemporaries were excluded from the Daughters' circle of southern virtue in the twentieth century, their enslaved ancestors held a central place in the mythology upon which this "tradition" rested, embodied particularly in the figure of the "faithful slave." Histories and anecdotes written by UDC members abound with stories of slaves who resisted the opportunities for freedom during the Civil War to protect and serve white women and children on the home front or who risked their lives to serve their masters in battle. These romantic fictions were intended to demonstrate that an affection and mutual understanding stood at the heart of slavery. They masked the coercion and brutalities of forced labor.

Spearheaded by the Jefferson Davis Chapter No. 1650 of Washington, D.C., the 1922–23 mammy commemoration drive grew out of nearly twenty years of discussion within the UDC about erecting a monument to the "faithful slaves" of the South. This debate had intensified between 1904 and 1905 in a series of exchanges printed in the *Confederate Veteran,* the national magazine of various Confederate patriot groups including the United Confederate Veterans (UCV) and the Daughters. In September 1904, Mrs. G. Gilliland Aston of Asheville, North Carolina, publicly appealed for a monument to "faithful slaves," a call endorsed by Mrs. Fred A. Olds, president of the North Carolina Division.

In an open letter to the UDC, UCV, and "all the women of the South," Aston argued that the Confederate Veterans' recent campaign to erect a monument to southern women should be redirected to fund a memorial to "faithful slaves." Aston juxtaposed the expectations placed on white southern women during the war with what she saw as the profoundly questionable support of enslaved people. White women, she said, had felt they were enduring the struggle "for the sacred ties of kindred and country. How different with the faithful slaves! They did it for love of masters, mistresses and their children. How nobly did they perform their tasks! Their devotion to their owners, their faithfulness in performing their labors and caring for us during these terribly disastrous years, and their kindness at the surrender, while we were powerless and helpless, have never been surpassed or equaled."[8]

At the same time, Aston's letter reveals a certain ambivalence about the nature of these cross-race relationships, usually described by the UDC as benevolent and noncoercive. While white women on the home front could be assumed to support the Confederacy, the letter implies, the actions of the enslaved were "different" because they worked against their own interests in astounding ways. Slaves who remained loyal when they had the opportunity to free themselves or to attack those who held them in bondage must have made their choice, Aston contended, out of genuine love for their masters. This, she declared, was a loyalty worthy of commemoration.

In keeping with the Daughters' desire to make visible their own work, Aston proposed an inscription for the statue that would highlight the women's activism: "Given by the Confederate Veterans as a memorial to the women of the South, and given by them in memory of the faithfulness of our former servants." Such an inscription would commemorate white womanhood as the UCV originally intended and also honor them for rededicating the sculpture. Note, however, that slavery itself would be written out of the monument, as "faithful slaves" were renamed "former servants."[9]

While Aston's plan garnered the support of her state division leadership, others found it highly inappropriate. In November 1904, Mrs. W. Carleton Adams of Memphis, Tennessee, denounced the proposal, writing: "This is not the time for erecting monuments to the old slave—if there will ever be a time. Our country is already black with their living presence. Shall there be a black monument erected in every southern city or state, when there is not a State in the South not in mourning for some beautiful woman whose life has been strangled out by some black fiend?"[10] Evoking the narrative of black sexual deviance that fueled so many lynchings in this period, Adams countered Aston's assertion of black people's supreme and selfless love for southern white women of the past. Instead she raised the claim that black men posed a present-day mortal and sexual threat. She wished for total black absence, in daily life as well as sculpture.

If this were not enough, Adams concluded that such a proposed monument would go widely unappreciated: "The negro of this generation would not appreciate any monument not smacking of social equality. The North would not understand the sentiment."[11] Seeing modern black freedom struggles as disloyal, Adams said African Americans did not deserve to be placed in the monumental pantheon of southern heroes. And the North, she concluded, would be incapable of comprehending such an act.

Adams's rage at the idea of a monument to faithful slaves was clearly motivated by racism, which shaped her belief that funds would be better spent on the care of Confederate women. "It is a woefully mistaken sentiment that would spend one dollar on a black monument when there are hundreds of women, young and old, descending from the Confederacy, who are in want because the homes and the incomes which should have rightly descended to them were swept away by the ravages of the foe," she wrote. These women would benefit more, Adams said, from a monumental home, built and staffed to care for them. "If any money is available for monuments, let a great Monumental Home be erected in some southern city, preferably selecting a mild climate where the orange blossoms and mocking birds fill the air with perfume and song, and help woo away sufferings past." Assessing the UDC's overall fund-raising program and goals, Adams asked which campaigns were most worthy of support.[12]

The dispute over a "faithful slaves" monument continued in 1905 when another Memphis woman, Mary M. Solari, framed her argument as an explicit response to Adams. In doing so, Solari retained Adams's presentist outlook, focusing less on the "faithful slaves" of the past than on the impact a monument might have on future generations of African Americans in the South. "To those slaves who watched the fireside, tilled the soil, helped spin, weave, and make raiment for the master and sons on the battlefield," Solari wrote, "to those slaves who protected and provided for the families at home is due a monument that will tell the story to coming generations that cannot be taught the lesson of self-sacrifice and devotion of the slave in any other way."[13] Bemoaning the loss of what she believed to be the civilizing function of slavery, Solari suggested that a monument to faithfulness might shape the behavior of future generations of African Americans living under southern apartheid. This notion of public sculpture as producing power relationships, rather than simply memorializing times past, would become the organizing principle of the 1922–23 mammy commemoration attempt.

Beyond the capacity to instruct African Americans, Solari insisted that such a commemoration also had much to teach white southerners: "If a time is ever ripe for a noble deed, now is that time, for the grand, courteous southern slave owner is fast passing away; and to erect the monument would be to hand down to posterity an open book, in which our southern children can learn that every negro is no 'black fiend.'" Solari countered Adams's racist venom with an alternative white supremacist illusion of race relations founded on paternalistic benevolence and maternal fantasy. Foreshadowing the 1920s monument drive in many ways, Solari concluded her call for a faithful slave memorial, which to this point had been primarily gender neutral, with a paean to mammies. Solari agreed that the North's reception of such a memorial would be negative. But she cared little, saying, "The North would not understand the sentiment. Of course not."[14]

Emerging from this ongoing debate about the "faithful slaves" monument, a proposal to erect the statue finally was made at the UDC's annual convention in Norfolk, Virginia, in 1907. The measure failed, however, as members voted to table the resolution. In her brief description of the proposal nearly thirty years later, Rassie Hoskins White said: "The organization was not ready for the work then and postponed consideration of it."[15] White's comment is suggestive in its vagueness. Given the contentious debates leading up to the 1907 convention, her comment does not appear to refer to the group's ability to raise funds for such a monument or commission a design. Rather it may describe members' inability to conceive of the "value" of such a commemoration at that time. In the early years of the twentieth century, the UDC could achieve no consensus on the need for a monument to enslaved black people. But changes in the social and political landscapes of the South and the nation at large would elicit a radically different response less than two decades later.

### *Ready for Mammy*

By the 1920s the UDC was ready to commemorate "faithful slaves," and some people beyond the South also were ready for such a monument.[16] The years surrounding the First World War were marked by increasingly visible black challenges to American racism and imperialism. Having rallied for what Woodrow Wilson described as a war to make the world "safe for democracy," many in the United States found this "democracy" still terribly wanting after the war. Black soldiers who served in the segregated U.S. military faced a grim reality: they were expected to fight for a country that refused to recognize them as citizens. Black Americans also witnessed the global, anticolonial struggles of other peoples of African descent.

The NAACP put its money and legal expertise behind antilynching legislation movements and in 1919 took a decidedly more militant stance in its public voice, *The Crisis.* Editor W. E. B. Du Bois, who had advised putting aside racial politics in favor of national unity during the war, now wrote: "We return. We return from fighting. We return fighting. Make way for Democracy!"[17] In that same year Du Bois hosted his first Pan-African Congress in Paris. With a distinctly different global vision and constituency, Marcus Garvey had shifted the base of his United Negro Improvement Association in 1916 to New York's Harlem, where its membership grew steadily during and after the war as black migrations from the South to northern and western urban centers escalated generally. This Great Migration and the twenty-five race riots that exploded in cities across the United States in 1919 were in the minds of many Americans in the 1920s. Confined to no single region, riots erupted in the North, South, and West; in Omaha, Nebraska; Chicago; New York; and Knoxville, Tennessee. NAACP Secretary James Weldon Johnson referred to the period between June and the end of 1919 as the "Red Summer"—a reference to the terror and bloodshed of that time.[18]

It was within this postwar American landscape of racial turmoil that leaders of the United Daughters of the Confederacy sought to construct their vision for future race relations—a "solution" of sorts, modeled on southern segregation and embodied in the mammy. Their decision to focus on this particular figure, rather than the more elusive and often gender-neutral "faithful slave," is telling. The broad national popularity of mammy imagery and its connotations of maternal tenderness and domestic labor were central to the Daughters' notion of affectionate segregation.

Mammy had always been, and remains, the product of a white racial imagination. Invented by southern proslavery writers in the late antebellum period, the figure was defined as a beloved cook, caretaker, and grandmotherly slave woman in response to abolitionists' charges that slavery was wracked with sexual depravity, including the rape and concubinage of black women by white men. Through the concept of the mammy, these theorists of slavery sought to legitimize relations between white men and black women as maternal and nurturing, not sexual. Their elaborate construction of mammy included not only physical attributes that stressed her old age or wide girth but also her character. She loved her white "family" and would protect it fiercely, but she was simultaneously a bit cantankerous and a disciplinarian of white children. Endearing in her gruff demeanor and unrefined features, mammy always was the antithesis of desirable white femininity.[19]

Images of mammy saturated early-twentieth-century American culture, promoting these notions of asexuality, big-hearted kindness, and Old South gloriana. This period saw the escalating production and consumption of racist imagery in everything from popular music and material goods to new forms of consumer advertising. The most prevalent representation of mammy was undoubtedly Aunt Jemima, who smiled from boxes of pancake mix in kitchens throughout the country while domestic worker Nancy Green toured the nation appearing at industry-sponsored pancake feeds as the embodiment of the still-popular trademark. In modern consumer capitalism, the mammy's southern origin was one of her key characteristics—she was (and is) an American icon, but always a southern figure.[20]

A front-page advertisement for a new culinary column in the January 1, 1923, *Richmond Times-Dispatch* (fig. 12.1) provides an example of mammy iconography at the time of the monument campaign. The ad announces the arrival of "Aunt Priscilla," identified as a black mammy figure pictured to the right. The image, her name, and the link to food preparation clearly draw upon the popularity of Aunt Jemima, illustrating the complex interchange of national and regional mammy narratives in this period. The southern character has been commodified on the national stage and then refracted back into a southern domestic science column, in which "Aunt Priscilla" instructs the white women of Richmond in the finer arts of southern cooking and hospitality.

It was within these interconnected contexts—increasingly visible black geographic movements and radicalism, and the wide, national popularity of mammy imagery—that the U.S. Senate concurred with the UDC that the "faithful mammies of the South" should be honored with a public monument in the nation's capital. Sen. John Sharp Williams of Mississippi had introduced his bill to set aside land for such a statue earlier that winter, the last piece of legislation of his thirty-year congressional career. Williams was one of a small cadre of Southern Democrats who had carved a significant, and often contentious, place for themselves in the Republican-dominated Senate. In his memoir, Sen. George Wharton Pepper, a Republican from Pennsylvania, marveled, "No

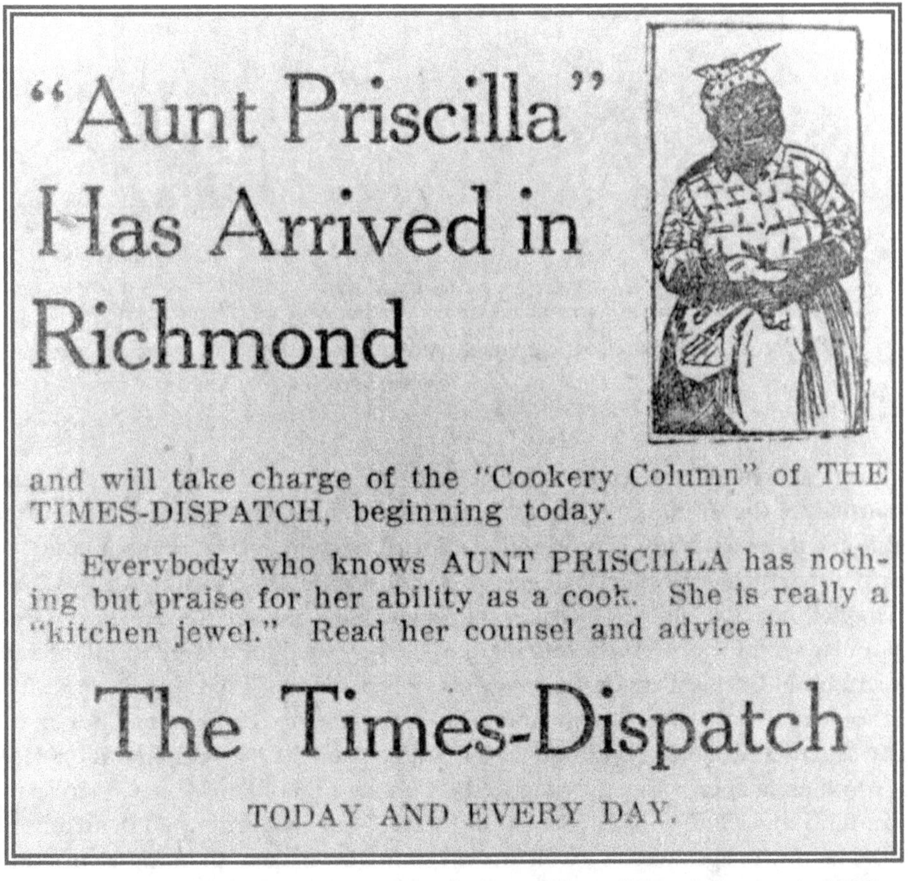


Fig. 12.1. "Aunt Priscilla" advertisement, *Richmond Times-Dispatch,* January 1, 1923. Courtesy of the Library of Virginia.

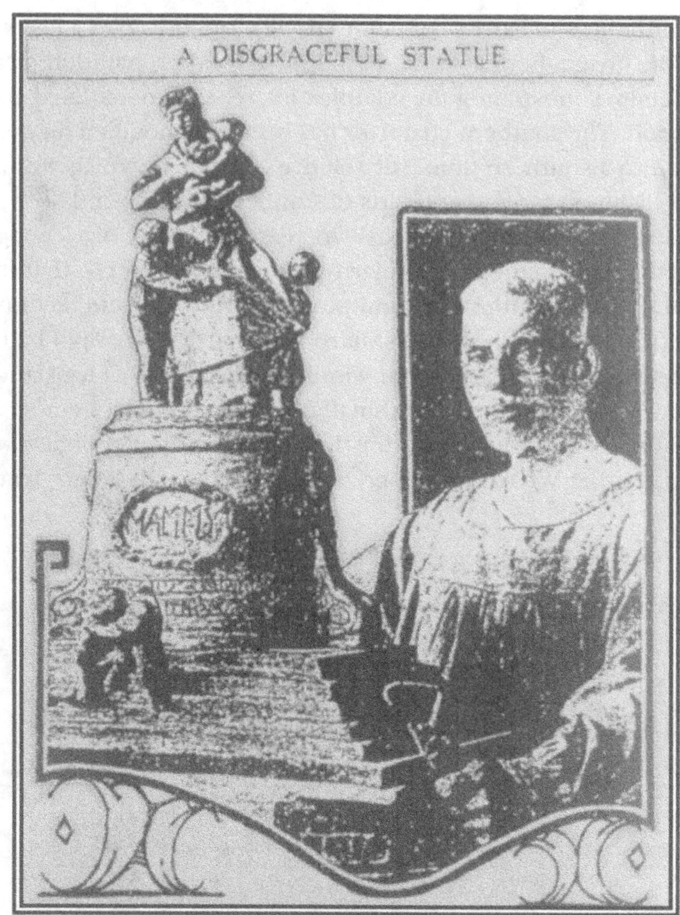


Fig. 12.2. Sculptor Ulric S. J. Dunbar with model for a mammy memorial.
"A Disgraceful Statue," *Chicago Defender,* July 14, 1923.

member of the Senate in my time approached in eloquence John Sharp Williams."[21] Senator Pepper was the chairman of the Committee on the Library, which initially reviewed the monument bill and passed it unanimously, sending it on to its ultimate passage in the Senate at large.[22]

Contemporary newspaper reports suggest that sculptors in the Washington, D.C., area began submitting model proposals to the UDC after the Senate bill's passage.[23] A design by George Julian Zolnay, a popular sculptor of Confederate memorials, provided for a large fountain and a seated mammy surrounded by three children. It was also reported that Ulric S. J. (Stonewall Jackson) Dunbar had renewed work on a mammy monument design (fig. 12.2) he had begun some years earlier.[24] The senators reviewed no designs for the monument as they debated Bill S4119, leaving ultimate governmental approval of the plan to the Commission of Fine Arts. Congress was to supply land, not fund the actual construction of the statue—a point reiterated in an amendment to the final bill. Mammy images were so well known to the lawmakers that no discussion of what a "faithful mammy" might look like was considered necessary at this stage.

## *The Limits of Citizenship*

The southernness of the mammy image invoked suggestions that segregation—the formal separation of white and black, with the disfranchisement of the latter—was the most desirable national order. Amid the massive migration of black southerners to urban centers in the East and West, ideas about the South infused racial discourses across the United States in the 1920s. They helped the white women of the UDC garner national support for a monument essentially commemorating the southern color line.

As a female slave, the mammy's domestic and maternal work had been intrinsically private, not public. In light of newly won female suffrage and continued struggles for full African American voting rights, the slave mammy delineated, for monument supporters, one group of women—and by extension an entire race—which they believed should not vote. Citizenship entails more than voting rights, however, and the image of the mammy as a domestic worker and surrogate mother to whites suggested a contained and sentimental notion of black public life. Though African Americans were not to share in the rights of full citizenship, in the monument proponents' view they nonetheless had a civic duty to labor for, support, and love those who did.

Recalling Solari's arguments of 1905, advocates hoped that a mammy statue would offer a lesson about appropriate black conduct and expectations. One supporter said: "If the negroes of the present generation and generations to follow, measure up [to mammy] in citizenship, character, intellect, dependability, industry and godly living, they, as well as the white people of this country, will have a right to feel that they are doing mighty well."[25] Note particularly in this passage the implication that black citizenship ought to be equivalent to the domestic labors of slavery. It was the monument's potential to solidify this intent, literally, within the national civic culture that so alarmed Neval Thomas as he wrote of its ability to "teach white and black alike that the menial callings are the Negro's place in the scheme of things."

This racialization of the domestic sphere had terrific potential for white women's reshaping of their own citizenship. In commemorating mammy, the UDC retained the maternal, feminine construction of domesticity through which "progressive" women's organizations had long articulated a gendered notion of political power in the United States while at the same time distancing white womanhood from private labor and the responsibilities of daily household upkeep. The UDC's construction of loving, servile blackness "emancipated" feminine whiteness from the domestic impediments to public activity.[26] In this manner, the Daughters campaigned to recast the gendered dichotomy of public and private space—with public life traditionally reserved for men, and women confined to the domestic sphere—into a bifurcated, racial division. For them, black people's labors could enable a new white public, composed of both men and women unified through racial homogeneity. The UDC hoped that mammy's mythic traits of loyalty and contentment with slavery might be a model for African Americans living in future eras of segregation, disfranchisement, and white privilege.

Read against Rassie Hoskins White's claims for the power of monuments to render visible the work of the white women of the UDC, the mammy commemoration campaign of 1922–23 marks an attempt to carry that logic to its most extreme conclusion. Of course, the work such a monument would make most visible was that of enslaved black women and, by extension, the labors of black domestic workers throughout the country in the 1920s. This profound racial visibility was essential to obscuring the gender constraints that made much of the UDC's public activism invisible. Black women's monumental labors, both literal and figurative, blunted the contradiction of the UDC members' reverence for the patriarchal tradition that confined them as gender inequality was displaced by racial segregation.

### *Monumental Violence*

The black press's challenge to this vision was swift as it opposed the monument bill and presented very different understandings of the enslaved, black mother's place in modern African American citizenship. In response to the Daughters' romanticization of slavery and their vision of "affectionate" segregation, black journalists focused on the abuses and sexual exploitation of slavery as well as the brutalities and disfranchisement of contemporary southern apartheid and the informal segregation prevalent across the nation. Assessing the controversy, one black newspaper, the *St. Louis Argus,* reported, "No subject has brought forth a more unanimous protest, except lynching, since the Civil War, than has the proposed Black Mammy statue."[27]

In drawing a historical trajectory back to the Civil War, the *Argus* cast the battle over the national mammy monument as one waged fundamentally over the meaning and substance of black freedom and full citizenship. In linking the controversy to lynching, the paper suggested the irony of monument supporters' desire to commemorate mammies while failing to challenge the continued lynchings of black men and women in the South, sanctioned by Federal indifference. By raising the issue of lynching—another arena in which black citizenship, particularly that of men, was violently contested—the editorial marked the erection of a statue in honor of mammy as a similarly brutal act of domination.[28]

Monument supporters proclaimed warm sentiment to be the wellspring of their campaign, but opponents saw incredible violence in the commemoration drive. Criticisms such as those made by the *Argus* suggested that the UDC's professed love for mammy swelled from the same blood lust and insidious white supremacist sentiment that fueled race riots, lynchings, rapes, and other abuses of African Americans. Rather than presenting an alternative to the testaments of affection promoted by the UDC, the monument's detractors argued that this affection *was* violence and the memorialization campaign itself profoundly vicious.

The black press wrote persistently of the injuries heaped upon the mammies of the past whom the Daughters professed to so love and honor. These newspapers often referred to mammies as tragic figures, unable to care for their own children or support their own black families as they were forced into mothering white children and as their labors were co-opted into the white family economy. Mary Church Terrell, one of the founders of the National Association of Colored Women, wrote in a widely printed editorial, for example, "The black mammy was often faithful in the service of her mistress's children while her heart bled over her own babies, who were thus deprived of their mother's ministrations and tender care, which the white children received."[29] Where Mrs. Aston had marveled at the expressions of "true love" the Civil War revealed in supposedly faithful slaves, critics in the black press spotlighted the pain and savage coercion that structured relations between enslaved black women and their white owners and charges.

Woven through these images of violence and tragedy were strands of the sexual exploitation of African American women, under slavery as well as in the early twentieth century. Focusing on predatory white men, these discussions linked the mammy figure as an embodiment of the history

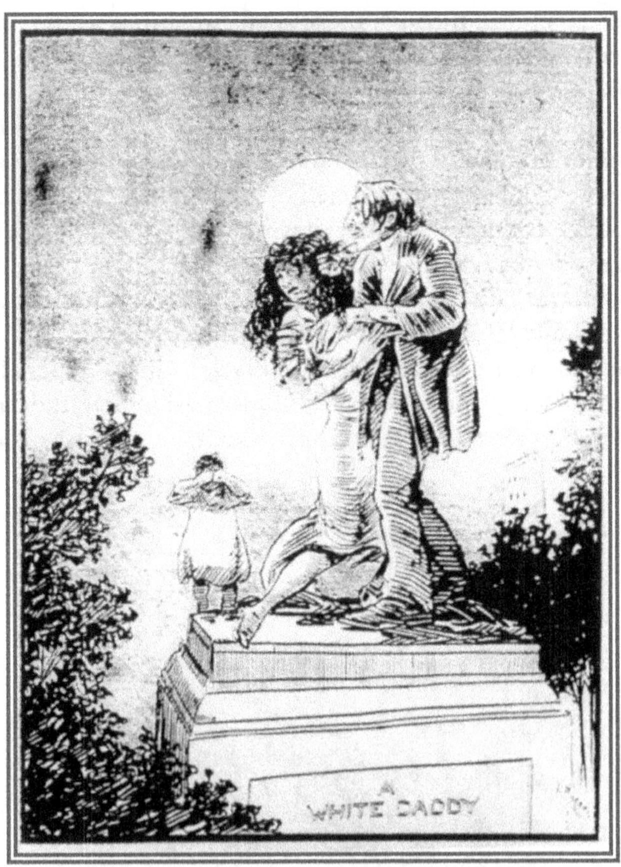



Fig. 12.3. "Since Statues Seem to be All the Rage, Suppose We Erect One." "A White Daddy," *Chicago Defender*, April 21, 1923.

of slavery with the position of modern-day African American women in a brutally segregated society. By drawing attention to the rape, exploitation, and endangerment of domestic workers, both enslaved and free, black journalists made it clear that the mammy figure was invented to conceal white desire and sexual violence.

Like other black papers, writers and caricaturists for the *Chicago Defender* argued that the UDC's mammy commemoration was an explicit attempt to deny the prevalence of interracial sex, forced and otherwise, in the South and beyond its regional boundaries. By putting a spotlight on sex across the color line, and placing the onus on white male aggressors, these journalists confounded the Daughters' vision of affectionate segregation. One editorialist charged: "Maybe the Daughters of the Confederacy wish to get their closets cleaned out by erecting a 'black mammy' statue in Washington. Pale-faced sheiks will tell them that one 'yaller gal' is worth a dozen 'mammy' statues."[30] While the mammy monument was intended to expel the skeleton of miscegenation from southern closets with its focus on maternal contact between the races, the *Defender* argued, the desire of menacing white "sheiks" would continue to blur racial boundaries and threaten black women. The reference to eroticized "yaller gals" compounds the argument, describing the children produced through these sexual relations as the most desirable to those who hypocritically decried racial mixing.[31]

A month later, the *Defender* made a similar argument in a powerful editorial cartoon (fig. 12.3). Under the facetious heading "Since Statues Seem to Be All the Rage, Suppose We Erect One," the paper proposed a countermonument, to the "White Daddy." The cartoon makes clear that "we" black Americans had quite a different story to tell of "affectionate" interracial contact by focusing on the white rapist and the children he fathered with black women. Its depiction of a nighttime scene also suggests the silencing and secrecy of black women's experiences of sexual assault within the dominant culture. This moonlit tableau is a richly layered critique that explodes the honeyed myth of fictive familial ties between black and white people.

By focusing on white men's sexual terrorism of black women, papers like the *Defender* disputed the assertions of black deviance and sexual transgression that underlay the brutal enforcement of southern segregation through lynching and assault. An expansive form of social control in

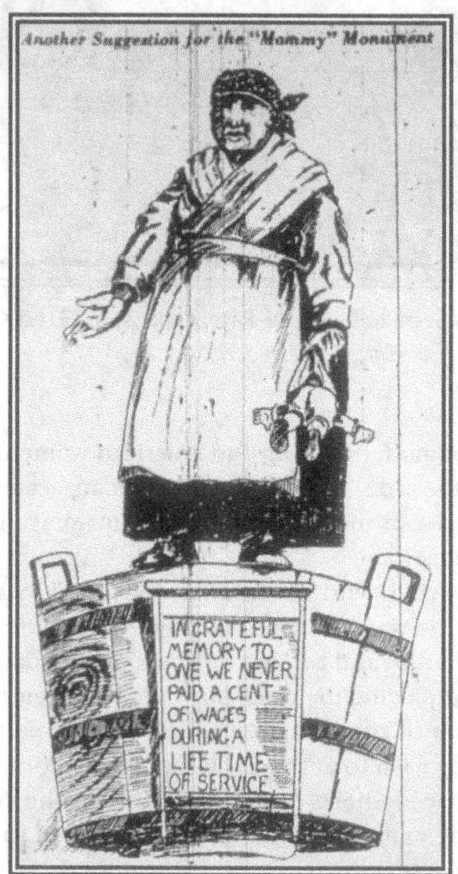


Fig. 12.4. "Another Suggestion for the 'Mammy' Monument,"
*Baltimore Afro-American*, March 30, 1923.

the South, actual violence and the constant threat of lynching enabled white, patriarchal domination, the denial of African American citizenship, and the continued coercion of black labor.[32] The black press sought to dismantle this system by turning the charges of rape against those who employed such accusations to fuel lynch mobs.

Journalists for the black press ripped away the veneer of maternal warmth and childlike innocence the UDC affixed to segregation and black exclusion in their drive to commemorate mammies. Exposing the white terrorism that enforced the color line, they also named as a form of violence the processes of denial, concealment, and domination that produced the mammy stereotype.

## *Conclusion: Monumental Vigilance*

As the monument controversy roiled, supporters and detractors of the statue agreed on one thing: The stakes were incredibly high. Both sides believed that national monuments could deeply influence American civic life. Commemoration was not a mere reflection of larger tensions over citizenship, race, and gender but stood at the heart of them with the potential to shape a new citizenry as well as new levels of oppression or freedom. Thus, much of the public discussion was about monumentality itself, reflected in the common use of monumental language and imagery to frame protests to the commemoration drive (figs. 12.3 and 12.4). The protest cartoons considered here make starkly clear the importance of the conflict over "representation," both visual and political. In critics' view, a public sculpture based on mammy imagery would give concrete form to dangerous ideas and imbue them with a kind of "official truth."

This facet of the conflict was clearly expressed in a fascinating editorial decision made by a prominent, Washington, D.C.–based black newspaper, the *Washington Tribune,* a month before the mammy monument bill passed the Senate. In January 1923 the paper, which would become a leading voice in organizing objection to the commemoration, began reprinting the text of *Emancipation and the Freed in American Sculpture: A Study in Interpretation,* written by the newspaper's president, F. Morris Murray. The timing of this reprint is too suggestive to be simple coincidence. In his introduction to the study, Murray argued for a keen critical vision in the face of public commemoration: "When we look at a work of art, especially when 'we' [black people] look at one in which Black Folk appear—or do not appear when they should—we should ask: what does it mean? What does it suggest? What impression is it likely to make on those who view it? What will be the effect on present-day problems, of its obvious and also of its insidious teachings? In short, we should endeavor to 'interpret' it; and should try to interpret it from our own particular viewpoint."[33] Like Rassie Hoskins White, Murray asserted the political and social power of monuments and counseled vigilance in reading their potential effects.

A month later, a front-page headline urged *Tribune* readers to "Voice Protest Against 'Mammy' Statue."[34] By framing its coverage of the monument campaign with this analytical study of artistic representation, the *Tribune* sought to provide readers with the conceptual tools for understanding the grave consequences of such a commemoration and for formulating a protest.

It was this fierce and varied protest that would ultimately spell the end of the mammy monument drive. The land grant proposal had never been as popular in the House. Drawing upon political and social relationships they had cultivated with southern lawmakers and journalists in Washington, the Daughters had won the Senate's backing in 1923. But the public controversy that followed Senate approval bolstered the representatives' lack of interest or active objections to the scheme, and the resolution was never allowed out of committee in the House. Quiet congressional inaction spared the city of Washington and the nation from witnessing construction of a memorial to the "faithful colored mammies of the South." The iconography of the mammy and the wider debate around it, however, would long remain powerfully present within American political culture.

## *Notes*

1. *Congressional Record,* 67th Cong., 1923, 64, pt. 5: 4839. Neval H. Thomas, "Want No Black Mammy Monument," *California Eagle,* Feb. 17, 1923. Portions of the letter were reprinted in "Thomas Against Mammy Monument," *Savannah Tribune,* Feb. 23, 1923. A note on usage: the term *mammy* stands in quotation marks (as it often did in the black press) to indicate that it was a representation or myth of a particular slave figure and should not be taken as a reference to identifiable, antebellum, historical actors. For the rest of this essay, the term will not appear in quotations unless in a citation, but the punctuation should be understood.

2. Kirk Savage, *Standing Soldiers, Kneeling Slaves* (Princeton: Princeton Univ. Press, 1997), 4.

3. This article is drawn from my "Monumental Citizenship: Reading the Mammy Commemoration Controversy of the Early Twentieth Century" (Ph.D. diss., New York University, forthcoming). Parts have been presented in 1999 papers at the Southern American Studies Association meeting, Wilmington, North Carolina, and the American Studies Association meeting, Montreal, Canada, and in a 2000 paper at the Southern Association for Women Historians conference in Richmond, Virginia. The essay has benefited from the critiques and questions of commentators and audience members.

4. Angie Parrott, "'Love Makes Memory Eternal': The United Daughters of the Confederacy in Richmond, Virginia, 1897–1920," in *The Edge of the South: Life in Nineteenth-Century Virginia,* ed. Edward Ayers and John Willis (Charlottesville: Univ. Press of Virginia, 1991), 221.

5. A number of scholars have explored the inconsistencies of the UDC's devotion to tradition and the Old South and its simultaneous promotion of public, political roles for women. See Drew Gilpin Faust, *Mothers of Invention* (Chapel Hill: Univ. of North Carolina Press, 1996), especially the epilogue; Karen Lynne Cox, "Women, the Lost Cause, and the New South: The United Daughters of the Confederacy and the Transmission of Confederate Culture, 1894–1919" (Ph.D. diss., Univ. of Southern Mississippi, 1997); Parrott, "'Love Makes Memory Eternal'"; Anastasia Sims, *The Power of Femininity in the New South* (Columbia: Univ. of South Carolina Press, 1997); and LeeAnn Whites, *The Civil War as a Crisis in Gender: Augusta, Georgia, 1860–1890* (Athens: Univ. of Georgia Press, 1995).

6. Quotations are from Mary B. Poppenheim et al., *The History of the United Daughters of the Confederacy* (Raleigh: Edwards and Broughton, 1938), 49, 92.

7. Sims, *The Power of Femininity,* 130.

8. Mrs. G. Gilliland Aston, "A Monument to the Faithful Old Slaves," *Confederate Veteran* 12, no. 9 (Sept. 1904): 443.

9. Ibid.

10. Mrs. W. Carleton Adams, "Slave Monument Question," *Confederate Veteran* 12 (Nov. 1904): 525.

11. Ibid.

12. Ibid.

13. Mary M. Solari, "Monument to Faithful Slaves," *Confederate Veteran* 13 (Mar. 1905): 123.

14. Ibid.

15. Poppenheim et al., *The History of the United Daughters of the Confederacy*, 77.

16. The UDC began its first official faithful slave memorialization campaign in 1920 to commemorate Heyward Shepherd. Shepherd, a black railroad employee, was the first person killed in John Brown's raid at Harpers Ferry, West Virginia, when, according to the UDC, he refused to join the abolitionist's attack. The campaign suffered a number of setbacks, including the discovery that Shepherd had not been a slave and protests from Harpers Ferry elected officials and students at Storer College, a black college near the monument site. After many changes, the monument (no longer to a "faithful slave") was erected in October 1931. Poppenheim et al., *History of the United Daughters of the Confederacy*, 77–79. See also the reports of the Committee for the Faithful Slave Memorial in *Minutes of the Thirty-Second Annual Convention* (1925) and the 1926, 1927, and 1931 conventions, and Mary Johnson, "An 'Ever Present Bone of Contention': The Heyward Shepherd Memorial," *West Virginia History* 56 (1997): 1–26. A "faithful slave" memorial including a mammy figure had been erected in Fort Mill, South Carolina, in 1898. In 1927 a monument depicting a diffident, aged black man was erected in Natchitoches, Louisiana, inscribed "in grateful recognition of the arduous and faithful service of the good darkies of Louisiana." Savage, *Standing Soldiers, Kneeling Slaves,* 151–61.

17. W. E. B. Du Bois, "Returning Soldiers," *The Crisis* 18 (May 1919): 14. On the NAACP and its antilynching activism, see Robert Zagrando, *The NAACP Crusade Against Lynching, 1909–1950* (Philadelphia: Temple Univ. Press, 1980).

18. On Marcus Garvey and the UNIA, see Irma Watkins-Owens, *Blood Relations: Caribbean Immigrants and the Harlem Community, 1900–1930* (Bloomington: Indiana Univ. Press, 1996), esp. chaps. 5 and 7. On the Great Migration, see Gretchen Lemke-Santangelo, *Abiding Courage: African-American Migrant Women and the East Bay Community* (Chapel Hill: Univ. of North Carolina Press, 1996); Carole Marks, *Farewell— We're Good and Gone: The Great Black Migration* (Bloomington: Indiana Univ. Press, 1989); and the essays collected in Joe William Trotter Jr. ed., *The Great Migration in Historical Perspective: New Dimensions of Race, Class, and Gender* (Bloomington: Indiana Univ. Press, 1991). On "Red Summer," see William M. Tuttle Jr., *Race Riot: Chicago in the Red Summer of 1919* (New York: Atheneum, 1970).

19. On mammy as a construction of antebellum whites, see Catherine Clinton, *The Plantation Mistress: Women's World in the Old South* (New York: Pantheon Books, 1982): 201–3; Elizabeth Fox-Genovese, *Within the Plantation Household: Black and White Women of the Old South* (Chapel Hill: Univ. of North Carolina Press, 1988): 137; Deborah Gray White, *Ar'n't I a Woman?: Female Slaves in the Plantation South* (New York: W. W. Norton and Co., 1985), 46–66.

20. On mammy iconography in the twentieth century, see Kenneth W. Goings, *Mammy and Uncle Mose: Black Collectibles and American Stereotyping* (Bloomington: Indiana Univ. Press, 1994); Thomas C. Holt, "Marking: Race, Race-making, and the Writing of History," *American Historical Review* 100 (1995): 1–20; K. Sue Jewell, *From Mammy to Miss America: Cultural Images and the Shaping of U.S. Social Policy* (New York: Routledge, 1993); Marilyn Kern-Foxworth, *Aunt Jemima, Uncle Ben, and Rastus: Blacks in Advertising Yesterday, Today, and Tomorrow* (Westport, Conn.: Greenwood Press, 1994); M. M. Manring, *Slave in a Box: The Strange Career of Aunt Jemima* (Charlottesville: Univ. Press of Virginia, 1998); Cheryl Thurber, "The Development of the Mammy Image and Mythology," in *Southern Women: Histories and Identities,* ed. Virginia Bernhard, Betty Brandon, Elizabeth Fox-Genovese, and Theda Perdue (Columbia: Univ. of Missouri Press, 1992), 87–108; and Patricia Turner, *Ceramic Uncles and Celluloid Mammies: Black Images and Their Influences on Culture* (New York: Doubleday, 1994).

21. George Wharton Pepper, *In the Senate* (Philadelphia: Univ. of Pennsylvania Press, 1930), 14.

22. There is no available record of the specific voting results in the Senate at large for Bill S4119, other than its passage.

23. It is unclear from newspaper accounts whether the design submissions arrived unsolicited or if the Daughters opened a formal competition. S4119 did not specify a site for the mammy monument, but it did outline clearly the places in Washington, D.C., where it could not be erected—the grounds of the White House, Capitol, Library of Congress, or Potomac Park. *Congressional Record,* 67th Cong., 1923, 64, pt. 5:4839.

24. "Southerners' Conception of Mammy Typical," *Washington Tribune,* Apr. 7, 1923; "A Disgraceful Statue," *Chicago Defender,* July 14, 1923. On Zolnay's plan, see David W. Blight, *Race and Reunion* (Cambridge, Mass.: Belknap Press of Harvard Univ. Press, 2001), 288–89, 459–60.

25. "For and Against the 'Black Mammy's' Monument," *Literary Digest* 28 (Apr. 1923): 48.

26. In her reading of *Imitation of Life,* Lauren Berlant argues that the white, female, adult character could only achieve disembodied, abstract, public authority and power by shielding her own gendered body "behind" the overdetermined racial body of the black domestic, a figure who is clearly coded in the 1933 novel by Fannie Hurst and first film version in 1934 as Aunt Jemima. See "National Brands/National Bodies: Imitation of Life," in *The Phantom Public Sphere,* ed. Bruce Robbins (Minneapolis: Univ. of Minnesota Press, 1993): 173–208. Grace Elizabeth Hale discusses links between white women's public activity and mammies in *Making Whiteness: The Culture of Segregation in the South, 1890–1940* (New York: Pantheon Books, 1998): 105–14.

27. Reprinted in "For and Against the 'Black Mammy's' Monument," 48.

28. My understanding of the commemoration as a form of violence has been shaped by Saidiya Hartman's notion of the violence of the banal in *Scenes of Subjection: Terror, Slavery, and Self-Making in Nineteenth-Century America* (New York: Oxford Univ. Press, 1997), 4.

29. "For and Against the 'Black Mammy's' Monument," 49.

30. Untitled, *Chicago Defender,* Mar. 3, 1923. Many thanks to Micol Seigel, who brought this citation to my attention and has enriched my work with her astute criticism, insight, and friendship.

31. The term *sheik,* drawn from the popular Rudolph Valentino film *The Sheik* (1921) and commonly used in the black press to describe womanizers and philanderers, reveals the complex racialization of sexual vocabularies in this period. Other references to "sheiks" can be found in "The Memoirs of an Ex-Sheik," *California Eagle,* Apr. 14, 1923, and the following *Baltimore Afro-American* articles: "Sheiks," Jan. 19, 1923; "A 'Sheik' Antidote," Mar. 23, 1923; and "Modern Sheik Killed in Bed While Asleep," Sept. 7, 1923.

32. For recent studies of lynching and citizenship, see Sandra Gunning, *Race, Rape, and Lynching: The Red Record of American Literature, 1890–1912* (New York: Oxford Univ. Press, 1996); Jacqueline Dowd Hall, *Revolt Against Chivalry: Jessie Daniel Ames and the Women's Campaign Against Lynching* (New York: Columbia Univ. Press, 1993); Martha Hodes, *White Women, Black Men: Illicit Sex in the Nineteenth-Century South* (New Haven: Yale Univ. Press, 1997); Bryant Simon, "The Appeal of Cole Blease of South Carolina: Race, Class, and Sex in the New South," *Journal of Southern History* (Feb. 1996): 56–86; and Robyn Wiegman, *American Anatomies: Theorizing Race and Gender* (Durham: Duke Univ. Press, 1995).

33. Freeman Henry Morris Murray, *Emancipation and the Freed in American Sculpture: A Study in Interpretation* (1916; Freeport, N.Y.: Books for Libraries Press, 1972), xix. Reprint in the *Washington Tribune,* Jan. 6, 1923.

34. *Washington Tribune,* Feb. 10, 1923.

# 13

# Granite Stopped Time

STONE MOUNTAIN MEMORIAL AND THE REPRESENTATION
OF WHITE SOUTHERN IDENTITY

*Grace Elizabeth Hale*

NOWHERE HAS the desire to naturalize culture taken a more literal form than in the carving of Stone Mountain, a bald bulk of granite sixteen miles from Atlanta. If the grandiose visions of the original planners had been realized, the Stone Mountain Confederate Monument would have stood with the presidential election of the southerner Woodrow Wilson, the unprecedented popularity of the film *Birth of a Nation,* and the segregation of Washington, D.C., as an early-twentieth-century symbol of the modern white South's triumphant coming of age.[1]

But a world war and the technological and financial hurdles of carving a mountain into a panoramic relief of Confederate heroism intervened. Atlanta attorney William H. Terrell proposed the project and Caroline Helen Jemison Plane, leader of the United Daughters of the Confederacy's Atlanta chapter, championed it in 1914. By 1916 the Stone Mountain Confederate Memorial Association (SMCMA) had incorporated, hired the internationally known sculptor Gutzon Borglum, and secured a deed from the mountain's owner, Samuel Venable, to the straightest face of the granite dome. Work on the mountain did not begin, however, until 1923. Conceived in the context of a national monument-building craze as an effort to ground in stone the courageous struggles of the Civil War generation and provide their offspring with the still-heroic role of memorialists, the Stone Mountain monument took shape instead within a decidedly different era.

Most veterans had passed away by the early 1920s and the memorialists, children during the Civil War and Reconstruction, now watched their own sons and daughters grow to adulthood in another postwar world. The South had fought on the winning side in this new conflict, and America's increased international stature brought greater economic opportunity even to the nation's poorest region. Race riots and widespread racial violence had followed African Americans' accelerated migration North, and in the immediate aftermath of this Great War many whites across the nation moved—much as white southerners had done after Reconstruction—to destroy blacks' wartime hopes for expanded freedom. The second Ku Klux Klan, reincarnated at the summit of Stone Mountain, gained membership throughout the country. A greater sharing of the "Negro Problem" as well as the wealth further reduced sectional tensions and made white southerners,

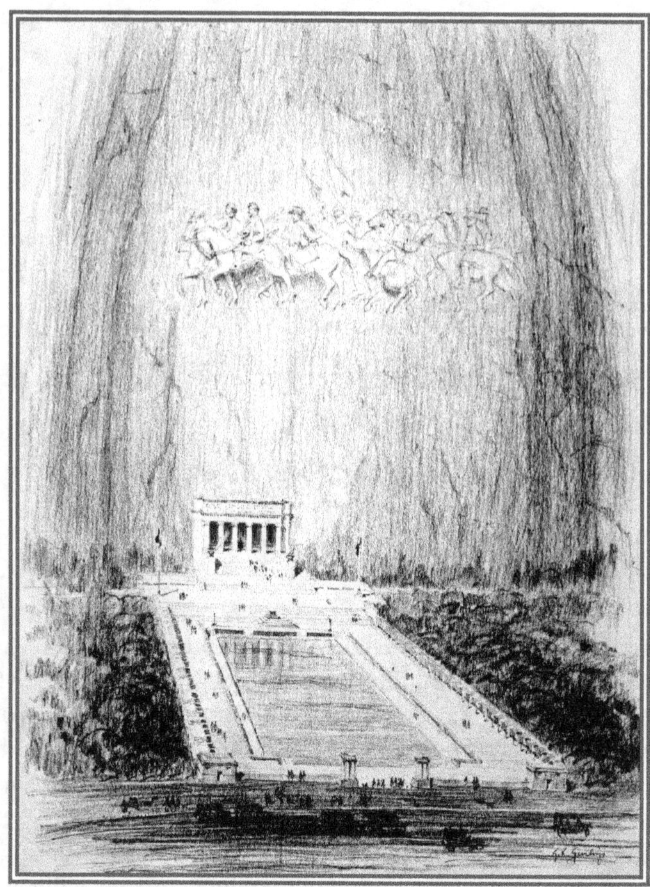

Fig. 13.1. Drawing of an early plan for the Stone Mountain Memorial near Atlanta, Georgia, showing Robert E. Lee, Jefferson Davis, and Thomas "Stonewall" Jackson leading Confederate cavalrymen across the mountain's granite face. Stone Mountain Collection, Robert W. Woodruff Library, Emory University.

especially an increasingly urbanized and educated middle class, secure within both their regional culture of segregation and their nation. With the original design for the Stone Mountain Confederate Memorial—Robert E. Lee leading a larger-than-life army across the mountainside—some southern whites hoped to capture their newfound sense of regional and racial serenity in stone (fig. 13.1).

Conceived as a symbol of the solid white South that anchored the segregated present in the Confederate past, the mountain as monument in progress, however, told a different tale. Granite proved strangely ephemeral as factions within the association squabbled over resources, plans, and sculptors, blasting the original design from the face of the mountain and leaving a second Lee's head floating disembodied above a shallowly etched torso and horse. Borglum's original design of Lee and his army riding silently across the mountain would later become a stylized flattened frieze of Lee, Confederate President Jefferson Davis, and Gen. Thomas "Stonewall" Jackson leading a less grand grouping of color-bearers and other generals. By 1970, when a new memorial association finally finished the project, only a triptych of Lee, Davis, and Jackson remained. The desire to ground white southern identity in stone and a sense that the figure of Lee somehow best served this intention remained unchanged over the course of the twentieth century, yet national and regional white support for the project waxed and waned. The ongoing incorporation of the region into the nation eroded modern southern whiteness externally as the continual resistance of black southerners undermined the culture of segregation from within. The halting progress of the carving of Stone Mountain into a memorial, then, provided a paradoxical measure of regional insecurity, nationalism, and ambition. Regardless of the desires of southern memorialists, granite could not stop time. Racial and regional identities could not be fixed in stone, and the story of the carving of the mountain revealed much more about white southerners than the memorial was intended to tell.[2]

## Borglum's Ambitious "Vision"

In 1915 Helen Plane and the Atlanta chapter of the United Daughters of the Confederacy (UDC) started the project when they called Gutzon Borglum to the city to survey Stone Mountain and discuss their memorial plans. Ironically, the sculptor the Atlanta Daughters chose was a "Yankee," or nearly one: he was born in Idaho in 1867 to Danish parents and trained in San Francisco and Paris. Borglum had achieved the national fame that brought him to the attention of the Atlanta UDC for his sculpted head of his hero Abraham Lincoln then on display in the rotunda of the U.S. Capitol. Who else could do justice to the South's own Civil War hero?

But the sight of all that untouched granite outside of Atlanta gave Borglum a vision. He quickly dismissed the organization's decision to carve a hundred-foot-high face of Lee seventy feet above the ground on the sheer northern face of the site. Seeing the immense block of faultless granite, Borglum shocked the Daughters by declaring that their head of Lee would look like a postage stamp stuck on a barn door. Instead of the tiny Lee head, he envisaged hundreds of Confederate soldiers marching across the steep dome of the mountainside, led by a fully figured Lee riding his horse Traveller and accompanied by Davis and Jackson on their mounts. Borglum described his ambitious plan for the *New York Times Magazine* in 1916 as "cutting a great frieze representing a moving mass of troops across its face in full or high relief, in such a manner . . . as to give the impression that they were in full relief and moving over the surface of the mountain. To the spectator, suddenly coming upon the mountain, in a dusk or soft light at a proper distance, the general appearance will be that of the natural mountain over which, silently, this great grey army moves." Without irony, newspapers and magazines compared the proposed memorial to the Sphinx, the pyramids, and other ancient wonders of other lost worlds, all of which it would outlast and dwarf. Borglum had transformed the UDC's modest plan into the "eighth wonder of the world."[3]

From the first, however, efforts to transfer the powerful presence the planners sensed in the mountain into the carved memorial proved difficult. The Daughters envisioned the sculpture in sectionalist terms, as a lasting tribute to the "heroes in gray." Mildred L. Rutherford, the historian of both the state UDC and the SMCMA, repeated the mantra of states' rights and the justice of the cause "not lost." But Borglum seemed more intent on his own rather than the Confederacy's glory. In December of 1922 he discussed the project with Angus Perkerson, editor of the *Atlanta Journal Magazine:* "The memorial as I plan it will without doubt be the greatest monument ever built. The single figures will dwarf other pieces of sculpture, and the entire effect of an army marching across the mountain in review before their leaders will be bigger than anything of the sort ever before attempted" (fig. 13.2). For Borglum, "my memorial" meant the artist's own as well as the Confederacy's eternity.[4]

Yet a theme of sectional reunion came through even Borglum's bloated egotism. When asked how he could reconcile his love for Lincoln with his work on the Confederate memorial, the sculptor answered that he shared "the deepest respect for the great men of the other side." More guarded when talking with his employers, officers of the SMCMA, Borglum modestly argued again for a national message. The project interested him, he insisted, because the Stone Mountain Memorial was "the first effort in America to build a monument to a nation, to a movement of a hundred thousand or ten hundred thousand people." Borglum's ability to reconcile these seeming contradictions and to couple American and Confederate nationalisms was emblematic of middle-class white thinking in the 1910s and 1920s. White southern interpretations of the institution of slavery, the war, and Reconstruction increasingly dominated amateur and professional histories as well as popular historical fiction. Lost no longer, a white southern nation had become by the

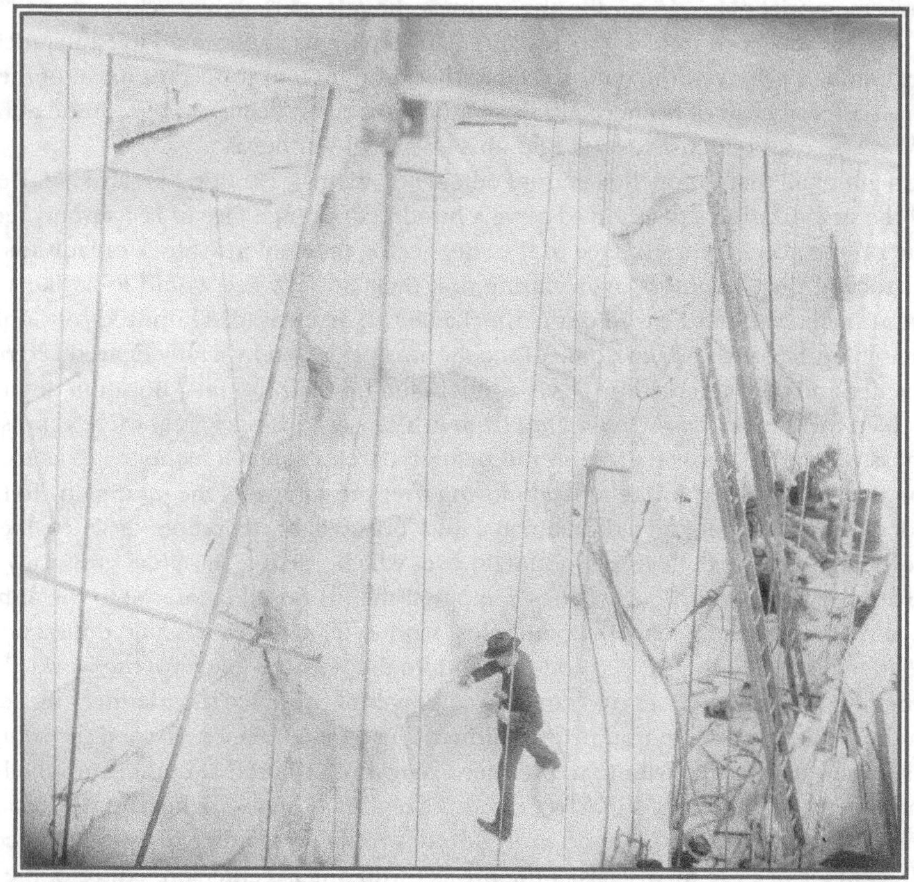

Fig. 13.2. Gutzon Borglum carves head of Robert E. Lee on Stone Mountain, completed January 19, 1924, and destroyed in 1928. Stone Mountain Collection, Robert W. Woodruff Library, Emory University.

1920s a respected part of the American past even for many white nonsoutherners, and the Stone Mountain Memorial would make sure that history entered eternity as art.[5]

The memorial association walked a difficult line, however, making arguments that would appeal to both Americans' expansive nationalism and the racialized regionalism of the most ardent Lost Cause supporters in fund-raising efforts. If many white Americans and a growing and increasingly powerful group of southerners saw no contradiction between "American" and southern loyalties, those whites maintaining the old southern militancy tended to be active members of the Confederate organizations. Shrewd enough to recognize that the money for the project could not be raised internally, however, the SMCMA from its inception carefully solicited a broad support. Politicians from across the country supported the effort, and in keeping with a national movement to reclaim Confederate military leaders, especially Lee, praised the planned colossal carvings of these great "American men." Even President Warren G. Harding complimented Borglum's design and wished "the people of the South" the aid and cooperation of "Americans everywhere" while stressing a message of reconciliation: "It will be one of the world's finest testimonies, one of history's most complete avowals, that unity and understanding may be brought even into the scene where faction, hatred, and hostility have once reigned supreme."[6]

In praising a gigantic carving of the Confederate army as a symbol of the nation, these men continued a theme of sectional reconciliation through a common white male martial ideal that had begun with the Spanish American War in the late nineteenth century and received new life through the film spectacle of *Birth of a Nation* in 1915. By January 21, 1925, Congress as well as President Calvin Coolidge had sanctioned the project by authorizing the U.S. Mint's coinage of five million silver half-dollars designed by Borglum to raise funds, inscribed as a "memorial to the valor of soldiers of the South," those "custodians of imperishable glory." The Sixty-eighth Congress passed the bill "to authorize the coinage of fifty cent pieces in commemoration of the commencement on June 18, 1923, of the carving on Stone Mountain, in the State of Georgia, a monument to the valor of the soldiers of the South, which was the inspiration of the sons and daughters and grandsons and granddaughters in the Spanish American and World Wars." Many white southerners praised the coin as the ultimate symbol of sectional reconciliation, the national government's homage to the Confederate past. The SMCMA continued this theme in other fund-raising activities, commissioning and selling songs and poems that validated the place of Confederate heroes within the nation as well as the region.[7]

The heroes in this story, however, were not all men. Borglum's design included a "symbolic sanctuary," a vast hall in white women's honor carved into the heart of the mountain below the sculpted army. The womblike space, a hall of records as well as a place of contemplation, would celebrate women's roles as the mothers and wives of soldiers and as the initial planners of the monument and keepers of the Confederate past. Borglum proposed to carve a massive seated figure of a white southern woman in the center of the hall out of the very rock of the mountain. Entitled *Memory,* the sculpture (fig. 13.3) would memorialize white women's wartime courage and suffering. Planners, however, chose an idealized rather than a specific Confederate "heroine," in contrast with the mountainside relief. Modern southern nationalism, in conjunction with the expansive American nationalism of which it was a part, symbolically provided an important place for white women, an inclusion that also marked off gender difference with its less dramatic, less visible interior space and generic woman.[8]

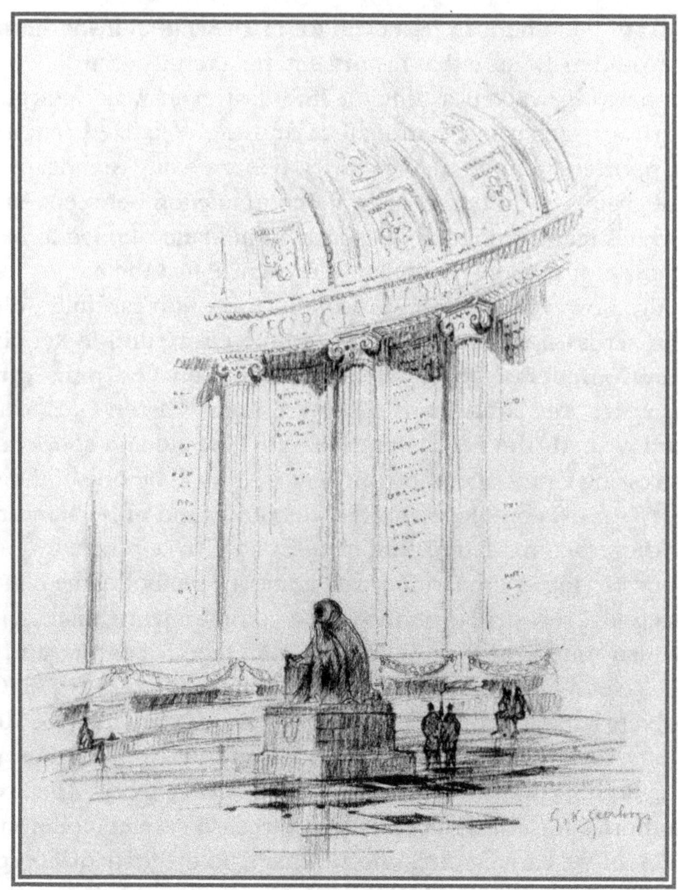

Fig. 13.3. Drawing for an allegorical sculpture of *Memory* that Gutzon Borglum proposed for a hall carved into the heart of Stone Mountain beneath his planned relief. Stone Mountain Collection, Robert W. Woodruff Library, Emory University.

## *Squabbling and Klan Politics*

On January 19, 1924, the completed head of Lee was ceremoniously unveiled. A stream of articles in popular national magazines as well as Borglum's successful lecture tours kept the country informed of the progress. Travel writers described even the unfinished carving as a tourist attraction. A letter to the *Atlanta Constitution* from a sympathetic northerner, reprinted under the caption "The Memorial's Cash Value," predicted that the mountain would make Atlanta the tourist "mecca of American and of other peoples for all times." In December 1925, *Forbes Magazine* hailed the project as a spectacular transformation of nature itself and as the creation of a truly American art, the nation's "answer to the ancient charge that the country is too absorbed in the pursuit of wealth to be interested in the more enduring things of the spirit."[9]

Yet by 1925 the Stone Mountain monument, planned to make the Lee-led Confederate army the symbol of sectional reconciliation and American international grandeur, competed with the

1925 *Scopes* trial for attention as a very different kind of symbol. Relations between Borglum and the SMCMA soured within months of the unveiling as technical problems at the mountain and miscommunication over medals to be given to young contributors delayed the actual carving. The 1924 presidential elections and the Ku Klux Klan's factional infighting greatly exacerbated tensions between Borglum and association president Hollins Randolph, reelected in April 1924 in ethically questionable circumstances. Borglum, a nationally active Republican, and Randolph, a member of the Georgia State Democratic Party with national ambitions, would have had difficulty getting along anyway, but the situation became exponentially more treacherous when combined with Klan politics. Borglum, Venable, and Randolph were all active Klan members but aligned themselves by 1924 with competing national Klan leaders. Randolph turned his anger over the defeat of his presidential candidate against his opponent both in national and Klan politics, Gutzon Borglum.[10]

By 1925 the squabbling became public and the national press hailed the infighting among Borglum, the UDC, the Memorial Association, and Venable, the mountain's owner, as an example of old-fashioned political machine patronage in the same league as the old-fashioned religion on display at the "Monkey Trial" in Dayton, Tennessee. That the allegations against the SMCMA (fig. 13.4) of corruption, theft, and mismanagement of funds involved charges of Ku Klux Klan involvement only made the story better copy. After all, the Klan, resurrected after the Atlanta lynching of Leo Frank in the same year as the memorial's birth, had marked its reorganization with a late-night ceremony atop Stone Mountain and continued to hold ceremonies and meetings there. Borglum, Venable, and the Atlanta chapter of the UDC, many of whose members had been purged from the executive committee, accused Randolph and his by then crony-packed association of both financial mismanagement and Klan membership. In its defense, the SMCMA countered that Borglum, not its board members, had joined the Klan; the association fired the sculptor in February 1925.[11]

With his flare for the dramatic, Borglum smashed his clay models with an ax (left photogenically at the scene) and fled the state. His supporters, seizing on Randolph's known Klan connections, claimed falsely that Borglum feared attack by the very Klan of which he was a member, and the Randolph-led SMCMA in turn sued the sculptor for destruction of property. While the governor of North Carolina provided him sanctuary, Borglum countered that his dismissal came after his departure. In keeping with his national interpretation of the memorial, he suggested that a national committee take over the work of Randolph's scandal-plagued board. The Atlanta UDC and Venable attacked the SMCMA for embezzlement and mismanagement of the hundreds of thousands of dollars donated for the project. In particular, the Daughters railed against the large commissions paid to fund-raisers who, the women believed, should have donated their services out of patriotism.[12]

Through the political allegiances of their editors, the Atlanta newspapers became involved in the battle as well. The *Journal* backed the association, while the *Constitution* sided with Borglum, the UDC, and Venable. Randolph and *Constitution* editor Clark Howell, who was a supporter of Venable and the Atlanta UDC's attacks on the SMCMA, denigrated each other's white manliness as they feuded. Exactly what the men said when Howell, in Randolph's words, invaded his office "without appointment" and "unannounced," remained in dispute. Howell insisted that he "flayed" the association president about the group's financial improprieties and that no "brave or self-respecting man would have sat in his chair and swallowed the rebuke I administered to that contemptible coward, as it was whiningly swallowed." Randolph countered that "no man who knows me, or no man who knows Clark Howell, believes for one moment that he could have called me a traitor and a renegade in my presence without suffering immediate chastisement. His statement is utterly and absolutely false." Both Howell and Randolph argued the authenticity of their descriptions of events by claiming that no white man would have behaved as the other described.[13]

With the Atlanta UDC having taken an important role in planning the memorial and then attacking the association's executive committee, the fight soon shifted from arguments about white manly behavior and Klan membership to competing conceptions of white womanly duties. In April of 1925 the association tried to bury the controversy and continue the fund-raising by swiftly hiring another sculptor, Virginia-born Augustus Lukeman, who was not as well known as Borglum. As a southerner, the SMCMA insisted, Lukeman would put patriotism before artistic ego, the glory of "the Southland" before his own fame. Lukeman cited artistic ethics in refusing to finish Borglum's work and instead began planning his own design and making new models for the carving. Lukeman and the SMCMA quickly unveiled the new plan, placing much more emphasis in their publicity on the women's part of the memorial. The Memorial Hall honoring white

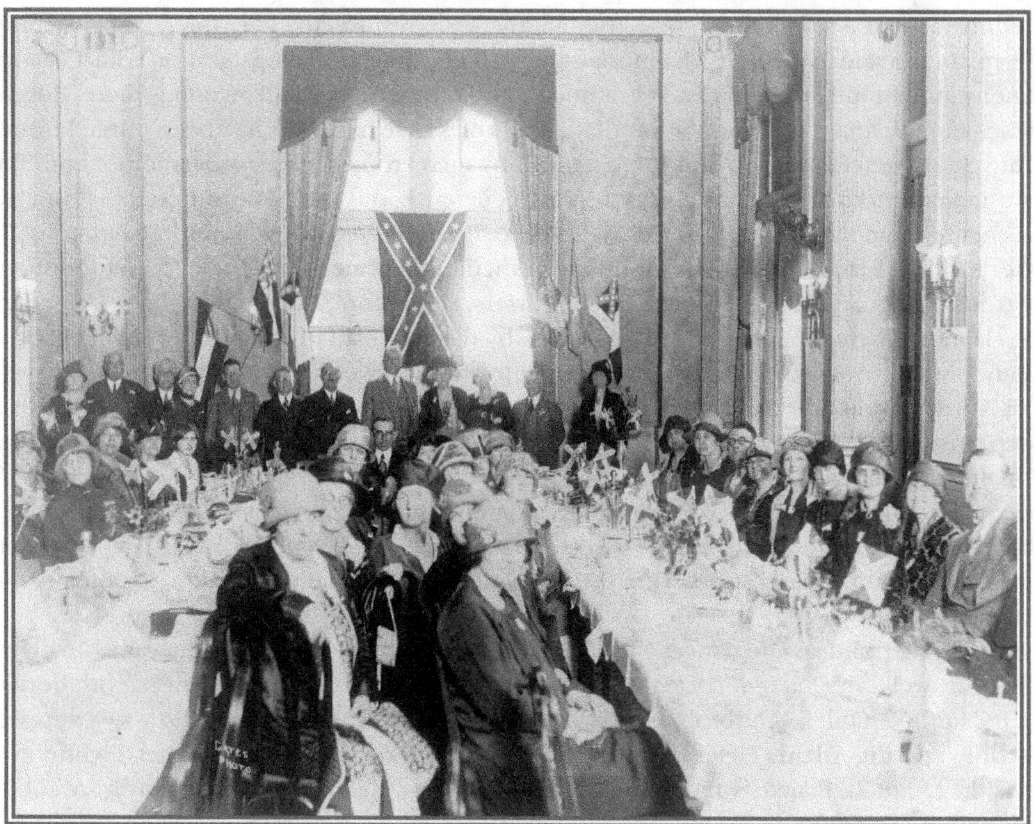

Fig. 13.4. Members of the Stone Mountain Confederate Memorial Association and other officials celebrate Georgia Day at a luncheon, probably February 12, 1925. Stone Mountain Collection, Robert W. Woodruff Library, Emory University.

southern women would still be hewn into the base of the mountain under the carving, the women standing symbolically beneath the men. Lukeman's carved figure of *Memory* no longer represented an anonymous woman, however, but became a likeness of the late Helen Plane. In the seemingly unending need for comparison of its plans to other American monuments, the SMCMA bragged that the statue of Plane would be at least two feet higher than the figure of the enemy president that graced the Lincoln Memorial in Washington. And that figure of Lincoln, an *Atlanta Journal* reporter emphasized, would eventually "crumble to pieces" as its sanctuary gave way, while "the figure symbolizing the bravery and sacrifice, the toil and privation of the women of the Confederacy, will remain untouched forever by the ruthless hand of time . . . enduring as long as the mountain endures."[14]

Whether intentionally or not, the new plans had the potential to split the Atlanta Daughters, who stood steadfastly behind Borglum and Venable, from other white women and their organizations, including other UDC chapters, who might decide to remain supportive of the SMCMA. After all, support for the memorial meant the glorification of white women too, as the association took pains to express publicly. Southern "ladies," the association pleaded in its revised plans, could trust it to fix not only men's but also women's place within history in stone. Neither the national nor state-level UDC had ever officially joined the Atlanta chapter in taking on the project, and some UDC chapters as well as Mrs. William A. Wright, state president for Georgia of the Confederate Southern Memorial Association, eventually sided with the SMCMA against the Atlanta UDC.[15]

As the association tried to win back support after the nationally publicized humiliations of 1925, it appealed to the nation, the region, and to these "true" upholders of white southern womanhood. The Lukeman design celebrated both the region and the nation, featuring two flags, Confederate and American, and two sets of thirteen and forty-eight stars, corresponding to Confederate and current states, leading to the Memorial Hall.[16]

Most significantly, however, the new executive committee of the SMCMA, purged by the reelected Randolph of all female members except Mrs. T. T. Stephens and Mildred Lewis Rutherford, demanded that the women leave the building of the memorial to the men. "The UDC are good women, all of them," stressed association attorney Reuben Arnold, "but they couldn't build the monument . . . . If Venable, Borglum, and the UDC could build the memorial I would be in favor of letting them do it." Hooper Alexander, the attorney for the Atlanta chapter of the UDC countered, "Do they mean to say that these good ladies can't finish the memorial? Whose patient toil and loving loyalty erected the monuments to Confederate valor that pierce the skies from every cemetery and almost all the country graveyards in Georgia? What money did these good women ever lose except the sums they put in the banks that failed through the mismanagement of men?" The UDC women, Alexander declared, were "like the real mother of the child Solomon threatened to cut in two." They did "not want to see the memorial destroyed." Had the men on the association's board been as self-sacrificing as these women, opponents implied, the goal of finishing the memorial while some Confederate Veterans still lived would have been realized.[17]

As funds ran out, the plan to carve white southern glory permanently in stone degenerated into a public squabble about the relative regional loyalties and selfless patriotism of white men and women. By April 9, 1928, the sixty-third anniversary of the surrender at Appomattox, Lukeman unveiled his own head of Lee atop a half-carved horse. The association, which had defeated the UDC's lawsuit to stop the destruction of Borglum's work, had the original head of Lee blasted off the mountain.

## *Waning Enthusiasm*

Along with the *Scopes* trial, the conspicuous failure of the Stone Mountain Memorial project provoked national criticism of the region, a sort of cynical new sectionalism. The momentum and national enthusiasm for the project had waned. And financial depression came early to the South, following the boll weevil east in the late 1920s and making a strictly regional funding of the carving impossible. Even the UDC's publicized endorsement of the SMCMA and the project in the late 1920s provided little help. The association eventually went bankrupt, and Lee floated vaguely above a ghostly Traveller until work resumed on the project in the 1960s. Borglum went on to plan and carve the much more explicitly national monument upon Mount Rushmore in the Black Hills of South Dakota. By the early 1930s the Stone Mountain Memorial's bickering factions represented the "Solid South" more accurately than the granite mountain. And visitors to the mountainside saw not "the eighth wonder of the world," but a "vaccination scar," that in the words of one critic made "the face of Stone Mountain immune from ever having a monument there."[18]

Ten years later tourists paid a dime to see through field glasses the white South's embarrassment rather than its glory. A sly reporter claimed that the folks running the concession assured guests that Lee's roughed-in companion was indeed Jefferson Davis and would not look so much like Abraham Lincoln when the bushy beard left by Lukeman was "chiseled down." Various groups of Atlanta businessmen and UDC officials tried from 1934 onward to raise funds and recommission Borglum. Riding a crest of fame from his ongoing work on the national memorial at Mount Rushmore, Borglum released to the news media several revised models that repositioned on the mountain his original plan for a granite gray army at double the scale.[19]

The vaccination that had made that scar seemed to make the mountain and the land surrounding it immune from national park status as well. By the late 1930s, Georgia state park officials were trying to get the federal government "to add Stone Mountain to its chain of natural wonders." The National Park Service's survey of the monolith, however, found that the scars in the granite from carving and quarrying destroyed the site's value as nature. The unfinished memorial in this case had become a liability.[20]

In 1941 Gov. Eugene Talmadge created a new group, the Stone Mountain Memorial Commission, to resurrect the carving project. This commission quickly persuaded the Works Project Administration to supply the labor. When Borglum died that year, the commission hired Julian Harris, a young Georgia sculptor, to redesign once again the mountain carving. Yet federal support as well as a proposed Reconstruction Finance Corporation loan disappeared in late 1941 as the nation directed its resources toward the war. As a well-known World War II veteran, Harris tried again four years later to jump-start the memorial in perhaps the last pre–Civil Rights era moment when the national and state governments might have come together to fund the project. Victorious Americans, however, were little interested in a Confederate past in 1945, and the state of Georgia got public projects in the form of expanded military bases instead. Lee on his watery Traveller, a faint Lincoln-like Davis at his side, rode on above the slag and weeds until the Second Reconstruction gave renewed impetus to the regional racial nationalism that had inspired the memorial more than forty years earlier.[21]

## *Finishing the Carving*

Across the South, the rising tide of African American activism in the wake of the 1954 *Brown* vs. *Board of Education* Supreme Court decision reignited broad interest in Confederate symbols as many white southerners girded up for battle with the nation again. In Georgia, Gov. Samuel

Marvin Griffin pledged in his 1955 campaign that "so long as Marvin Griffin is your governor there will be no mixing of the races in the classrooms of our schools and colleges of Georgia." By 1956 the new state flag, two-thirds of its area the "Battle Flag of the Confederacy," as approved by the Confederate states congress, flew over these still-segregated educational institutions. Two years later, Griffin and the Georgia general assembly formed the Stone Mountain Memorial Association (SMMA), which purchased the mountain for a state park with $1.1 million of public funds. Hoping to finish carving the Lukeman plan by 1961, the hundredth anniversary of the beginning of the War between the States, Griffin urged the staging of a "'Century of Progress' made in the South" celebration. While the use of prison labor to build the lake and other facilities might have suggested to some observers that little had changed in the region, it was little noted in print. For the governor and other supporters of the new plans, the completion of the carving would demonstrate instead to the rest of the nation that "progress" meant not black rights but the maintenance of white supremacy.[22]

State politicians formed Stone Mountain Park, then, as part of an effort to ground the white southern present in images of the southern past, a sort of neo-Confederatism, and to halt nationally mandated change in the region. Fittingly, planners added "as genuine a reproduction of a pre–Civil War Georgia plantation as research can make" to the other attractions such as the marina, game ranch, and aerial cableway that drew visitors to the park while the third sculptor, Walker Hancock, finished carving Lukeman's design. Pamphlets publicizing the plantation as an attraction sanitized slavery, while the plantation's buildings and landscape naturalized a hierarchical and yet peaceful antebellum racial order. The slave quarters were "neat" and well furnished, the promotional material insisted, and many masters in Georgia freed their slaves voluntarily before the "War between the States." Except to identify the two cabins themselves, park publications never used the term *slave;* instead, the park called bonds people "hands" and "workers."[23] Demonstrating their marketing genius when the plantation attraction opened in 1963, park officials employed a down-and-out Butterfly McQueen to live in the "Big House's" kitchen and greet visitors. Fusing regional and national versions of the "plantation romance" in its most popular representation, Atlantan Margaret Mitchell's *Gone with the Wind* and its Hollywood adaptation, the actress's reappearance as "Prissy" made Stone Mountain's plantation into *the* southern plantation, Tara. Stone Mountain Park dropped the original name of the site, Stone Acres, in advertising the attraction. Plans to build a Margaret Mitchell museum at the mountain never materialized, but through its "authentic" plantation, recreation park promoters capitalized on international interest in the novel and the movie anyway. McQueen stopped working at the park in 1965, and by 1968 her threatened lawsuit ended the park's use of her photograph to promote the plantation. Nonetheless, public perception of Stone Mountain's plantation as Tara remained. At this popular attraction, white southerners as well as other whites—the park was initially segregated—could visit an imagined time and place when white southerners created, in the guise of authentic recreation, their own racial utopia.[24]

Despite the violent resistance of many white southerners to southern blacks' demands for greater rights, the nation won this reconstruction. Atlanta seemed paradoxically both excited and embarrassed by the unveiling at last of the finished Stone Mountain Memorial in 1970 (fig. 13.5). When James Venable, Imperial Wizard of the Knights of the Ku Klux Klan and a descendant of Sam Venable, protested the inclusion of Dr. William Holmes Borders, the African American minister of the Wheat Street Baptist Church, on the program as "repugnant to a sense of respect due the memory of the confederates [*sic*] veterans," the SMMA ignored him. Park officials did protest the substitution of Vice President Spiro Agnew for President Richard Nixon, who had been scheduled

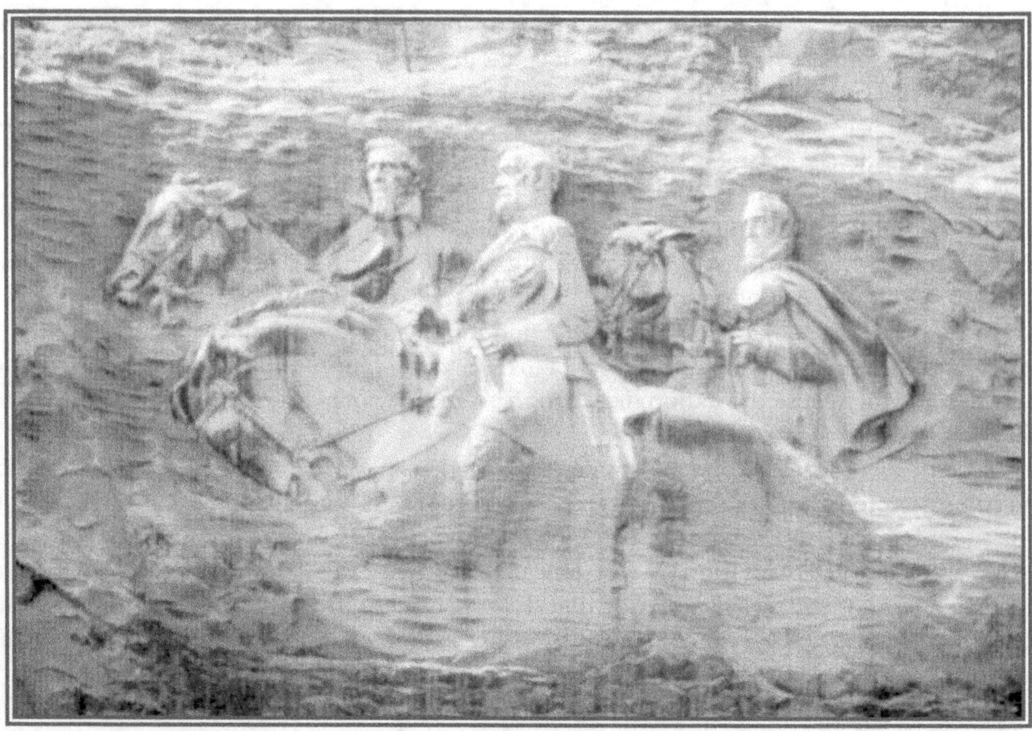

Fig. 13.5. The completed Stone Mountain Memorial, dedicated May 9, 1970.
Stone Mountain Collection, Robert W. Woodruff Library, Emory University.

to speak but canceled in the wake of the invasion of Cambodia. SMMA member and State Agriculture Commissioner Tommy Irvin demanded that Nixon appear and "afford the South the respect it deserves." Emory University historian Bell Wiley, another SMMA member, attacked Agnew's scheduled appearance directly as "an affront to General Lee": "General Lee believed in the right of dissent . . . and he did not believe that college students and teachers were bums." The *Constitution* editorially backed Wiley's position, proclaiming that Lee would never have "dismissed dissenters as 'effete snobs'" as Agnew had done, and reminding its readers that Lee had been a college president. While the SMMA passed a resolution welcoming Agnew anyway, Wiley had claimed Lee as a symbol of progressive protest in place of Griffin's white figures of reactionary resistance. At the unveiling, arch segregationists and southern Democrats Lester Maddox and Herman Talmadge shared the podium with the Republican Agnew, providing a dramatic glimpse of the not so distant regional political future. But in the *Constitution*'s editorial cartoon, behind the speaking Agnew the stone figures of Lee, Jackson, and Davis covered their faces with their hats.[25]

Confederate heroes did not, of course, become the cultural symbols that inspired American leftist and radical activism. Much more recent conflicts featuring fire hoses, protest signs, and unarmed African American civilians as well as white soldiers shaped the historical memories of the southern Vietnam War protestors who competed for attention with the memorial's unveiling. Advances in technology, however, allowed Stone Mountain Park to forgo another decade of carving. By the 1980s, the Stone Mountain Park laser show had become as big an attraction as the

Confederate heroes. Using the granite dome itself as a screen, the lasers painted another famous southern face right over those figures of Jackson, Lee, and Davis. When Martin Luther King Jr. said he had reached the mountaintop, he did not know how literally he meant it. The ever-changing laser imagery allowed the state park to be all things to all people by night even as the daylight face of the carving remained unchanged.[26]

## *Notes*

This article is reprinted, in slightly abridged form, from the *Georgia Historical Quarterly* 82, no. 1 (spring 1998): 22–44.

1. Mildred Lewis Rutherford, "The History of Stone Mountain," (n.p.: the Georgia Division of the United Daughters of the Confederacy, 1923), handwritten chronology and notes, and Ralph T. Jones, "Man's Brain Cannot Measure the Myriad Ages of Time Needed to Make That Block of Granite: The Monument Now Being Cut Will Remain for Millions of Years," *Atlanta Constitution*, Aug. 5, 1923, all in the Stone Mountain file, Hargrett Rare Book and Manuscript Collection, Univ. of Georgia, Athens (hereafter SMUGA). See also Historical Note for the Stone Mountain Collection and the correspondence of the Stone Mountain Confederate Memorial Association (hereafter SMCMA), 1915, in box 1, Stone Mountain Collection, Robert W. Woodruff Library, Emory Univ., Atlanta (hereafter SMEU).

2. Rutherford, "The History of Stone Mountain," and Craig F. Thompson, "The Stone Mountain Fiasco," *Plain Talk*, undated clipping, ca. 1928, both in SMUGA.

3. *New York Times Magazine,* Jan. 2, 1916. James C. Derieux, "A Sculptor Who Rode to Fame on Horseback," *American Magazine* (Jan. 1924): 12–14, 66, 68, 70, 72, quotation on 13; Rutherford, "The History of Stone Mountain," and "The Memorial Idea: A Brief Sketch of the Beginnings of the Movement for a Confederate Memorial," *Stone Mountain Magazine,* Apr. 20, 1923, 5, 6, all in SMUGA.

4. Angus Perkerson, "World's Biggest Photograph to Be Printed on Face of Stone Mountain," *Atlanta Journal Magazine,* Dec. 10, 1922, 1, 4. Rutherford, "History of the Stone Mountain Memorial," 3–5.

5. Derieux, "A Sculptor," 72; Don Winter, "Its Message and Its Memories," and "The Memorial Idea," 6, all in SMUGA. On Lee as a symbol, see Thomas L. Connelly, *The Marble Man* (New York: Knopf, 1977). On national reunification from the late nineteenth century through the 1920s, see Nina Silber, *The Romance of Reunion* (Chapel Hill: Univ. of North Carolina Press, 1994); Michael Rogin, "'The Sword Became a Flashing Vision': D. W. Griffith's *Birth of a Nation,*" in *Ronald Reagan, the Movie and Other Episodes in Political Demonology* (Berkeley: Univ. of California Press, 1987); and Nancy MacLean, *Behind the Mask of Chivalry: The Making of the Second Ku Klux Klan* (New York: Oxford Univ. Press, 1994).

6. SMCMA, "Custodians of Imperishable Glory" (Atlanta: SMCMA, 1925), 6; "The Memorial Idea," 6; and Warren G. Harding, Washington, D.C., Apr. 16, 1923, to Hollins N. Randolph, chairman, SMCMA, Atlanta, reprinted in *Stone Mountain Magazine* 3 (1923): 14; all in SMUGA. It is often difficult in the post–Civil Rights Movement era to remember the extent to which American and white southern nationalisms were not only compatible but often linked in the first half of the twentieth century. On nationalism in general, see Benedict Anderson, *Imagined Communities: Reflections on the Origin and Spread of Nationalism* (London: Verso, 1983). On the relationship between regional and U.S. nationalisms, see Nell Irvin Painter, *Standing at Armageddon: The United States, 1877–1919* (New York: W. W. Norton, 1987); and Silber, *The Romance of Reunion.*

7. Frederic J. Haskin, *Savannah News,* Dec. 15, 1925; "Custodians of Imperishable Glory," 2; SMCMA letter to "Banks, Bankers, and the General Public," n.d.; SMCMA, "Stone Mountain Belongs to the Nation," n.d.,

attached to previous letter; SMCMA, "Buy Confederate Memorial Coins: The Nation's Tribute to the South," undated promotional pamphlet; Association for the Information of the American People, "The Confederate Memorial Half-Dollar," undated pamphlet; Rogers Winter, "The Founders Roll," undated pamphlet; SMCMA, "The Children's Founders Roll," undated pamphlet; SMCMA, "A Plan for the Children of the Confederacy . . . ," undated flyer; "The Memorial Song," 15–17, and Herbert Myrick, Springfield, Mass., "Patriot's Day, 1922, to the *Atlanta Constitution,*" reprinted as "The Memorial's Cash Value," in *Stone Mountain Magazine* 1 (Apr. 20, 1923): 12; Virginia Milmow, *Stone Mountain: A Song and March* (Atlanta: SMCMA, 1926), all in SMUGA.

8. Rose V. S. Berry, "Gutzon Borglum and His Stone Mountain Plan," *Art and Archaeology* (May 1923): 229–332; Winter, "The Founders Roll"; SMCMA, "A Plan for the Children of the Confederacy"; and A. J. Hain, "The World's Most Wonderful Memorial: The Great Borglum Sculpture on Stone Mountain, Georgia," *Landmark* (June 1924), all in SMUGA.

9. Richard Peckham, "Commemorating a Great Lost Cause," *Travel* (Oct. 1924): 21–22; "The World's Most Wonderful Monument," *McClure's Magazine* (Jan. 1924); Forrest Dunne, "A Mountain Speaks for America to a World of Critics," *Forbes Magazine* (Dec. 1, 1925): 15–16, 67, quotation on 15; "Making a Monument Out of a Mountain," *Scientific American* (Aug. 1924); Hain, "World's Most Wonderful Memorial"; and other 1923–25 clippings, all in SMUGA.

10. Craig F. Thompson, "The Stone Mountain Fiasco," *Plain Talk,* undated clipping ca. 1928; "Borglum and Tucker Are Sought on Warrants Following Destruction of Memorial Models," *Atlanta Constitution,* Feb. 26, 1925; "Stone Mountain Not Given to Daughters of Confederacy, Memorial Historian Shows," *Atlanta Georgian,* Mar. 14, 1925; "Howell's Statement False, Says Hollins N. Randolph in Card to the Public," *Atlanta Journal,* Mar. 29, 1925; Walter Davenport, "The Battle of Stone Mountain," *Liberty* (May 16, 1925): 13–16; and "Notable Work of New Mountain Sculptor," *Atlanta Journal,* Apr. 19, 1925; all in SMUGA. On the founding of the second Klan at Stone Mountain in 1915, see Kenneth T. Jackson, *The Ku Klux Klan in the City* (New York: Oxford Univ. Press, 1967), 5. For sorting out the complicated infighting, I am grateful to David B. Freeman, whose *Carved in Stone: The History of Stone Mountain* (Macon: Mercer Univ. Press, 1997) was published while I was editing this piece.

11. Craig F. Thompson, "The Stone Mountain Fiasco," *Plain Talk,* undated clipping ca. 1928; "Borglum and Tucker Are Sought on Warrants"; "Stone Mountain Not Given to Daughters of Confederacy"; "Howell's Statement False"; and Walter Davenport, "The Battle of Stone Mountain," *Liberty* (May 16, 1925): 13–16.

12. Thompson, "The Stone Mountain Fiasco"; "Borglum and Tucker Are Sought on Warrants"; "Stone Mountain Not Given to Daughters of Confederacy"; "Howell's Statement False."

13. "Howell's Statement False."

14. Quoted from Frances Newman, "300,000 Visitors at Stone Mountain Each Year," *Atlanta Journal,* June 20, 1926. "Etching by Sculptor Lukeman Shows How Figures Will Appear High on Stone Mountain Precipice," *Atlanta Journal,* Jan. 17, 1926; and "Fifty Year Quit Claim Deed to Stone Mountain Is Owned by Association, Letter Says," *Atlanta Constitution,* Aug. 15, 1927. See also Frederic J. Haskin, "Stone Mountain," *Savannah News,* Dec. 12, 1925; and Augustus Lukeman, "An American Monument to Surpass the Pyramids," *World's Week* 51 (Mar. 1926): 488.

15. Quotation from "Etching by Sculptor Lukeman." See also "Fifty Year Quit Claim Deed to Stone Mountain"; and Frederic J. Haskin, "Stone Mountain," *Savannah News,* Dec. 12, 1925; and Augustus Lukeman, "An American Monument to Surpass the Pyramids," *World's Week* 51 (Mar. 1926): 488.

16. "Etching by Sculptor Lukeman" and Lukeman, "An American Monument to Surpass the Pyramids," 488.

17. Quotations from "Stone Mountain Measure Argued before Committee," *Atlanta Journal,* July 8, 1927. "Buy Confederate Memorial Coins," undated pamphlet, SMUGA; "Memorial Body Is Out of Funds, Venable

States," *Atlanta Journal,* Sept. 30, 1928; and Lamar Sparks, "Stone Mountain Memorial Gains Support of Georgia Division UDC," *Atlanta Journal,* undated clipping from late 1928 or early 1929.

18. Quotation from "Stone Mountain Measure Argued before Committee." Thompson, "The Stone Mountain Fiasco"; "Borglum and Tucker Are Sought on Warrants"; "Stone Mountain Not Given to Daughters of Confederacy"; "Howell's Statement False"; Davenport, "The Battle of Stone Mountain," 13–16; and "Notable Work of New Mountain Sculptor," *Atlanta Journal,* Apr. 19, 1925; all in SMUGA. On the founding of the second Klan at Stone Mountain in 1915, see Jackson, *The Ku Klux Klan in the City,* 5.

19. "Memorial to Confederate Dead May Be Completed," *Macon Telegraph,* Apr. 24, 1937; and "Borglum Plans New Carving," *Atlanta Journal,* July 3, 1932.

20. "Stone Mountain May Become a National Park," *Southeast Georgian,* Dec. 14, 1939; *Athens Banner,* "Stone Mountain Memorial," Apr. 8, 1940.

21. "Stone Mountain May Become a National Park"; "Stone Mountain Memorial," *Athens Banner,* Apr. 8, 1940; "Harris Outlines Memorial Project as Defense Recreation Center," *Dekalb New Era,* Sept. 18, 1940; Sgt. Walter Paschall, "Post-War Stone Mountain," *Atlanta Journal Magazine,* May 11, 1945; and Freeman, *Stone Mountain,* 133–34.

22. James F. Cook, *Governors of Georgia* (Huntsville: Strode, 1979), 272–76; Oscar Johnson, "Griffin Says He's Ready to Buy Stone Mountain, Finish Project," *Atlanta Constitution,* undated clipping from 1957 or 1958; *Encyclopedia of Georgia* (New York: Somerset Publishers, 1993), 3, 73; "Historical Note," box 1, SMEU, and "Stone Mountain to Echo Prison Choir's Songs," *Atlanta Journal,* undated clipping from early 1960s.

23. On the Stone Mountain Plantation, see "Souvenir of Stone Mountain Park," Plastichrome Travel Series; and "The Ante-bellum Plantation," undated pamphlets published between 1962 and 1969, in SMUGA.

24. Juanita Karpf, "Thelma 'Butterfly' McQueen," in *Notable Black American Women,* ed. Jessie Carney Smith, 710–15 (Detroit: Gale Research, 1992); "Butterfly McQueen Wins GA High Court Plea," *Jet* 33 (Mar. 28, 1968): 55; Freeman, *Stone Mountain,* 149; and "Stone Mount Would Affix Memorial to Margaret Mitchell," *Eastman Times-Journal,* Sept. 1, 1949.

25. Program, "Stone Mountain Memorial Carving Dedication," May 9, 1970, SMUGA, error not the paper's but Venable's; Gene Stephens, "100,000 Due at Stone Mountain Ceremonies," editorial, "Shame and Disgrace," and editorial cartoon by "Baldy," all in *Atlanta Constitution,* May 9, 1970; and Don Winter, "Mountain Carving Has Day of Glory," *Atlanta Journal,* May 9, 1970.

26. In his 1963 "I Have a Dream" speech at the Lincoln Memorial in Washington, D.C., King declared, "Let freedom ring from Stone Mountain of Georgia!" The controversies over Stone Mountain's delineation of history continue in the new millennium. In the fall of 2000 a company announced plans to build a $100 million southern history theme park at the site. See Somini Sengupta, "Georgia Park Is to Hail 'Southern Spirit,'" *New York Times,* Oct. 8, 2000. Critics warned that commercialization of the 3,200-acre park might endanger its natural beauty. "Georgia Park Adds Features as Critics Fret," *New York Times,* Nov. 25, 2001.

# 14

# Contesting the Sacred

PRESERVATION AND MEANING ON RICHMOND'S MONUMENT AVENUE

*Brian Black and Bryn Varley*

ON JULY 10, 1996, history was made in Richmond, Virginia, by an event incongruous with the city's past role as capital of the Confederacy. Five impressive statues dedicated to Confederate heroes had imbued the city's Monument Avenue with sacred meaning for many southern whites over the last century. But on this day more than two thousand people looked on as Monument Avenue's mandate expanded to include a sculpture of a black man in sweats: Arthur Ashe, the tennis champion of the 1970s. Reactions to the addition of his image were mixed indeed.

Since the dedication of its first statue in 1890, this grand Richmond avenue had served as a central symbol of the Lost Cause, a defense in stone and bronze of the honor and heroism of Confederate participants in the Civil War. Thus the installation of the Ashe monument outraged many southerners. One protester explained: "My ancestors fought with the twenty-first Virginia Infantry . . . and I think this place is inappropriate." Before the unveiling, hate fliers attributed to the Ku Klux Klan were distributed throughout the neighborhood, referring to Ashe as "an AIDS infected nigger."[1]

L. Douglas Wilder, the former Virginia governor who led the effort to memorialize Ashe on Monument Avenue, acknowledged the controversy with wry sarcasm in his address to the diverse dedication-day crowd (fig. 14.1). "Some say he doesn't deserve to be here," said Wilder. "Some say he deserves better." Ashe's widow, Jeanne Moutoussamy-Ashe, chose not to attend the unveiling, commenting that she was "afraid that a statue of Arthur Ashe on Monument Avenue honors Richmond, Virginia, more than it does its son, his legacy, and his life's work."[2] Some Ashe supporters wished the sculpture to be placed in another part of town where more of the city's black population lived. As one of Ashe's early classmates said of the elite white neighborhood, "We couldn't ever go to Monument" while growing up in Richmond.[3]

The conflicting views about the Ashe monument's placement, together with earlier debates about Monument Avenue, offer a dramatic case study of how the meaning of a public site can change over time. Further, Monument Avenue is a prime example of "sacred space." Historians including Edward T. Linenthal and David Chidester have argued that in modern society such special spaces have been set apart from ordinary environments to provide arenas for human ritual, or

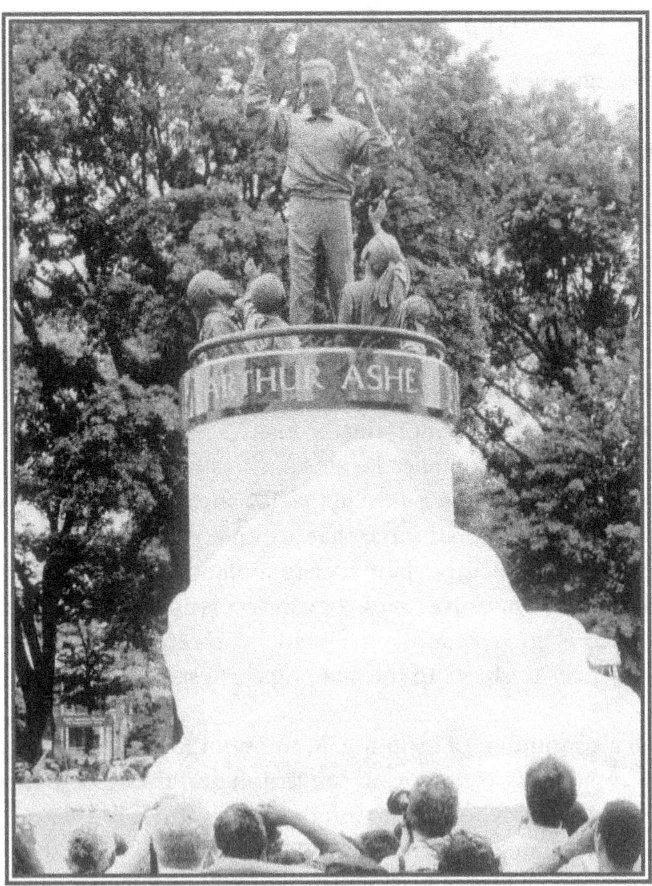


Fig. 14.1. Unveiling of the Arthur Ashe Memorial by Paul DiPasquale, Monument Avenue, Richmond, Virginia. *Richmond Times-Dispatch*, July 10, 1996. Photograph by Alexa Welch Edlund.

"extraordinary" patterns of action.[4] Defining a ritual site helps a community express its vision of what is important. But these locales can become sites of controversy later when decisions must be made about historic preservation—decades after original notions of consensus have faded. That happened along Monument Avenue in the 1990s.

Throughout the twentieth century, the avenue's larger-than-life statues of Confederate icons helped assure that the Lost Cause was not forgotten, but how it was to be remembered remained open to debate. Memory of place is not static but is constantly being contested and redefined. A community seeking to maintain a sacred site must constantly reaffirm its attitudes toward the past.

By the 1990s, Monument Avenue summoned up ideas about racial oppression and exclusion for some residents of Richmond, while for others it evoked a proud Confederate heritage. This volatile combination created a hard-fought controversy over the location of the new monument. Just how did an African American tennis player end up memorialized on the city's most stately street, amid battle-seasoned Confederate generals on horseback? The answer says a great deal about American memory and the New South.

## *The Convergence of Space and Meaning*

Symbolic behavior distinguishes humans from other species. When we consider our immediate surroundings, for example, our perceptions blend with an abstract network of signs and symbols that we call myths, legends, and science. Geographer Yi-fu Tuan identifies the intellectually constructed worlds that result with a naturalistic term indicating their ability to protect or shield: he refers to them as cocoons. These interminglings of perception and cultural embellishments, he suggests, can alter the significance of our natural surroundings and stir an entirely new range of emotional reactions. Details of place in a church, school, or favorite meeting site, for instance, may influence our definitions of the sacred and profane. Our personal levels of interaction with a site also may cause us to look beyond its original significance. We try to explain ourselves through stories of place, which often become myths. They grow out of humans' desire to resolve psychic dilemmas of some kind—to cope with mortality or loss.[5]

This process of defining meaning makes locales such as battlefields, speech or demonstration sites, and Monument Avenue particularly instructive for students of cultural discourse. Some layers of meaning possess such emotional force that groups or individuals strive to preserve these sites or try to change them. This is especially true in a place like Monument Avenue, where passionate responses derive from opposing points of view on issues essentially unrelated to the natural site. Meaning of place is created subjectively and is rarely universal; it may be difficult for people of diverse experiences to share. In the ensuing contest, the sacred site becomes the trophy to be won.

Viewed against such a continuum of meaning, Monument Avenue's significance, then, begins in April 1861 with the secession of Virginia from the Union and the state's invitation to make Richmond the capital city of the newly formed Confederacy. As the rebel capital, Richmond took on symbolic importance immediately. Defended until the closing days of the war, the city fell into Union hands on April 2, 1865, just six days before Gen. Robert E. Lee's surrender at Appomattox. Union Gen. William Tecumseh Sherman's march to the sea marked the final decimation of southern commerce and culture, but the Confederacy's defeat was not consciously admitted until its heart—Richmond—was stilled. The city's importance was underscored when President Lincoln arrived April 3 to survey the regained territory and made his way directly to the Confederate White House. Lincoln sat in the chair behind Jefferson Davis's desk, demonstrating the Union's reestablished control.[6]

With this history, it made sense to many Virginians to pay homage to leading Confederates from this same site and to perpetuate a mythology about the war long after Lee's surrender. While this mandate has been clear throughout Monument Avenue's history, the Ashe debate was not the first attempt to modify the Confederate character of Richmond's central avenue.

Monument Avenue has been Richmond's proudest thoroughfare since it was created in the last decade of the nineteenth century to hold its first monument, that of General Lee, but it was never intended to be an avenue for all people.[7] Developers of the avenue, a westward growth of fashionable Franklin Street, took great care in designing the landscape that was to surround the huge shrine to Lee. Early property deeds literally kept Monument Avenue off limits for any but the most affluent of white citizens. Building restrictions, created to measure and check the growth and style of this new urban neighborhood, included prohibitions against renting or selling to blacks. African Americans were not welcome on the avenue, at least not at the front doors. Inherent in the avenue's design and layout are many back alleys created so that African American servants could enter and leave the elite homes without setting foot upon the avenue.

The land surrounding the monuments to the Confederate chieftains was treated as sacred from its inception. The large-scale commemoration of Confederate heroes that began with the huge Lee memorial (figs. 0.2 and 6.2) also signified the white establishment's resistance to the new interracial era proposed for a reunited nation's future. Many blacks were astounded by the scope of the unveiling celebration at the Lee monument in May 1890, decades after the abolition of slavery. The *Richmond Planet,* an African American newspaper published from 1883 to 1938, commented on the lack of social progress signified by the celebration in the southern capital. The event was scheduled to coincide with a Confederate veterans' reunion and the grandest parade ever seen in the South. Confederate flags were unfurled by thousands of veterans and supporters. These emblems, according to the *Planet,* "told in no uncertain terms that they still clung to theories which were presumed to be buried for all eternity."[8]

The *Planet,* an important public voice for the black population in Richmond at this time, published several articles arguing that the South's progress in the nation as a whole was retarded by this new commemoration of the Lost Cause and display of extreme views. Rather than aid national unity and patriotism, such efforts served to further alienate the South from the rest of the country. Memorialization of men such as Lee who fought for the states' rights doctrine would only hand down to future generations "a legacy of treason and blood," the paper said.[9]

The warnings and expressions of discomfort from the black community were largely ignored as the grand tributes to Confederate heroes continued. It would be many decades before the black population, which held little political or economic power, could organize or rally enough support and authority to make a significant stand against the commemoration of these heroes. Until that time, the sanctification of a history not their own was imposed upon all by the lessons in stone around the city.

Far from being reconciled into a single nation with joint causes, many white Richmonders continued to sanctify the Lost Cause in the next decade, and Monument Avenue expanded as a Confederate pantheon. By idealizing the past, supporters rallied for a segregated city. Over the years, the *Planet* repeatedly criticized the white governing bodies for being behind the times, calling segregation plans against all reason.[10]

In 1907 a second great reunion of Confederate veterans was marked by the dedication of two new monuments to such heroes. An equestrian statue of cavalry commander J. E. B. Stuart (fig. 6.4) rose east of the Lee memorial. West of the Lee monument, the president of the Confederacy, or as the *Planet* described him, "the President of the Lost Cause," Jefferson Davis was honored with a sixty-seven-foot-tall architectural monument (figs. 4.3 and 6.5) designed by the city's most prominent artist, Edward V. Valentine. The *Planet,* however, did not address the issues head-on as it once had; no campaign was launched against the Stuart and Davis memorials. The *Planet* coverage instead assumed that this kind of nostalgia was winding down as the "remnants of the armies of the gray" passed away.[11]

An article in the *Planet,* reprinted from the *Richmond News-Leader,* described some events that held out hope for a "healed" future for Richmond's black and white communities. On the same afternoon as the Davis monument unveiling, a contingent of black southerners and local Federal veterans decorated the graves of Federal soldiers in the National Cemetery and marched back through the city. A group of Confederate veterans who wandered from their own celebration were welcomed by these former enemies and slaves, the newspaper said. It described a similar inclusive spirit at the Confederate proceedings along Monument Avenue and Franklin Street: "Many Negroes were in the crowds along the sidewalk and they were among the most enthusiastic in applauding notable individuals and organizations as they passed." In its account, the *News-Leader* commented upon the "absolute good will that exists here in Richmond and in Virginia."[12]

As Richmond developed westward, Monument Avenue grew with it. Despite the declining health and number of Confederate veterans, memorial groups continued to flourish and another monument was proposed. In 1915 a black settlement was displaced in preparation for the arrival of Thomas "Stonewall" Jackson on horseback (fig. 6.6), a monument not unveiled until 1919. In spite of years of delay and desperate fund-raising, the event again attracted veterans nationwide and was celebrated with citywide pageantry.[13]

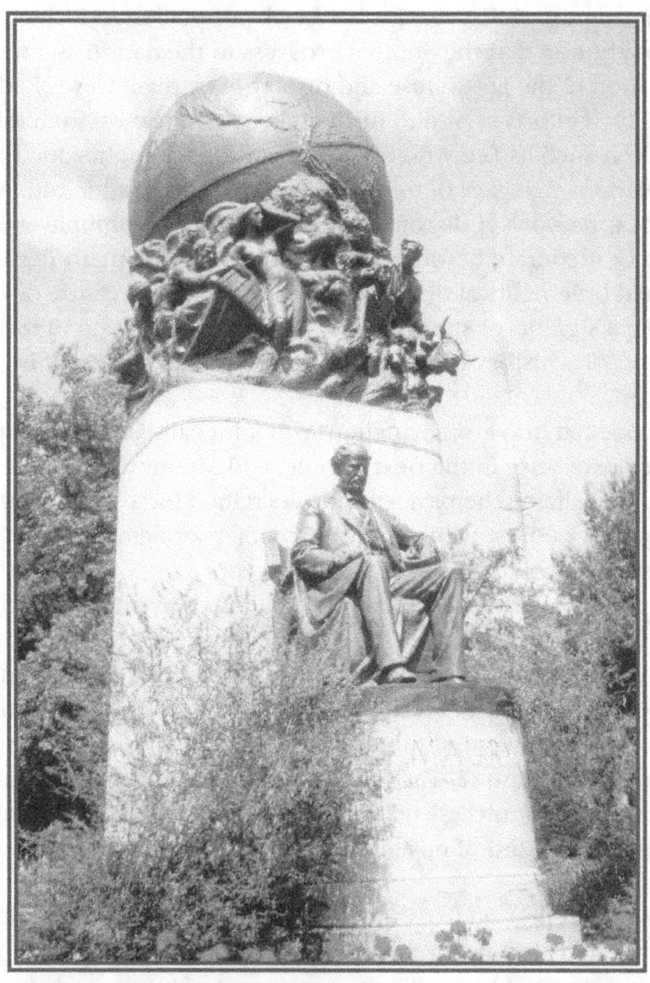

Fig. 14.2. Matthew Fontaine Maury Memorial, sculpted by William F. Sievers and unveiled November 11, 1929, Monument Avenue, Richmond. Photograph by Bryn Varley.

The final Confederate monument on the avenue was not unveiled until 1929. The occasion was again a reunion for those few veterans who survived. Matthew Fontaine Maury's memorial (figs. 14.2 and 6.7) was different in style and feeling from the equestrian statues, however. This figure sits calmly beneath a large globe, a rolled-up chart in his hand and a book at his feet. Although he served as a Confederate naval officer, Maury was best known for his oceanographic work, including wind and current charts of the Atlantic Ocean in the years before the conflict. This Pathfinder of the Seas was a source of international pride for the South. Yet his monument also was erected amid much Confederate pageantry.

The various reunions drew veterans from all over the South, often wearing their old Confederate uniforms. For a number of days, these aging men watched and marched in parades, attended meetings, and listened to addresses that focused on past military bravery and camaraderie. Their reunions, according to historian Edward L. Ayers, "seemed to validate the racial and political order that had emerged since the Civil War, de-emphasizing the fight to end slavery and replacing it with an emphasis on the shared experience of battle."[14]

## *Change in the Wind?*

Monument Avenue continued to grow westward and prosper throughout the twentieth century as the city's best-loved avenue. Over time the street itself had become a monument, retaining aspects of sacred space. But time did not stand still, and in 1965, amid the centennial of the Civil War and the Confederacy, Richmond's City Planning Commission suggested a major improvement and expansion scheme for Monument Avenue. In addition to upkeep and beautification, the report suggested slightly moving some of the existing statues for better public viewing or traffic flow. The question of the appropriate placement of the Maury statue also was reopened.[15]

The main focus of the CPC report, however, was a proposal for adding seven new monuments to the avenue, each with a Confederate theme. The public was deeply divided. Many descendants of veterans' groups such as the United Daughters of the Confederacy and the Sons of Confederate Veterans favored an extended Confederate commemoration but strongly opposed altering the existing cityscape—now viewed as a historically significant space that merited preservation.[16]

Other groups, such as the National Association for the Advancement of Colored People (NAACP), opposed any continuation of a theme that could be linked with the subjugation of an entire race. "We feel that the spirit of Richmond at the present time should be reflected," said Henry L. Marsh III, NAACP representative and future mayor. "We have no objection to honoring true heroes and founding fathers, but we object to continuing the Confederate theme."[17] Groups such as the NAACP did not yet exist during the early development of Monument Avenue, decades characterized by the expansion of Jim Crow laws, lynchings, and segregation. In the 1960s, however, a more powerful black community could and did speak out against the ideals celebrated on Monument Avenue.

Others agreed that a continuation of Richmond's Confederate memorialization would be backward-looking. Although Richmond was a stronghold of segregation throughout this era, being one of the last cities to desegregate its schools, the pressures upon its old ways, ideals, and ties grew stronger. The nation was in the midst of tumultuous change in the mid-1960s. The number of African Americans going to the polls was increasing significantly, and some members of the black community were winning public offices. Their new political clout fueled both sides of the debate.[18]

Seeing the changes and possibilities of truer equality close at hand, both the emerging black community and the threatened white establishment pushed their contrasting agendas forward.

When the City Planning Commission held an open forum on the suggested plans, more than half of the twenty speakers opposed continuing the Confederate theme along Monument Avenue. Most people attending the meeting favored opening up the famous street to other representations of Virginia's long and proud history. This would allow tributes, for example, to the many Founding Fathers and U.S. presidents who hailed from Virginia. Dr. J. Rupert Picott was quoted later in the *Times-Dispatch* as declaring, "The concept of the Confederate theme is out of order with the present time: let's include some northern generals to be fair, and perhaps some Negroes. The existing monuments should be maintained, but this is a great city and it must be greater. We must think of Richmond today, not as it was a hundred years ago."[19]

A *Times-Dispatch* editorial also asked why the city would want to continue such a limited theme when it could capitalize on Virginia's rich history to gain a more progressive world image. Citing Jefferson, Madison, Monroe, and Wilson, the newspaper said: "Such men as these are among the greatest of all Americans. Their presence in marble or bronze on Monument Avenue would tend to give Richmond a more diversified and forward-looking 'image.'"[20]

Pockets of resistance remained within Richmond. One resident wrote the *Times-Dispatch* to lament what he saw as a terrible loss of the state's Confederate character. Virginians, he argued, were seen by other southerners as Yankees and needed to reassert their true Confederate nature and resolve. This man could not understand the NAACP's objections to the continuing veneration of the Confederacy, saying some blacks did fight for the South in the Civil War and "I would like to think that the erection of more monuments to the Confederate Virginians would do honor to all individuals and races who participated in the conflict."[21] Most black "participants" were slaves, however, forced by their owners to defend their own subjugation, and the irony of this suggestion was not lost on many.

In 1965 many people in Richmond affirmed that it was time to break with the Confederate emphasis of Monument Avenue. Rev. Chas L. Stigger publicly asked why great black leaders were being overlooked in the selection debates and proposed that Anthony Binga Jr., an educator and author working just after the Civil War, be included on Monument Avenue. His suggestion was ignored. But the concerns expressed about diversity and a national perspective did affect subsequent planning. In an effort to diversify the avenue within the Confederate scope of meaning, the planning committee sought a monument to the women of the Confederacy. Capt. Sally Tompkins, a nurse who ran a hospital in Richmond during the Civil War, was selected as the heroine to be honored in the newest Monument Avenue statue. The committee in charge of raising funds and choosing the sculpture asked Spanish artist Salvador Dali to create a design. Dali created a plan for an aluminum monument of Tompkins, like Saint George and the dragon, fighting a giant germ, perched upon a twenty-foot model of the artist's little finger. Confronted with such an option, the committee dropped the entire matter.[22]

Monument Avenue did not stay quiet for long. The "battle of the Belgian blocks" in 1968 and 1969 brought much attention to the avenue. When the city threatened to pave over the original Belgian paving blocks along the early sections of Monument Avenue, residents of the street publicly protested, and one homeowner literally placed herself between the paving truck and the well-loved blocks. The new Monument Avenue Association launched a campaign over the next year to preserve the stateliness that loyalists insisted the blocks communicated. In a full-page advertisement in the *Richmond News-Leader,* the association commented: "The handsome and unique paving blocks on historic Monument Avenue have been threatened with destruction for ten months. Three years ago, the Monuments themselves were under threat of being moved. This splendid boulevard in its totality . . . is a priceless treasure of the entire Commonwealth and the nation." After a long battle, the blocks were saved and some that had earlier been paved over with asphalt even were uncovered. The city also designated Monument Avenue as an official historic district. The sacred nature of the avenue was saved again, and this time formalized.[23]

The designation of Monument Avenue, its houses, paving blocks, and statues, as a historic district in 1969 confirms that despite a marked growth in the black community's political and social influence, the prevalent historical outlook continued to sanctify the Lost Cause. Historian Charles P. Roland argues that this "history with a southern accent" persisted most strongly through physical reminders, such as the atmosphere and monuments along this avenue. Many white southerners revered the Confederate heroes although they no longer supported the causes associated with them. Some reformers in the New South tried to link their modern objectives to these idealized and romanticized visions of the Old South, "forming a 'vital nexus' between the epochs."[24] Even progressives in the New South, one hundred years after the war had ended, were not secure enough in the rapidly changing American culture to proceed without their sanctified Confederate history.

Throughout the 1970s and 1980s, the racial balance of power continued to shift. This process did not occur easily in any part of the country, but Richmond's history and the persistence of its influence exacerbated racial stratification there. In an interview with *Sports Illustrated* in 1971, the up-and-coming Arthur Ashe spoke of this: "I have thought sometimes that I might like to be a Senator, but, let's face it: Senator Ashe from Virginia—even in twenty years that's an unlikely possibility."[25] As the population changed to favor African-American communities, however, black politicians did gain prominent and powerful city positions.

City officials did not try to change Monument Avenue again until 1991. That is when Chuck Richardson, a black councilman, suggested the addition of a monument to African American civil rights leaders to balance the white-establishment view of history he perceived on the avenue. The majority of Richmond residents responding to a survey about this idea backed the creation of such a new monument.[26] Richmond was not yet ready, however, to bring this kind of plan to fruition, even though over half of its population was African American. The century-long history of Monument Avenue was still venerated by powerful sections of the citizenry of Richmond. But the groundwork had been laid for a new effort.

## *Contesting the Man in Sweats*

Arthur Ashe Jr., born in Richmond in 1943, showed a great talent for tennis at a young age. Growing up in a segregated city, he was prohibited from practicing on the whites-only courts in Byrd Park and from competing in critical matches. Although he had earlier fled Virginia and its racial burdens, Richmond declared a day honoring Ashe after he achieved champion status in 1968. Ashe went on to greatness, winning both the U.S. Open and Wimbledon and captaining the Davis Cup team. Five years after Ashe underwent a heart bypass operation in 1983, he discovered he was infected with HIV, which was traced to a blood transfusion needed for the surgery. In the final years of his life Ashe became widely renowned outside of the sports world, fighting for human

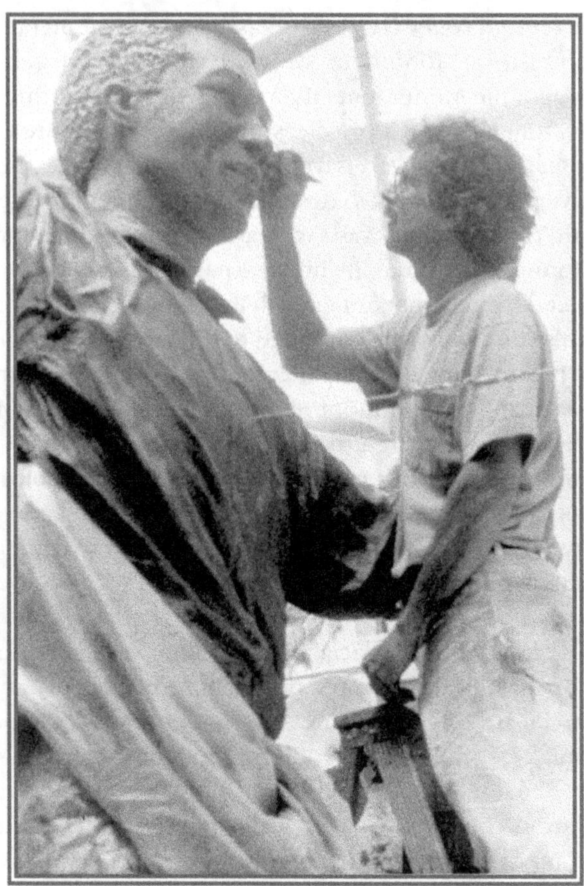

Fig. 14.3. Sculptor Paul DiPasquale putting finishing touches on the Arthur Ashe memorial.
Photograph by Jay Paul.

rights and against prejudice and apartheid. After he succumbed to the AIDS virus in February 1993, many residents paid last respects to Ashe, whose body lay in state in Virginia's Executive Mansion in Richmond. Despite the city's ambiguous support for Ashe during his life, Richmond was eager to claim him as a native son after his untimely death.[27]

The idea for an Arthur Ashe memorial in the Cradle of the Confederacy came from Ashe himself in the weeks before his death and from sculptor Paul DiPasquale (fig. 14.3). Ashe and DiPasquale discussed plans for a statue to be erected in front of a black athletes' sports hall of fame that Ashe wished to see built in Richmond. The sculptor said Ashe wished to be depicted with children and books, emphasizing the value of education to youth, and also with a tennis racquet, dressed casually in a sweat suit. When he later defended his design against art critics and politicians, DiPasquale said his goal "was to create a monument that acknowledged the man's vision. When he talked about the monument before he died, Ashe said, 'I want to be involved with children in some way and I want to have books with me. I want to show that books are the most important part of whatever discipline you choose.' This piece has Arthur Ashe's input."[28] DiPasquale and Ashe hoped that Ashe's statue before the sports hall would inspire future generations.

It was Wilder, the first elected black governor in the nation's history, who suggested a different, much more controversial placement—Monument Avenue. With the site's continuing ties to a glorious, or as some like Wilder now suggested, significantly inglorious, Confederate past, this proposal sparked a year of racially and politically driven debate.

More than 250 people—some in African garb, others in Confederate regalia—attended a public hearing held by the Richmond City Council on July 17, 1995. Leonidas Young, the city's black mayor, opened the forum by emphasizing the gravity of the debate. He noted that it raised "some of the most essential questions of our collective identity—the meaning of our traditions and symbols, the nature of heroism, the relation between our white and African-American populations and the function of public art in expressing the soul of a community."[29] Creating a consensus about Richmond's collective identity would not be a simple task. Each of these issues would gain prominent attention in the following months of debate.

Ideas abounded for other sites for the Ashe monument. Mayor Young repeatedly proposed that the city raze two empty downtown buildings and construct an Arthur Ashe park in which the statue would be placed. A suggestion that the sculpture stand in front of the Arthur Ashe Jr. Athletic Center (fig. 14.4) met much criticism despite its apparent appropriateness. The athletic center was

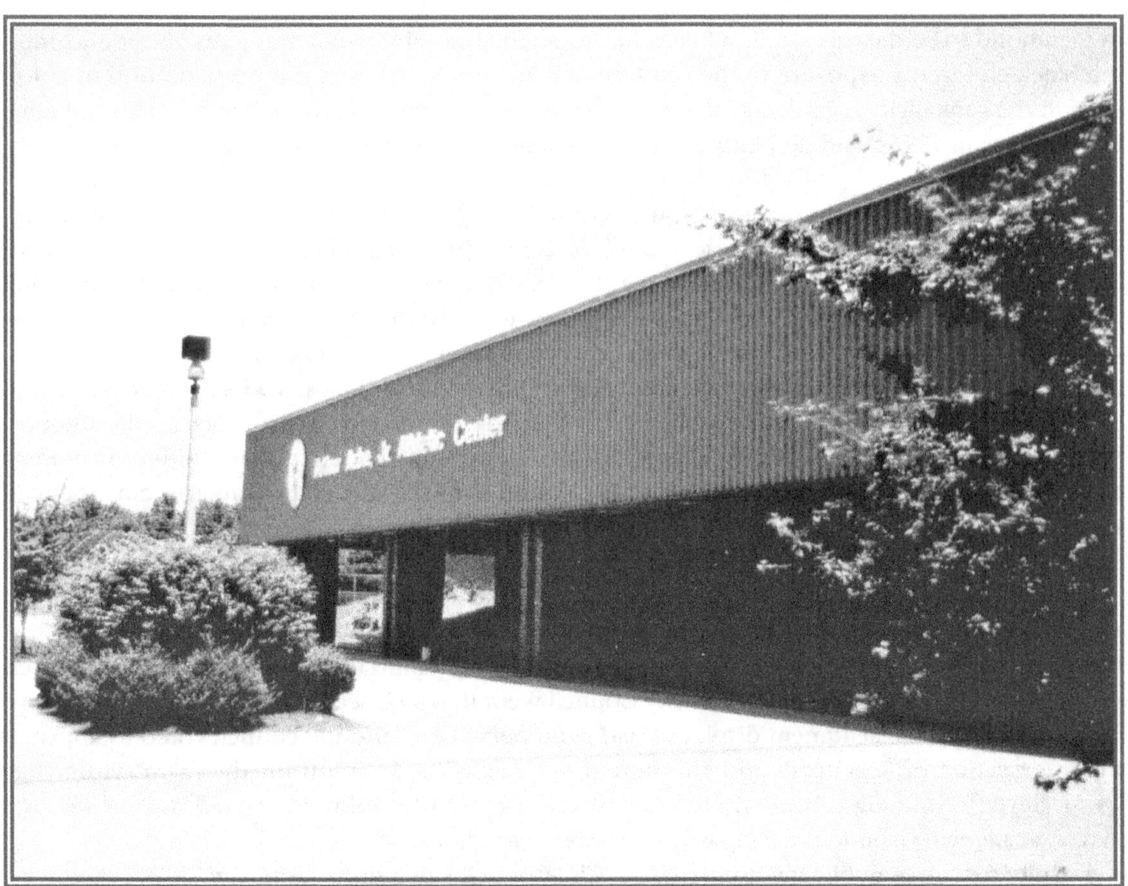


Fig. 14.4. Arthur Ashe Jr. Athletic Center, Richmond, Virginia. Photograph by Bryn Varley.

outside of the protected and well-kept historic district; opponents bristled at the thought of placing this tribute to Ashe and what he had overcome across from the city's Greyhound bus station.[30] Throughout the brainstorming process, the question remained: Why not Monument?

Suggestions came from both the black and white communities that Ashe be placed in a part of town, such as Jackson Ward, where more of the city's black people lived. That way, advocates of this idea said, black children would more frequently see his image, an inspiration for honorable behavior and success. Why memorialize Ashe in a hostile environment such as the historic Monument Avenue district, some asked, when in an area such as Jackson Ward, a bastion of the city's black community, he would be home, in the place where he grew up? Ashe's contemporaries declared that as children they never visited Monument Avenue. Eugene Price, an early classmate, demanded of the Planning Commission: "Why not put the monument where he came [from]?"[31]

Opposition sprang not just from those who believed it was offensive to Ashe to place his likeness alongside those of Confederate chieftains or who thought another place in the city would be more appropriate. Many organizations and individuals spoke up to defend the historic integrity of the stretch of road. One protester at the Ashe memorial ground breaking in August 1995 commented: "If you're going to put up a black monument here, put one up to those [blacks] who fought in the Confederate Army. A lot of fellows in the city feel this way."[32]

Journalist Michael Paul Williams had much to say about keeping Ashe eternally off the last street in Richmond to be desegregated. While acknowledging the validity of arguments about maximizing black children's exposure to the nobility of Ashe, he questioned the perpetuation of color lines in the capital city regarded as the last stronghold of segregation in the South. "This thinking has no place in 1995," and no place in a city with a now predominately black population and city council, he said.[33]

Among those present at the Ashe monument public hearing in 1995 was Tony Horwitz, a former war correspondent who was researching the remaining Confederate ties in the South. In his firsthand account, Horwitz stated that some "blacks could barely contain the rage they felt about Monument Avenue and the decades of Confederacy-worship they'd suffered through before the civil rights struggle. For them, putting Ashe on Monument Avenue represented emotional payback, an in-your-face gesture that would salve some of the insult blacks had so long endured. 'I want my hero's statue as tall as Lee's,' one man shouted. 'I want Ashe to be as big as all outdoors. Arthur Ashe is bigger than Lee!'"[34] This angry sentiment was echoed at many different points. Some college-age white students called for the removal of the Confederate statues, seeing them as representing treason and oppression, but their appeals to dispose of the past, glorious or inglorious, were booed by the mixed audience.[35]

Although originally in favor of the Monument Avenue site, the City Council, especially Mayor Young, had been leaning toward selecting a new location. Now public opinion expressed at the hearing strongly favored Wilder's idea to place the Ashe memorial on Monument Avenue. After seven exhausting hours of debate, the City Council went into a closed executive session to discuss the possibilities. The sentiment displayed had been persuasive, and the council voted to approve the intersection of Roseneath and Monument Avenue as the location for the Ashe statue (fig. 14.5). Seven of the eight council members voted for the site; John A. Conrad, the white vice mayor, abstained. Ground breaking was set for one month later.[36]

Despite extensive public involvement, the City Council's decision was not readily accepted by all the people of Richmond. Three days before the groundbreaking ceremony, a group calling itself the Heritage Preservation Association held a news conference on Monument Avenue, amid a display of Confederate flags. Its leaders insisted that their concern about the site was not racially motivated and only promoted preservation of the historical focus already established along the thoroughfare.

On the day of the ground breaking, August 15, 1995, two dozen protesters hoisted Confederate flags around those gathered for the ceremony. The protest, organized by the Council of Conservative Citizens in Richmond, was silent but highly visible, quite like the monuments down the street that the demonstrators were defending. Although the monument was supposed to help bring people together and heal racial divisions, one reporter noted that the protesters' presence "showed that resolution still may be a long time off."[37]

Neighborhood reactions were mixed. One woman living near the Ashe site deplored the decision to honor a man she considered merely a sports hero on a street such as Monument Avenue. The distribution of propaganda targeting the Ashe monument site was reported just days after the ceremony. Several neighbors were quoted in the press, however, as saying that the extremist and bigoted sentiments slipped under their doors did not represent their attitudes. Some area residents favored the monument and some did not, but no one living close to the site publicly reacted with the vehemence of the anonymous fliers.[38]

The ceremony also drew supporters from some unlikely arenas. One member of the Sons of Confederate Veterans came to lend support, stating that "a hero is a hero." Addressing the divisive nature of the new monument, Wilder said: "[W]e are breaking ground on this site. We are breaking new ground . . . . We are breaking the myths and the shibboleths that have tied us to a past that in too many instances truthfully has been inglorious." The placement of the Ashe statue

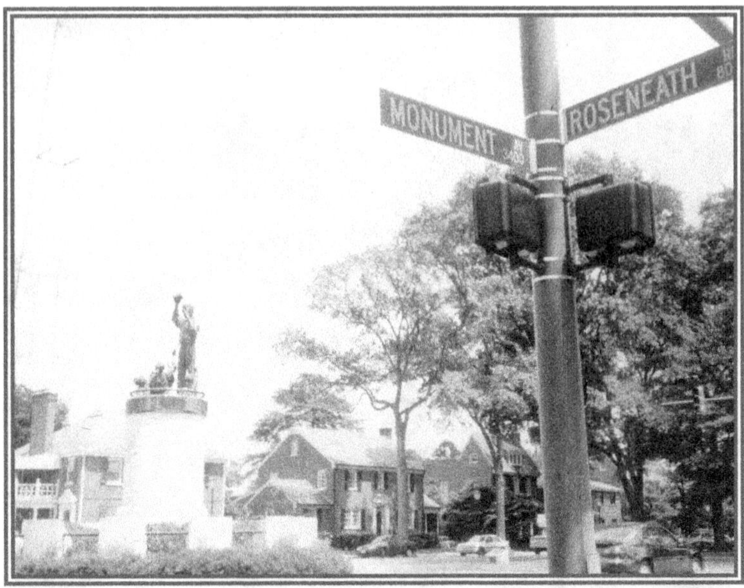


Fig. 14.5. The Arthur Ashe Memorial as seen from the intersection of Roseneath Road and Monument Avenue. Photograph by Bryn Varley.

seemed inevitable. As DiPasquale finished his creation—the bronze figures of a larger-than-life Ashe surrounded by four schoolchildren, to be set atop a tall marble base—the city waited.[39]

In January of 1996 the debate was revived when Ashe's widow, Jeanne Moutoussamy-Ashe, complained that the site controversy had overshadowed her husband's achievements and appropriate memorial. In a letter to the people of Richmond printed in the *Times-Dispatch,* Moutoussamy-Ashe noted that the original intention of a sports hall of fame had been lost. Surprising those planning the memorial, Mrs. Ashe remarked: "No, I am not in agreement with the decision to place the 'Arthur Ashe monument' on Monument Avenue. My reasons are not politically driven; nor are they artistically or racially motivated. I have always felt that in all this controversy, the spirit that Arthur gave to Richmond has been overlooked."[40]

This letter stunned the City Council, which had believed the Ashe family supported the site. After revisiting its position, the City Council decided to proceed with a compromise plan for the monumental integration of this historic street. A two-site proposal was agreed upon, in which plans for the Hard Road to Glory Sports Hall of Fame would move forward, albeit slowly; upon completion of the hall, the statue of Ashe would be moved to that location. The site at Monument

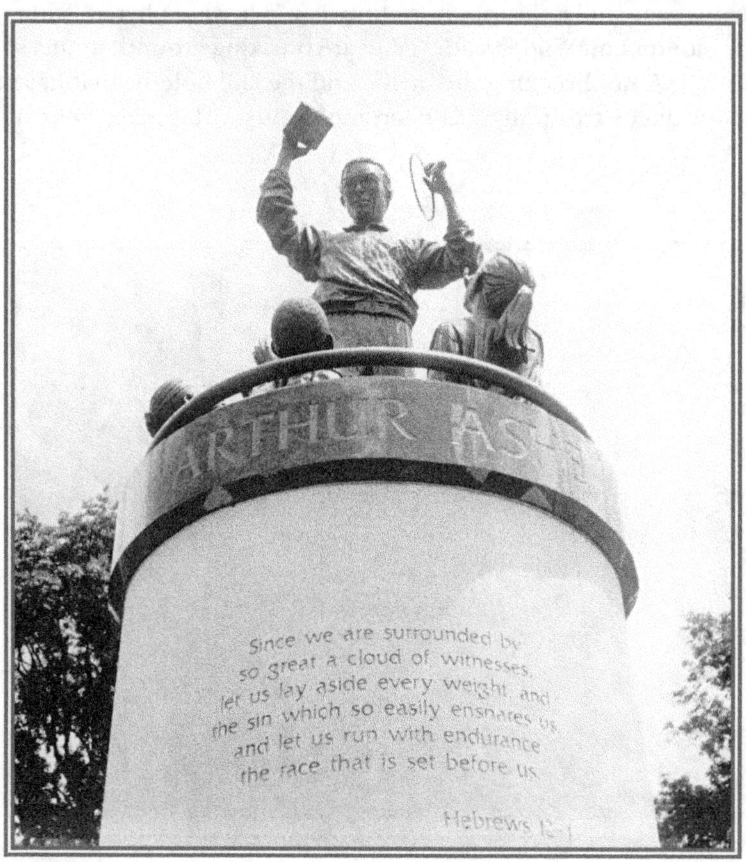


Fig. 14.6. The Arthur Ashe memorial, Monument Avenue, Richmond. Photograph by Bryn Varley.

and Roseneath, however, would not be left bare. A committee calling itself Citizens for Excellence in Public Art would mount a campaign to raise funds for a replacement monument, which the City Council insisted represent civil rights leaders. This plan has yet to move forward. But with its dedication in July 1996, the Ashe memorial broke the hegemony of Confederate monuments on the avenue (fig. 14.6). Many of the City Council members wish to maintain their advantage.[41]

## Continuity of Meaning and Place

The changes on Monument Avenue that resulted after the 1965, 1969, 1991, and 1995–96 debates reveal a great deal about contemporary attitudes toward Richmond's past. Historian David Lowenthal argued that "the links [to the past] are unbroken only so long as no one realizes how unlike the present the tangible past is."[42] Much of the debate in 1965 acknowledged the outdated thinking of memorializing Confederate heroes, just as it did thirty years later. But the controlling city forces had changed. In 1965 a predominately white-establishment Richmond government suggested commemorating the hundred-year anniversary of the Confederate States of America and their valiant leaders. In the 1990s—after desegregation, the dawn of affirmative action, and a move to inclusiveness—a new government, more representative of Richmond's majority-black population, could control the city's public icon-making.

Richmond's prime tourism book, *Old Richmond Today,* written in 1988, touches upon the delicate balance of power: "As a city that honors heroes of the American Revolution and still argues the relative merits of Jefferson's and Marshall's precepts of government, Richmond is able to put its tumultuous Civil War history into perspective. The appropriation of funds by a city council with a black majority to conserve the statues of southern generals exemplifies the strides in sensitivity and understanding achieved in a city that has endured and survived epic social change."[43] Although this account might be overly idealistic about the willingness of the black community and local government to preserve the Confederate statues, its overall message of a respect for history is supported.

In a letter to the *Richmond Times-Dispatch,* Councilman Chuck Richardson commented upon the distress that African Americans in Richmond endured for more than a century as they walked past the "symbols of subjugation of our race." He noted that many in the city wondered about the fate of such monuments after the change in government that occurred in 1977 with the election of more black leaders to key city positions. Yet the old symbols were respected and preserved from the "orgy of desecration" that occurred in many other cultures when power changed hands. Tony Horwitz explained it this way: "Whatever one felt about the Confederates, their enshrinement on Monument Avenue was historic in its own right, a unique museum piece of the Lost Cause mentality."[44]

Yet to many, Monument Avenue was more than this. This grand thoroughfare and the Confederate heroes enshrined upon it embodied the collective identity embraced by many southern whites for generations following the Civil War. At the turn of the twentieth century, the ideals of the lost Confederacy were still held strongly by a majority of Richmonders. The sacred nature of Monument Avenue was established by the people's ongoing preservation of their cherished ideals displayed along this landscape. The debates that began in the 1960s and that continue today challenge the old ideologies of post–Civil War southern thought. In 1965 the beginnings of a new southern memory influenced by a budding national unity appeared to be gathering support in

Richmond. By the mid-1990s, the Lost Cause mentality seemed defused enough to allow the Ashe monument to be placed in Richmond's highest row of honor.

The different heroes and ideologies now seem to coexist peacefully together along Monument Avenue. At least one Richmonder, whose great grandfather fought "nobly for the Cause in the War between the States," honored his memory yet expressed a belief that the city has room on Monument Avenue for all of its history and memorials: "My great grandfather's past actions, however, take nothing away from the vast accomplishments and legacy of Arthur Ashe. Neither does Arthur Ashe's memorialized presence take anything away from the honor and integrity of my ancestor's deeds or memory."[45] This writer said Richmond can simultaneously pay homage to the city's old and new beliefs on this sacred landscape. Such views demonstrate the slow diffusion of the modern national consciousness into the long-held Confederate loyalty.

Still the ambiguity expressed along the two-mile stretch of memorials makes one question whether the avenue illustrates a new ideology in the southern capital or whether Monument Avenue has become the manifestation of Richmond's dual personality under a new political power. Does a progression down Monument Avenue show a marked growth in ideals, attitude, and community inclusiveness—and reveal a new southern ideology replacing the Lost Cause? Or rather than signifying the achievement of unity and acceptance, does the addition of Arthur Ashe show a Richmond more divided than ever before? Two divergent sets of ideals and idols still exert power in the southern culture, and one no longer dominates to the relative exclusion of the other. Is Richmond weakened by the undermining of the historical focus that engendered its collective consciousness, or is it strengthened by standing on a broader base, which encompasses all its citizens and their history?

The addition of a statue to honor Arthur Ashe on Monument Avenue could well signify a new relationship in Richmond between the city's Civil War history and its Civil Rights era, and between its white and black populations. If Ashe were indeed added to the line of Confederate heroes to honor the man and express the city's united support, this debate may be a positive sign of Richmond's century-long healing and growth. How would that black tennis champion in sweatpants feel about his new place on Monument Avenue? In his final memoir, Ashe wrote: "I see nothing inconsistent between being proud of oneself and one's ancestors and, at the same time, seeing oneself as first and foremost a member of the commonwealth of humanity, the commonwealth of all races and creeds."[46]

## Notes

The authors are grateful for the support of Skidmore College's Keck Collaborative Research Grant Program. This work would not have been possible without the support and input of Mary C. Lynn and Candice Varley.

1. Protester's quotation from "Race and Memory in Richmond," *Washington Post*, July 21, 1995. Michael Paul Williams, "Hate Fliers Target Ashe Statue Site," *Richmond Times-Dispatch*, Aug. 29, 1995.

2. Wilder quotation from Spencer S. Hsu, "Breaking Ground in a Divided City," *Washington Post*, Aug. 16, 1995. Jeanne Moutoussamy-Ashe, "A New Year's Wish for Richmond: Accept Gift of Arthur's Vision," *Richmond Times-Dispatch*, Jan. 1, 1996.

3. As quoted in "Placement of Ashe Statue a Matter of Richmond Controversy," Associated Press, June 20, 1995.

4. David Chidester and Edward T. Linenthal, *American Sacred Space* (Bloomington: Indiana Univ. Press, 1995), 9.

5. Yi-fu Tuan, *Topophilia: A Study of Environmental Perception, Attitudes, and Values* (Englewood Cliffs, N.J.: Prentice-Hall, 1974 ), 17.

6. Geoffrey C. Ward, *The Civil War* (New York: Knopf, 1990), 374.

7. Kathy Edwards, Esmer Howard, and Toni Prawl, *Monument Avenue: History and Architecture* (Washington, D.C.: U.S. Dept. of the Interior Historic American Buildings Survey, 1992), 83.

8. "Thousands Present—Confederate Flags Everywhere Displayed," *Richmond Planet,* May 31, 1890.

9. "What It Means," *Richmond Planet,* May 31, 1890.

10. "Still Kicking," *Richmond Planet,* Oct. 2, 1907.

11. "From Women of the South: Memorial Raised to President of the 'Lost Cause' at Richmond," *Richmond Planet,* June 8, 1907.

12. "Racial Harmony," *Richmond Planet,* June 8, 1907; reprinted from the *Richmond News-Leader,* May 31, 1907.

13. "Great Improvement," *Richmond Times-Dispatch,* Mar. 14, 1915. For the Jackson celebration, see the essay by Richard Guy Wilson in this anthology.

14. Edward L. Ayers, *The Promise of the New South* (New York: Oxford Univ. Press, 1992), 338.

15. City Planning Commission Minutes, Dec. 6, 1965, 4–6. Vertical file, Valentine Museum, Richmond.

16. "United Daughters of the Confederacy Backs Monument," *News-Leader,* Mar. 24, 1966.

17. "State Heroes of Other Eras Urged for Monument Avenue," *Richmond Times-Dispatch,* Dec. 7, 1965.

18. Charles P. Roland, *The Improbable Era: The South since World War II* (Lexington: Univ. Press of Kentucky, 1976), 186.

19. "State Heroes of Other Eras Urged for Monument Avenue."

20. Editorial, "Why a Confederate Emphasis?" *Richmond Times-Dispatch,* Nov. 27, 1965.

21. R. Roland Reynolds, "Deep South Thinks of Virginians as Yankees," *Richmond Times-Dispatch,* Dec. 24, 1965.

22. Charles L. Stigger, "Voice of the People," *Richmond Times-Dispatch,* Dec. 16, 1965. Karen Schultz, "Statue Backers Study Dali Verses Captain Sally," *Richmond Times-Dispatch,* Apr. 4, 1966; other coverage throughout April; Robert J. Alexander in "Voice of the People," June 9, 1966, argued that a sculpture by Dali would hold the interest of the people and bring tourists to Richmond while breaking from the hero-on-horseback monument mold. A fanciful drawing for the Tompkins monument is included in Sarah Shields Driggs, Richard Guy Wilson, and Robert P. Winthrop, *Richmond's Monument Avenue* (Chapel Hill: Univ. of North Carolina Press, 2001), 237.

23. Quotation from advertisement, *Richmond News-Leader,* July 23, 1969. "Monument Ave. Old and Historic District," *Richmond News-Leader,* Feb. 9, 1971.

24. Roland, *The Improbable Era,* 193. Monument Avenue became one of the first districts entered on the National Register of Historic Places in 1969, and in 1998 was designated a National Historic Landmark. See Driggs, Wilson, and Winthrop, *Richmond's Monument Avenue,* 233.

25. Arthur Ashe as quoted in "The Once and Future Diplomat," *Sports Illustrated,* Mar. 1, 1971.

26. Michael Paul Williams, "Arthur Ashe Deserves Place on Monument," *Richmond Times-Dispatch,* Dec. 12, 1994.

27. *Richmond Times Leader,* Dec. 18, 1966. Ashe describes being forbidden to use the segregated tennis courts in Arthur Ashe and Arnold Rampersand, *Days of Grace* (New York: Alfred A. Knopf, 1993).

28. Doug Smith, "Sculptor Believes Ashe Would Approve of Statue," *USA Today,* Feb. 7, 1996. For background on Paul DiPasquale, a New Jersey–born sculptor who graduated from the University of Virginia and Virginia Commonwealth University and settled in Richmond, see entry in *Who's Who in the South,* 1998.

29. "Hearing Puts Focus on City," *Richmond Times-Dispatch,* July 18, 1995.

30. Ibid.

31. "Placement of Ashe Statue a Matter of Richmond Controversy," Associated Press, June 20, 1995.

32. Hsu, "Breaking Ground in a Divided City."

33. Michael Paul Williams, "A Monument to Richmond's Racial Strife," *Richmond Times-Dispatch,* July 3, 1995.

34. Tony Horwitz, *Confederates in the Attic* (New York: Pantheon Press, 1998), 250.

35. Ibid.

36. Minutes, Council of the City of Richmond, July 17, 1995, City Clerk's Office, Richmond.

37. Hsu, "Breaking Ground in a Divided City."

38. Williams, "Hate Fliers Target Ashe Statue Site."

39. Wilder quotation from Hsu, "Breaking Ground in a Divided City." The base of the completed monument bears the inscription from Hebrews 12:1: "Since we are surrounded by / so great a cloud of witnesses / let us lay aside every weight and / the sign, which so easily ensnares us / and let us run with endurance the / race that is set before us."

40. Jeanne Moutoussamy-Ashe, "A New Year's Wish for Richmond: Accept Gift of Arthur's Vision," *Richmond Times-Dispatch,* Jan. 1, 1996.

41. Gordon Hickey, "Site Sale Plan Received Favorably," *Richmond Times-Dispatch,* Jan. 10, 1996; Hickey, "Always Rancor and Race?" Jan. 30, 1996; and Hickey, "Ashe Contest Proposal Doused," Mar. 26, 1996.

42. David Lowenthal, "Age and Artifact: Dilemmas of Appreciation," in *The Interpretation of Ordinary Landscapes,* ed. D. W. Meinig (New York: Oxford Univ. Press, 1979), 124.

43. John G. Zehmer, *Old Richmond Today* (Richmond, Va.: Historic Richmond Foundation, 1988), introduction.

44. Chuck Richardson and Michael Paul Williams, "Richardson Vision Step in Respect," *Richmond Times-Dispatch,* July 22, 1996. Horwitz, *Confederates in the Attic,* 251.

45. Jane G. Atkinson, "Letter to the Editor," *Richmond Times-Dispatch.* Undated article in vertical file, Valentine Museum, Richmond.

46. Ashe and Rampersand, *Days of Grace,* 167.

# Selected Bibliography


### *BOOKS*

Ayers, Edward, *The Promise of the New South: Life after Reconstruction.* New York: Oxford Univ. Press, 1992.

Blight, David W. *Race and Reunion: The Civil War in American Memory.* Cambridge: Harvard Univ. Press, 2001.

Bodnar, John E. *Remaking America: Public Memory, Commemoration, and Patriotism in the Twentieth Century.* Princeton, N.J.: Princeton Univ. Press, 1992.

Brundage, Fitzhugh, ed. *Where These Memories Grow: History, Memory, and Southern Identity.* Chapel Hill: Univ. of North Carolina Press, 2000.

Campbell, Edward D. C. Jr., and Kym S. Rice. *A Woman's War: Southern Women, Civil War, and the Confederate Legacy.* Richmond: Museum of the Confederacy, and Charlottesville: Univ. of Virginia Press, 1996.

Chidester, Lilenthal, and Edward T. Linenthal, eds. *American Sacred Space.* Bloomington: Indiana Univ. Press, 1995.

Clinton, Catherine. *Women, War, and the Plantation Legend.* New York: Abbeville Press, 1995.

Confederated Southern Memorial Association. *History of the Confederated Memorial Associations of the South.* New Orleans: D. Graham Press, 1904.

Connerton, Paul. *How Societies Remember.* Cambridge: Cambridge Univ. Press, 1989.

Driggs, Sarah Shields, Richard Guy Wilson, and Robert P. Winthrop, with photographs by John O. Peters. *Richmond's Monument Avenue.* Chapel Hill: Univ. of North Carolina Press, 2001.

Edwards, Kathy, Esme Howard, and Toni Prawl. *Monument Avenue: History and Architecture.* Washington, D.C.: National Park Service, 1992.

Eicher, David J. *Mystic Chords of Memory: Civil War Battlefields and Historic Sites Recaptured.* Baton Rouge: Louisiana State Univ. Press, 1998.

Emerson, Bettie Alder Calhoun. *Historic Southern Monuments: Representative Memorials of the Heroic Dead of the Southern Confederacy.* New York: Neale Publishing Co., 1911.

Ezekiel, Moses Jacob. *Memoirs from the Baths of Diocletian.* Joseph Gutmann and Stanley F. Chyet, eds. Detroit: Wayne State University Press, 1975.

Faust, Drew Gilpin. *Mothers of Invention: Women of the Slaveholding South in the American Civil War.* Chapel Hill: Univ. of North Carolina Press, 1996.

Foster, Gaines. *Ghosts of the Confederacy: Defeat, the Lost Cause, and the Emergence of the New South.* New York: Oxford Univ. Press, 1987.

Freeman, David B. *Carved in Stone: The History of Stone Mountain.* Macon, Ga.: Mercer Univ. Press, 1997.

Gallagher, Gary W., and Alan T. Nolan, eds. *The Myth of the Lost Cause and Civil War History.* Bloomington: Indiana Univ. Press, 2000.

Gelbert, Doug. *Civil War Sites, Memorials, Museums, and Library Collections: A State-by-State Guidebook to Places Open to the Public.* Jefferson, N.C.: McFarland and Co., 1997.

Hale, Grace Elizabeth. *Making Whiteness: The Culture of Segregation in the South, 1890–1940.* New York: Pantheon Books, 1998.

Horwitz, Tony. *Confederates in the Attic: Dispatches from the Unfinished Civil War.* New York: Pantheon Press, 1998.

Kammen, Michael. *Mystic Chords of Memory: The Transformation of Tradition in American Culture.* New York: Knopf, 1991.

Jacob, Kathryn Allamong, with photographs by Edwin Harlan Remsberg. *Testament to Union: Civil War Monuments in Washington D.C.* Baltimore: Johns Hopkins Univ. Press, 1998.

Levinson, Sanford. *Written in Stone: Public Monuments in Changing Societies.* Durham, N.C.: Duke Univ. Press, 1998.

Loewen, James W. *Lies Across America: What Our Historic Sites Get Wrong.* New York: New Press, 1999.

Martin, David G. *Confederate Monuments at Gettysburg. The Gettysburg Battle Monuments.* Vol. 1. Hightstown, N.J.: Longstreet House, 1986.

Martinez, J. Michael, William D. Richardson, and Ron McNinch-Su, eds., *Confederate Symbols in the Contemporary South.* Gainesville: Univ. Press of Florida, 2000.

Mitchell, Mary H. *Hollywood Cemetery: The History of a Southern Shrine.* Richmond: Virginia State Library, 1985.

Neely, Mark E. Jr., Harold Holzer, and Gabor S. Boritt. *The Confederate Image: Prints of the Lost Cause.* Chapel Hill: Univ. of North Carolina Press, 1987.

Piehler, G. Kurt. *Remembering War the American Way.* Washington, D.C.: Smithsonian Institution Press, 1995.

Poppenheim, Mary B., et al. *The History of the United Daughters of the Confederacy.* Raleigh: Edwards and Broughton, 1938.

Rable, George C. *Civil Wars: Women and the Crisis of Southern Nationalism.* Chicago: Univ. of Chicago Press, 1989.

Savage, Kirk. *Standing Soldiers, Kneeling Slaves: Race, War, and Monument in Nineteenth-Century America.* Princeton: Princeton Univ. Press, 1997.

Schedler, George. *Racist Symbols and Reparations: Philosophical Reflections on Vestiges of the American Civil War.* Lanham, Md.: Rowman and Littlefield Publishers, 1998.

Silber, Nina. *The Romance of Reunion: Northerners and the South, 1865–1900.* Chapel Hill: Univ. of North Carolina Press, 1993.

Sims, Anastatia. *The Power of Femininity in the New South: Women's Organizations and Politics in North Carolina, 1880–1930.* Columbia: Univ. of South Carolina Press, 1997.

Valentine, Elizabeth Gray. *Dawn to Twilight: The Work of Edward Valentine.* Richmond, Va.: William Byrd Press, 1929.

Widener, Ralph W. Jr. *Confederate Monuments: Enduring Symbols of the South and the War between the States.* Washington D.C.: Andromeda, 1982.

Wilson, Charles Regan. *Baptized in Blood: The Religion of the Lost Cause, 1865–1920.* Athens: Univ. of Georgia Press, 1980.


## *DISSERTATIONS*


Clark, Kathleen. "History Is No Fossil Remains: Race, Gender, and the Politics of Memory in the American South, 1863–1913." Ph.D. diss., Yale Univ., 1999.

Cox, Karen Lynne. "Women, the Lost Cause, and the New South: The United Daughters of the Confederacy and the Transmission of Confederate Culture, 1894–1919," Ph.D. diss., Univ. of Southern Mississippi, 1997.

McLean, Ann Hunter. "Unveiling the Lost Cause: A Study of Monuments to the Civil War Memory in Richmond, Virginia, and Vicinity." Ph.D. diss., Univ. of Virginia. 1998.

Mills, Cynthia J. "Frederick Wellington Ruckstull: In Pursuit of the Ideal." Master's thesis, Univ. of Maryland, 1988.

Panhorst, Michael. "Lest We Forget: Monuments and Memorial Sculpture in National Military Parks on Civil War Battlefields, 1861–1917." Ph.D. diss., Univ. of Delaware, 1988.

Williams, Lewis Waldron. "Commercially Produced Forms of American Civil War Monuments." Master's thesis, Univ. of Illinois, Urbana, 1948.

## *ARTICLES*

Bishir, Catherine W. "Landmarks of Power: Building a Southern Past, 1855–1915." *Southern Cultures,* inaugural issue (1994): 5–46.

Coulter, E. Merton. "The Confederate Monument in Athens, Georgia." *Georgia Historical Quarterly* 40 (Sept. 1956): 230–47.

Davis, Stephen. "Empty Eyes, Marble Hand: The Confederate Monument and the South." *Journal of Popular Culture* 16 (winter 1982): 2–21.

Gulley, H. E. "Women and the Lost Cause: Preserving a Confederate Identity in the American Deep South." *Journal of Historical Geography* 19 (1993): 125–41.

Jones, Richard W. "Confederate Cemeteries and Monuments in Mississippi." *Publications of the Mississippi Historical Society* 8 (1904): 87–119.

Knox, Joseph T. "Le Général Lee: A Design for the Future." *Virginia Cavalcade* 38 (autumn 1988): 76–85.

Moore, John H. "The Jefferson Davis Monument." *Virginia Cavalcade* 10 (spring 1961): 29–34.

Price, Edward T. "The Central Courthouse Square in the American County Seat." *Geographic Review* (Jan. 1968). Reprinted in *Common Places: Readings in American Vernacular Architecture,* ed. Dell Upton and John Vlach, 124–45. Athens, Ga.: Univ. of Georgia Press, 1968.

Smith, Elise L. "Belle Kinney and the Confederate Women's Monument." *Southern Quarterly* 32, no. 4 (summer 1994): 7–31.

Towns, W. Stuart. "Honoring the Confederacy in Northwest Florida: The Confederate Monument Ritual." *Florida Historical Quarterly* 57 (1978): 205–12.

Winberry, John J. "Lest We Forget: The Confederate Monument and the Southern Townscape." *Southeastern Geographer* 23 (Nov. 1983): 107–21.

## *JOURNALS*

*American Architect and Building News* (1876–1908)
*Confederate Veteran* (1893–1932)
*Monumental News*
*Southern Historical Society Papers* (1876–1959)

# Contributors

CATHERINE W. BISHIR, a native of Lexington, Kentucky, is senior architectural historian with Preservation North Carolina and adjunct professor in the Department of Architecture at North Carolina State University. She has degrees in English from the University of Kentucky and Duke University. A founding member and former president of the Vernacular Architecture Forum, she served in various capacities in the North Carolina Historic Preservation Office from 1971 through 2001. She is author and coauthor of several prize-winning books and articles including *North Carolina Architecture* (1990); *Architects and Builders in North Carolina: A History of the Practice of Building* (1990); a three-volume series of regional guides to the historic architecture of North Carolina (1996–2003); and "Landmarks of Power: Building a Southern Past," *Southern Cultures* (1993), republished in W. Fitzhugh Brundage, ed., *Where These Memories Grow: History, Memory, and Southern Identity* (2000).

BRIAN BLACK is a landscape and environmental historian at Pennsylvania State University, Altoona, and editor of *Pennsylvania History: A Journal of Mid-Atlantic Studies.* He is the author of *Petrolia: The Landscape of America's First Oil Boom* (2000) and is currently writing about the changing ideas of the sacred at the Gettysburg National Military Park.

W. FITZHUGH BRUNDAGE, William B. Umstead Chair of History at the University of North Carolina–Chapel Hill, previously taught at the University of Florida. He edited *Where These Memories Grow: History, Memory, and Southern Identity* (2000) and is at work on a study of black and white historical memory in the South from the Civil War to the present. Brundage, who received his Ph.D. from Harvard University, is also the author of *Lynching in the New South* (1993), *A Socialist Utopia in the New South* (1996), and editor of *Under Sentence of Death: Essays on Lynching in the American South* (1997).

KATHLEEN CLARK received her Ph.D in American Studies from Yale University in 1999 and is now assistant professor of history at the University of Georgia. She is the author of several articles on African American historical memory in the post–Civil War South and is currently completing a book manuscript, tentatively entitled "History Is No Fossil Remains: Race, Gender, and the Politics of Memory in the American South, 1863–1913."

KAREN L. COX is assistant professor and director of public history at the University of North Carolina at Charlotte. She has been engaged in the scholarly study of the Lost Cause for several years and has completed a book entitled *Dixie's Daughters: The United Daughters of the Confederacy and the Preservation of Confederate Culture* (2003). She earned a Ph.D. in U.S. history from the University of Southern Mississippi.

DAVID CURREY holds an M.A. in public history from Middle Tennessee University and is principal at Frontier Interpretive Resource and Media, a consulting company in Nashville that works with historic sites, museums, and preservation organizations in designing interpretive programs, preservation plans, and heritage tourism materials. His academic work has focused on collective memory, specifically how the South remembered the Civil War. His article on Franklin, Tennessee, is taken from his thesis, completed in 1996.

M. ANNA FARIELLO is an independent curator with Curatorial InSight and associate professor at Virginia Polytechnic Institute and State University. She also is curatorial co-chair for the Smithsonian Folklife Festival and a former research fellow with the Smithsonian American Art Museum. She is visual arts editor for the *Encyclopedia of Appalachia* and co-editor of the forthcoming volume *Objects and Meaning: Readings that Challenge the Norm.* She holds an M.F.A. from James Madison University and an M.A. in Art History/Museum Studies from Virginia Commonwealth University.

GRACE ELIZABETH HALE is an assistant professor of history at the University of Virginia and an Atlanta native who grew up visiting Stone Mountain Park. She is the author of *Making Whiteness: The Culture of Segregation in the South, 1890–1940* (1998).

MICKI MCELYA is a doctoral candidate in American history at New York University, where she is studying the history of women and gender, the U.S. South, and the history of sexuality. Her dissertation is entitled "Monumental Citizenship: Reading the Mammy Commemoration Controversy of the Early Twentieth Century." She also has contributed to *Our Monica, Ourselves: The Clinton Affair and the Public Interest* (2001).

CYNTHIA MILLS is executive editor of *American Art,* the scholarly journal of the Smithsonian American Art Museum in Washington D.C. She earned her Ph.D. in art history from the University of Maryland with a dissertation on cemetery sculpture of the late nineteenth century, and she has written and lectured widely on that topic. She is at work on a manuscript entitled *Beyond Grief: American Funerary Sculpture in the Gilded Age.*

WILLIAM M. S. RASMUSSEN is Lora M. Robins Curator of Art at the Virginia Historical Society. His publications include coauthorship of five books that have served as exhibition catalogs: *The Making of Virginia Architecture* (1992), with Charles Brownell, Calder Loth, and Richard Guy Wilson, recipient of the Society of Architectural Historians' Architectural History Catalogue Award; *Pocahontas: Her Life and Legend* (1994), with Robert S. Tilton; *George Washington: The Man Behind the Myths* (1999), with Robert S. Tilton, recipient of the Award of Merit from the American Association for State and Local History; *The Virginia Landscape: A Cultural History* (2002), with James C. Kelly; and *Lost Virginia: Vanished Architecture of the Old Dominion* (2001), with Bryan C. Green and Calder Loth. He has published articles in the *Journal of the Society of Architectural Historians, The Magazine Antiques,* the *American Art Review, ARRIS,* and the *Virginia Magazine of History and Biography.*

PAMELA H. SIMPSON is the Ernest Williams II Professor of Art History at Washington and Lee University in Lexington, Virginia, where she has taught since 1973. She received her Ph.D. in art history from the University of Delaware. Her books include *The Architecture of Historic Lexington* (1977), with Royster Lyle; *Cheap, Quick and Easy: Imitative Architectural Materials, 1870–1930* (1999); and *The Sculptor's Clay: The Work of Charles Grafly, 1862–1929,* a 1996 exhibition catalog. In 1995 she was given a Virginia State Outstanding Faculty Award.

BRYN VARLEY is currently working on her doctorate in the History of American Civilization program at the University of Delaware. She is a part of the university's interdisciplinary Center for American Material Culture Studies and also studies at Winterthur Museum. She has been associated with Saratoga National Historical Park and the Historical Society of Delaware.

RICHARD GUY WILSON holds the Commonwealth Professor's Chair in Architectural History at the University of Virginia. A frequent lecturer for universities, museums, and professional groups and a television commentator, his publications include *McKim, Mead and White Architects* (1983); *The American Renaissance, 1876–1917* (1979); *The Machine Age in America, 1918–1941* (1986); *The Art That Is Life: The Arts and Crafts Movement in America* (1987); *The Making of Virginia Architecture* (1992); and *Richmond's Monument Avenue* (2001). He is also editor of the Society of Architectural Historians volume *Buildings of the United States, Virginia: Tidewater and Piedmont* (2002).

CATHERINE W. ZIPF received her doctorate in American architectural history from the University of Virginia in 2001. Formerly a visiting assistant professor at the University of Virginia School of Architecture, she is cofounder of CMZ Collaborative, a firm specializing in architectural history and preservation consultation. Although her essay in this volume focuses on nineteenth-century mortuary design, Zipf's primary area of research has centered on women's participation in the decorative arts and architecture. Her research on the work of Hazel Wood Waterman, Mary Louise McLaughlin, Adelaide Alsop Robineau, and Candace Wheeler will be presented in a forthcoming book on women and the arts and crafts movement.

# Index

Illustration numbers are in *italics*.